WITCH

WITCH

The True Story of Las Vegas's
Most Notorious Female Killer

GLENN PUIT

BERKLEY BOOKS, NEW YORK

THE BERKLEY PUBLISHING GROUP
Published by the Penguin Group
Penguin Group (USA) Inc.
375 Hudson Street, New York, New York 10014, USA

Penguin Group (Canada), 90 Eglinton Avenue East, Suite 700, Toronto, Ontario M4P 2Y3, Canada
(a division of Pearson Penguin Canada Inc.)
Penguin Books Ltd., 80 Strand, London WC2R 0RL, England
Penguin Group Ireland, 25 St. Stephen's Green, Dublin 2, Ireland (a division of Penguin Books Ltd.)
Penguin Group (Australia), 250 Camberwell Road, Camberwell, Victoria 3124, Australia
(a division of Pearson Australia Group Pty. Ltd.)
Penguin Books India Pvt. Ltd., 11 Community Centre, Panchsheel Park, New Delhi— 110 017, India
Penguin Group (NZ), Cnr. Airborne and Rosedale Roads, Albany, Auckland 1310, New Zealand
(a division of Pearson New Zealand Ltd.)
Penguin Books (South Africa) (Pty.) Ltd., 24 Sturdee Avenue, Rosebank, Johannesburg 2196,
South Africa

Penguin Books Ltd., Registered Offices: 80 Strand, London WC2R 0RL, England

WITCH

A Berkley Book / published by arrangement with the author

PRINTING HISTORY
Berkley mass-market edition / December 2005

ISBN: 0-425-20719-6

BERKLEY®
Berkley Books are published by The Berkley Publishing Group,
a division of Penguin Group (USA) Inc.,
375 Hudson Street, New York, New York 10014.
BERKLEY is a registered trademark of Penguin Group (USA) Inc.
The "B" design is a trademark belonging to Penguin Group (USA) Inc.

PRINTED IN THE UNITED STATES OF AMERICA

10   9   8   7   6   5   4   3

This book is dedicated to my late grandfather, Glenn Edick, and my mother, Dolores Hicks, who currently lives in upstate New York. Without you two, who knows where I'd be.

Author's Note

In the spring of 2001, I was assigned to cover the criminal case of Brookey Lee West for Nevada's largest newspaper, the *Las Vegas Review-Journal*. I had no inkling at the time that the assignment would prompt a tumultuous, three-year personal odyssey—some would say obsession—to document the most remarkable criminal case I've ever come across in my journalism career.

West was a successful technical writer who seemed to have it all when she was arrested in Vegas on charges she killed her own mother. Following her arrest, authorities detailed a suspected crime spree spanning two decades and two states, and when it was over, two were dead, one was missing and at least two others were victimized in frightening acts of violence.

The seeds of the mayhem, according to Las Vegas authorities, can be traced to the occult, and more specifically, witchcraft and Satanism.

In 2003, I met with Brookey Lee West at the Southern Nevada Women's Correctional Center in North Las Vegas, and despite an avalanche of evidence against her, she denies all of the accusations. For the record, she denies being a witch, a Satanist or a killer. I'll let you decide on each of those issues.

In 2004, I spent nearly two days with West discussing her life in tape-recorded interviews, and she is an enigma of a human being. To this day, after three years of researching her life, I still haven't quite figured her out, and many of the police officers who investigated her for a decade in California and Las Vegas will tell you the same thing.

But there are three things I can say about West with absolute certainty. First, she is extremely intelligent. She is not your typical criminal defendant. Second, West has a history of mental illness—she herself will tell you as much. And third, she had a truly horrible childhood. In my humble opinion, it was her mental illness and her upbringing that played a huge role in determining why she ended up where she is today.

Before we get to West's story, however, I need to give you a primer for what is coming. For you to fully comprehend the contents of this book, you have to understand Brookey Lee West's family, and to do that, you must familiarize yourself with the basic players in the West clan.

West's mother is Christine Smith. Her father is Leroy Smith. Her brother is Travis Smith, and her stepmother is Chloe Smith,* i.e., Leroy Smith's second wife. If you can keep West and these four family members straight in your mind, you should have no problems following the complex series of events documented in this book.

I used the standard news-gathering principles in putting together *Witch*. The book is based on two years of interviews with dozens of witnesses and approximately 3,000 pages of law enforcement and court documents gathered in Nevada and California through open-record laws. Unlike other true-crime books, you will find no re-created conversations in *Witch*. The quotes in this book came either from my interviews with witnesses or from the police reports, although I have edited some quotes for the sake of clarity and brevity.

For a handful of witnesses in the book, I was obligated to use false names, or pseudonyms, to protect their privacy. Each pseudonym is noted by an asterisk. However, I used false names very, very sparingly. I used them only for witnesses who were the victims of a violent crime and who requested anonymity, or for those who are the subject of allegations made by West herself, and the veracity of those allegations could not be verified in any other independent way.

Otherwise, if someone gave a statement to the police in the Brookey Lee West case, then their name is in this book. Their comments are, by law, a matter of public record.

It is also important for you to understand that the contents of this book are not meant to demean the legitimate Wiccan following in the United States. There are hundreds of thousands of people in the United States who identify themselves as Wiccans or witches, and they do not use the craft for evil.

Special thanks go to: Brookey Lee West, who was kind enough to meet with me so her side of the story could be told; literary agent Jim Cypher, who helped make all this possible; Samantha Mandor, my editor at Berkley Books; the *Las Vegas Review-Journal*'s editors, who gave me my chance at the big time in the news business nearly a decade ago; former Clark County, Nevada, district attorney Stewart Bell, who granted my massive records requests; Nevada prosecutor Frank Coumou, who guided me through the mass of paperwork; Clark County deputy public defender Scott Coffee, who is a true professional and a hell of an attorney; former Tulare County, California, homicide detective Daniel Haynes, who was kind enough to meet with me although he still cannot discuss facts surrounding the slaying of West's husband; Las Vegas homicide detective Dave

Mesinar; the Indiana State University journalism program in Terre Haute, Indiana; and all the other witnesses who gave their valuable time. I especially want to thank my wife, Tina. Only she knows what I've been through in making this dream a reality.

*Give me your blessing; truth will come to light; murder
cannot be hid long.*

—William Shakespeare, *The Merchant of Venice*

The downtown corridor of Las Vegas is a sinner's paradise.

In the shadows of the Las Vegas Strip, a tourist can slip
a cabbie $20 and, within minutes, be smoking a rock of
crack bought from a dealer in the city's projects. On Fremont Street in the center of downtown, streetwalkers troll
in front of run-down weekly-rent motels, copping sex acts
for cash at all hours. Or a $50 bill to a bouncer at most of
the city's strip clubs will secure a hand job from a volup-
tuous stripper in a back room.

While other cities boast fine arts and entertainment, Las
Vegas prides itself in its industry of flesh. It even adver-
tises it. "What happens here, stays here," the Las Vegas
Convention and Visitors Authority said in a recent national
television advertisement aimed at luring tourists to Southern Nevada.

At the city's casinos, greed is the game. Customers fill up
on free alcohol and throw away their cash at the gaming tables. The casino offers credit when the money is gone, and
the legalized loan-sharking not only helps gamblers chase
their lost money, it helps makes Nevada the nation's suicide

capital, where destitute drunks and drug addicts routinely take fatal plunges off casino parking garages.

The sex. The alcohol. The drugs. The gambling. They blend together, forming an economic juggernaut that draws some thirty-five million out-of-towners to Vegas annually. They pack flight after flight into the city's McCarran International Airport, where jumbo jets line up in the southeast Vegas sky like huge mechanical birds descending upon Sodom.

But there is another side of Vegas few tourists see.

Within a few hundred yards of the downtown corridor begins a massive, rolling expanse of residential development that houses the Las Vegas Valley's 1.6 million residents. The most pristine portion of the city is about fifteen minutes from the Strip in northwest Las Vegas, where upscale homes sit at the base of the towering, rusty brown Sierra Nevada mountains to the west. Life here is a world away from Sin City—it is suburbia, an existence of stucco homes, grocery stores, libraries and golf courses.

Soccer moms whisk their kids to and from $15,000-a-year private schools in luxury sport utility vehicles. Casino workers take their families to church on Sunday. Gaming executives and Vegas lawyers find refuge from the city's twenty-four-hour hustle in their ultra-exclusive gated country club communities.

Murder is a rarity here.

Las Vegas police dispatch received the call at 1:31 p.m. on February 5, 2001. On the phone was Bill Unruh, general manager of Canyon Gate Mini Storage on West Sahara Avenue in northwest Las Vegas.

Unruh was calling to report a terrible smell floating in the air at the business.

"People were complaining about it," Unruh said. "It

started getting worse and worse. You'll never forget it. The smell."

Unruh, sixty-three, keeps a watchful eye over Canyon Gate, an expansive, two-story storage facility sitting in the middle of suburbia. Las Vegans can rent storage sheds to stash their excess belongings at Canyon Gate for twenty dollars a month. Kitty-corner to Canyon Gate is a luxury 24 Hour Fitness gym, where BMWs, Jaguars and Hummers fill the parking lot. Down the block a few hundred feet is a series of upscale shopping complexes catering to the Vegas rich.

Unruh told police the smell at Canyon Gate was so pungent he and coworker Greg Stoner made like makeshift bloodhounds and trailed the smell to the second floor of the business. They tracked the stench to storage unit #317, a tiny, five-by-five-foot storage locker rented by a woman named Brookey Lee West. West could not be reached despite repeated phone calls to the number she listed on her Canyon Gate rental sheet.

"My manager and I went out there, and we found the unit where it was smellin' the worst, and we cut the lock," Unruh said.

Under a cool, cloudless winter sky, the men rolled open the white door to unit #317, and a sickening odor rushed out in a thick, invisible fog.

"We opened up the door, and the smell hit us," Unruh said. "That's when I said, 'This is not one for us. It's for the police.'"

The men peered into the storage unit and noticed boxes and boxes of shoes lining the interior of the shed.

"Shoes, and there was a potty in there for older people to use for a bathroom, for anybody that's crippled or anything like that," Unruh said.

The men noticed something else, too. A large green plastic garbage can was in the back left corner of the storage shed.

It was leaking.

"We noticed a green plastic trash can with blackish fluid coming out of the sides and the bottom," Stoner wrote in a police statement.

Unruh and Stoner scrambled back to Canyon Gate's main office and dialed 911. Patrol officers arrived and knew immediately from the smell something was dead and decaying inside unit #317. The officers contacted dispatchers and asked for Detective Todd Rosenberg and sergeant Jim Young of the Las Vegas police General Assignment Detail to respond to the scene.

"As soon as you entered the storage building, it was an unmistakable smell of decaying flesh," Young said.

Young, forty-three, is a detective with a shock of grayish-brown hair, and Rosenberg, thirty-nine, is a clean-cut, brown-haired Indiana native with a wife and kids at home. Together, Rosenberg and Young have a combined quarter century of experience working the night shift on the General Assignment Detail for Vegas police. It is a grisly endeavor, encompassing the investigation of seven hundred death scenes annually in Las Vegas and the surrounding desert of unincorporated Clark County, Nevada.

"When you get to the scene, all you know is somebody is dead," Young said. "You don't know whether it's natural death, accidental, homicide or suicide, so you have to figure it out."

Their job is to determine whether a death is suspicious or not and whether homicide detectives need to conduct further investigation. On average, approximately 140 of the death scenes general assignment detectives investigate each year in metropolitan Las Vegas and the surrounding desert turn out to be murders.

Rosenberg and Young arrived at Canyon Gate in their unmarked Crown Victorias and were directed by patrol to unit #317. They smelled the odor, too, but at first, they were not convinced this was necessarily a dead-body call.

"Just two weeks earlier, we were called to another storage shed across town for a similar smell," Young recalled. "We investigated and found a huge cache of used medical waste from some health insurance scam, so we figured we were probably dealing with another one of those cases."

The detectives then saw the leaking can, however, making it clear that crime scene analysts were needed. CSIs Joe Matvay and Robbie Dahn arrived at Canyon Gate in about twenty minutes.

"When we got there, Joe looked at me and said, 'That smell is the unmistakable smell of death,'" Dahn said. "It was everywhere."

Matvay, forty-eight, is a legend in Las Vegas law enforcement circles, a walking encyclopedia of evidentiary expertise with thousands of crime scenes investigated and solved during his twenty-four-year career. The devout Catholic is tall and thin haired, a thick black beard accenting a face that shows no evidence of his being a crime scene investigator.

"I derive a lot of satisfaction from knowing I was the one who solved a case, whether it was fingerprints, hair, blood, fiber, tool marks, whatever," Matvay said.

Dahn is an attractive redhead who spent eighteen years as a manicurist in Las Vegas until deciding, at the age of forty, that it was time for a career change. She enrolled at the criminal justice program at the University of Nevada, Las Vegas, and now makes a living dusting for prints, scanning for fibers or tire tracks and gathering DNA to catch killers.

"I used to sit inside doing nails all day, and I wanted to be out there," Dahn said. "I was going nowhere fast, and I felt I had a lot more to offer."

"My friends say, 'Oh, crime scene investigation, that is

so cool,' and this and that," Dahn said. "They have no idea. There is no glamour."

The general assignment detectives and the CSIs gathered in front of the unit and started their investigation. The first step was seeking permission from the renter to enter the shed, and Unruh provided the cops with rental sheets identifying the renter as a Brookey Lee West, forty-seven. West, according to her rental agreement, started renting the shed on June 26, 1998. West wrote on the rental sheet that her mother, Christine M. Smith, was the only other person who was allowed access to the shed. West also listed her address as a post office box on Industrial Road in downtown Las Vegas, a seedy strip of earth where all-nude strip clubs and pornography shops sit next to plumbing stores and greasy auto repair shops. Unruh told the police West paid her monthly rental fee in cash. She usually paid ahead of time and the rent was current. There was a phone number for West on the rental sheet, but it was a bad number.

"Our manager had been calling numbers, and we never got anything," Unruh said. Rosenberg directed dispatchers to run West's name in a driver's license database, and it came up as an address listed in Santa Clara, California.

"We called the police out there and asked, 'Can you track this woman down? We need to have permission to go into her storage unit,' " Rosenberg said, "They came back and they said it wasn't a good address. The dispatch said the address doesn't even exist."

Immediately locating West and obtaining consent to search the shed looked unlikely, so Matvay and Dahn started a preliminary search of the premises. They had solid legal ground to do so, given their responsibility to try to pinpoint the source of the smell. Matvay crouched down and walked inside, waving his black flashlight back and forth in the light-starved shed. He noticed a potty chair and a shower chair built for senior citizens. Looking closer, he saw stacks and stacks of shoe boxes on the right interior of the storage shed. The boxes appeared to be wrapped with a green-tinted plastic wrap. A wooden cane was leaning up against some of the boxes, and a black trunk was visible under others.

Gradually, Matvay focused on the garbage can in a back corner as Dahn trailed behind, snapping photos with her department-issued camera.

"The trash can was a forty-five-gallon green Rubbermaid trash can on wheels," Dahn said. "The left side was buckled at the bottom. It appeared there must have been some crack or something, because there was fluid coming out."

The origin of the smell was unmistakable—it was coming from the trash can.

The can's lid was sealed tight with duct tape. A large amount of what appeared to be the light green plastic wrap on the shoe boxes was wrapped around the top of the can, and garbage bags were taped together and placed over the top of the plastic wrap.

"Big-time problem," Matvay said. "I know there is something dead in there. I just don't know what it is."

Matvay initiated a presumptive test for blood on the black, crusty fluid spilling from the can, and also on the wood floor underneath. It's a test he's done hundreds of times. He squeezed a drop of distilled water onto the tip of a cotton swab to moisten it. He applied a liquid chemical called phenolphthalein to the tip of the swab and rubbed it through the black fluid. Next, he dripped a droplet of hydrogen peroxide on the swab. If the swab turned purple, blood was likely present in the fluid.

"I repeated the process five times, and on one of the tests the swab turned purple," Matvay said. "At this point we're thinking there may be someone in this can and this could be a homicide. I told Rosenberg about the test results, that we had a marginally positive test for blood, and he proceeded to get a telephonic search warrant."

The ability to secure a search warrant over the phone is a godsend for Las Vegas police. Instead of having to leave the scene and drive back to the detective bureau to type up an affidavit detailing why police believe they have probable cause, detectives call a judge and tell them the facts of a case in a tape-recorded conversation.

Rosenberg called Las Vegas justice of the peace Deborah Lippis to request a warrant to search unit #317.

"I went back to the office at Canyon Gate to use the phone because the last thing you want to do is apply for a telephonic search warrant on a cell phone," Rosenberg said. "Number one, it could be intercepted, but more importantly, cell phones drop calls."

"You could be right in the middle of an application for a search warrant and the phone disconnects, and you've got to call back, then explain later to a defense attorney why the call disconnected," Rosenberg said.

Lippis approved the search warrant almost immediately. It was a logical move given the facts detailed for the judge.

"We had a storage shed that has been paid for several months in advance," Rosenberg said. "The information the renter has left with the storage business, her contact numbers and a contract address, were faulty. There's a terrible smell coming out of there; you can see some stuff leaking out of the plastic drum; and we have a positive presumptive test for blood, so any prudent person is going to think maybe someone's dead in there."

The search warrant cleared the way for Matvay to cut open the can, but he first had to figure out how to pry off the lid without destroying the wrappings. They might contain valuable evidence.

"The lid was secured all the way around the circumference of the lid with duct tape," Matvay said. "Then there were three large green plastic trash bags duct-taped together, and those were wrapped around the lid and upper portion of the can. And then there was this greenish-tinted plastic wrap, sort of like Saran Wrap, and it was wrapped all around the circumference of the lid and upper portion of the can," Matvay said. "A lot of thought went into this."

Matvay retrieved a box cutter and slowly started to cut through the wrappings.

"When I made the first incision on the plastic wrap, the plastic bag and duct tape, some liquid emanated from the can, as did dead maggots," Matvay said.

Matvay proceeded like a surgeon, slicing through the light green plastic wrap, preserving the evidence as much as possible. The three green trash bags were next, then the duct tape.

"Once I cut through the duct tape, I removed the lid," Matvay said.

Matvay looked inside and saw something so horrible, so gruesome, so frightening that it startled even the veteran crime scene investigator.

"There's a body in here," Matvay said. "Another homicide! It's a homicide."

In the bottom of the can was the badly decomposed body of what appeared to be an elderly woman. She was up to her shoulders in a thick, brown, soupy mix of human decomposition topped with a layer of insect larvae. A white plastic bag was tied tightly around the victim's face and a long stretch of gray and black hair descended into the pool of decomposition. The victim was leaning over in death; all that was left of her face was a partial, thin layer of skin on top of her skull, her head against a folded elbow as if resting her head for the last time.

"It appeared to be a woman from the hair," Young said. "The size was of a very small person. The thought had crossed our mind this could even be a child."

Young called Las Vegas police lieutenant Wayne Petersen on his cell phone so he could notify one of his sergeants, Kevin Manning, that homicide detectives were needed.

"It is clearly a homicide," Rosenberg said. "If you knew someone who died, you wouldn't say, 'Hmm, let's put her in a barrel in a storage shed.' It was bizarre."

Even more bizarre to the investigators was the bag tied over the woman's mouth.

"There was a portion of this white plastic bag knotted at the back of the head with the remainder of the bag going toward the front of the lower portion of the face," Matvay said.

Young wondered how someone could do something so heinous. Whoever the killer was, he or she stuffed a senior citizen in a garbage can like a piece of trash, then left her corpse to rot. It looked to the detectives as if the body had been there for years.

"It must take a pretty indifferent person to do something like that," Young said. "This person is out there, going to work, interacting with people, hanging with friends, and this garbage can is in there the whole time. This has to be someone who is pretty psychologically warped."

2

Dave Mesinar is a Vegas homicide cop who has spent the last three decades tracking down bad guys, leaving him no stranger to the brutality of Vegas' underbelly. Shootings, dismemberment, drug deals gone bad, domestic violence murders and deadly trick rolls are all on the homicide detective's resume of investigated murders.

"It's a noble profession," Mesinar said. "The victims can't tell you what happened, so you do right by them."

At six foot one and 220 pounds, he is a man who, like many cops, lives two lives. To his wife, Linda, and his two grown boys, he is a caring husband and father who worries about them constantly.

"It takes a special person to put up with someone who works homicide, with someone who does this for a living, and my family is very special to me," Mesinar said.

At work, he is far different: a human robot void of emotion, out of necessity. They say murder doesn't kill just one person—it kills everyone who knows the victim, too. Mesinar, fifty-eight, learned a long time ago you care about the deceased and their loved ones, but you don't get too close. It will destroy you.

"You get used to it after a while," Mesinar said. "I do it because someone has to speak for the victims."

He is an imposing, salt-and-pepper-haired figure with a stare capable of cutting straight through a suspect's bullshit. It is a valuable skill that has served him well as lead detective on some of Vegas' most high-profile murders.

In June 1999, a man named Zane Floyd walked into an Albertsons grocery store on West Sahara Avenue in Las Vegas and, with a shotgun in hand, started blasting at everyone in sight, leaving a trail of blood up and down the store's aisles. Floyd's rampage was Las Vegas' most prolific spree killing. One victim, Albertsons employee Lucille Tarantino, sixty, was shot in the face as she begged for her life. Another store employee, Dennis Troy Sargent, was cut down in his prime. He left behind a seven-year-old son. Victim Thomas Darnell was shot in the back, and Floyd's fourth murder victim, Carlos Leos, forty-one, had just celebrated his first wedding anniversary.

"This guy was just shooting throughout the store," Mesinar said. "The bread rack was full of shotgun pellets, and there was blood and dead bodies all over the place. It really enraged me to think one human being could do something like that."

The work of Mesinar and his now retired partner, Paul Bigham, yielded Floyd a spot on Nevada's death row.

In another case of Mesinar's that drew headlines, Mesinar was assigned in August 1998 to investigate the discovery of a body at a Las Vegas motel on the north end of Las Vegas Boulevard. The Del Mar XXX Motel is a sex addict's dream come true. Its rooms feature beds surrounded by mirrors and twenty-four-hour broadcasts of graphic sex flicks. Prostitutes regularly walk the surrounding streets, hoping to find work from the likes who frequent the Del Mar.

The body at the Del Mar was found by a guest who noticed a putrid smell in his room and called the police. Detectives snooped around to identify the source of the smell, and they found the body of Patricia Margello, forty-five, stuffed in an air-conditioning duct. The corpse had been in the duct for days.

Margello appeared at first to be just another dead hooker or drug user headed for a slab at the Clark County coroner's office. A blurb about the slaying in the city's largest newspaper, the *Las Vegas Review-Journal*, stretched a mere four paragraphs the next day. But within weeks, a trail of clues led Mesinar to the front door of one of America's richest families.

Mesinar learned that Margello's boyfriend was a man named Dean MacGuigan, the son of a woman named Lisa Dean Moseley. Moseley, in turn, is a direct descendant of the DuPont family, which founded the largest chemical company in America. MacGuigan told the detective that Moseley's husband, Christopher, hated Margello because he believed she was demeaning the family's prestigious name. Christopher Moseley was soon the prime suspect in Margello's slaying, prompting Mesinar to fly to the DuPont family estate in Delaware.

"Money," Mesinar said. "Their estate and the mansion they lived in were massive. The driveway leading to their home was at least a half mile long."

Christopher Moseley eventually confessed to carrying out a murder-for-hire plot culminating in Margello's body being stuffed in the air-conditioning duct. Moseley said he paid an over-the-hill porn star, Diana Hironaga, forty-one, and two other street thugs $15,000 to strangle Margello at the Del Mar.

"That was a crime that made no sense at all," Mesinar said. "These people were so rich they could buy anything they wanted in the world three or four times over. There was no need for it."

Mesinar was at home on the eve of February 5, 2001, getting ready to have dinner with his wife when his Homicide supervisor called.

"You are not going to believe this," Sergeant Kevin Manning said. "They found a body in a trash can."

Mesinar agreed to meet Manning and another Vegas police homicide detective, James Vaccaro, at Canyon Gate.

"Kevin said they found a body in a trash can, so I'm thinking, 'All right, it's a body in a Dumpster,'" Mesinar said. "Nothing unusual."

The idea of Mesinar, Manning and Vaccaro working together is a scary proposition for criminals. Combined, they've investigated nearly a thousand murders. Vaccaro, a cop with more than five hundred homicide investigations under his belt, is as good a detective as they come. He is best known in Las Vegas for his work in the "Black Widow" case of Margaret Rudin, who killed her millionaire husband, Ron, in 1994.

Manning is a crucial cog in the Las Vegas police Homicide Section and one of the most respected cops in the 2,500-member force of the Las Vegas Police Department. A former cop in Cape Cod, Massachusetts, he still has a slight New England accent. At about five feet seven inches tall, he supervises some fifty homicide investigations annually, monitoring teams of detectives like a father imparting wisdom to his sons.

"A lot of guys that I used to work with in narcotics ask me if it is fun to work homicide," Manning said. "I could never use that word to describe working homicide. It's one of two things—it's either very frustrating or extremely satisfying. It's very frustrating on the cases where you don't have cooperative witnesses, or caring families, or where you don't have much evidence at all."

Mesinar drove his police-issued Ford Expedition from his northwest Las Vegas home to Canyon Gate on West Sahara. He met with Manning and Vaccaro, and the three were escorted by patrol officers to an elevator. From there, the three were led to the front door of unit #317, where Matvay was waiting. Matvay sent Dahn home for the night because she was going to be needed the next morning at the autopsy.

"The odor of death and decomposition was overwhelming as soon as we arrived," Mesinar said. Matvay, Young and Rosenberg briefed the homicide detectives on what they knew so far. Brookey Lee West was the renter of the shed, but she couldn't be found. A corpse was in a can in the rear of the storage shed, and no one had an inkling as to who the victim was.

"I looked in there, and I saw a whole bunch of fluid in the can," Mesinar said. "There was this body in somewhat of a fetal position. There was some clothing on the body, there were insects on the victim and there was the back of a plastic bag sticking out from behind the head."

Mesinar has witnessed the result of hundreds of acts of violence in his career, but nothing as gruesome as this. His thoughts were racing.

Nobody deserves this. This woman should be buried.

Vaccaro was astonished at the contents of the makeshift tomb.

"In this business, you get to see a lot of people in pitiful positions," Vaccaro said. "But I was thinking, 'My God, I have never seen one like this, decomposition at that level, where all of the body fluids had stayed contained in a can like that with the victim.' "

Mesinar took special notice of the bag over the victim's face.

This lady was likely suffocated. This murder was pre-

meditated. We are dealing with something out of the ordinary, something personal.

Matvay walked the detectives through the crime scene, pointing out how the can was sealed with green wrapping, duct tape and plastic bags.

"It was like a cocoon wrapped in all this plastic wrap," Mesinar said. "It was taped real tightly. Whoever did it knew they were going to have an odor. They took a lot of time."

The first step, the four men decided, was to get the body to the Clark County coroner's office for autopsy, but this was not your typical crime scene. The body could not be lifted and placed in a body bag. There was a can full of decomposition fluid to deal with, and that fluid might contain clues like bullets, a broken knife or evidence of drugs.

"How do we move this package?" Manning asked. "We started to talk about it, and eventually we decided to give Vaccaro the police department–issued credit card, and we sent him to Home Depot to buy a huge roll of plastic."

The detectives decided they would wrap the garbage can in a plastic tarp and lift it onto a gurney, then roll it to an awaiting mortuary van for shipment to the coroner's office.

"We are going to wrap it up like you would a Christmas package," Manning said. "Wrap the plastic all the way around the can, tie it together with flex cuffs, and then actually put the toe tag on the package.

"It was a first for us," Manning said. "That's the creative part of the job."

Vaccaro made the five-minute drive to a Home Depot on West Charleston Boulevard to buy the tarp.

"I got this huge tarp. I went up to the counter and I presented the clerk with the credit card, and it actually says 'Homicide Section' on the credit card," Vaccaro said. "The clerk says, 'Plastic tarp? Homicide? Oh, I hope you are not buying this for some investigation.' I said, 'Lady, you don't even want to know what I'm going to do with this.'"

Vaccaro drove back to Canyon Gate, the 1,156-foot Stratosphere Tower rising into the skyline to the east, the glow of the Strip illuminating the clear winter night. He arrived at Canyon Gate, and the cops wrapped the huge tarp around the garbage can and tied it with plastic handcuffs.

"I thought it looked like an Easter basket," Mesinar said.

The can was heavy. The detectives, patrol officers and mortuary workers gradually got the can onto the gurney, and they wheeled it down to the coroner's van.

Whoever did this had to have help getting that body up here.

Manning, Matvay, Vaccaro and Mesinar started canvassing the contents of the storage shed for clues. There were at least two dozen boxes to search through, many containing shoes. There were enough shoes in here to last a woman a lifetime. Dress shoes, casual shoes, high heels, sneakers, loafers. Some looked like they were never worn or even taken out of the box.

"The green wrapping on many of the shoe boxes was the same width as the wrapping on the can—five inches," Matvay said. "It was the same color, same tinting, so whoever owns the shoes is the one who wrapped up the can."

The men opened each of the boxes and the black trunk. In the trunk, Matvay found a section of the *Las Vegas Review-Journal*, dated August 7, 1998. In a box that appeared to be a produce box from a grocery store, Matvay found a series of books, their covers worn thin: *The Satanic Bible*, *The Geography of Witchcraft*, *Necronomicon*, *Studies in Astrology*.

Manning, searching through a large box, found more books: *The Book of Black Magic*, *Amulets and Talismans*, *Jews for Jesus*.

"What is this stuff?" he said.

Mesinar found even more: *Satanic Rituals*, *Personal Aura*.

"Look at this," Mesinar said. "Here's a book on devil worship!"

This is unbelievable.

Vaccaro tried to comprehend the crime scene he was standing in the middle of. An elderly woman sealed in a garbage can, a bag over her face and books about Satanic worship and witchcraft near the body.

"How bizarre is that?" Vaccaro said.

Most homicide detectives will tell you they have a sixth sense about them, a feeling in the gut, so to speak, in assessing a crime scene. When the books were found, the instinct hit Vaccaro like a sledgehammer. He just knew there was a strong likelihood the perpetrator was a woman. "There's a female inside the can; there's all these women's shoes," Vaccaro said. "The whole thing had a female gender feel to it."

No one said a word about how strange this crime was. There was no need to—it was better left unsaid, because no one needed the distraction.

The men continued their search.

In one box, Manning and Mesinar found Social Security documents in the name of Christine M. Smith, date of birth February 15, 1932. She was a senior citizen, just like the woman in the garbage can appeared to be.

This may be our victim.

In a bag, Mesinar found a lady's wallet and a picture ID. It was a Citizens Area Transit bus pass for an elderly woman, Christine Smith. The picture on the bus pass showed a fragile, elderly woman. She was thin; her dark hair appeared to be long and bundled in back, just like the hair of the woman in the garbage can. She wore a wool knit cap on her head, and she was smiling. She looked happy.

3

Just one last chance before you go
You hold the secrets and I must know
Just one last chance to right the wrong
Before the clues are buried and gone

—"Speak for You," by Clark County deputy
medical examiner Gary Telgenhoff, aka Skinnerrat

In the early morning hours of February 6, 2001, a team of Las Vegas police and crime scene analysts gathered at the Clark County coroner's office on Shadow Lane in downtown Las Vegas. They were about to witness one of the most macabre autopsies in Southern Nevada history.

The victim in question was the nameless female found sealed in the garbage can at Canyon Gate Mini Storage. A toe tag was tied to the flex cuffs securing the tarp around the garbage can, and it read JANE "MINI STORAGE" DOE, a temporary label used to identify the woman until dental records and fingerprints could be secured.

Detective Mesinar arrived first. CSI Dahn arrived soon after, and she was joined by veteran Las Vegas police crime scene investigator Sheree Norman and coroner's office technician Damon O'Brien.

The job of determining the manner and cause of death for Jane "Mini Storage" Doe on this day would fall to veteran Clark County deputy medical examiner Dr. Gary Telgenhoff. He is stocky, mildly rotund, forty-six years old, with long gray hair and blue eyes that suggest he gets plenty of sleepless nights. He readily admits he is a man interested in death.

"I'm a dark person," Telgenhoff said. "A heavy thinker, and death fascinates me. It does everyone to a degree, but I think I was a little excessive with it."

By day, Telgenhoff makes a living dissecting dead bodies to determine the cause of their demise. He makes it clear he is not in law enforcement, but instead medicine.

"My job is not to convict anyone," Telgenhoff said. "It is not to set them free or anything else. I just want to make the best assessment I can. You learn right away, keep your mouth shut, observe, be methodical. I want all the information. I want to synthesize it and boil it out."

By night, Telgenhoff rocks. He has converted his garage into a soundproof music room. It is completely black inside, with a silver drum set in one corner and a keyboard with thousands of dollars of computerized recording equipment in the other. He retreats to his music room every night, writing dark, foreboding songs about murder and death.

"I compose on my keyboards, I record them on a computer, I lay down drum tracks, I play the bass and I sing," Telgenhoff said.

He calls his one-man band Skinnerrat, and it is music not for the faint of heart. It is heavy Alice Cooper–style rock-guitar riffs, drums, haunting synthesizers and grisly lyrics. In the background of one of Skinnerrat's songs is the sound of the whiz of a bone saw, which Telgenhoff uses at work to slice open human skulls like coconuts. It is as if all the ugliness he sees at work exits from his body and into his keyboard or drums. There, the ugliness is recast and reemerges via Skinnerrat.

I'll speak for you when your lips are cold and blue
Dead men do tell tales, and I'll speak for you
I know your soul is seeking some kind of rest
But you'll be unaware of my inquest
Our exchange will be somewhat extreme
But you won't feel my crude, cold sharpened steel

"The song is called 'Speak for You' because it's what I do," Telgenhoff said. "I speak for the dead."

Telgenhoff's song "Speak for You" was recently played on an episode of the national hit television show *CSI*. Telgenhoff has even served as an unpaid consultant for the show's producer.

"I like dark, and the lyrics are important to me," Telgenhoff said. "This is my real love."

The road to becoming a medical examiner was a long and difficult haul for Telgenhoff. As a boy raised in a strict Baptist home in Michigan, he was always interested in trying to figure out how things work. By the age of eight, he was taking apart toys or old appliances he found sitting around the home to see what made them tick.

"I like to tear things apart to see how they work, but I don't really care to put them back together," Telgenhoff said.

Telgenhoff snuck Beatles albums into his home during his teen years without his father knowing. His first love was music, and he pounded the drums throughout high school. He dreamed of rock superstardom and, after high school, played with famed guitarist Dick Wagner and his band Frost.

"One band led to another, and another, and another, and eventually I ended up in a traveling type of band, a small trio that ended up playing canned cover tunes," Telgenhoff said. "We ended up playing Holiday Inns and hotels and motel chains. It was a good living for me. I didn't have any bills, all the hotels were free and it was a nice, free lifestyle. All the money we made was just cigarette and beer money. I loved my life, but eventually I realized I'm going to get old, and I'm probably not going to be able to do this when I'm fifty. This was not going to work anymore, and I didn't want to end up a vagabond or street urchin."

Telgenhoff decided to pursue a career in medicine. He completed four years of undergraduate school, three years of graduate school, four years of medical school, a one-year internship and four more years in a pathology residency.

The worst time in those sixteen years, Telgenhoff said, was interning in a hospital during medical school.

"I hated my miserable life," Telgenhoff said. "You go in at five a.m. and leave at nine p.m. and the whole day is scorn, ridicule, abuse. Mental abuse and intimidation. It's like going to boot camp and having a sergeant in your face, but it continues for four or five years."

It was too late to quit, though, Telgenhoff said.

"Once you are there, you are so far in debt that there is no turning back," he said. "By the time I was done with everything, I had $100,000 in debt."

Telgenhoff ended up studying at the Cuyahoga County coroner's office in Cleveland, Ohio, where he started to entertain pathology as a possible career field.

"I didn't think some of the smells and stuff were tolerable," Telgenhoff said. "But then I got over that, and I thought, 'Hmm, I could probably do this.' I might have found something that is away from the hospitals, where they run around like Energizer bunnies on meth. Here, I can go home at four p.m., and it's still medicine."

He said the most important part of the job of medical examiner is pathology, because most of what Telgenhoff sees on the steel gurney at the coroner's office is natural death and disease.

"Any idiot can count bullet holes," Telgenhoff said. "It

is a special study to identify entries and exits. That's complicated, but most people can even figure that out with a little training. Where the doctor part comes in is diagnosing disease under the microscope. It is seeing a thousand livers and noticing that this one just isn't right," he said.

Telgenhoff landed his first job at the Clark County coroner's office in 1997. He performs about five hundred autopsies a year, and it is work that leaves him with a few dark stories to tell. One is of a woman who lost it mentally and locked herself in her Las Vegas home during the city's scorching-hot summer months. She took towels and stuffed them in the window cracks, and she barricaded the windows and doors like a horror-flick actress trying to fend off the bogeyman. She turned the heater and oven on full and lay down on the kitchen floor next to the open oven. The cops found her body a few days later.

"She was cooked like a Christmas ham," Telgenhoff said. "She had been there for two weeks like that. I went to move an arm, and it tore off like a drumstick. On the floor, there were drippings, just like in a broiler pan."

In another case, cops called Telgenhoff to the scene of a suicide on U.S. Highway 95 in northwest Las Vegas. A man took a steel cable and put it around his neck with a slipknot, then tied the other end to a freeway overpass and jumped.

"Pulled his head right off," Telgenhoff said. "The cops said, 'You've got to come out here and look at this.'"

Telgenhoff drove to the scene and saw a group of cops standing around in a circle.

"It looked like a coven or something, so I went over there and I couldn't believe what I saw," Telgenhoff said. "The guy's head was looking back at his ass."

Telgenhoff's dark sense of humor keeps him sane in an environment of horror and tragedy. Like Mesinar and the CSIs, he sees up close the murder, mayhem and grief of Las Vegas.

"I don't see any rhyme or reason to the daily tragedy I see except for stupidity," he said.

The garbage can containing the body of Jane "Mini Storage" Doe was rolled into the well of the coroner's office on a flat steel gurney at eight thirty a.m. Telgenhoff and Mesinar knew by the sight that this wasn't going to be a routine day at the office.

"The garbage can came in, the whole damned thing," Telgenhoff said. "I'm used to the odors, but this one was a little different. A little more intense. The average person wouldn't be hanging out. They'd be looking for the door, maybe on their hands and knees."

Dave Mesinar stood in the well of the coroner's office and ran the facts of the case through his head. A woman dead in a can. The identification next to the body was of Christine M. Smith. Her daughter, Brookey Lee West, was the renter of the storage shed.

We need an identification of the victim.

The can was in almost the exact same condition as it was when it was found. It was square and buckled at the bottom. It was covered with the green plastic wrap, duct tape and garbage bags.

Telgenhoff decided not to open the lid until after the fluid from inside the can was drained.

"Shit, how we are going to approach this?" Telgenhoff asked. "It's not something you get everyday, so you start thinking, 'What would be the best way to do this?'"

The challenge, Telgenhoff said, was to get the body out of the can without losing any potential evidence in the fluid. Coroner's office medical technician Damon O'Brien came up with a novel solution. Telgenhoff would use a drill to punch a hole in the bottom of the can, and then O'Brien would hold a strainer at the bottom and let the liquid strain through it into a sink. This way, if there was a bullet fragment or knife tip in the liquid, O'Brien would catch it before it entered the sink.

"Dr. Telgenhoff had a spaghetti strainer, but we knew that wasn't going to be big enough, so Sheree traveled back to the lab," Dahn said. "We do have a large sifter we use out at crime scenes in the desert, and she went and got that and came back with it."

O'Brien, Telgenhoff and the CSIs perched the can on the ledge of a deep, stainless steel sink and Telgenhoff used the drill to punch a four-inch hole in the bottom of the can. The can was stinking, and Jane "Mini Storage" Doe's body was sloshing about inside.

"I cut the hole in the can, and all of this spooge comes out," Telgenhoff said. "There is no way to describe it. Very thick fat mixed with fluids you've never seen."

The can kept tipping back and forth from one side to another, and Telgenhoff worried the can might fall over and spill its contents out onto the floor. Two medical students were in the building, so Telgenhoff asked one of them to help hold the can at the top so it wouldn't tip over.

"This one medical student was actually stabilizing the can from one side, and as we are working on it, his eyes are huge," Dahn said. "It was really smelly, and he is getting exposed to all this."

O'Brien was at the bottom of the sink with the strainer, sifting the soupy brown contents for any potential evidence.

"He got the good job," Telgenhoff said. "He will always remember that day. He still talks about it, because he had to shower twice and throw away his clothes."

After the initial rush of liquid and fat emanated from the bottom of the can, the flow of fluids slowed to barely a drip.

"It didn't really work because the body was blocking the hole," Mesinar said.

Telgenhoff gave the go-ahead for the group to crack the

lid and lift it up, then slowly pour the contents onto the gurney in a slow, methodical fashion. Slowly, they gained leverage on the can and angled it at forty-five degrees, causing the plastic container to cast out the victim like a cannonball. Jane "Mini Storage" Doe plopped down on the gurney, and Telgenhoff witnessed something he had never seen before. Jane "Mini Storage" Doe was almost completely skeletonized, and her corpse was morphed into a large, round, gooey, smelly, Jell-O–like, half-oval ball.

"It looked like a white, waxy, smelly, cheese ball," Telgenhoff said. "You had to be there."

Telgenhoff's blood was flowing. This was something new.

"Sweet screaming Jesus!" he recalled thinking. "Wow, this one is a top five. I've got to write this one down in the journal."

Mesinar was shocked at the sight of a woman shaped into a gelatinized ball of human decomposition. Some bugs were on the outer layer of the body, too.

"They removed the body, and it came out in the shape of the can," he said. "I remember thinking to myself, 'This is amazing.'"

Dahn was snapping photos to document the bizarre sight.

"It was kind of like a rubberized, solidified block," Dahn said. "Actually, when it came out of the can, it didn't bounce, but it was like a blob and it just laid out. It was a cubicle square of a person."

The woman had long gray hair, and she was clearly old. Her hair was more than eighteen inches long, and it was tied in the back with a pink scrunchie. She was curled up in the fetal position with her hair draping backward into the block. Her hands were gnarled, and her eyes and mouth were wide open in an expression of horror.

Who could do something like this?

"The head was on its way to complete skeletization,"

Telgenhoff said. "Kind of like something you'd see in *Tales from the Crypt*."

There was one detail about the woman's body that immediately caught the medical examiner's eye. A common household trash bag covered the victim's face, and the bag was tied in a knot at the back of her head.

"It was white, and it was tied over the nose and mouth area," Telgenhoff said. "It wasn't real tight, but some of the hair in back was caught up in the knot."

Telgenhoff believed the bag may have been tied tighter when the body was originally placed in the can, but decomposition may have caused it to loosen slightly. Any doubt in Mesinar's mind that this was anything other than murder evaporated at the sight of the bag.

"The bag would cut off her air, especially with the assistance of a pillow or strangulation," Mesinar said.

It wouldn't have taken too much to kill a frail woman like this.

"When I saw the plastic bag, I said, 'I can't believe it,' " Dahn said. "I said, 'It's a homicide.' "

Telgenhoff and O'Brien worked the corpse by bending the arms and legs at an angle to flatten it out on the gurney. They had to repeatedly break the stiffness of the woman to get her supine on the gurney.

"We stretched it out, and it took more than one person," Telgenhoff said. "It tried to spring back."

Telgenhoff told his colleagues to collect samples of the insects.

"I suggested we collect all the maggots," Telgenhoff said. "Insects are very important. Only a couple of times in your career will they make a difference, but when they do, it is monumental."

Another fact that stood out to Telgenhoff from the gurney was a white, gooey substance adhering to much of the corpse. The material was adipocere—the first time Telgenhoff observed it during an autopsy. The gooey substance is the body's fat after it breaks down and is traditionally only found in bodies stored in moist environments.

"Usually, it's in cold waters, deep waters when the body has been there for a long time," Telgenhoff said. "They pull up a lot of bodies with adipocere in the Chesapeake Bay. I assumed I would never see it in the desert. One place where it also happens a lot is in the mausoleums," Telgenhoff said. "There have been people who go into a mausoleum and they've been in one hundred years and they pull them out. Their facial features, everything, is preserved in wax—a cheesy wax. It retains the shape of whatever it was."

A darkened, humid corner of a storage shed would provide the perfect moist climate for the phenomenon.

"It tells me the body has been there for quite some time," Telgenhoff said. "Most of the textbooks say it requires a good six months to form a layer of adipocere, but it is variable. This was the first time I had ever seen that," he said. "It took me a moment, looking, saying, 'What is that odd stuff?' This is different—a white, waxy, musty, earthy smell. 'Oh, yeah, this is what I read in the books.' It is exciting when your training clicks in."

The woman had on a pair of underwear, a bra, a thermal undershirt and a light-colored long-sleeved sweatshirt.

"When I saw the bikini underwear, I've got to admit, right away I thought that was strange," Dahn said, unable to envision an elderly woman wearing bikini underwear. "But maybe it's an elderly woman wearing bikini underwear all her life, and she just never switched," Dahn said. "To me, though, I found it odd that it wasn't high-topped underwear. Generally, they [older women] get a pooch on their belly, and they just—I don't know—go to the higher-topped underwear. As a woman, it is something I would think about."

Dahn said the victim was wearing was the type of clothing one would wear to bed.

"The first thing I thought was she was sleeping when she was killed," the CSI said. "They looked like sleep clothes. She had a long-underwear top on and a sweatshirt, then underwear. No pants or shoes."

Dahn photographed every inch of the body, the clothing and the bag. She and Norman also took DNA samples.

Upon closer inspection of the corpse, Telgenhoff concluded that determining a cause and manner of death was going to be a challenge. All of the internal organs were liquefied, including the brain. Telgenhoff had no gunshot or stab wounds to identify. Because of the decomposition of the throat, eyes and lungs, he could not tell if the woman was suffocated or drowned. The bag tied over the victim's face led him to believe the woman was suffocated, and he told Mesinar of his suspicions.

Telgenhoff was not ready, however, to issue a ruling on cause and manner of death. He needed to see the results of toxicology tests—if they were even possible—and he figured it was going to take several weeks to determine if there was evidence to prove murder.

"I couldn't be sure yet if this was just a bizarre way of disposing of somebody who had died naturally, or if a person was killed and then put in the can," Telgenhoff said.

But even though Telgenhoff stopped short of saying the case was definitely murder, the autopsy provided one instantaneous benefit to Mesinar. The lower mandible of the woman's jaw was still present, and when those teeth were compared with dental records of the woman whose identification was found next to the body, the coroner's office got a match.

The teeth from the woman in the can and the dental records from Christine Merle Smith, age sixty-five were identical. Mesinar's hunch at the storage shed was right—the items of identification found next to the body belonged to his victim, Christine Smith. The home address listed on her bus pass and Social Security documents found at Canyon Gate was the Orange Door apartments, 2829 West Sahara Avenue, apartment #1.

Mesinar now had some solid leads to work on. He had an official victim identification, he had her home address and he knew from the Canyon Gate records that the victim was the daughter of the shed's renter—Brookey Lee West.

"Based on Telgenhoff telling me he believed it was a homicide, I made a decision it's definitely time to start looking for Ms. West," Mesinar said. "Our whole focus was going to be trying to find her, This was definitely someone we wanted to talk to."

After the autopsy was over, Mesinar walked to his vehicle in the parking lot of the coroner's office. Even though he didn't have a cause of death, in his heart he knew he was on the hunt for a killer, whether it was West or someone else. He also wondered who could take an elderly woman like Christine Smith, put a bag over her face and store her in a garbage can for what appeared to be an extended period of time. In Mesinar's mind, the age of the victim made the killing particularly heinous.

No one deserves this. She was probably a sweet little old lady.

4

A decomposing corpse in a garbage can is the perfect story for television news. It is bizarre, gruesome and shocking—a guaranteed ratings-booster that seizes on the morbid curiosity found in every one of us. The idea of someone melting away in a garbage can is unfathomable, an image of brutality beyond the everyday human experience, and when we see such horrors on the six p.m. news, we predictably react with disgust, condemnation and outrage. But deep down inside, we want more. We crave for the latest update like a crackhead searching for the next hit off that glass pipe.

A television news producer couldn't ask for more.

On the night Christine Smith's body was found, homicide sergeant Kevin Manning typed up a press release confirming the gory details of the discovery. He faxed it out to the three main Las Vegas television news stations, but he withheld the fact that books about Satanism and witchcraft were next to the body. Even without this salacious detail, the Vegas television media gobbled up the story like wolves sinking their teeth into an animal carcass. It was a damn good news story, and everyone knew it. Each Vegas news station ran sensational blurbs about Jane Doe in the garbage can on their morning, lunch and evening broadcasts, and in death Christine Smith was big news in Sin City.

Detective Mesinar usually pays little attention to the media coverage while carrying out a homicide investigation. He said the wave of stories rarely hurts an investigation, and in only a few cases does it help—namely, when a victim is unidentified or when a crazed killer is on the loose and the cops need the public's help tracking them down.

"I really don't think about the media a lot, because I don't have to deal with them," Mesinar said. "Either our lieutenant or sergeant deals with the press, and that allows us to focus on the job at hand. But in the same breath, I knew this case would be of interest because of the oddity."

In the case of Christine Smith, the media coverage was a mild concern for Mesinar during the first forty-eight hours of the investigation. The stories about the corpse in the can were flooding the television screens in the Las Vegas Valley, and the police hadn't found the renter of the shed yet. West was, at a minimum, a potential suspect in the eyes of police because, as the renter of the shed and the daughter of the victim, she had to have relevant information about her mother's death.

Mesinar was concerned West might see the news and flee before the cops could find her.

"I figured there is a good chance she was going to watch the news and see what was happening," Mesinar said. "She was either going to run or she was going to call us, and she never called us, so we started looking for her."

Mesinar said it was important to find West even if it turned out she wasn't the killer. If she was, by chance, simply a daughter whose dead mother was hidden in her storage shed without her knowledge, Mesinar wanted to tell

West about her mother's horrifying fate before she saw it on television.

"I knew it was important to try to find her," Mesinar said. "I know what happened to her mother, and in case she didn't know her mother was dead, I could give her the death notification."

Mesinar drove from the coroner's office to the Las Vegas police Homicide Section office on West Charleston Boulevard to begin the search for West. The Homicide Section is a nondescript, single-story office building offering no indication from the outside that it is home to some three dozen of the most veteran detectives in Las Vegas. The detectives work themselves to the point of exhaustion week after week in the never-ending pursuit of killers. Each detective is given a computer, a small work desk, a filing cabinet and a spot in the office not much bigger than your average walk-in shower. There aren't even any partitions to separate the detectives.

A detective who accepts the assignment to Homicide knows the investigation comes first and, on many occasions, his family comes second. The murder calls come in at all hours, and if a dead body is found sixty miles away in the desert outside Las Vegas at three a.m., the detective assigned to the case is expected to be at the crime scene as soon as possible. On some especially busy weeks at the Homicide Section, the sleep-deprived detectives look like walking zombies. If the trail for the killer is hot or the crime scene is especially complex, they may not see their wife and kids for days, but Homicide is still the most prized assignment in the Las Vegas Police Department because the detectives have, over the years, played a repeated role in history.

Perhaps the most well-known murder case involving Las Vegas police was the infamous 1959 murders of the

Clutter family in Holcomb, Kansas. The shootings of wealthy wheat farmer Herbert Clutter, his wife and two children inspired Truman Capote's classic true-crime book *In Cold Blood*. Kansas police successfully cracked the case with evidence linking career criminals Perry Smith and Dick Hickock to the shotgun slayings, but it was Vegas cops who helped collar the killers. The two thugs ended up swinging from the Kansas gallows for the heinous murders.

The cycle of high-profile homicides in Vegas is nonstop. In 1996, gangster-rapper Tupac Shakur was gunned down on the Strip in a case that remains unsolved to this day. In 1997, Las Vegas Homicide made news by solving the murder of seven-year-old Sherrice Iverson, an innocent little girl who was lured into a casino restroom, sexually assaulted and strangled to death by well-to-do Southern California teen Jeremy Strohmeyer. Strohmeyer is serving life in prison. And in 2002, Las Vegas Homicide carried out a massive investigation into a deadly riot between the Hells Angels and Mongols motorcycle gangs at a motorcycle run in Laughlin, Nevada. The two outlaw biker gangs clashed in a bloodbath inside the Harrah's Laughlin casino on the Colorado River. They shot, stabbed and bludgeoned one another in a chaotic melee captured on casino surveillance video, and when it was over two Hells Angels and a Mongol were dead. A two-year investigation by Vegas cops resulted in a 2004 indictment charging seven Hells Angels and five Mongols with murder.

Mesinar knew he had another high-profile case on his hands with Christine's death. It is not everyday you find an old lady melted in a garbage can. By midmorning on February 7, Mesinar arrived at the Homicide Section office and consulted briefly with his lieutenant, Wayne Petersen, and Sergeant Manning, about the results of the autopsy. He then started his search for West with a call to the Nevada Department of Motor Vehicles, and he learned West did have a driver's license in Nevada. A picture of West from the license showed an attractive, brown-haired, professional-looking forty-seven-year-old. The license, like the rental sheet at Canyon Gate, listed a post office box on Industrial Road as a home address for West. West was continually listing a post office box for a home address, and it left detectives wondering if she was trying to keep the location of her residence a secret.

Mesinar and Vaccaro drove to the address on Industrial and found it to be a traditional private mailbox business.

"The owner knew who Brooke West was, and she said West was living both here and in California, commuting back and forth between Las Vegas and San Jose," Mesinar said. "She said West was recently in to pick up her mail, and there was mail waiting for her. The employees of the business agreed to let us know when she came in again.

"We did have her driver's license picture, so we knew what she looked like," Mesinar said. "We decided to set up surveillance on the post office box, hoping she would come back, but she never showed up."

The next step was serving a subpoena in the name of Brookey Lee West with Nevada Power, which is the power company serving all of Southern Nevada. This time, Mesinar got a hit.

"I was able to locate power service in the name of Brookey West to an apartment complex located at 8000 West Spring Mountain Road in Las Vegas," Mesinar said.

"That was a big shot in the arm for us," Vaccaro said. "We've confirmed she's got a place here, and it gives us a chance to start looking into who this Brookey West really is."

The $1,200-a-month apartment West resided in was at the upscale San Croix condominiums in northwest Las Vegas. San Croix sits just a little more than two miles from the Canyon Gate Mini Storage where Christine's body was found, and most residents at San Croix can look out their window or back patio and immediately see the beautiful Sierra Nevadas to their west. To the east is the Las Vegas Strip and its magnificent lights, which radiate out of the sand like supernova emerging from the desert floor.

It appeared to the detectives Brookey West was living a comfortable life at San Croix with access to an elegant pool, fitness center and spa.

"The management said she still lived there, so we knew we had something to work with," Mesinar said. "We went ahead and got a search warrant for the apartment."

With the search warrant in hand, the detectives got a key for the apartment from San Croix management and entered apartment #2122. Vaccaro quickly noticed how nice the place was. Much of a homicide detective's work involves trolling through the gutters of humanity, and this was no gutter.

It appeared West was well-off financially.

"I was impressed with the apartment," Vaccaro said. "I thought it was a neat, well-kept place with nice stuff. It seemed like there was a little bit of money involved here."

There was a black couch and black love seat with a footrest in the living room. Long golden drapes lined the windows, and there was a television set, a boom box and a brand-new laptop computer in the central quarter of the apartment as well. The master bedroom was lived in, but the second bedroom was empty of furniture.

"The whole apartment had sort of a one-person-living-alone feel to it," Vaccaro said.

There was an easel with a half-finished pencil sketch on it in one corner of the apartment, leading Vaccaro to conclude West was a sophisticated woman and talented artist.

"This person was involved with doing sketches and art with pastels," Vaccaro said. "There were several works of art on the floor."

Mesinar sensed West was recently in the residence.

"There was food in the refrigerator, food in the cupboards," Mesinar said.

The two detectives proceeded to pore over the contents of the apartment like hunting dogs sniffing the trail of a wounded animal. In the spare bedroom, Mesinar found a garbage bag containing a crucial clue—bank statements from Nevada State Bank in the name of Christine Smith. The bank statements showed West's mother was receiving monthly Social Security deposits from the U.S. Department of Treasury, and the deposits were made within the last month.

How could this be? This woman has been dead for years.

More important, the records showed withdrawals were being made from Christine's account within the last few weeks.

Someone is stealing her money.

Some of the withdrawals from Christine's account were made at ATMs, and there were also point-of-sale purchases, known as debit card purchases, made within the last couple of weeks. Each of the purchases was made between Las Vegas and San Jose, California, each communities West had ties to. West resided in Las Vegas, and San Jose was in Santa Clara County, where a prior address for West had popped up when the cops at the storage shed ran her name through the police computer database.

The information in Christine's bank records immediately raised red flags in Mesinar's mind. Telgenhoff had been clear in his opinion that Christine Smith had been dead in that garbage can for at least six months, if not years, and the bank statements showed someone was spending Christine's Social Security money while she was rotting in the storage shed.

This lady is dead. She shouldn't be getting Social Security. All this stuff is in her daughter's apartment, and the money's being used.

"It really fueled our suspicions," Mesinar said. "Why is she getting Social Security when she is dead?"

West was now the number one suspect in her mother's murder.

This woman may have killed her mother for the Social Security money.

Mesinar and Vaccaro continued their search in West's kitchen, and while rummaging through the kitchen drawers Mesinar found a key and a roll of duct tape. The duct tape looked identical to the duct tape used to seal the garbage can containing Christine's corpse, and the key looked as if it would fit a lock that Unruh had pried off the door of the storage shed at Canyon Gate. Mesinar decided he would give the duct tape to the CSIs later to see if it matched the duct tape on the garbage can, but the detectives would not have to wait to see if the key could further link West to the shed.

"We still had the lock from the storage shed, so we put the key in the lock, and it worked," Mesinar said.

All of the facts were pointing to West as the killer of her mother. She was the renter of the shed, her mother's bank records were in her apartment and the records showed Christine was getting Social Security money long after her death. Someone was spending Christine's money in San Jose and Las Vegas, both communities where West listed an address. In the drawer in West's apartment was duct tape similar to duct tape at the crime scene, and the key in the drawer fit the lock to the storage shed.

"At this point, we're thinking Brooke is the suspect," Vaccaro said. "This lady has obviously got some explaining to do. I remember thinking, 'If this is the woman who did this, how bad is it to put your mom in a garbage can, store her away in a storage shed and not treat her remains with some decency and respect?'" Vaccaro said. "This is the person who brought you into the world? What do we owe our parents—storage in a storage shed?"

After concluding their search of West's apartment, the detectives started knocking on the doors of West's neighbors, and in minutes they came across a friendly, polite woman named Carole H. Wolf in a downstairs apartment at San Croix. Wolf said she'd known West for about a month, and she agreed to give detectives a taped statement.

"She was walking out front of my apartment, uh, hunched over with a bag, as if she was having problems . . . and I went out to help her," Wolf told the detectives. "And she brought me up the stairs to her apartment, and she invited me in for a cup of tea."

Wolf told the detectives West drove a small black pickup truck with gold trim and that West was probably still in the area. She knew West had an adult daughter who did not live in Las Vegas.

"She did say the other day she had four or five husbands," Wolf said.

Wolf told police West commuted back and forth to a second residence in the San Jose area of Silicon Valley, and West worked in the San Jose area as a technical writer before losing her job the week prior.

"A technical writer, writing books for computers, is what she explained to me," Wolf said.

Vaccaro's suspicion that West was a woman of financial means was correct. Technical writers prior to the dot-com bust in the Silicon Valley made good money, and it was clear their suspect was well-off compared to most of the dirtbags Vegas detectives deal with on a daily basis.

Wolf said she and West went to lunch together recently, and the two also went to a local oxygen bar called Breathe on Sahara Avenue at Decatur Boulevard in Las Vegas. Instead of bellying up to the bar to drink alcohol, Breathe patrons, known as clients, place a tube hooked to an oxygen tank over their noses and inhale oxygen in a Zenlike social setting symbolic of the West Coast's health-conscious populace.

On one of their trips to the Breathe oxygen bar, Wolf said West started reading peoples' psychic futures.

"She did a spiritual psychic reading for a client, and the owner at that time pulled her aside and said she was gonna give her free oxygen in lieu of her coming down to read for clients of Breathe," Wolf said. "God help us."

"So she does psychic readings?" Mesinar asked.

"Yes, she does," Wolf said. "And she does them correctly."

Wolf told the cops West used marbles to perform the psychic readings. She took the marbles and rolled them back and forth in her hands as if rubbing dice at the craps table for good luck. West said the caressing of the marbles magically transferred the psychic vibes from the universe into her body, mind and spirit.

"She reads what comes off the marbles," Wolf said. "However, she can also read anything you ask about her. She never did a reading for me here," Wolf said. "It's funny, because I never asked her to when she was in my house. But the first time we went into Breathe, she reads marbles—she carries marbles in her pocketbook, and she reads them."

"Does she charge for this service?" Mesinar asked.

"No," Wolf said. "She says . . . she does it for free as her gift."

Wolf said West talked to her about having some spiritual books in storage on Sahara Avenue, and West was apparently not shy about promoting her psychic talents—she was proud of it.

"She said she's seeing a doctor who was studying her because of her psychic abilities," Wolf said. "In fact, she even said, 'Oh, my doctor should come down and watch me when I give readings at Breathe. He'd be really impressed.'"

The detectives asked if West ever talked about her mother, and Wolf told police West repeatedly spoke negatively about her mother.

"Uh, [she] just said that she was a bad influence on her and she couldn't, [she] chose not to be around her," Wolf told the detectives.

"Did you get the impression that her mother was alive?" Mesinar asked.

"I didn't get the impression she was not alive, but I don't remember," Wolf said.

Wolf then remembered a specific conversation in which West had, in fact, indicated her mother was alive.

"'When my mother calls, I'm just very aloof,'" Wolf quoted West as saying.

The idea of West claiming her mother was alive in a recent conversation with Wolf intrigued detectives because medical examiner Gary Telgenhoff had indicated Christine must have been in the can for several months, if not years. It was clear West was deceiving people about the wellbeing of her mother, and such a deception would be completely unnecessary if West wasn't involved in the killing. But Wolf had more. She said West told her a multitude of problems in her life were because of her mother. West said she suffered a nervous breakdown because of her mother, and that being around her mother caused her to be physically ill.

"The reason for her breakdown and the reason for her not being well was her mother," Wolf said. "All her friends told her this, and she now has gotten away from her mother. She doesn't see her mother, [and] she doesn't allow her mother in her life in any way."

West's dislike for her mother sounded to the veteran detectives like a motive for murder. West's venomous criticisms of her mother went beyond the tensions normally found in a mother-daughter relationship. This sounded like blood-boiling hatred.

"She just said, 'I don't let her into my life,'" Wolf told police, quoting West. "[She] said, 'She's been a very dark force, a very negative force in my life, and I no longer allow that in my life.'"

The case was quickly coming together like a jigsaw puzzle. Mesinar had a dead elderly woman in a can in a storage shed rented by the victim's daughter. The body was surrounded by books about witchcraft, and West just happened to be a proclaimed psychic. West's apartment contained duct tape similar to duct tape found at the crime scene, and a key in her drawer fit a lock to the shed. West was telling at least one woman her mother was alive when she was dead, and to top it off she was bad-mouthing her mother as a "very dark force."

This is the strangest case I've ever had.

5

Joe Matvay may be the best crime scene analyst in the state of Nevada. He has, over the last quarter century, helped solve hundreds of criminal cases for Las Vegas police, putting dozens of killers in the Nevada state penitentiary. He is a tall, soft-spoken man, and one of his greatest skills as a CSA is an uncanny ability to lift fingerprints from evidence. In one criminal case, Matvay lifted a perpetrator's fingerprint off a brick. In another case, he retrieved a fingerprint from a tree branch, and he has even plucked a perpetrator's print off a piece of smooth leather at a crime scene.

"With today's technology, we can pretty much get fingerprints from anything except shag carpet and water," Matvay said.

The science of processing crime scenes for fingerprints has come a long way over the last century. The first person widely credited with recognizing the value of fingerprints to the criminal justice system was an Englishman named Sir Edward Henry, who in the 1890s oversaw the Bengali police in the East Indies. Henry was an acquaintance of a scientist named Francis Galton, and Galton had success-fully documented how each human being has unique, iden-tifiable patterns on the tips of his or her fingers. Henry was convinced fingerprints could offer a new way for Bengali officers to keep track of the people they took into custody, so he ordered his officers to start keeping records of prints gathered from suspects.

Henry then took the technology a step further by devel-oping his own system of identifying and classifying finger-prints, and in 1901 he was named an administrator to Scotland Yard, where he ordered his investigators to begin collecting fingerprints, too. The program was an over-whelming success, and word of the new crime-solving technique quickly spread to police departments across the Atlantic.

In 1911, an American man named Thomas Jennings was arrested in Chicago for the fatal shooting of a home-owner during a residential burglary. Police found Jennings' fingerprints on a stairway railing in the victim's home, making Jennings the first person in the United States to be convicted of murder because of fingerprints left at a crime scene. Jennings appealed the conviction to the Illinois Supreme Court, and the court ruled fingerprints were cred-ible evidence in a court of law in a ruling that cleared the way for fingerprint evidence to become a staple of the American criminal justice system.

For Matvay, fingerprint processing is part art, part sci-ence. The key, he said, is knowing what method will best highlight the presence of a print otherwise invisible to the naked eye. Some prints are best exposed when sprayed with chemicals. Others are revealed with powders, and some surface when exposed to alternate light sources. The temperature of the environment at a crime scene, the type of surface the print is on and the age of the print are variables the CSA needs to consider as well when determining what method to employ on a particular print.

"There are a lot of different techniques we can use," Matvay said. "It depends on the texture of the item, and it depends on how old we think the print may be, as to what techniques we'll use. So literally, we could use twenty or thirty different techniques on one item. It's called sequential processing, and with the advent of technology, there is more and more we can do everyday."

Matvay's intricate knowledge of the different methods of fingerprint processing has repeatedly produced results for Vegas homicide investigators. In 2002, Matvay's skills were crucial in solving the murder of a Cuban drug dealer named Enrique Caminero Jr., who was brutally strangled and shot in a drug robbery at the Capri Motel on Fremont Street in downtown Las Vegas. Caminero's killers carried out an extensive cleanup of the room after the slaying, but Matvay's persistence turned up a hidden bloody palm print on a bathroom countertop, and the print led to the arrest of three suspects. One, Sally Villaverde, was convicted of the crime and is now serving a life sentence. Two other suspects are awaiting trial.

The case Matvay is most proud of solving unfolded in 1986. Sylvia Pena, the operator of Richard's Produce, a small produce and nut shop in northeast Las Vegas, was butchered with a bread knife in her business during a robbery. It was a senseless, horrific crime.

"She wasn't well known, wasn't popular," Matvay said. "Just a hardworking woman. What the perpetrator did was take a bread knife, and he just slashed her face and her neck and chest. She was cut up badly—cut to shreds."

The brutality of the crime left Matvay with an extremely bloody crime scene. It took him hours to process the store for evidence, but while dusting the inside of a cabinet door in the rear of the business, Matvay found a single bloody fingerprint. He removed the cabinet door from its hinges, took it back to the police crime lab, photographed the print and preserved it. It was promising evidence that held the potential to identify the killer, but the print matched none of the hundreds of thousands of prints stored in Las Vegas police files.

Pena's murder went unsolved for the next seven years, until, in 1993, a woman in North Carolina went to police and said her boyfriend, Jeffrey Lark, told her he once carried out a robbery in Las Vegas in the mid-1980s.

"She said this guy was involved in some robberies in Las Vegas, specifically a robbery of a fruit and nut stand," Matvay said. "She knew he had done a robbery, but he never told her he committed a murder."

Police in North Carolina phoned Las Vegas authorities about the woman's information, and Las Vegas authorities started probing their old unsolved robberies. The murder of Pena was one of the old cases reviewed by detectives, and fingerprints from Lark were compared to the prints left behind by the killer at the fruit stand seven years earlier.

"I was on vacation at the time, and I was called in to do the fingerprint examination," Matvay said. "Lo and behold, seven years later, it was him."

On February 7, 2001, two days after the discovery of Christine Smith's corpse, Matvay and CSA Robbie Dahn met at the Las Vegas police crime lab on West Charleston Boulevard to process the evidence from the Canyon Gate storage shed for fingerprints. There were four items in particular from the crime scene the CSAs thought might yield fingerprints. The first was the bag tied tightly around Christine's decomposed face, but the bag was covered with human remains, and the thick, crusty material eliminated any chance of prints being retrieved from the bag.

"We are talking thick, caked, fatty tissue covering the bag," Dahn said. "It was like Crisco oil."

The other items from the crime scene, however, were ripe for processing. They were the 21 strips of duct tape used to seal the garbage can containing the body; the 151 feet of long green plastic wrap the killer wrapped around the can to contain the odor; and three green garbage bags placed on top of Christine's makeshift tomb.

"To do the plastic wrap, the plastic bags and the duct tape, it took about three days," Matvay said. "Some people may think that is tedious, and it is a little bit slow. But there are two keys I always say are necessary to be successful in crime scene investigations. Number one is thoroughness, and number two is paying attention to detail.

"You don't have to be a brain surgeon to do this job," Matvay said. "Of course, intelligence is important, but if you are thorough and pay attention to detail, you can be successful."

For the duct tape, Dahn took fingerprint powder known as sticky-side powder, and she mixed it with water and Ivory dish soap to produce a black, pancake-like batter. Dahn brushed the sticky-side powder mix on the adhesive side of the strips of duct tape, and an ultraviolet light was shone on the nonadhesive side of the tape. The processes turned up a single partial palm print, but the palm print was never identified.

Matvay now set his sights on the garbage bags and the plastic wrap, and he knew the best way to process the two was with a device known as a super glue chamber. The device is a three-foot-long glass container resembling a square fish tank. To use the chamber, the CSAs squeeze globs of clear super glue into a small cup inside the chamber. The glue is heated with an open flame until it melts, and vapors from the glue adhere to fingerprints, making them visible on the clear plastic.

"Most fingerprint experts would agree a good way to start with plastic wrap is to go ahead and super glue it," Matvay said.

Matvay is a master with the super glue chamber. He was the first in the state of Nevada to use the chamber to recover a print from plastic in a homicide case, and the print resulted in the arrest of a cold-blooded murderer.

"It was a case where this guy killed his girlfriend, and what he had done is he had gone into their kitchen and pulled off a bunch of plastic wrap, and he covered her face with it," Matvay said. "I made him on prints using super glue on the plastic wrap."

In the case of Christine Smith, Matvay placed the garbage bags from the top of Christine's garbage can in the super glue chamber, melted the glue and waited for a print to appear. None did.

The CSAs finally set their sights on the 151 feet of green plastic wrap. Because the wrap was so long and the super glue chamber so small, the CSAs had to cut the wrap into five-foot-long segments.

"We ended up with about twenty-four sections, and we did two sections at a time," Matvay said.

The first section of plastic wrap was placed in the chamber and produced no prints. On the second section of wrap, Matvay melted the glue, pulled the plastic out of the chamber and held it up to the light.

"After fuming it in the super glue chamber, we removed the plastic wrap, and, lo and behold, there it was—a beautiful print," Matvay said.

"I remember we were handing every sheet back and forth, and Joe was looking over this one piece and he said, 'Oh, my gosh, Robbie. Look at this!'" Dahn said.

The excitement from the discovery was palpable. Dahn and Matvay knew whoever left the left thumbprint on the wrap was either the unluckiest person in the world, or was involved in the disposal of Christine Smith's corpse.

"I was very thankful for finding the print, because a print like that is obviously a big part of the puzzle," Matvay said.

The print was photographed and preserved, and the CSAs proceeded with processing the rest of the plastic wrap. For the next two days, they meticulously fumigated the wrap with super glue fumes and found nothing. Their three days of work produced only one crystal clear print.

When Matvay and Dahn were finished with their work, the CSAs called Mesinar to inform him of the new evidence. The detective was ecstatic over the find, and he started searching to see whether the fingerprints of his prime suspect, Brookey Lee West, were on file. He learned West had a long criminal history in California, and police records showed she was once arrested in the shooting of a spouse in California. Mesinar had no details on that case yet, but he was able to get West's fingerprints from police records.

Matvay then compared the left thumbprint from the plastic wrap to West's prints on file.

They were a perfect match.

LOVED ONES

6

Tornadoes in North Central Texas usually crop up in the spring or summertime. They are the product of some of the most powerful and frightening forces in nature—extremely strong winds, thick black thunderstorm cells and updrafts of air combine to form a rotating mass of terror. The most powerful tornadoes rumble like freight trains, with wind speeds in excess of 250 miles an hour, and they kill at random, destroying communities and leaving behind a zigzagging path of chaos.

In February 1932, North Central Texas experienced the arrival of a rare winter tornado. Her name was Christine Merle Smith, and she was born February 14, 1932, to Clyde and Annie Sands in the city of Ennis. Ennis is located in Ellis County, in Texas's Blackland Prairie, where expansive flatlands serve as fertile ground for corn, soybeans, grain and hay. The origins of the small city date back to 1871, when the Houston and Texas Central Railroad made it a stop on a rail line connecting Houston to the heart of rural Texas. The railroad came through Ennis for one reason and one reason only—to get the cotton grown in Ennis' dark-soiled fields. Ennis produced some of the world's finest cotton crops, and Ennis soon became known as the city where the railroads and cotton fields meet.

One man who called Ennis home was Christine's father, Clyde Sands. He was a tall, slender man who spent years earning a living as a lineman in the depths of the Great Depression. One of Clyde Sands' six children—Christine's brother Billy Sands—said his daddy helped stretch power lines throughout the nation, and it was hard physical labor that required Clyde Sands to spend long stretches of time away from home.

"Work was a little tight," Billy Sands recalled. "So he had to leave home a lot in order to get work. It was a good job and it paid well, but he had to leave home an awful lot."

When Clyde Sands wasn't working as a lineman, he was driving a truck and hauling freight, and he worked for several years as a truck driver for Planters Cotton Oil Mill in Ennis, where he hauled cotton lint and seed to the plant so it could be crushed and refined into valuable products like cottonseed oil.

Clyde's wife, Annie, was a housekeeper and, by all accounts, a loving woman who gave birth to six healthy children. The Sands' first child was a beautiful little girl, Trudy, born in 1911. Their first boy, Woodrow, followed; then came Lawrence, Richard Bob, Billy and, finally, the baby of the family, Christine. She was a blond-haired child who was rambunctious from the start.

"I remember hearing my parents talk about how tight money was," Billy said. "When they done work for somebody, they did it in trade for garden vegetables, livestock, meat, something of that nature, because nobody had any money."

Billy Sands said Christine had a normal childhood growing up in Ennis. He and his sister successfully made it through Alamo Elementary School on the city's west side, and Sands said his parents were never abusive to him or his sister. It seemed like Christine was on the right track in life as a child.

"As far as I know, me and her both had a pretty good life," Billy said. "We had plenty of food, and our mother was home with us. Most of the time, we played in the neighborhood, things like that. . . . We went to movies a lot, normal things. To the best I remember, it was about eleven cents to get in the movie. Christine was happy, and she was mostly a good girl."

But while everything may have been perfect in Christine's early childhood, things started to go downhill in a hurry near the age of ten. Her daughter, Brookey Lee West, said her mother told her she was repeatedly molested by a family member when she was a young girl.

"He had been molesting her since she was eight," West said.

Billy Sands said he never heard about the molestation allegation involving his little sister and a family member. Molestation was something rarely talked about in Texas in the 1930s, but if Christine was molested, it would have been a terrible trauma for such a little girl—a trauma Christine would have carried with her for the rest of her life. Billy Sands said he and Christine both dropped out of the Ennis school system by the eighth grade. Looking back, their decision to drop out was likely a result of childhood rebellion and a lack of emphasis on the importance of schooling from Clyde and Annie Sands.

"There didn't seem to be enough pressure put on the kids to educate themselves," Billy said. "They could have put a little more pressure on us for that."

Christine's decision to drop out of school at the age of thirteen was just the beginning of a series of bad decisions that would end up scarring her for life. Within three years, Christine's wild side took off like a crop duster climbing into the rural Texas skyline.

"I think personally she was restless at home by herself," Billy said. "She was looking for anything that come along so she could grab a hold of it and get out of little old Ennis."

At the age of sixteen, Christine married Tommy Harris,* who was described by Billy Sands as a muscular, dark-haired, Ennis-area thug who was always up to no good. Against her parents' strenuous objections, Christine and Harris ran off to Houston and the big city.

"He was a bad character," Billy said. "I don't know what in the world she ever seen in him, because he was really something. . . . It was bad from the word go. Several people said he treated her like a dog."

"He abused her very badly," said Billy's wife, JoAnn Sands.

Within months, Christine's new husband forced her into prostitution on the streets of Houston, leaving Christine ashamed, degraded and angry. She knew she had to get away from Harris, so she called her daddy and asked Clyde Sands to come rescue her from Harris.

"She wanted somebody to get her," JoAnn Sands said. "So her daddy and [one of] her brothers went down and got her and brought her back to Ennis."

Christine was saved from her husband, but the damage was already done. A victim of childhood molestation and now a divorcée with a history of prostitution, Christine was already a young woman whose psyche had suffered some serious blows.

If life were a game of poker, then Brookey Lee West's father, Leroy Smith, was dealt a pair of twos as a kid. A child of Russian immigrants who emigrated to the United States when he was a baby, Leroy was just five when his father butchered his mother during a domestic dispute at the family home in the hills of Tennessee.

"He cut her head off with a machete in Tennessee," West said. "My dad said his father went to prison for about ten years."

Following his mother's murder, Leroy was left in the care of his three older sisters in Tennessee, and Leroy's siblings had little time to care for their brother. They put Leroy on a bus and attached a note to his jacket explaining the boy was orphaned by the murder of his mother. Leroy ended up on a street corner in Tennessee, where he was noticed by a caring stranger. The woman gave Leroy to another woman with the last name of Smith.

"My dad told me they took him to Arkansas, and they gave him the name of Leroy," West said.

Leroy's adoptive mother was an alcoholic woman unable to have children, but she and her husband took Leroy in because they worried how society would view a childless couple in the prime of their lives. Leroy later told his loved ones that he spent much of his early life living out of tents and shacks in Arkansas, and it was apparently not a good life. By the age of sixteen, Leroy was desperate to get away from his family, so he lied about his age and enlisted in the army. Leroy thrived on the structure and discipline of the military, and he also discovered a lifelong love—firearms. Leroy was an avid collector of guns, and he loved the power and control they offered. With a gun, Leroy Smith could instill fear.

"My dad liked shotguns, and he had some pistols, too, but my dad always had a big gun collection," West said.

The guns served to soothe a raging personality lurking deep inside Leroy. Leroy was an angry human being likely because of his troubled childhood, and anyone who came to know Leroy as an adult concluded he had a defensive, reclusive, antisocial personality. He was also extremely racist. He hated blacks, Mexicans and Jews, and racism flowed through Leroy Smith like rainwater rushing through a gutter in a summer downpour.

"My dad didn't like nothing that wasn't white," West said. "That's just the way he was. I used to tell him, 'You know what, Dad? If you tried to join the skinheads, you would be president of them in six months.' He would be like, 'Yeah, I would be.' He just felt that way."

Leroy Smith was stationed at Fort Bliss in El Paso, Texas, when he met his bride to be, Christine Merle Sands, at a skating rink in downtown El Paso in 1947. Leroy Smith, at eighteen, was a blond-haired military man in a crisp U.S. Army uniform, and he was quickly captivated by Christine. Her long blond hair, blue eyes and shapely figure got the army man's hormones flowing.

"Gee, I think you are beautiful," Leroy told Christine.

"I know it," Christine said.

"Oh, I've seen better," Leroy said.

"Well, not around here," Christine said.

There was an immediate animosity between Christine and Leroy, and the tension left Leroy filled with lust. This sexy little thing in a tight red dress had an attitude, and it made him want her.

"The fight was on right away," West said of her parents' first meeting.

It wouldn't take long for Leroy to have his way with the infatuated teen. On weekends away from Fort Bliss, he would take Christine to a picture show costing a couple of dimes, they would spend a few hours at a soda joint and then they'd set out for the local lover's lane. To Leroy, Christine was likely just a tramp culled from the roller-skating rink to screw. For Christine, however, Leroy was a handsome, wavy-haired military man, and she wasn't about to let this one get away. Within weeks of their meeting, Christine told Leroy she was pregnant even though she wasn't.

"My dad said that's why he married her," West said. "He told me he wanted to divorce her after he was married to her for about three months. He said, 'I knew I'd been had.'"

Leroy Smith told his daughter he was also dismayed at Christine's level of intelligence.

"He said he went to some smoke shop with her, and she bought a book called *Nobody's Doll*," West said. "It was a second-grade book you would buy for a little kid, and that's when he realized my mother could barely read. My parents didn't know each other very well when they got married."

7

Within a year of his marriage to Christine Smith, Leroy's commitment to the army expired, and he promptly hired on as a patrol officer with the El Paso police department. The new job seemed a perfect fit for Leroy. The boy who came from modest, chaotic beginnings in life had seemingly gotten past his mother's murder and traded in his army uniform for a badge.

But according to Leroy's daughter and the woman who would become his second wife years later, Chloe Smith, Leroy's good intentions were quickly corrupted patrolling the streets of El Paso. El Paso in the late 1940s and 1950s may have been traditional Southern Americana, but like most cities of reasonable size, El Paso still had its fair share of pimping, prostitution and drugs, and Leroy indulged like a college boy in a whorehouse.

"This is when my father started using drugs, and this is also about the time my mom started using drugs, too," West said.

Leroy spent much of his time collaring drug dealers who were running drugs back and forth from Mexico through El Paso, and the busts provided him a prime opportunity to make a little extra cash to line his pockets.

"He'd take dope from some suspect and give it to some snitch to sell it to somebody," West said.

"He said it [police work] wasn't all organized like it is now," West said. "You just took care of whatever you wanted to take care of as a cop. There were a lot of drugs coming through El Paso, and he said he dealt with a lot of snitches."

Leroy's drug of choice was speed. He liked the energy it gave him on the night shift, and he was soon popping pills every day.

"He was a cop with a drug problem," West said.

"He used to tell me some awful things," said Chloe Smith. "He said they used to sit on the other side of the border, just on the other side of the river, and shoot the Mexicans' horses and donkeys. They did it for target practice. Not very nice things."

Leroy Smith told his daughter he patrolled the streets of El Paso with a heavy hand. The avowed racist had the ability to stop anyone he wanted in a city filled with Mexican Americans, and if you back-talked Leroy Smith, a beating or worse was likely.

"He said it was getting to the point where he was getting really violent," West said. "My dad wouldn't back down from anybody, and he had a real bad temper."

Christine, like Leroy, was doing drugs, and she was also starting to exhibit some very strange behavior. People who knew her noticed she was lying constantly, and one of her favorite lies was that she was a Native American. At times she claimed to be Apache. At other times she claimed a Cherokee heritage, and Christine's fascination with Native American culture did not go over well with her racist, hate-filled husband.

"He called them savages," Chloe Smith said.

"He told me he cheated on her all the time, and he made no bones about being a philanderer," Chloe said. "Leroy led me to believe Christine was crazy. So he cheated on her all the time, and he admitted to it. He said she had absolutely zero interest in sex, and he had lots of interest in sex. And he had a lot of availability for it as a cop."

When Leroy was away at work, Christine spent most of her time either in the downtown bars or at home in the couple's apartment, popping amphetamine pills, drinking liquor and smoking Camels as she waited for Leroy to get home. Slowly, the drugs and the alcohol started to wear on the couple, and by 1951 the two were fighting constantly. Following one of their episodes of domestic violence in their El Paso apartment, Christine sought out her husband's gun and, in a drunken stupor, crawled into bed next to her sleeping husband.

She put the gun to Leroy's head and pulled the trigger.

"He was a very light sleeper, and he heard her come into the room," West said. "She stuck the gun to my father's head and pulled the trigger. The gun was empty, so she just put the gun underneath his pillow and went to sleep.

"Who knows why?" West said. "But my mother didn't really need a reason to kill anybody. My mother was a very devious person. When you would get to know her, you would see that."

In 1952, Leroy decided to leave his wife once and for all and move on with his life. Problem was, Christine had bigger news.

She was pregnant.

"She never got pregnant, she never got pregnant, never got pregnant," Leroy told Chloe Smith years later. "Then, when the pressure was on, suddenly it happened."

Leroy was skeptical of the pregnancy. After all, he'd already bit once on Christine's pregnancy bait and got yanked into a miserable marriage, but any doubts about the pregnancy dissipated when Christine's belly started to bulge like a balloon.

"He always thought the baby may have been some other guy's," Chloe Smith said. "He always wondered about that."

Brookey Lee Smith, later to be known as Brookey Lee West, arrived in the maternity ward of an El Paso hospital on June 28, 1953. She was a beautiful, healthy baby with light brown hair and hazel eyes. West was, by all accounts, a sweet-natured child, and despite the differences between Christine and Leroy, both immediately fell in love with their little girl.

As a toddler, West was a bright child set on pleasing her mother and father. She loved her mommy and daddy, and when Christine wasn't partying, she took West to the park to play or to her aunt Trudy's house for dinner.

Any sense of normalcy in West's childhood, however, was short-lived because both her parents were raging alcoholics and drug addicts, and as a result West was frequently left home alone for hours on end.

"My parents both had their positives and negatives," West said. "The negatives were they drank and used dope."

In 1956, Christine got pregnant again.

"My dad was furious with her," West said. "My dad preached her up and down to no end, saying, 'You just did this to put another rope around my neck!' I heard that for years."

The couple's second baby, Travis Smith, arrived August 29, 1956, when West was three.

"My brother was a chubby, heavy baby," West said. "They put these striped shirts on him, and he looked like a wrestler."

But unlike West, Travis was a handful from the very beginning. He wore out three mattresses running in circles on

them as a young boy, and West believes her brother probably had attention deficit disorder long before the condition
was diagnosed.

"He would chew on Sheetrock," West said. "I'm serious. He was something else. He was like my mother in that
he did not have a good disposition. Him and my mother
adored each other."

Travis suffered from another pronounced medical problem as a child. His tongue was too long for his mouth. The
disability left him with a pronounced speech impediment
through much of his life.

"It made it hard for him to suck a bottle, and he couldn't
talk right, so he developed his own language," West said. "It
was like b'la ugh blabel ble. Instead of calling me Brookey,
he called me 'Kikey.' It was like speaking Chinese. He had
his vowels mixed up. People thought he was retarded, but he
really wasn't," West said. "He just had a speech impediment. He had to take speech classes throughout school."

As a toddler, Travis was also a biter. He regularly
chomped on the flesh of his sister or neighborhood kids
who got in his way.

"If anyone took something away from him, my mother
would say, 'Go bite them!'" West said. "So they used to
call my brother the snapping turtle. She couldn't take him
anywhere because he'd bite the hell out of you. My mother
would get invited to someone's house down the street, and
the neighbors would say, 'Don't bring him [Travis] over
here.' He'd draw blood."

Despite all the negatives in the Smith household, however, there were moments during West's childhood when
she and her brother were happy children. Family snapshots
show West dressed in an innocent cotton dress, her curly
brown hair combed until it looked just right. Christine
dressed Travis in fancy dark overalls over a white shirt,

and she would take the children outside and snap their photos in the hot Texas sunlight.

"My sweet little babies!" Christine wrote on the back of one black-and-white snapshot of the smiling children taken in the late 1950s.

The photos of smiling children masked the real truth. Mostly, the childhoods of West and her brother were of abandonment and loneliness. When West was left at home alone, she passed the time making paper dolls, dressing them like a princess or queen in a fantasy world far away from the solitude of her family's empty apartment. She had only one birthday party as a girl because her parents were too busy partying, and she remembers having to care for her brother for days while her parents were out barhopping.

"We had all kinds of medications in our cabinets," West said. "Speed, then tranquilizers to calm [my parents] down. My mother told me [years later] that they were both strung out, and they couldn't handle it [being parents]."

In the mid 1950s, Leroy bottomed out and was fired from his job as a police officer.

"My dad said he borrowed money from the police department, but if you borrowed money, you had to have people vouch for you that you would pay it back," West said. "If you didn't pay it back, they sort of blacklisted you, and blackballed you, is what he told me."

Leroy didn't pay the money back and he was booted off the force.

The story about failing to pay off a debt was the explanation Leroy gave his loved ones for losing the job he loved, but Leroy's family suspects it was only a partial explanation. Chloe Smith said years later, after she married Leroy that the firing from the El Paso police department remained a sore topic with her husband.

"My guess is he got in some trouble and he got kicked

out or pressured to leave," Chloe said. "That's my gut feeling. I don't think he ever wanted me to see him as a bad guy, so he whitewashed it somewhat."

In an act of desperation, Leroy packed up his family and headed to Bakersfield, California, for a fresh start.

8

Leroy Smith realized it was time to get out of El Paso for good. His prized job as a city cop had blown away with the Texas winds, so in 1959 Leroy, his wife, Christine, and their two children, Brookey and Travis, packed up their belongings and headed west. They stopped briefly at low-rent motels in New Mexico and Ventura, California, before finally settling in Bakersfield.

The municipality of 234,000 sits at the southern tip of California's four hundred-mile-long Central Valley, where thousands of acres of flat farmlands produce oranges, grapefruit and almonds in abundance. The picturesque Central Valley is responsible for more than 60 percent of the state's agricultural production, and its farms contribute to roughly a quarter of the nation's food supply, making California one of the most prolific farming states in the country.

Bakersfield, however, is largely a city still dependent on what the locals call "black gold." Derricks on the outskirts of the city pump for oil; producing some 570,000 barrels of oil a year, and some of the nation's largest oil companies, including Chevron-Texaco and Shell, carry out huge extraction and refining operations in Bakersfield.

In 1959, Leroy and Christine were a perfect fit for Bakersfield. The city was home to thousands of Oklahomans and Texans who fled their native states during the Great Depression of the 1930s. Bakersfield was also in the midst of a honky-tonk heyday fueled by the Oklahoma and Texas transplants. The city's nightclubs were overflowing with couples yearning for the twangy, unique brand of Bakersfield country music, and Christine and Leroy spent plenty of nights drinking and dancing at downtown bars like the Cellar and the Blackboard, where Buck Owens and Merle Haggard made history developing the sounds of the legendary Bakersfield musical scene.

Leroy found work in Bakersfield laying carpet in homes. The job didn't pay a lot, but it was a steady income, and it allowed the Smiths to rent a house in a lower-income section of the city.

"Bakersfield is where it got interesting and sort of strange for my family, because we had a lot of neighbors who were Oklahomans, and if you've never been around Okies, they are a real experience," West said.

"Most of them are just like my parents," West said. "Alcoholics, drinkers, partiers, sitting out in front of their homes drinking and working on some old wrecked-out car, saying, 'Go in the house there, baby, and get daddy a beer! Go in there and get me my shotgun!' They'd all be out there shouting at each other in the yard with their rifles pointed at each other," West said. "That's what I'm talking about when I say, 'If you've never been around Okies, it's a real experience.'"

Leroy and Christine tramped through the Bakersfield bar scene night after night, and the nonstop partying made for a volatile home life for West and her brother. At seven, West said she was pretty much solely responsible for taking care of four-year-old Travis while her parents were hitting the bars.

"We had periods where we were left home alone for two to three days," West said. "I always took care of my brother."

When Leroy was at work laying carpet, Christine usually spent her days in bed recovering from self-inflicted headaches and a bloodstream filled with liquor.

"My mother was always in bed sick, and she had turned this really dark gray—weird looking," West said. "She was always, 'This hurts, that hurts.' Then my dad would come home after work and say, 'You want to go out tonight?' And all of the sudden, my mother would pop right out of bed and say, 'Let's go.'"

Leroy chugged wine like water, and his kitchen cabinet was filled with a large stash of amphetamines and tranquilizers. Leroy was driving himself into the ground with drugs and alcohol, and he didn't seem to care.

"That's about the time when my parents started going to doctors to get more and more pills," West said. "They were writing prescriptions for my parents for painkillers, and then my parents would sell them. Sell them to their friends or whoever wanted them. A buck for this, a buck for that, and that's how they made their money.

"I took care of them and all their problems," West said. "If I could hide something for them, I did. If they told me to lie, I lied. Someone would call up and say, 'Can I speak to your dad?' And I'd say, 'Well, he's not here. He went to a doctor.' Meanwhile, my dad was right there smashed out of his mind."

Leroy could be frightening during his drunken rages. On more than one occasion, his anger was unleashed on the children in the form of violent spankings that left bruises in the shape of handprints on their bottoms.

"One time, my dad came home from work with a box

of chocolates for my mother on her birthday, and I said,
'Oh, can I have some?' " West recalled. "My dad just lost
it, and he spanked me so hard I had his whole handprint on
my butt.

"There were times that he would spank us with a two-
by-four," West said. "I'd go to school with bruises all over,
but no one ever said anything."

Guns were everywhere in the house—handguns, shotguns, rifles. The firearms were tucked underneath couch
cushions or hidden beneath the bed. Leroy regularly carried a gun on him, and it was well known in Bakersfield
that Leroy was an individual to be feared.

"My dad didn't back down from anybody," West said.

West remembers witnessing her father chase down a
man he noticed driving too fast through his Bakersfield
neighborhood.

"My dad actually went out and physically pulled this
guy out of his car," West recalled. "He said. 'You see all
these kids around here? If you want to run over somebody's kid, make sure you run over somebody else's, because if you run over one of my kids, I'm going to twist
your head off your shoulders and use it as a doorknob.'

"If my mother was angry, you couldn't talk to her,"
West said. "She wasn't bad about hitting, but she was a
screamer, saying things like, 'Shut up! Turn that damned
television down!'

"I was frightened of both of them," West said. "I had to
be careful because they both had their idiosyncrasies about
things. My parents were not educated people, and they
didn't know anything about encouragement and praise.
They basically treated me how they were treated when they
were children. They saw you as an object. 'What do you
know? You are only seven.' "

The home life of violence, alcohol, drugs and arguments left West and Travis emotionally damaged inside.

Especially hurtful for the children was the fact that their parents were continually separating and getting back together. Christine would run off for days, and when she came back, Leroy would disappear. There were continual threats of divorce between the husband and wife, and West and her brother wondered whether they were the problem.

The stormy relationship between Leroy and Christine seemed to come to a boiling point in 1961 when Leroy left his wife for a cocktail waitress named Faye. Leroy took his daughter and son with him, and they moved into Faye's home in Bakersfield, where the waitress was already living with her six children. West and Travis were suddenly living in a large family with a new mother figure.

Christine, meanwhile, replaced her missing husband with a married man. David Gilmore* was a mason by trade, and for a few months Gilmore and Christine burned up the Bakersfield nights together in a steamy hot romance. They dreamed of running off together and leaving their spouses behind for a new life someplace else.

"He was married and I was married, and we snuck around," Christine would later tell Bakersfield police in a taped statement.

The affair between Christine and Gilmore was so torrid, Christine told police she and Gilmore once plotted to kill his wife, Susan.*

"He wanted me to kill her, and I thought, 'You son of a bitch, if I killed her, where would I be with you?'" Christine said in the taped statement. "Who would he get to kill me? That's the way I felt about it."

She said the plot to murder Susan Gilmore involved "sleeping medicine, a lot of sleeping stuff."

But before any plot to kill his wife was carried out, David Gilmore had a change of heart. He decided he was going back to his wife, and he told Christine of his decision in the first few weeks of 1961.

Christine was enraged.

"I said, 'Well, you know, you can take me to the water, you son of a bitch, but ain't going to drown me because I'll kill your ass,' " Christine told the police.

David Gilmore was about to learn a very valuable lesson: No one fucks with Christine Merle Smith.

9

In 1961, Christine Merle Smith was the meanest, angriest bitch in all of Bakersfield, California. Her secret lover, David Gilmore, had promised to leave his wife for her, then dumped her, so on January 24, Christine called Gilmore and asked if he would meet with her one last time at the Cellar bar in downtown Bakersfield.

At about seven thirty p.m., the five-foot-four-inch Christine walked into the lounge at 1918½ Eye Street with a loaded shotgun tucked underneath her jacket.

"I had the gun under there," Christine told police. "It was a sawed-off shotgun. [Had] it over my shoulder. I had a shoulder strap."

Christine sat down at a table in the bar and rested the 16-gauge shotgun on her lap underneath the table. The bar was nearly empty, and the few who were there didn't notice Christine covering the weapon with a sweater and her jacket.

Gilmore showed up at the bar with his wife, Susan, just after seven thirty p.m., and the couple sat down across from Christine.

Christine grasped the shotgun, leveled it at Gilmore and pulled the trigger.

"I reached under the table, I had the gun under there . . . and I shot him!" Christine said.

The blast ripped into David Gilmore, who was sitting just two feet from the end of the barrel of the gun. Shotgun pellets shattered his right arm and tore a sizeable chunk of flesh from his torso. He slumped to the floor of the bar in a pool of blood, his horrified wife looking on in shock.

Gilmore, thirty, was rushed to Bakersfield's Mercy Hospital where he underwent surgery. His life was saved, but his arm would never be same. He was maimed for life.

"It hurt him bad," West said. "He was in a cast for months, and he was a brick mason, so I'm sure it took a toll."

City police had no problems apprehending Christine, who was hauled away from the scene in handcuffs to the Kern County jail. She was fingerprinted, photographed and booked on a felony charge of assault with a deadly weapon with intent to commit murder, according to police records.

"I didn't have the least feeling of sympathy," Christine told the cops. "Hell, no."

When asked by a California homicide detective what she'd intended to do to Gilmore that day, Christine said simply, "Kill him."

The shooting was big news in Bakersfield, and the city's newspaper, the *Bakersfield Californian*, ran a front-page account of the crime the next day.

Woman Held in Shooting at Downtown Café
Wednesday, January 25, 1961

Police today were holding Mrs. Christine M. Smith, 28, of 1019 Casa Loma Dr., mother of two small children, for investigation in the shooting of David Gilmore, 30, of 1013 Sandra Drive. Gilmore was reported in "good" condition in Mercy Hospital with shotgun pellet wounds in the side and the right arm. Police said they were told the arm may have to be amputated.

Mrs. Smith is in Kern County jail on suspicion of assault with a deadly weapon with intent to commit murder. Police said she fired a single blast from a 16-gauge sawed off shotgun at Gilmore in The Cellar, 1918½ Eye St. The incident occurred about 7:30 p.m. Tuesday.

Lt. Richard Mason said Mrs. Smith told him she carried the shotgun into the cafe under a coat draped over her arm. She waited nearly half an hour to meet Gilmore and his wife, Susan.

Mrs. Smith, separated from her husband, told Mason she had been dating Gilmore during his separation from his wife. Earlier Gilmore had told her he was reconciling with his wife. At Mrs. Smith's request, the Gilmores were to discuss with her how she might win back her husband, Leroy.

Mrs. Smith told officers she did not know where Leroy Smith and the children, ages 7 and 4, were living.

Investigators said she was seated at a table with the gun under the coat and a sweater when Gilmore sat down next to her, his wife across the table. Officers said he was about two feet away when Mrs. Smith, without warning, pulled the trigger of the gun in her lap.

Asked if she would deny the shooting, Mrs. Smith said she would not. Asked the reason for it, she was reported to have said "that will come out later."

Christine went to trial in downtown Bakersfield in March 1961. The mother of two was convicted by a jury of assault with intent to commit murder and sentenced to fourteen years in prison.

Years later, Christine the ex-convict bragged about the shooting to dozens of people, saying it was the greatest accomplishment of her life.

"My mother talked about that shooting like she was some sort of movie star," West said. "The first thing out of her mouth about it was, 'Well, you know, I went to prison because I shot that son of a bitch. He deserved it. Every pellet he got."

10

One would think Leroy Smith would have completely disowned his wife, Christine, when he learned of the shooting of David Gilmore, but he did the exact opposite. His relationship with Faye the cocktail waitress crumbled, and he went running back to Christine with his daughter and son in tow.

"It was traumatic," West said of her mother's arrest. "It was on TV and everything. A lot of people knew about it."

At the age of eight, West was deeply ashamed of her mother. She remembers going with her father to visit her mother at the Kern County jail in downtown Bakersfield following her arrest, and she also remembers going to see her mother during Christine's trial at the Kern County courthouse.

"My dad took a dress down to her, and it was a honkytonk dress with no back, so her lawyers put a sweater around her because they didn't want her in court in that thing," West said. "They wrote in the paper that she was a Lolita."

Christine was convicted and sent to the California Insti-

tution for Women (CIW). The prison is a cold, hard expanse
of concrete and prison bars built in 1952 on 120 acres in
Riverside County, just outside of Los Angeles. CIW was
originally called "Frontera," which the California Department of Corrections says is a reference to the inmates' hope
for a new beginning. But to this day, there are plenty of inmates at CIW who have no hope of ever being released.
CIW is home to some of the state's most notorious female
killers and thieves, and perhaps the most famous resident of
CIW is Leslie Van Houten, who participated in the 1969
stabbing murders of Rosemary and Leno LaBianca with the
followers of Charles Manson.

Christine fit in well at CIW.

"My mom somehow had a thing with these people,"
West said. "She understood them. It was some sort of un-
spoken communication."

Christine worked in the prison kitchen serving food.
She would sneak some inmates pies or sweets, and she became so popular in the cafeteria that the inmates were furious when she was moved to another job in the prison.

"So when they took my mother off that detail, and another inmate tried to serve them, they threw hot coffee all
over this new server," West said. "My mother had that in
her. I don't know what it is, but she had that thing where
she could connect with people, and she manipulated them."

West said losing her mother to CIW as a little girl was a
life-changing event, and there was no escaping it no matter
how hard she tried.

"I knew exactly what was going on," West said. "I failed
the second grade, and they couldn't understand why. But it
was because my mother was in prison, and I couldn't think.
I couldn't learn.

"I didn't talk to anybody about my mother being in
prison," West said. "I didn't tell the teachers, I didn't talk
to my friends and I didn't tell anyone about it because peo-

ple would make fun of you and be rude about it, so I just grinned and bore it."

Travis was crushed as well, and his emotional trauma was exacerbated by Leroy's method of dealing with Christine's imprisonment. Instead of telling now five-year-old Travis his mother was going to be gone for fourteen years, Leroy instructed West to tell Travis his mother was dead and buried.

"'You just tell your little brother your mom died,'" West quoted her father as saying.

"My dad felt he wouldn't understand it. My brother cried and cried when I told him our mother was dead," West said. "I felt bad about lying to him, but I didn't know how else to handle it, you know? It was the wrong way to do it."

Having his eight-year-old daughter tell her little brother their mother was buried and gone was perfectly acceptable in Leroy's mind. It was a way of making sure West was developing from child to woman.

"I was supposed to understand everything," West said. "I was to take care of my brother, and my dad was like, 'If you want to be treated like an adult, then act like an adult.'"

It was a terribly turbulent time for West and her brother, but it was about to get worse. Within a year of Christine's incarceration, Leroy took his children to Fresno for a few months. Then they moved to Oregon, where they stayed for five months, and then it was to San Luis Obispo, California, and finally back to Bakersfield.

"We were always going through something, or we were always worried about something, and we were always moving," West said of her childhood. "There was always some trauma in our lives all the time.

"Drink all day and half the night," West said of her father. "It was getting to where he couldn't even work anymore. We were living in another run-down motel, and he

was feeding us crackers for dinner. Pillar to post and motel
to motel. If you didn't have something to eat that day, you
asked the neighbors for something."

In 1962, Leroy decided the children would be better off
without him, so he took his son and daughter to a local orphanage in Bakersfield. West was eight and Travis five
when they were dropped off at the Baptist Sunnycrest
home for youths.

"My dad told us he was going to have to put us there,
and I just started screaming," West said. "I thought it was
something I did, and that he was going to have to put me
there because I did something wrong. I said, 'I'll be good,
I'll do what you tell me,' but it wasn't that," West said. "He
just couldn't take care of his kids."

The abandonment of the children was now complete.
Christine was serving hard time at CIW, and West and her
brother had not heard from their mother in nearly two
years. To make matters worse, their drunken father felt his
drinking was more important than his kids.

But in the months that followed, West and Travis
quickly came to love their new home at the orphanage. The
orphanage housed about twenty children in two single-
story buildings adjacent to a large playground, and the facility was run by an older husband and wife who took the
time to show each child the love they were starving for.

"We started going to school regularly at the orphanage,
and everything got a little better for me," West said. "My
grades were good, I had clothes to wear, and they fed me
right."

Travis immediately warmed up to the orphanage as
well, and the five-year-old gravitated to the husband and
wife who ran Sunnycrest.

"My brother became attached to both of them," West
said. "The woman, she was sort of a big, buxom type, very

motherly, and she would hold him a lot. He became very attached to her."

For the first time in their lives, West and Travis were in a nurturing environment that allowed them to blossom. The orphanage's managers may not have been the children's parents, but they treated West and her brother like kids are supposed to be treated. They fed and looked after the children, and when West or her brother were sad, they showed them unbridled love. West realized she really didn't miss her mother and father at all, and as far as she and Travis were concerned, they were content staying at Sunnycrest for as long as the church would have them.

And then, Leroy came back.

West's father drove into the driveway of the orphanage with a woman in the front seat of his car. The woman was thin, blond haired, with tight black pants and an even tighter black sweater. A pair of dark sunglasses covered her eyes, and as she got out of the car, West recognized who it was: Christine.

"My parents show up—both of them," West said. "I didn't want to leave the orphanage, but we had to. My brother's screaming and crying, and he didn't want to leave, either. My mother actually wanted to leave my brother there and let him adjust, but my dad wouldn't have it."

Christine was fresh out of prison just two years into her fourteen-year sentence. The parole board released her on her first appearance, and her chance at freedom mandated she complete only a five-year parole.

"I think [my parents] sought each other out after my mom got out of prison because it was one of those types of relationships, like when an abused woman keeps going back to her husband," West said. "They didn't want each other, but then, when they were apart, they really did. And then, they didn't want each other again. That's the way their relationship was. On and off all the time."

The stability West longed for in her childhood was gone again. She and her brother were whisked out of the orphanage by their parents, and the family moved north to San Jose. It was the city where West grew into a woman, and it was the city where West's father dedicated himself to the Prince of Darkness.

DEVIL WORSHIP

11

Sitting forty-five minutes south of San Francisco in the center of the Santa Clara Valley is the city of San Jose, a municipality that gets little attention when compared to the other major cities of California. There are no golden beaches like the ones found in San Diego. There is no Golden Gate Bridge, no Hollywood and no massive state government center like in nearby Sacramento. But San Jose may still be the most pleasant place to live in all of California.

The city's diverse population is extremely congenial, and anyone who visits immediately recognizes San Jose has struck a perfect balance between country living and big city. On the outskirts of the city, one is greeted with a charming view of green pastures and farmlands leading to lush, even greener hillsides. In the interior of the city, downtown is a wonderful mix of modern office complexes, shops and restaurants offering exotic cuisine from around the world. San Jose's residents and tourists seem to act as if they are in paradise as they walk through the city's downtown Center Plaza, where commuter trolleys whisk by every few minutes.

Founded in 1777, San Jose is one of the oldest communities in the western United States, and much of San Jose's cultural and religious history can be traced to the Spanish missions, which spread across California like wildfire to teach the Catholic faith to the Native Americans. Today, the city's economic power can be traced to its massive technology industry, which has earned San Jose the internationally recognized nickname "Silicon Valley." Hewlett-Packard was started here in the 1930s, and some of the brightest computer programmers on the planet come to San Jose and surrounding areas from India, China and other countries to work at companies like HP, Sun, Cisco and Apple, where monitors, hard drives and programs are churned out like nowhere else in the world.

In 1965, Leroy Smith and his family were attracted to San Jose by its beauty and economic opportunities. Leroy quickly found another job laying carpet, and the Smith clan eventually settled into a single-story rental home on Lafayette Street, near Santa Clara University, in a mostly Hispanic neighborhood.

West said she always felt like she never quite fit in her neighborhood as one of the few white kids in the entire community. She ended up spending much of her grade school years playing alone or with her little brother in a grassy field of a Catholic church near her family's house.

"The kids weren't very friendly to me," West said. "I was always big for my age, and by the time I was twelve, I was tall. I didn't look twelve, and I didn't look like everyone else."

West's little brother didn't fit in, either. By the age of nine, Travis was acting out, fighting with neighborhood boys and engaging in self-destructive behavior uncommon for a child so young.

"My brother started using drugs when he was nine," West said. "Pills right out of the cabinet. The bathroom cabinet couldn't hold all these pills. Any color you wanted."

One of the Smiths' family friends in San Jose was a buxom woman West knew only as "Mrs. Beauford." She lived in a Victorian house about six blocks away from the Smiths, and she was especially close to Leroy. According to West, Beauford was a practicing witch, and West's father was captivated by Beauford's proclaimed ability to cast spells on others.

"She was from Kentucky," West said. "Her husband and two of her sons had been murdered, and they had run her out of Kentucky."

West said she was thirteen when her mother asked her to go to Mrs. Beauford's home to return a dish Christine had borrowed.

"I knocked on her door, the door sort of came open and I said hello, and nobody answered," West said. "I stood there for a second, and I hear this moaning, groaning, kind of like screaming. It's coming from the basement," she said. "You had to go to the back of the house, so I walked in, went down the stairs, looked around the corner, and they have all these black candles. This son of hers, who was going to Santa Clara University, was doing some sort of spell or something."

Spells and witchcraft quickly became Leroy's passion, according to West. He was consumed by the premise that, with a spell, he could make his enemies suffer. By the late 1960s, Leroy was meeting regularly with Mrs. Beauford and a network of San Jose occultists. They gathered to carry out secret, candle-lit ceremonies in which they wore dark robes, practiced spells, recited chants and worshipped the devil.

"He'd go to these meetings, and he got to where he was crazier, meaner, doing more dope, drinking heavier," West

said. "A lot of people that are alcoholics and dopers, especially mixers of the two, have tendencies to get into weird
things like that."

Covens of Satanic worshippers were not necessarily unusual in Northern California in the late 1960s and 1970s.
In fact, the region was a hotbed for the movement. The
modern day Church of Satan was founded in nearby San
Francisco in 1966 by a man named Anton LaVey. LaVey,
an ominous-looking creature with shaved head and goatee,
played the part perfectly, wearing black robes, wielding
long swords and giving countless media interviews promoting the worship of Satan. The sins of the flesh were to
be indulged in, LaVey said, in a message that shocked
mainstream Christian America.

But LaVey's words struck a chord with thousands in the
late 1960s. One estimate put LaVey's followers at 25,000,
and the movement even attracted some Hollywood elite.

LaVey's book, *The Satanic Bible*, is widely regarded as
the religion's gospel. It is an intensely dark and frightening
mantra outlining the tenets of the religion and its ceremonies.

Leroy read every word.

Of Christ, Leroy said, "I don't believe it. I think he was
just a man, nothing more than a rabble-rousing trouble-
maker, and that's why they crucified him."

Leroy started calling himself a "warlock," and he saw
himself as a high-ranking male witch in Satan's legion.

"He had books, knives and other stuff," West said.
"They wore their robes, almost like the Ku Klux Klan, and
it was a secretive organization. You had to be taken in by
someone who was already in.

"It was about worshipping Satan and being as faithful to
him as Christians are to the Lord," West said of her father's
beliefs. "Like it says in the Scripture, when he [Satan] had
Jesus on the mountain, Satan tells Jesus, 'I'll give you all
the world, bow down and worship me. The power was

given to me, and I can give it to anyone I wish.' My dad identified with that stuff. He didn't go around killing people, but he believed Satan was the ruler of this world, and he could give you anything you wanted. You just have to know how to get in touch.

"He never took me to any of these meetings," West said. "My father was the type of person who believed you should just find your own road. He wasn't forceful like, 'I like baseball, so you'll like baseball.'

"I understand all of it," West said. "I know what their belief systems are. I know how they meet. I know what they do. Is there any validity to it? Yes, there is. There are people who are true Satanists, who are faithful to him. Can they cast a spell? Can they wreak havoc in your life? Absolutely. It's real. Their spirits are real. But not your average person or everyday Joe, some guy who buys some book, is going to be able to do that.

"But, I have to tell you, it works just like any other faith," West said. "If you are a Christian and you have the faith, the Bible speaks of the faith and you must have faith. Well, its the same way with the other side. You have to be given to that. You have to belong to it, or it won't work for you.

"Have I practiced it?" West said. "No. But I've read about it, and I've done a lot of in-depth study on all of it. I can't go that way, because it is just not my path. I know it is a reality, and I know that it works for them. I know people that are in it, people in very high positions."

12

A witch is one who worketh by the Devil or by some curious art either healing or revealing things secret, or foretelling things to come which the Devil hath devised to ensnare men's souls withal unto damnation. The conjurer, the enchanter, the sorcerer, the diviner, and whatever other sort there is encompassed within this circle.

—George Gifford, a British clergyman in the sixteenth century

In Salem, Massachusetts, in 1692, two little girls decided they were going to dabble in the occult. One of the children was Betty Parris, the nine-year-old daughter of Salem village reverend Samuel Parris, and the second was Elizabeth's eleven-year-old cousin, Abigail Williams.

The two children loved to listen to stories told to them by the Parris' Caribbean family slave, Tituba, who weaved for the little girls wild tales of sorcery. The children were captivated by Tituba's stories, prompting them one day to try their own brand of sorcery. In a haphazard experiment, the girls dropped hot wax into a glass of water, and Betty then peered into the water with the hope of seeing what the future held for her and Abigail. But instead, Betty saw the image of death, frightening the two children out of their wits.

Soon, Betty and Abigail's behavior was out of control.

They were observed going into convulsions and wildly thrashing back and forth. The village doctors were summoned and provided a disturbing diagnosis for Reverend Parris and his loved ones—the children were suffering from a witch's spell.

Within days of the diagnosis, other children in Salem started to suffer as well. The children talked gibberish or blasphemy, and their bodies contorted at all angles. The leaders of Salem quickly realized something had to be done.

Carrying torches to illuminate the pitch-black night, they searched through the village and the dense New England woods for those responsible. The first to be charged with crimes of witchcraft were Salem residents Sarah Good, Sarah Osborn and Tituba. Tituba confessed to consorting with the devil under questioning from religious leaders, and her life was spared. The others were taken to trial, convicted and hanged in front of angry mobs on Witch's Hill in Salem.

"I am no more a witch than you are a wizard," Good said prior to her hanging. "If you take my life away, God will give you blood to drink."

When the mayhem was finally over, nineteen suspected witches were hanged, and a man was pressed to death. It was the deadliest witch hunt in American history.

Sonny Armas is a pack rat. In the garage of his single-story home in rural Central California, Armas keeps boxes and boxes of stuff stacked on top of one another like cord wood. Most of the boxes are filled with tapes, CDs, books, tools, hardware and various other knickknacks he's collected over the years.

Armas, thirty-nine also collects furniture at his Los Banos, California, home. The admitted clutterbug said most of the items he's gathered were given to him by family and acquaintances.

"I'm always helping someone move, so I get a lot of the stuff that way," Armas said. "I guess I keep stuff because, once I get rid of something, I usually find out about a week later that I needed it."

In 1994, Armas and his wife, Genia, bought their Los Banos home from its original owner—Brookey Lee West. When West moved out of the residence, she left behind stacks and stacks of boxes in the garage. In one box, Sonny Armas found a book titled *The Truth About Witchcraft Today*. The cover of the book consists of a glossy photo of an attractive female model in a business suit, and she is holding a briefcase in her hand. The message from the cover of the book makes clear that witchcraft, in the author's opinion, is an acceptable religion practiced by modern professionals.

The Truth About Witchcraft Today was written by the late Wiccan author Scott Cunningham, who spent much of his literary career trying to dispel the premise that witchcraft is a form of devil worship. Instead, he worked to promote the idea of witchcraft as a respected religion that honors the natural universe. Tragically, he died young at the age of thirty-seven.

But *The Truth About Witchcraft Today* wasn't the only odd item Sonny Armas found in his garage. In a toolbox, Armas found a handful of items belonging to West's father, Leroy Smith. In the box was a black knit ski cap, commonly referred to as a burglar's cap, and an electronic listening device capable of picking up the conversations of unsuspecting people from hundreds of feet away. It was as if Leroy was equipped to be a professional burglar.

There were weapons in the garage, too. They consisted of a series of long, steel, curved knives with gothic handles, and next to the knives was a brown leather pouch with a drawstring. When the drawstring was loosened, the pouch produced a macabre, miniature white skull with long, protruding fangs. The skull looked like something a Satanist might wear around his neck during a ritual.

"I thought, 'Wow, this is some really weird stuff,'" Sonny Armas said. "It totally tripped me out."

And finally, Armas found a black leather notepad in Leroy's belongings. The notepad, containing about eighty sheets of paper, was the type of tablet a cop might fit in a shirt or pants pocket.

One entry in Leroy's notepad listed the address for a gun parts store in Glendale, California. The entry is followed by a drawn red cross, and there are then a series of writings on the final three pages of the pad. The writings can only be described as a succession of sinister-looking symbols and letters that come together to craft a secret code.

The code is written in black ink on stained, faded white paper, and a close inspection of the letters show them to be of the ancient Theban alphabet, which is commonly referred to as the "witch's alphabet."

"I thought maybe it was a foreign language when I first saw it," Sonny Armas said.

The Theban alphabet first surfaced during the medieval period, and today it is an alphabet claimed by witches and Wiccans. The alphabet, according to myth, adds a powerful, mystic quality to a witch's spell.

"It is an old, hieroglyphic-type writing put together by witches in this country when they first came here in Salem," West said. "It's like a secret language. My dad always used it, and he had a special book to translate it."

The writings in Leroy's notepad, when translated from the witch's alphabet, are a series of prayers. Like the image Betty Parris observed in the water glass, the contents of the prayers are an ominous foretelling of the future, because they show that Leroy knew one day his wife, Christine, and his daughter were going to desperately need the favors of his God.

The prayers read:

> *Please, oh God, take care of my loved ones.*
> *Dear God, please take care of Brooke*
> *and her mother Chris, Christine.*

13

At age fourteen, Brookey Lee West enrolled in Santa Clara High School in San Jose, and she was no longer the awkward-looking girl of a few years ago. Puberty had morphed her into an attractive, well-built young girl on the verge of womanhood.

"I was a dancer when I was a teenager," she said. "Ballet, and I was really built because of it. I had gorgeous legs."

With her curly brown hair, beautiful hazel eyes and shapely figure, West was starting to attract the attention of several boys at Santa Clara High. What really made her attractive to the opposite sex was the way she dressed—she donned tight-fitting sweaters and short skirts, just like the outfits her mother wore in the Bakersfield honky-tonks nearly a decade earlier.

"I dressed very sexy," West said. "I was a looker. The boys all wanted a date with me, but I didn't want to go. I was very standoffish about men. Probably because of the way my home life was, I couldn't invite anybody home. I couldn't have a normal life. I didn't really do well in school, too, because I had so much stress."

West got less than average grades throughout high school, and she was pretty much an aimless teen without a plan for the future. Her underachieving was probably attributable to the tumult in her home, which came to a head when she was in high school. In the late 1960s, her parents' marriage hit the rocks for good when Christine caught Leroy in a series of affairs he wasn't even trying to hide.

"My mom moved out," West said. "My dad was running around with other women, and he was drinking heavily, and my mother was always trying to change him, and she never could."

The couple divorced in yet another emotional trauma for West and her brother. The divorce was especially hard on Travis, who dropped out of high school to pursue a life of doing drugs.

"My brother loved speed," West said.

Leroy tried to convince his son to work with him laying carpet, but Travis had little interest in working for a living. Travis was constantly lying and stealing to get drugs—mostly methamphetamine—and he ended up repeatedly in trouble with the San Jose police department and the Santa Clara County sheriff's office.

There were, however, positive developments stemming from Christine and Leroy's divorce. Christine, tired of feeling poorly from drinking and drugging seven days a week, swore off all drugs and alcohol. She started attending Alcoholics Anonymous, was gradually successful in giving up her bad habits, West said.

"My mother cleaned herself up, and she got off the dope," West said.

Christine, now sober, decided she was going to come to terms with her sinful past by attending a little Episcopalian church called Faith Temple in San Jose with her daughter.

For Christine, religion was a chance to try to find answers to some of the most perplexing traumas in her life. Why was she molested as a child? Why had she, at age sixteen, married a wife beater, Tommy Harris, who forced her into prostitution? Why, when she finally escaped that abusive relationship, had she hooked up with Leroy, an avowed womanizer and Satanist? And why, with two small children, did she shoot a man in Bakersfield and go to prison?

In short, it was time for Christine to find God. Christine was soon talking regularly about the word of God and the power of Jesus. But according to West, Christine was still far from a perfect Christian. She wanted to be forgiven, but she didn't want to put in the work. She paid attention to the teachings of the Gospel, yet she was still a bitter woman filled with spite and anger for anyone who crossed her.

"My mom started going to church with me when I was in my teens, but she still viewed religion as a matter of convenience," West said. "She wasn't book smart enough to learn the Bible, or even read it, and she didn't apply herself."

By the late 1960s, Christine was also on the verge of another personal revelation—she was mentally ill. While at a local doctor's office for one of a dozen or so mysterious ailments she complained about constantly, a doctor referred her to a mental health professional.

"My mother was always going to doctors because she always had something wrong with her," West said. "Her back hurt. 'My foot hurts, my earlobe hurts.' She was always in bed, always had some sort of chronic cough, and doctors would always tell us, 'I've given her enough medicine to cure a horse.'

"It was finally determined all her ailments were psychosomatic," West said. "There wasn't really anything wrong with her."

Christine was sent to a mental health clinic in San Jose,

and during a screening interview with a psychologist, she attacked her doctor with her boot.

"She took her boot heel, and she beat him over the head with it," West said. "He had this big old gash in his head, and he's running around, screaming in the hallway."

The attack led authorities to send Christine to a state psychiatrist, Sidney Goldstein, who concluded Christine was mentally unstable. Christine visited Goldstein for the next ten years, and during one visit to Goldstein's office, West realized just how seriously ill her mother was during a conversation with Goldstein's secretary.

"She said, 'Oh, um, well, anyone who sees Dr. Goldstein has got a real screw loose,'" West said. "'He only takes the sickest patients.'"

Moments later, the secretary left her mother's psychiatric case file open in front of West, and West scanned her mother's diagnosis.

"Sociopath with psychopathic tendencies," West said. "That was my mother's diagnosis . . . someone who cares for nobody but themselves. They see the world as a place to be manipulated for their own comforts and use.

"She was a total sociopath," West said.

14

I was about thirty and I was going to work. I got out of my car, and I felt this wind. I stood there for a moment, and it was like I was watching a movie. I could see this man, and there was a little girl behind a green sofa. She was five years old, and she was watching this guy in a Halloween costume kill her pregnant mother. I see this guy cutting her open and taking the baby out. This is not my imagination—I knew I was having a premonition. The next day, the whole thing is on the news. It happened on Halloween night.

—Brookey Lee West

The premonitions usually come without warning to Brookey Lee West. Her mind flashes like a time machine, and a whirling sensation takes her into the future, allowing her to witness events yet to occur. When TWA Flight 800 plunged into the Atlantic Ocean in 1996, killing all 230 passengers, West knew the tragedy was going to happen before it actually unfolded. In San Jose, West said she witnessed the murder of a pregnant woman in her mind the day before news of the slaying showed up on her television screen.

"It's like I'm watching a movie," West said. "It's not something I acquired. I was born this way."

West said she's had the premonitions since she was a little girl growing up in San Jose. The phenomenon can likely be traced to West's father, who actually encouraged his child to explore the occult and different methods of predicting the future. When West was eleven, Leroy Smith bought his little girl two gifts used to tell the future—a crystal ball and some tarot cards. The tarot cards were West's favorite, and they remained a fascination for her throughout her adult life.

"I know all about those cards, and I have studied them for years," West said. "They are valid. The only issue I see about those cards is that what the books say they mean, and what they really mean is much more vast."

Tarot cards are twenty-two pictorial playing cards dating back to fifteenth-century Europe. The cards feature elaborate picture designs of several symbols, including the Moon, Justice, Hanged Man and the Devil card. The most ominous card in the deck is the Death card, which is adorned with a skeleton riding a horse.

"An amateur person does not really understand the depth of the cards," West said. "They can be helpful, and they can also be very dangerous. I take the deck, cut the cards, and I just lay them out in a certain format," West said. "Each position of the card means a certain thing, and each card means a certain thing. The cards are all interlinked."

West does not call herself a psychic. She prefers the term "empathic," meaning she draws upon the feelings of other people to see what the future holds.

"If I meet someone, or if I'm in the presence of someone for a long time, I take on how they feel," West said. "If they are angry, I feel their anger. Or if they are upset, I feel that."

And in Las Vegas in the late 1990s at the oxygen bar Breathe, she used marbles to predict futures.

"I'll usually do one marble at a time," West said. "I have the person hold it, then they lay it down, and I pick it up.

It's like a camera, and I see things. But I could pretty much use anything to do it. I can do the same thing with straws. I just use marbles because they are easy to carry around.

"I do run into skeptics, but after they get to know me for a while, they know I'm for real," West said.

"I always wanted to try and help the police, because I know about all kinds of stuff before it happens," West said. "Murders, bank robberies, plane crashes, assassinations. TWA 800?" West said. "I knew about that one. The plane that crashed into the Potomac River? I knew about that. The assassination of that guy over in Israel a number of years ago? All of it, I know. I know it is going to happen.

"This thing that happened in New York, September eleventh? I knew that," she said.

"But the problem is, you can't help the police with this stuff, because you can never trust the police."

15

In 1971, Brookey Lee West graduated from Santa Clara High School in San Jose and decided it was finally time to get away from her nutty mother, her devil-worshipping father and her high school dropout brother. But with less than average grades in high school and no plans for college, West had few career options in front of her, so she joined the army.

"I signed up for military intelligence," West said. "I wanted to be a spy. I thought I'd make a good spy, and what got me on that track was my dad. He loved war stuff and cop stuff on television, and basically to have any kind of relationship with him, I'd watch these shows with him. So I would watch combat shows, shows like *Secret Agent Man*, with my dad. I had all these visions of glory in the army, and I was going to do all this interesting stuff."

West enlisted in San Jose, was shipped out to basic training and then was stationed at the now closed Fort McClellan in Alabama. It didn't take long for West to realize that military life was not the glamorous existence depicted in the television shows. "All the restrictions were stupid to me," West said. "It didn't have the sophistication I thought it would, and I like to do my own thinking. I was like, 'Why do I need to follow what everybody else thinks?' But that is the way they do it, the military, the government, the FBI, the CIA," West said. "So when I really found out the way it was, I said, 'I'm not doing this.'"

West was begging for a discharge from the army within nine months of her enlistment, and remarkably, the military agreed to cut West loose with an honorable discharge even though her only reason for wanting out was disillusionment. Broke, disappointed and without any post–high school education, West returned home to San Jose to live with her mother.

It was a depressing time for West. She took odd jobs as a waitress and a legal secretary, and at just twenty years old West was paying all the bills and taking care of all her unemployed mother's needs. Deep down inside, West was desperate to get away from Christine.

In 1973, West thought she found the perfect chance to escape in the form of a man named Ray Alcantar.* Alcantar was a parishioner at the Faith Temple church attended by West and her mother, and West soon came to believe Alcantar was the love of her life. "One night, I came home from church, and Ray asked me, 'Do you want to go out and have something to eat?'" West recalled. "So we went out, and we had something to eat, and we started going out."

Alcantar was a handsome, smooth-talking man who was three years older than West. He had dark skin, deep brown eyes and dark hair parted down the middle.

"He was good-looking, he was charming, so we dated for a while," West said. "We dated maybe six or seven months, and I was wild about him. I was in love with him. Completely gone."

Alcantar, however, didn't see the relationship that way. In a statement later given to California detectives investigating West, Alcantar said of the relationship, "I visited with her a few times, not a whole lot of times. Maybe seven times total, visiting and talking."

In 1973, West and Alcantar went on a weekend trip to Los Angeles and it was there, in the City of Angels, that the couple first made love. Within a few months of returning from Los Angeles, West started feeling ill, and a doctor confirmed she was pregnant.

Alcantar, according to West, wasn't excited about the news, and his disappointment crushed West's dreams of a storybook relationship with Alcantar.

"I just told him I was pregnant, straight up, and it was over the phone, because he called me to see how I was feeling," West said. "That's when he gave me this snotty-assed remark, saying, 'How do you know it's mine?' I'm naïve up to this point. I think I knew in my heart he was already out seeing other women on the side, but I really couldn't face that.

"As soon as I told him I was pregnant, he was gone," West said.

Abortion was not an option for West, and she knew she was going to have to tell Christine and Leroy she was pregnant. As expected, they were furious.

"My parents crucified me," West said. "They called me all kinds of names. Bitch, whore, slut, a tramp. 'Why don't you have an abortion?'" West quoted her father as saying. "'You don't need that baby. He doesn't love you.'"

West gave birth to a beautiful baby girl at O'Connor Catholic hospital in San Jose in 1974, and she named her blue-eyed daughter Susie Alcantar.* West loved her child, but when her daughter was born, she was not ready to be a mother. She was immature, emotionally unstable and suffering from extreme mood swings.

"I was having a nervous breakdown," West said. "I got to where I was having [mental] episodes, and I couldn't stand being around people. I couldn't do my job. I made a bunch of mistakes, I couldn't remember things and I was highly temperamental . . . it was getting to where I was out of control. I knew I was spinning down. I felt like I was going to crash."

West worked long hours as a legal secretary in a law office to support her daughter and her mother, and all the while West was struggling with the pressures of being a single mom. She worried about leaving her daughter alone at her apartment with Christine for hours on end. By the time Susie was four, West had had enough of motherhood, so she sent her little girl off to a boarding school in Arizona.

"To protect her, I sent her to school really so I could have someone take care of her," West said. "I was working two and three jobs, and I wanted her to have a good environment. The teachers at this school took good care of her. It cost me a lot of money to put her in private school. It was a hard decision, but I was never emotional like a lot of people are over their kids," West said. "I look at things over the long range."

With West's decision to send Susie off to private school out of state, history was repeating itself. Nearly two decades earlier, Leroy had dropped West and her brother off at an orphanage in Bakersfield. Now the same thing was happening to West's daughter.

"I went down for her communion, but I didn't have a lot of time or money," West said. "She would come home on holidays. I'd make airline reservations, and she'd fly by herself. She was in school about five years."

By the time Susie was nine, West had no plans to bring her daughter home from private school. Instead, she decided she was going to give Susie to her teachers at the private school. Suffering from increased mood swings and mental instability at the time, West said she did not think she would be a good parent for Susie.

"They [Susie's teachers] were good people," West said. "They had two teenage children, they had a younger daughter and they wanted her. It was the best thing for my daughter because it was a stable environment. She was not used to living with me, and my environment was not stable."

There was one problem, though, with West's plan to give Susie away. Susie's father, Ray Alcantar, still had parental rights to the child, so West approached Alcantar and asked him to relinquish his parental rights.

He refused.

"I asked him to sign the papers, and he goes, 'No, I won't sign that,'" West said. "And I thought, 'Well, okay, don't sign it.' He didn't understand I didn't need his signature. I got this lawyer who knew the law about adoptions."

West initiated legal proceedings in the San Jose courts to terminate Alcantar's parental rights to Susie.

Alcantar, meanwhile, offered a different account of his confrontation with West over Susie's fate. He said in a statement to police that he was mortified at the idea of Susie being sent away to a private school in Arizona, and he was even more shocked at West's intentions to give away their daughter. He told West he would never sign any papers relinquishing his parental rights to Susie.

"She was wanting me to sign over legal guardianship papers to her, [so] that she would be able to put her up for adoption," Alcantar said. "She wanted me to be in agreement with it. I didn't agree with it . . . I said I would adopt her."

It was a decision that infuriated West, and it enraged West's father, too. No Mexican was going to tell Leroy Smith's daughter what she could or couldn't do.

"I wanted to have custody of my daughter, full custody," Alcantar said. "It was not up for conversation with them. It wasn't in their heads."

16

Ray Alcantar's decision to maintain parental rights to his daughter, Susie, infuriated Brookey Lee West and her father in 1984. Weeks later, on the night of January 14, 1985, a man paid a visit to the home of Alcantar's eighty-six-year-old grandmother, Juanita Alcantar, in Sunnyvale, California. The man knocked on the door of Juanita's residence, and when the elderly woman emerged onto her front porch, she was confronted by a man dressed completely in black.

"Is Ray here?" the man asked.

"No," Juanita Alcantar responded.

The man lifted his arm, pointed a handgun at Juanita Alcantar's chest and pulled the trigger at point-blank range. A bullet from a .22-caliber handgun pierced the elderly woman's torso, knocking her backward. She regained her footing and stumbled inside the home to a nearby bed, where she collapsed in a pool of blood. Juanita Alcantar's daughter happened to be inside the house and called 911 while comforting her gravely wounded mother. Juanita Alcantar was rushed by ambulance to nearby

Kaiser Hospital in Sunnyvale, and remarkably, her life was saved during surgery.

Sunnyvale police immediately kicked off an extensive investigation to identify the gunman, but from the beginning of the case, police had little evidence to work with. According to police reports, a witness got a brief glimpse of the gunman fleeing in a light-colored foreign car. A forensic examination of the crime scene turned up no fingerprints on the front door of Juanita Alcantar's residence, and one of the few physical clues available was a faint tire impression left on the side of the road by the gunman's vehicle.

There was not even a shell casing at the scene. It was as if the gunman knew to retrieve the shell casing in order to eliminate any evidence.

The gunman was described as a thin, white male, possibly in his thirties, and he may have had a mustache. One account given to the police indicated the gunman may have been wearing a Halloween mask. He spoke in Spanish, but it was clear that Spanish was not his native language.

Juanita Alcantar, described as senile by one family member, wasn't much help to detectives, either. She could never identify her attacker, and her version of the shooting changed over time.

Ray Alcantar was devastated by his grandmother's shooting, and his pain was only exacerbated a month later when he received a letter in the mail that scared the living hell right out of him. The letter arrived in the mail at his home on the 100 block of Browning Way in Vallejo, California, on February 13. The letter was in an envelope with no return address, and it was postmarked the day before in Vallejo.

The letter consisted of a single piece of paper adorned with a handwritten pentagram and a series of Satanic chants predicting the murder of his entire family.

"Satanic chants and curses . . . the letter was a threat,

[a] threat, you know, to kill me and my family," Ray Alcantar told the police.

You pray to your God, I'll pray to mine. We'll see whose God is stronger.

There was little doubt in Ray Alcantar's mind as to who sent the letter. Ray Alcantar told police when he dated West briefly in the 1970s, West talked as if she had intimate knowledge of the occult.

"She would speak of different demons, that they would attack people and afflict them physically," Ray Alcantar said. "She had a knowledge of that kind of thing, you know, things I've never heard anybody else talk about."

Ray Alcantar also told police West's father was a follower of Satan, and Leroy Smith was the only person he knew who was capable of sending such a letter.

"She had said that her father was a warlock, or you know, something like that, in the religion," Ray Alcantar said. "I didn't feel like they were the kind of gang that I wanted to hang out with." Ray Alcantar and his wife turned the letter over to authorities investigating his grandmother's shooting. The letter was processed for fingerprints, according to police reports, but produced no results.

After the shooting of his grandmother and his receiving the letter, Ray Alcantar was shaken to the core with fear. He abandoned his attempts to keep his daughter, and the little girl was adopted by her teachers in Arizona within the year.

"After that, I never tried to get in touch with them. Never," Alcantar said.

The shooting of Juanita Alcantar remains unsolved to this day.

17

By the early 1980s, Christine Smith was a lonely, fifty-year-old woman hungry for a man's tender touch. Leroy was no longer in the picture following the couple's divorce, and for Christine, having a big, strong man around to satisfy her physical needs was an absolute necessity.

Christine's loneliness caused her to make several romantic overtures to strange men. One man who came over to fix an appliance at the house that Christine shared with her daughter was suddenly subjected to not-so-subtle hints that Christine was yearning for a man's company.

"I came home from work, and my mom said, 'There was a real good-looking man who came out here today,' so she started in on him," West said, quoting her mother. "'You know, if you are not married . . .'"

But time and again, Christine's efforts were rebuffed by members of the opposite sex, who saw her as strange and, sometimes, downright creepy. Christine eventually started to focus on her chiropractor, David Hobson.* Hobson was a divorced professional with children, and Christine regularly visited his office for what she said were numerous back ailments. After a few visits, Christine was enamored with her chiropractor, and she made it clear to Hobson that he could have her if he wanted.

"He was not interested in my mother, but in my mother's mind he was," West said. "She wanted him because he was successful, and he had money."

Hobson's lack of a romantic interest in Christine didn't deter Christine, and she literally believed she could make Hobson love her. She started going to the chiropractor's office more and more often, and Christine was interpreting every hello and good-bye from Hobson as covert overtures that he wanted to have sex with her.

" 'I know he loves me, and pretty soon he's going to ask me to marry him,' " West said, quoting her mother.

Christine was so hot for Hobson, she decided to make a pornographic audio cassette tape of herself masturbating, and she planned to give the tape to the doctor. On the tape, Christine can be heard moaning and groaning as she fondles herself, and in between her sounds of orgasmic ecstasy Christine narrates her love for Hobson in a slow, sultry Texas drawl.

You [Hobson] are probably gone to your son's [house] by now. I hope you enjoyed yourself. I hope you caught lots of fish. You sounded quite tired, Doc, on the phone. I know you really needed to get away, and to be more rested when you come back.

Oh! Doc! Ohhh. God. Come on. Fuck me. I love the way you make love to me. Oh! Baby! Oh! Oh, God. Oh! Ohhh! Come on. [Panting] Ohh! Ohhh! Ohhhhhh! Oh! Oh! Oh! Oh! Oh, God! Ohhhh! [Heavy breathing]

Oh! [Heavy breathing] Oh, God! Ohhh! Call me a bitch! Ohhh! [Heavy breathing]

Christine's sex tape seems to offer a rare insight into her twisted mind. Hobson has no interest in her, yet Christine talks as if they are in a consensual, passionate relationship. She actually sounds like she is fucking the doctor on the tape.

Baby, I'm laying here just thinking about you. You know you just drive me crazy. Had breakfast with you. Then you took us over to the office. Ohhh, God. I wanted you so bad! I don't think you realize how much I love you. I want your body. Do you know, Doc, that's a form of love, too, when a woman wants you, and desires you that much?

I've never felt this way toward no man in all my life until I met you. You kind of rubbed my ass in there, and then you come up. Ohh, God. Oh, my God, Doc. I wanted you!

I wanted to rub your legs. Oh, Doc, it's different with you and I. You know that. You know you want me. You know you want me. It is not a friendship with you and I. You don't [touch] your friend's ass. You don't accept porno tapes from them. Don't tell me you don't want to fuck me. You do. Ohhh, Doc. Don't wait. Don't let this fire inside of my belly die!

Christine, it seems, is in a delusional state. She is overcome by sexual fantasy and desire for a man who, in real life, has no interest in her.

Oh, I want you, oh, God, how I want you! I can hardly stand it. I'll get on you so bad. Oh, Doc, there's so many men who wish they could have a woman who wanted to love them like I want to love you. I desire you sexually. I love you as a person, as a man, as a doctor. I love you, period. I wish I could just say, 'Okay, I'll be your friend,' and just treat you like you do a friend, and walk away. Hello, every now and again, but, oh, Doc, I can't treat you like a friend. No, it has gone too far between you and I. I don't want to be treated like a friend. I want you to love me.

I want our love to be kept a secret, because I know it may touch your life. It would never be told. I would never tell. I would never cause you trouble.

A promise of secrecy. A sexual relationship that will never be revealed. Christine's lust for Hobson and her promise that no one will ever know sound familiar, of course, when compared to the tryst Christine had with her married lover, David Gilmore, in Bakersfield. Christine will do whatever it takes to get her man, even if it means blasting him with a shotgun and then going to prison.

Oh, I just want you to put your cock in my belly! I want you to fuck me! I want you to make me feel good! I want you to make me holler. I'm fixin' to do it in a few minutes. I start thinking of you, and I rub my ass . . . and I just climaxed all over the place. Don't take much from you to pop my nuts. Ohhh, my baby! Ohhh, Doc! Don't give up a wonderful love because of some man-written ideal, that if you are a doctor, you can't touch your patient. They do all the time. [Heavy breathing] So what. I want to love you, and that's all I want.

I don't want your money, I don't want nothing else. Just to love you, and have you fuck the hell out of me. Oh, God, Doc. You just have the wildest imagination. Oh, I want to get all over you, and just suck you good. You know, you need to be sucked. Fucked and sucked. Oh, baby. Oh, damn, when you get around me, I just can't take it. I get so hot. Just pretend that you're not a doctor and I'm not your patient. I'll love the hell out of you.

Did you know there was a man who wanted to climb Mount Kilimanjaro? He saved his money all his life, and by the time he got to the mountain, the guy there told him he couldn't because he was too old. Well, Doc, don't wait until you are too old to love me. Don't wait until you don't have a home run left in your lovely legs down there. There has to be a place you would meet me. A place where we could be together. Oh, Doc, don't take this away from me. I've never wanted a man like I wanted you. I've never been loved by no one in my whole life. Oh, Doc. Please, love me. I beg you to love me. I'm so hot, and there is so much desire and passion for a man.

Ohhh. Ohhh. [Heavy breathing] Ohhh. Ohhh. Ohhh. Ohhh. Ohhh. Ohhh. Love you. Fuck me. Oh, God Ohhhh. [Heavy breathing] Ohhhh! Ohhhh! Ohhhh! Baby! [Heavy breathing] Baby. Oh.

What can be heard next on the tape is truly bizarre. On the tape, Christine interrupts her orgasmic sex sessions to record a twenty-minute television sermon proffered by an unidentified televangelist. The televangelist is an African American man, and he was apparently recorded off Christine's television set. The unidentified preacher is heard screaming at the top of his lungs as he praises God during a Fourth of July celebration.

For 210 years, we have been led by the inspiration of the Constitution of the United States. It is the only document existing in the world today that has gone 210 years that a revolution has not substituted. We have amended it, but we have not destroyed it, because God started it, and God's going to end it.

We've got our share of sinners, but we've even got them under God. We have our agnostics, but we are working on them. They are beginning to believe. For no man can look at a black cow who eats green grass and gives white milk and churns yellow butter, and not know, there is a God somewhere. [Crowd applauds, yells Amen]

Christine's taping of the preacher's religious rantings in the middle of her sexual fantasy tape is, by all accounts, strange. But those who knew Christine—including her own daughter—could hardly have been surprised she mixed sex with God in her private life.

Christine, West said, was a woman obsessed with religious imagery, and even though she was a sinner, she talked about Jesus regularly. Taping herself masturbating, then splicing it with a preacher's sermon, seems to offer prolific insight into the twisted workings of Christine's mind and her maddening, grandiose obsessions in life.

> We've made progress. We have a nation. We've got Chicago. We've got New York. We have Miami. We've got Los Angeles. We've got San Francisco. We've got Orange County. We are a nation. We have an army, we have a navy, we have all kinds of military preparedness. But thank God, we have steeples on almost every block, calling on the name of the Lord, Jesus Christ.
>
> God bless you, America. You are just a little baby. I'm going to give you time to grow up. I may not be here, but when you get a little bit older, you will perfect your vision. One nation, under God, indivisible, with liberty and justice for all. You are going to do it! You are going to do it! You are going to do it! And I'm going to help you do it! I'm going to pray for you. And I'm going to ask God, God bless America! [Crowd cheers]

Christine's voice then returns to the tape, and she begins to talk to her doctor again as if he was with her. She explains to Hobson how the preacher is a favorite of hers, and she resumes her sex-crazed fantasy for the doctor.

> Hello there. It's me again. I hope you enjoyed what he had to say. I like his teaching, I like his preaching. I hear him

every once in a while on TV. He speaks a lot of truth. He don't butter everything up. He puts it out like it really is. That's why I like to hear him. He's a great big, heavyset, fat black man. He's really a minister, and one of the few that don't beat around the bush. He tells it like it is. Well, baby, it's getting late. I'll sign you off. I'll talk to you, maybe about three o'clock in the morning. I really feel that way.

Christine wants to fuck this man, and she wants to fuck him hard—even if it is all in her mind.

Ohhh, I sure do. I'll get you at about three o'clock in the morning. I'll just come right into your bed, and you won't even know it. Just start loving you. Ohhh, I'll just get all over you. It's so much fun, because you can't stop me in my mind. Ohhh, sweet thing. I could just stick my tongue in your mouth and suck your tongue. Oh, God. Just suck your cock. Oh, you are so sweet. You are sweet all over. I'll just kiss you, love the hell out of you. You are so sweet, so wonderful. I just want to feel that hair on your chest, stick my tongue in your little navel hole. Suck your little balls. Just tongue and love the hell out of you.

Oh, please don't keep turning away from me. Don't cheat yourself. All you have to say is, 'I'm going to make love to you.' Do it! You don't have to make it so damned complicated. We'll do it however you want to do it, wherever you want to do it. I know, you probably think I'm being pushy again. I don't mean to be pushy, I just want you so bad. I've never had a burning desire to want anybody in my whole life like I've wanted you. I want to start munching on you. Kiss those sweet ears. You have the sweetest little mouth. I just want to search down in there and find that tongue. We can get away, and you can take me somewhere.

Oh, Doc. Think about it. Just think about it. I just want

you so bad. You think about it. Oh, my baby, sleep tight. I want you so bad.

End of tape.

Christine never gave the tape to Hobson. Before she could, her dreams of a romance with the chiropractor were crushed when his secretary informed Christine that Hobson was in love with another woman.

Christine was fuming over the slight, even though her relationship with Hobson had been a figment of her imagination.

"My mother came out of his office and she was as white as a ghost," West said. "She was shaking, and she said, 'Take me home.' We get home and I said, 'What happened? Did they hurt you?' She goes, 'No, that son of a bitch is leading me on. That damned doctor, he loves me, and he's been advancing toward me, putting his arm around me, and I know he loves me, and that son of a bitch has another woman.'"

West was stunned.

"I was looking at her, like, 'Mom!'" West said. "It was in her mind, but she believed it. She said, 'I'm going to get me a gun, and I'm going to shoot that son of a bitch, just like I shot that other one.'"

But unlike the revenge Christine exacted on David Gilmore, Christine never followed through on her promise to shoot her chiropractor.

That's because West wouldn't let her.

"She wanted me to get her a gun, and I said no," West recalled. "I never would have no guns around her, because she meant it. I said, 'No, I won't let you do that. If I know about it, it's not going to happen. He didn't do anything to you.'"

18

In late 1975, Chloe Smith was a woman in desperate need of money. The twice-divorced thirty-four-year-old was working as an accounts payable clerk in San Jose, and the few hundred dollars a month she was making was hardly enough to support herself. As a result, Chloe started looking for a second job, and she found one slinging beers at a hole-in-the-wall tavern near Santa Clara University.

"I had a friend who was a bartender, and she knew somebody who had just taken over a little beer bar down by the San Jose bus depot," Chloe Smith said. "This guy needed a barmaid part-time, and I was like, what the hell? It's money. I can do that."

At first glance, Chloe Smith doesn't seem the type to sling beers at a juke joint. A soft-spoken woman with a diminutive figure and short, grayish hair cut at the neckline, she is quiet and extremely polite, making her seem more like a librarian, than a cocktail waitress.

But Chloe Smith needed the money, so she took the job, and it was a decision that changed her life forever. Within a few weeks of starting work a patron of the bar, Leroy

Smith, was courting her, and within two years Chloe and Leroy married.

"It was not love at first sight," Chloe Smith said. "I was very much not interested in getting involved again at all."

Despite Chloe Smith's resistance to Leroy's advances, he was persistent in his attempts to get to know Chloe, and over time, she recognized there was something about Leroy that made him different from the rest of the men in her life. He glowed with affection for her, and his fondness made Chloe Smith feel special. She realized Leroy genuinely cared for her, and during a slow-moving two-year courtship, Leroy convinced Chloe Smith to believe in his love.

"He was wonderful," Chloe Smith said. "He was very loving to me. In fact, that is what finally attracted me to him. Very affectionate, very protective. Just a feeling he gave me."

Leroy's affection was a much-needed boost for Chloe Smith given her prior struggles in life. Chloe was born in Massachusetts to an alcoholic father who moved Chloe and her three siblings to rural, middle-of-nowhere Arizona when she was a little girl, in the 1940s.

"We lived in a place called Apache Junction when there was nobody there but the Apaches, the junction and me," Chloe said. "It was pretty desolate and pretty awful. The nearest neighbor was several miles away, and my dad was somewhat reclusive. My sister and two brothers and I had to take the bus into school, and it was like an hour ride to Mesa, and an hour back," she said. "We were the last ones on and the last ones off the bus. It was not fun, and I hated it.

"We had no television and no telephone in the house," she said. "Once school let out for summer, I never saw my friends until the fall. To this day, if you say 'Arizona' or 'cactus' to me, I shudder. I would never live there again, and I would never wish it on anybody."

Chloe Smith escaped Apache Junction by marrying her

high school sweetheart when she was just sixteen. She and her husband, a military man, jumped from state to state, and the marriage produced two beautiful children. But the relationship soon soured, and Chloe found herself a single woman. A second marriage followed on the rebound, and after that relationship failed as well, her children, ages thirteen and fourteen went to live with Chloe's first husband in Texas.

With Leroy, Chloe Smith was holding out hope that things would be different. The two married in 1977, and the couple rented a small house on Lawrence Street in San Jose. Chloe called Leroy by his last name, Smith, and he in turn called her by her middle name, Jean. Leroy, the mustachioed, sturdy-framed carpet layer with a turbulent history, seemed to thrive on Chloe's stability, and Chloe grasped on to Leroy's unconditional love. But, without question, Leroy brought a great deal of baggage into the relationship. Chloe Smith knew Leroy had a history with women and that he had been a womanizer throughout much of his life.

"He had a way of lighting up when a woman would walk in the room, and he was very attractive to women," Chloe said. "A woman would come up to him, and he'd just sparkle. I thought it was amusing. It didn't bother me, because I felt very secure about how he felt about me. But he just had a way of twinkling around the opposite sex."

Leroy was socially dysfunctional to an extreme. He was defensive in public, and he was rarely interested in talking to other people.

"He was very defensive, very hostile to guys probably," Chloe said. "It depended on the circumstances. If he were meeting you, and you were a friend of somebody, he would be polite, but he didn't have any friends. He could only be outgoing for very short periods. A very short attention span for being social. He didn't trust people."

During one particularly heated argument with Chloe, Leroy made mention of his mother's murder in Tennessee.

"We were arguing and he said, 'You are going to make me so mad that I'm going to do what my dad did. I'm going to chop your head off,'" Chloe said. "I was like, 'Okay.' It was something he never wanted to talk about."

There were other faults, too, such as his avowed racism and hatred of minorities.

"There was no one more racist than Smith," Chloe said.

And he was a recovering alcoholic who was routinely falling off the wagon.

"He was an alcoholic, and he had to fight it a lot," Chloe said. "He would fall off the wagon once in a while, but then he would fall off the wagon and he was like off for two weeks. But then he was back on the wagon, and he got it back together."

Leroy also kept a large stash of firearms in their residence. At any given time, there were usually about twenty guns in the house. Some guns were stored under the cushions of their couch. Others were stashed in the bedroom, and there was always one handgun on the nightstand. Leroy kept a firearm in the kitchen "just in case," she said.

"He certainly had plenty of guns, and he could be a hostile person . . . [and] I don't think he would have a fear of shooting people," she said.

When asked whether her husband was ever a follower of Satan, Chloe said her husband dabbled with multiple religions throughout their twenty-year marriage. She never saw Leroy involved in devil worship, but in retrospect she can remember two instances that hinted at the possibility her husband was once involved in Satanism. The first incident, in the 1980s, involved a Mexican couple who lived on Lawrence Street, just a few houses down from them. The neighbors had spent thousands of dollars landscaping their front yard, and after they were done they started parking their cars in front of Leroy's house so everyone on the street could have a full view of their prized new yard.

Leroy was pissed.

"He wrote them this awful, devil-threatening letter," Chloe Smith said. "They turned it over to the police, and the police came to the house."

Like the letter sent to Ray Alcantar, it threatened the neighbors and mentioned the powers of Satan. Chloe didn't learn of the letter until the Santa Clara deputies came knocking on her door. Dismayed and shocked, she confronted her husband after the officers left.

"What are you thinking? Are you insane? This is so stupid," she said to her husband.

Leroy's response was somewhat cavalier.

"He said they were Mexicans, and he figured they were real religious and just talking about the devil would scare them," she recalled. "That's what he told me."

The second incident unfolded when Leroy was given some furniture by his ex-wife, Christine, and his daughter, Brookey West. Chloe said Leroy was moving the furniture into his garage when she noticed Leroy placing a large, "grotesque" Halloween mask into a secret compartment he had built into a cabinet in his garage.

"It [the secret compartment] was open, and he was putting a mask of some sort in it," Chloe recalled. "All I know is, it was ugly. It was very dark. A very dark and grotesque face. I said, 'What in the world?' And he says, 'This isn't mine. This is Brooke's and her mother's. You never saw this. It has got to do with devil worship, and you don't want to get involved. I'm just sealing it up in this wall.' I was like, okay, and that's the only time I ever saw anything."

Chloe Smith didn't pursue the matter further, and despite these strange events, she loved Leroy, and he loved her. Leroy certainly had his faults, but he was still a good husband.

"He always made me feel loved," Chloe said.

Chloe said the best example of Leroy's love was demonstrated when she decided she needed to get a college education. Chloe is an especially intelligent woman and was tired of working dead-end jobs in the 1980s, so she headed back to school. Leroy offered his full support for her decision to get a degree in business.

"He was very supportive when I decided I needed to go back to school because I only had a high school education and I knew I wasn't going to get anywhere," Chloe said.

"He encouraged me to go to school, and I ended up actually getting a four-year college degree. He took over everything in the house while I was at school. I would come home [from school] and say, 'I'm tired. I can't take it anymore,' and he would say, 'The longer you put this off, the worse it is going to be. You're never going to go back,'" she recalled.

Leroy's treatment of Chloe Smith was the exact opposite of the way he treated his first wife. It was as if she had married a man far removed from the Leroy Smith of the 1960s in Bakersfield and the early 1970s in San Jose. If he was still active in the Satanic church, it was on a much more covert level. He was not drinking all the time, and to Chloe Smith, at least, he was a kind, considerate and compassionate man.

"He didn't like to talk about his prior life," Chloe said. "It was like it was another time, another place, another world."

But deep down inside, the old Leroy was really still around. It would take two decades of marriage for Chloe Smith to come to the conclusion that she never really knew her husband and that, in fact, Leroy Smith had a frightening side to him.

"I think he was two different people," Chloe said. "That wasn't the guy I knew."

*   *   *

Throughout Chloe Smith's marriage to Leroy, he always made sure his wife followed one very simple rule—under no circumstances was Chloe to associate with his ex-wife, Christine.

"They had been apart a lot of years and divorced a long time before I met him," Chloe said. "He told me she was crazy and that I didn't want to be around her."

Leroy also instilled in his wife the belief that his daughter, Brookey Lee West, was to be kept at a distance.

"I always thought it would have been very nice if we all could have gotten together. . . . I asked him, 'Why can't we get together on the holidays?'" Chloe recalled. "He would say, 'Nope. No, no. You are not going to get involved with them. They are crazy. You are not going to get involved with them . . . they are not very nice people.'"

In fact, Chloe didn't even meet West until approximately three years after she married Leroy.

"He knew she was coming over to the house, and he answered the door, and they just let it be known that I wasn't needed," Chloe said. "It didn't necessarily strike me as anything strange, because he had already told me he didn't want me around his family."

West visited her father's house from time to time, but she rarely spoke to his wife. When West would show up at the house, she went directly into her father's office and they closed the door to talk.

It was as if Chloe Smith wasn't even there.

"He didn't think it would be good for our relationship," Chloe said. "He just kind of explained that it would cause all kinds of problems for us."

There was one person in Leroy's family, however, with whom Chloe did have some contact during her marriage, and that person was Leroy's son, Travis. A towering figure with long, bushy, black hair, Travis was hopelessly addicted to drugs, unable to hold a job and often homeless.

"I don' think he even graduated from the seventh grade," Chloe Smith said. "He started using drugs very young, and I think he burned himself out. He did poorly in school, and I just don't think he was very smart. He didn't get it."

When Travis would show up at the Smith household, like his sister, he would go into Leroy's office, where his father would shut the door behind them. At first, Chloe Smith had only minimal interaction with Travis, but she did see a noticeable difference in the way Leroy treated his son compared to the way he treated his daughter. West, Leroy believed, could take care of herself, but Travis was in constant need of his help, prompting Leroy to do whatever he could to make his son's life easier. He bought Travis a truck, got him several jobs in the flooring industry and set up his son in one apartment after another. But Travis was too busy partying to maintain any semblance of a normal life, and Leroy was in misery as he watched his son's slow decline.

"He despaired for his son," Chloe Smith said. "He tried so hard to make things easier for his son, and he ended up only making things worse. Buying cars, giving him cars. An enabler. He didn't give to Brooke like he gave to his son. He made excuses for his son. He didn't for Brooke. My view is, he absolutely favored his son."

Out of concern for his son's future, Leroy even started his own flooring business in San Jose. He called the business Smith's Floor Covering, and he hoped to give the business to Travis one day. But just like all the other dreams Leroy had for his son's future, the idea of leaving a legacy for his son quickly evaporated.

"He hoped to start something for his son," Chloe said. "And his son told him, 'Dad, I have no interest in this at all.'"

Leroy disbanded the business within a few months of starting it.

"He was doing it for his son, and after six months it was real clear that his son didn't want any part of it," Chloe said. "He told his dad, 'I don't want to do this. It's too hard.' So Leroy said, 'Why am I doing this? Why am I killing myself?' So he just gave the business up, and he started doing security work."

Travis hit rock bottom by the early 1980s, when he was in his late twenties and early thirties. Completely overcome by drugs and alcohol, he lived on the streets. Any money he had he spent on drugs, and he survived by eating a meal a day at the local missions. It was a sad existence, likely due to a childhood of undisputed emotional pain. His mother was not affectionate and was in prison during his developmental years, and Travis likely questioned his own self-worth. To kill the pain and self-doubt, Travis turned to methamphetamines and the streets.

Police records show Travis was arrested at least ten times in seven years by the San Jose police and the Santa Clara County sheriff's office. Many of the offenses were drug related. Others consisted of arrest for public intoxication and for loitering by a homeless drug addict.

But two of Travis' arrests were particularly serious. In one instance, Travis was found incoherent and rambling in front of a low-rent motel. Delirious on drugs, he had taken a chair from his hotel room and set it on fire in front of the motel, prompting police to take him into custody on an arson charge.

In another instance, Travis attacked an ex-girlfriend in a methamphetamine-induced rage.

"My brother liked speed, meth, and he had some guns," West said. "He and a friend went over to this gal's house, and they broke in, and she was in bed with this other guy. So my brother strips them all down naked, and he goes in another room, and he gets this woman's little boy, and he brings him back in, and he says, 'Now you see what a whore your mother is?'"

A neighbor heard the commotion and called 911, and Travis was arrested at the scene by Santa Clara County authorities.

"The cops tracked him down, but it took six cops to take him down," West said. "By the time he calms down in jail, his hand is broke, his nose is broke, and they were like, what do you expect? So he was going to go to prison for a long time."

But Travis's arrest record was so long and these two crimes so bizarre, he was examined by a state psychiatrist and diagnosed as being schizophrenic. A Santa Clara County judge deemed him criminally insane, and Travis was committed to the Atascadero State Hospital for the criminally insane in San Luis Obispo County. The hospital houses some of the craziest, most dangerous people in the California criminal justice system, and a third of Atascadero's patients are some of California's most violent sexual predators.

Chloe Smith said Travis rarely received visitors at Atascadero. Leroy went to visit his son about once a month at the hospital, and at first Leroy wouldn't let Chloe go with him. But shortly before Christmas, she baked a huge batch of Christmas cookies for Leroy to take to Travis, and on this occasion Leroy invited her to go along with him.

"I went in, and I saw him, and he was this big huge guy," Chloe said. "He came across as a big guy with all this hair, but to me he just seemed like this big, harmless woolly bear."

Touched by Travis' fate, Chloe walked across the room, gave him the cookies and then gave him a big hug.

The response she got from Travis startled her.

"Do you know what he did?" Chloe Smith said. "He cried. It was like nobody had hugged him in God knows when. It was the saddest thing. It was just an automatic thing for me, and I was like, 'My God.' It was like I was the first person who had done anything nice for him."

The tears streaming down Travis's face were likely the result of a lifetime of emotional emptiness. His mother was a crazy bitch who had no need for him, yet his father's second wife—a woman who had no investment in Travis—took the time to bake him cookies and give him a hug.

"Maybe he never remembered even having a hug," Chloe said.

Travis was eventually released from the state mental health system, and he immediately went back to the streets. Every now and then, Travis would come by his father's house with a little gift for Chloe Smith.

"He brought me little presents, probably stolen from somewhere, but whatever," she said. "He knew I collected little [figurine] elephants, so he'd find elephants, and he'd bring me ones he found around in different places. I don't think he had a mean bone in his body. In fact, I think that is part of why his dad despaired so much. He didn't protect himself. He was just there. He was out on the streets, and people could take his money, people could take his drugs. He wasn't a hurting kind of person."

Leroy continued to try to help Travis after his release from Atascadero. But Travis had used so many drugs that he developed severe swelling in one of his legs and there was little hope he would ever work again, because of the condition. He was eventually deemed disabled by the state of California, and he started receiving monthly disability checks from the Social Security Administration. Leroy made sure his son had access to the money by getting the checks automatically deposited for Travis in an account at the Bank of Santa Clara in San Jose.

In the early 1990s, Leroy tried to help his son one last time. He sought his son out on the streets of downtown San

Jose, trying to see if he could convince Travis to come home. It ended up being an encounter that crushed any hope Leroy held of rescuing his boy. "[Leroy] told me the last time he saw his son, his son said, 'Dad, I don't want you coming down here anymore,'" Chloe Smith said, quoting Travis. "'I like living on the street. I've got lots of friends. When you come down here, you just bother me, you disturb me. I don't want you coming down here anymore. I want you to leave me alone.'"

Leroy's encounter with his homeless son may have been the last time anyone saw Travis Lee Smith alive.

19

They will steal anything, and call it [a] purchase.

—William Shakespeare, *Henry V*

On July 21, 1985, Brookey Lee West walked into the Nordstrom department store on Rio Vista Avenue in San Jose, and almost immediately store security took notice.

Security employee Ann Vallier watched as West picked up three black blouses and two gold ones from two circular clothes displays. West walked with the clothes into a fitting room, where she remained for a few minutes. When West emerged, she was carrying more clothing—one black blouse, one gold blouse, two plaid skirts, a vest and a pair of pants.

Vallier was at first confused, but she soon became convinced West was engaged in some sort of ruse. West was leaving the fitting room with items she didn't go in with, and two of the blouses she was originally carrying were missing.

Vallier stopped West with a security officer as West left the store, and Vallier suspected they were about to catch West with a blouse stashed underneath her clothing.

"She came back to the security office willfully, and in the security office I asked West if she would like to give back [the] Nordstrom merchandise, and she said yes," Vallier wrote in a statement for San Mateo police.

To Vallier's surprise, however, West didn't just have a blouse.

"In her purse, she had four blouses—two black, one rust colored, and one gold," Vallier wrote. "She also had in her possession one scarf and six necklaces. West [also] pulled two blouses out of her pants that she was wearing."

When asked by police why she took the items, West responded, "They were my size."

West was booked at the Santa Clara County detention center on two counts of felony grand theft. Court records show one charge was dismissed, and West pleaded guilty to a misdemeanor theft charge. She was ordered to pay a fine.

Three months later, West was at it again, and this time she was with her mother, Christine.

The mother and daughter strolled into the Emporium department store in a Palo Alto shopping mall on November 20, 1985. The two women started rummaging through a display of high-priced sweaters, causing store employee Jane Casas to take notice. Casas saw the two take four expensive sweaters into a fitting room, and when they exited, it appeared Christine was wearing one of the sweaters. Casas quickly checked the fitting room, and the three other sweaters she saw the women with were not there.

Casas called Emporium security, but officers were busy at the time responding to another theft incident. When the officers finally did meet with Casas, Smith and West were long gone, and the Emporium figured it had been swindled.

But the very next day, the thieves returned. Casas saw West and Christine walk through the front door of the store, and she called security immediately. She and officers watched from a distance as West grabbed a white-and-tan wool Evan-Picone sports coat off a hanger. Two security officers also saw West pick up two identical pairs of tan pants and a gray shirt from a nearby hanger. They watched West go into a fitting room, then emerge with only one pair of tan pants.

West browsed through the store some more, picked up a white sweater and returned to the fitting room again. She walked out of the fitting room carrying the sweater, and now she had a black purse and a red-handled shopping bag. The purse and the bag, officers believed, were smuggled into the store under West's clothing so she could then use them to carry the stolen items.

West found her mother inside the store, and they exchanged words before separating again. The security officers watched Christine go into a restroom and walk out; West then approached her mother again and handed her a purse. Christine then left the store.

It appeared to the officers the women were trying to carry out an elaborate game of deception in case anyone from the store was watching.

One security officer trailed Smith out of the Emporium to a nearby Macy's store, while another officer trailed West as she walked through the Emporium. Gradually, West made her way out of the store to Macy's, and she met up with her mother in the women's shoe department. Christine and West were on their way out of Macy's when the Emporium security officers stopped them and identified themselves.

"Go ahead, call the police!" West said loudly. "I have a receipt for everything in that bag!"

West was being difficult. She asked to use the restroom, but the security officers told her she would have to wait until police arrived. West started screaming and making a commotion so nearby customers would take notice.

"Do you want me to pee my pants! I have to use the restroom!"

West was allowed to use the restroom, and the two women were then escorted to the Emporium's security office. Inside West's bag, officers found the blazer, a skirt, two hangers and a used pair of pants.

"We then noticed that [Christine] was wearing a pair of pants that looked like the pants I had seen West with," security officer Joshua Cohen wrote in a report for Palo Alto police.

A search of West's purse revealed a pair of heavy-duty scissors with marks on them suggesting they had cut the metal fasteners off sensor tags from the store. Those sensor tags were subsequently found in a fitting room. Also in West's possession were a series of return-exchange receipts from various stores dated over the previous five days, but they had nothing to do with the clothes West and Christine were caught with at the Emporium.

A Palo Alto police officer arrived at the scene and separated the two women. He interviewed both, and each denied any wrongdoing. Christine and West each told identical stories—they were doing Christmas shopping. Yet the officers took notice of the fact that both were unemployed at the time but carried $500 in cash each.

The officer wrote in a report that West had a prior arrest history for theft. Christine's criminal history came up empty, but she was quick to correct any notion that she had no arrest record.

In fact, she started bragging to the officer about having once shot a man.

"She stated she had been arrested for attempted murder a long time ago," the officer wrote in his report.

Both women were transported to the Santa Clara County detention center and booked on charges of burglary and conspiracy. The mother-and-daughter theft team pleaded guilty to felony burglary charges, and each received thirty days in jail followed by two years of probation.

HOWARD

20

Sequoia National Park and Forest is a magical stretch of wilderness located just west of the California-Nevada border. The 866,000-acre park features some of the state's most beautiful natural wonders, including the Kaweah and Tule Rivers, which bubble over rocky terrain and through thick woodlands as they flow south into Central California. There are dozens of rugged trails featuring spectacular, breathtaking views of the park's immense forest and snow-capped Mount Whitney, which, at 14,494 feet, is the tallest mountain in the lower forty-eight states.

But without question, the most amazing feature of Sequoia National Park is its grandiose sequoia trees. The sequoias are the largest living trees on the planet, and they grow only on the western slope of the park's forest. Many of the trees grow up to forty feet in diameter at their base, and one particular giant sequoia in the park, the General Sherman Tree, has an astonishing circumference of 103 feet at its base, making it the largest tree on the planet.

The beauty of the trees, the mountains, the rivers and forest-lined canyons draw visitors from around the world to a place that defines God's grace—a place of peace and serenity.

It is not the type of place you would expect to find a dead body.

On the morning of June 6, 1994, California outdoorsman Jerry Doyle was scouting out a potential fishing hole with his wife, Doris, when he pulled his three-quarter-ton 1975 Chevy pickup into the Lower Coffee Camp recreational area in Sequoia National Forest. It was 9:25 a.m., and it looked like a beautiful morning to try to land a rainbow or brown trout in a nearby fork of the Tule River.

Doyle got out of his truck, and within a few steps, he noticed what appeared to be a corpse stretched out on a sloping bank leading to the river.

"Immediately, upon spotting the body, Jerry turned to his wife and told her to get back in the vehicle, but he did not tell her why," an officer wrote in a Tulare County sheriff's office report. "Doris assumed that Jerry had possibly seen a rattlesnake."

Jerry Doyle rushed to a nearby park attendant, Michael McTighe, and told McTighe of the grisly discovery. McTighe then flagged down a passing California Department of Forestry van loaded with prison inmates, and a supervisor in the van called the authorities.

As they waited for the police to arrive, the Department of Forestry supervisor, Kevin Martin, and an inmate retrieved a blanket from the bus and covered the corpse.

The body was clearly that of a long-haired man, and his pants were halfway down his legs. A plastic bag partially covered the victim's face.

* * *

The investigation of the dead body at the Lower Coffee Camp recreational area was assigned to Detective Daniel Haynes of the Tulare County sheriff's office's violent crimes unit in Visalia, California.

"We were still in the office, drinking our first cup of coffee, when the call came in," Haynes said.

Haynes, forty-five, is a bulldog of a detective. A short, thin-framed man with brown hair and mustache, he is a native of Tulare County who was born in the nearby city of Exeter. His father supported the family with a job as a mechanic; his mom was a housewife.

Haynes said he never figured he would end up spending his entire professional life as a police officer, but as a young man working construction in Tulare County, he stumbled across a career in law enforcement. A friend convinced him he should take a law enforcement class at the community college in Visalia, and within weeks of starting the class, Haynes was hooked. He joined the police reserves in the small city of Wooklake, doing volunteer work to help the local cops while still keeping his forty-hour-a-week construction job to support his wife and two children.

"I never had any intentions whatsoever of being a full-time police officer," Haynes said. "But one night, I came home [the police department] called and they asked me to go talk to the chief. I did, and he offered me a job.

"The job provided benefits when I was raising my children," Haynes said. "That's not something you can usually get working in construction. Hindsight is 20/20, but thank God I did it."

Haynes was quickly promoted to sergeant, and when a coveted spot in the Tulare County sheriff's office opened up, he jumped at the chance. The sheriff's office is based in Visalia, a city of 92,000 that serves as the central hub of Tulare County. The county itself is home to some of the state's most productive farmlands and borders the Sequoia National Forest on three sides.

"It's just a nice, slower pace of life," Haynes said of life there. "It's an agricultural area that is not nearly as populated as other areas of the state."

Haynes was promoted to detective by the county in 1991, and in 1994 he was assigned to the violent crimes unit of the sheriff's office, the unit responsible for investigating all homicides in the county. On June 6, 1994, the dead body at Lower Coffee Camp officially became Haynes's case.

On that morning, Haynes and his fellow detectives in the violent crimes unit—Detective Greg Hilger and Sergeant John Zapalac—headed out to the Sequoia National Forest to begin their investigation. They drove west from Visalia in their Chevrolet Luminas, speeding down state Route 190 for a little more than an hour, passing through the tiny community of Springville before arriving at Lower Coffee Camp.

"Coffee Camp is a day-use recreational area, almost like a rest area," Haynes said. "It's on a two-lane, real winding, narrow road, with water on one side and mountains on the other. There are picnic tables on the edge of the water, there are restrooms, and that's about it."

Haynes is limited on what he can say about specific evidence he observed at the crime scene, but in a sheriff's office police report, Tulare County deputy Joe Teller memorialized his observations of the victim and his surroundings.

I observed the adult male victim to be lying on his back approximately 20 feet below the asphalt parking area. Victim was wearing a light green T-shirt and black jeans. Victim's pants were down almost to his knees, and his belt was still buckled. The pants appeared to be still zipped up and buttoned. Victim's underpants were pulled slightly down, but not as far down as his pants. Victim had no shoes or socks. Victim had a plastic bag covering his face.

To Haynes, it clearly looked like Coffee Camp was not the site of the murder.

"It wasn't a crime scene as much as it was a dump site," Haynes said. "It wasn't like we had extensive evidence lying around. It looked like someone had backed up [a vehicle] to the edge, and the body was pulled from a vehicle."

The detectives interviewed Jerry Doyle, his wife and any park workers familiar with the operations of the campsite. Witness statements were taken, and one witness, Michael Seymour, said he had helped pick up trash from the camp at five p.m. the prior day. He told the Tulare County investigators the body was not at the site at that time.

This information led Haynes and his fellow detectives to suspect the body was dumped by the killer or killers sometime overnight. It seemed plausible the killer or killers may have also been to the area before, because Coffee Camp is a remote place and is sparsely traveled at night.

"It's not a road that you would go up unless you had a reason to be up there," Haynes said. "It's very steep, very crooked. It is a highway, state Route 190, and it does lead into the park, but unless you were specifically going there as a tourist, you wouldn't be going up there."

While Detective Hilger and Sergeant Zapalac helped crime scene analysts process the crime scene, Haynes drove to a nearby trash collection area and started poking through the bags of trash collection at Lower Coffee Camp during the previous twenty-four hours. It was a smelly, stinky job, but it needed to be done in case the killer or killers carelessly discarded evidence in a public trash bin.

"I thought it sucked," Haynes said of the task. "But as they say, no job is perfect."

Haynes found nothing of value in the trash. Upon returning to the location of the body, Haynes, Hilger, Zapalac and crime scene analysts meticulously scrutinized every potential piece of evidence. They collected beer cans, paper debris and various pieces of clothing from the ground surrounding the corpse. It appeared the victim had been shot, but the detectives would rely on an autopsy for a formal cause of death.

"You don't take anything for granted," Haynes said. "I'm big on believing you don't take anything at face value. Wait until you get the big picture."

Of interest to the detectives was the plastic bag, according to police reports. The bag was partially on the victim's face, and detectives hoped the bag might have fingerprints on it. It was collected and processed for prints, but it turned up nothing, according to police documents.

Haynes said detectives had very little to work with at the crime scene. Their victim had no identification on him, and there were no obvious clues to immediately lead them to any suspects.

"We didn't know who he was and how he got there, but obviously the body didn't fall out of a plane," Haynes said. "He had to be hauled there in a vehicle, and that was really about all we had to go on."

But within a few hours, the detectives got a big boost. Zapalac rolled the victim's fingerprints at the crime scene, then returned to the sheriff's office in Visalia to enter the prints into California's computerized fingerprint identification system. Within hours, the victim's prints were matched to a Native American man named Howard Simon St. John.

St. John was from San Jose, which is about a five-hour drive northwest of the Sequoia National Forest and Tulare County. The detectives wondered what St. John was doing so far away from home.

The fact that their victim was a Native American, however, did offer one possible explanation. Just a few miles away from Lower Coffee Camp is the Tule Indian Reservation, and the detectives speculated St. John might have some connection to the reservation.

"We have an Indian male, and a reservation is on the other side of the ridge, so obviously it's something to think about," Haynes said.

Over the course of the next day, Haynes gathered more details about St. John. He was thirty-five years old, five feet ten inches tall and weighed 230 pounds. He had brown eyes and black hair, and an autopsy showed he had been shot in the back with a .38-caliber handgun.

Curiously, St. John also had a .32-caliber bullet in his neck, and the autopsy indicated the .32-caliber bullet was from a shooting prior to the one that killed him.

Haynes learned through background checks that St. John was a former parolee whose arrest record showed apprehensions for approximately fifteen misdemeanor arrests. The crimes included drunken driving, public drunkenness and drugs. St. John had only one felony—a drug charge. The background checks showed St. John had eight different aliases.

Haynes contacted St. John's parole officer, Richard Toledo, in San Jose, and the detective learned St. John was not a native of the Tule Indian Reservation. In fact, St. John was a Sioux Indian who hailed from South Dakota. As far as the parole officer knew, St. John's father, Sylvester, still lived on the reservation in South Dakota.

"We contacted the sheriff in South Dakota where he lived, and they tracked down the father on the reservation, and they got a number for me," Haynes said.

Haynes called Sylvester St. John to find out as much as he could about his victim. Haynes said it was immediately apparent Sylvester St. John had a distant relationship with his son. Sylvester St. John told Haynes that Howard had

struggled with alcohol and had at times lived in a rehabilitation center for alcoholics in San Jose.

Sylvester St. John also told the detective that his son
was married to a woman who lived in Los Banos, and the
couple had an apparent history of domestic violence.

Howard's wife was Brookey Lee West.

21

Tyla Knotchapone attended Alcoholics Anonymous meetings at the Native American Indian Center in downtown San Jose in 1992 because they allowed her to enjoy life again. No more partying in Knotchapone's life—just clean, day-to-day living that allowed Knotchapone to cherish the clarity that comes with being clean and sober.

At the meetings, Knotchapone made several friends. One was a man named Howard Simon St. John, a full-blooded Sioux Indian from South Dakota. Quiet and shy, he was also a man whose noble heritage had been ravaged by substance abuse. St. John had a huge beer belly, at times looked dirty and had rotted teeth. But Knotchapone said she could see behind St. John's weathered exterior, and to her there was a kindhearted, soft-spoken man inside who needed a little sobriety to shine.

"I was close with Howard," Knotchapone said. "I used to laugh with Howard. I used to cry with Howard, and we enjoyed our friendship."

Knotchapone, a Zuni Pueblo from New Mexico, said she bonded with St. John immediately. They enjoyed discussing their heritage and often attended powwows together throughout the Northern California region.

Knotchapone and St. John also had another thing in common—they were both recovering alcoholics, and throughout their relationship St. John sought out Knotchapone for advice and counseling. But St. John was consumed by the bottle, and despite repeated attempts to quit, booze had ruined him by early 1992.

"He was very honest about it," Knotchapone said. "He would say, 'I have no excuse for drinking, for doing this to myself, but yet I find myself doing it.' He was the kind of guy who was very honest about his faults."

St. John was born in Redwood City, California, on May 15, 1958, to Sylvester and Katherine St. John. The second oldest of seven children, Howard was born into one of the most prestigious Native American tribes, the South Dakota Sioux. The Sioux ruled the plains of North America for hundreds of years, and their most famous leaders, Crazy Horse and Sitting Bull, were known for their courage, bravery and fighting skills.

After Howard's birth in California, the St. John family moved back to an Indian reservation in South Dakota, and Howard spent much of his early life growing up on the reservation. It was there, in the 1970s, that tragedy struck the St. John family when one of his brothers, Michael, was killed in a car accident. His cousin Elmer "Sonny" St. John told police Michael was killed when he slipped and fell underneath his friend's car in the driveway of his home following a night of drinking.

"He was drinking with them, I guess, and they took him home to drop him off, and he didn't want to stay there," Sonny St. John said in a taped statement. "So when they went to drive off, he [Michael] was arguing with them, I guess, and he hung on to the car. He slipped under the car."

Michael St. John was crushed by the weight of the vehicle, and his death was devastating for Howard. But the loss of his brother wasn't the only event that left him scarred emotionally.

Friends said he had a disastrous relationship with his own father, Sylvester. When Howard was a young man, he badly beat his father during a domestic dispute. Such violence and disrespect to the family's paternal figure was not tolerated on the reservation, and Howard was ostracized from the family.

"He beat up his dad pretty bad, and he sent him to the hospital," Sonny St. John said. "I guess it was the drinking and stuff like that. He didn't get along with my cousins back there [in South Dakota] and they told me they didn't get along with him, so I didn't have much to do with him, either."

By the 1970s, St. John's family left the reservation and moved back to California. They settled in the tree-lined, lower-middle-class neighborhood of Northwood Park in San Jose. One of their neighbors, Thomas Gutierrez, who is now a forty-two-year-old cement mason and father of three in San Jose, said he became close childhood friends with St. John while growing up in the neighborhood.

"I used to play with my cousins, and Howard lived next door," Gutierrez said. "We all played baseball, football in the street, what have you. Howard loved playing sports and stuff. He was a nice, average kid, and he was a good person."

Gutierrez said the St. Johns were nice people as well, but Howard and his brothers had a reputation for partying in their neighborhood. By the age of sixteen, Howard was drinking regularly.

"He started [partying] young, and it got out of control," Gutierrez said. "I don't think he had a proper upbringing to where he was told, 'Hey, these are the things you do, these are the things you don't.' "

St. John dropped out of Piedmont High School in San Jose during his sophomore year, and when his family decided to move back to South Dakota, Howard stayed behind.

"There was [another] incident with his parents," Gutierrez said. "They threw him out. They didn't want him back, and he sort of got abandoned. He just started living on his own."

With his family now thousands of miles away in South Dakota, St. John lived with neighbors and family friends as a teenager.

"He was sleeping in his car, sleeping at friends' houses and partying," Gutierrez said. "That was his lifestyle from that point on. He would wait for his friends to come out of school, and when they did, he'd say, 'Lets go get some beer now.' "

St. John did, however, have one true passion in life. He was fascinated by cars. He spent countless hours working on vehicles, tweaking them to run as fast as possible, and some of his best times in life were spent running his souped-up cars through the rural countryside of Northern and Central California with another friend, Tony Mercado.

"One time, Howard and I went to a powwow in Sacramento right after high school," Mercado said. "He had an old Dodge, a former police car, and he had this car all pumped up. It usually takes an hour and a half to get from Sacramento to San Jose, and we made it in like forty minutes. We were going like a hundred something miles per hour."

Mercado, an expert mechanic, said he and St. John worked on vehicles in front of Mercado's home on Postwood Avenue in San Jose almost every day. Mercado imparted his wisdom about cars to his friend, and the two gained a reputation in the neighborhood as quality mechanics.

The experience led St. John to dream of a career as a mechanic.

"He was a good mechanic, a good helper and a good handyman when we worked on cars," Mercado said. "He never said no when I would tell him to go get parts. We were partners, and we were making good money at the time."

But slowly, St. John's boozing became more important than work. His alcohol consumption was completely reckless, and St. John was starting to experiment with cocaine as well. By his mid-twenties. St. John drank himself into unconsciousness almost daily, and those who saw him drink were amazed at the amount of alcohol he consumed during his binge drinking.

"He would take a bottle of tequila, and he would down it," Gutierrez said.

"He could hold a lot of liquor," said Gutierrez's wife, Dana. "It was unbelievable."

St. John was living on the streets by his late twenties because of his alcohol abuse. His teeth were rotted, and his beer belly protruded more than a foot over his waistline. He was often unkempt, and friends said he was at the bottom of the human barrel when he turned thirty, in 1988. His drunkenness resulted in multiple arrests for public intoxication, robbery, assault and battery, and drunk driving, and a felony conviction resulted in a sentence of probation. In a report crafted by his probation officer, St. John confided in the officer his grave concerns over his drinking.

"[Howard] believes [his drinking] is a problem," the officer wrote. "[He] consumes three to four bottles of hard liquor per week; five cases of beer per week. Drug usage includes peyote during Indian ceremonies only. Cocaine began in 1983. Occasional use. No marks on arms."

During some of St. John's binges, he would walk the streets of San Jose for hours on end or hang out in city parks to pass the time while the alcohol wore off.

"I think in his early twenties it was more beer and drugs, and by his late twenties and early thirties he started drinking more and more liquor," Thomas Gutierrez said. "Alcohol was his problem. It was eating up his liver, and he'd get in fights, he'd get beat up, or he used to get rolled. He would get rolled a lot on the streets. He would pass right out, and people would take his money. He'd be walking downtown, and he would just pass out against a building or something."

Watching St. John's decline was an extremely sad affair for Gutierrez and his wife, Dana. The couple liked St. John, and they allowed him to visit their home regularly despite his troubles, because they recognized St. John was a decent man suffering from a terrible disease.

"He was never violent," Dana Gutierrez said. "He was actually a very good guy. I would never have someone around my children who I felt fear from. He liked our kids, and if you needed something, he'd do it for you. He helped work on our car, and he'd do whatever you asked him to do. Never, at any given time, would you feel fear from him."

By the mid-1980s, St. John's life was in shambles, and he recognized he needed help to overcome his addiction. He started frequenting the Native American Indian Center on Rhodes Court in San Jose, and he enrolled in an alcohol rehabilitation program at the center called the Four Winds program, which specifically helped Native Americans recover from substance abuse. As part of the program, St. John moved into a house adjacent to the center, at 109 Rhodes Court in San Jose, where he lived with eight other recovering alcoholics. The home was the end of the line for the men—it was either quit drinking and stay at the house, or go back to the bottle and live life on the streets.

"He cleaned himself up, so he was trying," Thomas Gutierrez said. "He was saying, 'Okay, I'm on the right path now.'"

Part of his enrollment in the Four Winds program required St. John to attend the AA meetings, and while attending them, he met Knotchapone. Knotchapone said that during their first meeting, St. John volunteered to fix her car for free.

"I had this little old sports car, and sometimes I needed a tune-up, a tire change or an oil change," Knotchapone said. "Howard always had himself under a hood, and he was a good mechanic. He was always working on my car, and he never, ever asked me to pay him a penny."

Knotchapone and St. John became close friends, and he was always asking her to cook up his favorite food, her deep-fried bread.

"Howard would always tell me, 'Tyla, I want you to make a dozen of that fry bread for us,'" Knotchapone said. "'We are going to have it for dinner. We don't want no white bread slices, and we don't want no regular bread. We want some of that fry bread.' I would never turn him down," Knotchapone said. "I would say, 'Howard, here I come with my one dozen fry bread,' and he would really appreciate that."

To Knotchapone, St. John was a good spirit trying to cure himself of his alcoholism, but in the end, Howard couldn't stop drinking. He was constantly falling off the wagon, and Thomas Gutierrez said he knew of at least seven occasions in which St. John quit drinking for a few weeks, only to go back to the bottle.

"He was a depressed person," Thomas Gutierrez said. "He was a sad person because of his life. He would break down and cry when he got real drunk, and he would talk about his dad, and his family, that they don't love him, and how come."

To those who knew him, St. John was a desperate man. He was desperate for sobriety, he was desperate for hope and he was especially desperate for genuine, unconditional love.

Brookey Lee West met the first of her four husbands through a classified ad in the *San Jose Mercury News*. The advertisement sought a female vocalist for a country-western band, and at twenty-four-years old, West's curiosity was piqued.

"I thought, 'Well, I'll make some extra money or something'—that's the way I was thinking about it," West said. "I wasn't really interested, because it was country music, and I loathe country music."

But West responded to the advertisement anyway, and the decision kicked off a brief, ill-fated romance with a man nearly three decades older than West. The person who placed the ad was country music promoter David Cray,* a fifty-eight-year-old native Oklahoman with a shock of red hair. Cray was infatuated with West, and in Cray's mind, West's sex appeal might make her America's next big country music star.

The two married within a few months of meeting.

"He was real good to me at first," West said. "The one thing I always thought was real good about him was he never tried to hit me, never tried to raise his hand toward me, even though we had some nasty arguments. That's the good thing I can say about him. But he had drinking issues, dope issues, same thing all my husbands had. I guess it was the caretaker syndrome."

West sang lead vocals in Cray's country band, and she sang songs about heartache, broken love and drinking at a handful of redneck bars in Central and Northern California.

"You have to be drunk to sing that trash, it is just so depressing," West said. "My wife left me, etc."

But after a few weeks on the country music circuit, it quickly became apparent to West that country music stardom was little more than a pipe dream. The same could also be said for her marriage to Cray, and West divorced her husband within three months of their wedding.

"I married him, and then I divorced him," West said. "I sang in his band, but my heart wasn't in it, and I guess it wasn't what I really wanted. After about six weeks, I looked at him and I said, 'Who the hell are you? What do I want with you? This is just not working.' I'm the kind of person that when I make up my mind it's done. I'm done."

In retrospect, West said her decision to marry Cray was a rash impulse caused by mental illness. She said she is a bipolar manic-depressive who, without medication, has trouble resisting impulsive decisions like a quickie marriage.

"He seemed like a nice enough guy, but what was really going on was this disorder I have," West said. "When you have this disorder, you do all kinds of strange things. You get married, you get divorced. You buy stuff, and then you go, 'What did I buy that for?'

"I have a disorder in my brain," she said. "People will equate that with you being incapacitated, being stupid or being crazy, but it isn't that at all. It's really a disorder in the brain where the chemicals are not balanced."

After her divorce from Cray West took a job as a security guard at a Palo Alto computer company called National Advanced Systems. West was quickly promoted from security guard to secretary, and while working at the company West met her second husband, Gerald Herbert West.* Gerald West was an administrator at National Advanced Systems, and like Cray he was an older man infatuated with Brookey West.

"He was tall, slender, very Norwegian, with sharp features," West said. "Good-looking, blond haired. I was about twenty-eight, and he was twenty-one years my senior."

Like her marriage to Cray, the courtship with Gerald was extremely quick.

"I was working in a different area of the company, and I took some papers to his office," West said. "That was the first time I ever met him, and when he looked up at me, he was just staring at me, and he goes, 'Would you like to go out for a drink?' "

West accepted the invitation, and the two left work for a bar in downtown San Jose.

"We are having a drink, and he looks at me and goes, 'Will you marry me?' " West recalled. "And I looked at him, and I said, 'Are you serious?' And he goes, 'Yeah, I'm serious. So I said, 'Yeah, sure.'

"It was our first date, and we got engaged," West said.

The two were married in five months, and at first West was happy with her marriage to Gerald, but her mother did not approve of the relationship with such an older man. Gerald, in turn, couldn't stand Christine, whom he viewed as a mean-spirited, wacko bitch. The two fought constantly, and Gerald found himself having to bring Christine along on any social outing with his wife.

"Mom was always hanging around," West said. "She didn't live with us, but she was always there, and we would all go out to functions together. Gerald was, quite frankly, irritated with her, and they did not like each other. My mom did not like to share me, and she was a man-hater to start with. She used to tell me, 'I don't care if he's next door to Jesus. I don't like him.' "

The dispute between Gerald and Christine came to a head during a dinner outing just a few months after the marriage. Brookey, Gerald and Christine were having dinner at a San Jose restaurant when a waitress approached the trio's table and mistakenly addressed the older Gerald West as if he were Christine's husband—not Brookey's.

"I looked at the waitress and I said, 'Well, I'm his wife,'" West recalled.

"And my mother goes, 'Well, that's what you get for marrying some old man,'" West recalled. "Gerald was sitting there, and she says to Gerald, 'And that's what you get for robbing the cradle, for trying to marry some young woman when you are old enough to be her father. You look ridiculous, and the waitress thinks you look ridiculous.' I was red in the face, and Gerald was upset," West said.

Christine wanted to know if Gerald was going to leave her daughter any money in his will.

"She started ragging on him," West said. "'Aren't you going to leave my daughter any money?' Blah, blah, blah."

Within months, the marriage was over. Once again, West's pursuit of an older man ended in divorce, and once again, West said her decision to marry Gerald West was due to her manic-depressive condition.

"I wasn't stable back then," she said.

But unlike Cray, to this day, West speaks with great disdain for her second husband. She said after the marriage was over, she heard rumors Gerald molested her daughter while Susie was visiting during a weekend visit from the Arizona boarding school.

"I found out about the molestation years later," West said. "If I would have found out about that at the time, I think I might have killed him. I think I might have."

The molestation allegations against Gerald West, however, were never reported to police and are unsubstantiated.

"If I would have had a reason to kill somebody, it would have probably been Gerald," West said. "If I wanted to kill him for money, it would have been ideal, because he had $250,000 in life insurance."

West said that before he changed his wills, Gerald's estate was designed to be given to West if he died.

"He signed everything over to me in case of his death, so if I had a reason to kill somebody, it would have been him," she said.

Brookey Lee West's decision to take a job at National Advanced Systems was an extremely beneficial career move over the long run. West was quickly promoted from security guard to secretary, and then to the company's hardware and mainframes division, even though she had never even gone to college to study computers. West's increasing work responsibilities convinced her to pursue a career in the computer industry, and she started studying computers extensively on her own time. She checked out books on computer programming and engineering from the Stanford University library, and she read them tirelessly to prepare herself to work in the Silicon Valley's bustling computer industry.

"Computer engineering, I don't know why, but it was just in my head," West said. "I can read that stuff, I understand all the logic, how to troubleshoot computers, how they work, everything."

West gravitated to the field of technical writing. She enrolled in a series of classes to learn the job, which involves writing complex instructional manuals for purchasers of computer software. By the late 1980s and early 1990s, West was landing technical writing jobs for San Jose's most renowned computer companies, and by all accounts West was a whiz at the job.

"She was very good at her job, and she was very talented," said Natalie Hanke, who was one of West's technical writing supervisors. "One of the best I've ever worked with."

West, Hanke said, understood computers, and she had a knack for using the printed word to explain in simple terms the intricacies of computer software.

"My resume is about eight pages," West said. "I worked for all of the best. I worked for Sun, Intel, and I did a lot of stuff for Cisco. I'm a contractor, and they hired me for short periods of time. Sometimes, the contract would be for a few weeks, and sometimes it would be six months."

The jobs brought in a lot of cash for West—she was making $65 to $100 an hour—and the money offered her a chance at a lifestyle she previously never dreamed of. She bought a Jaguar; she owned expensive clothing; she bought a house on Fir Street in Los Banos, California, which allowed her to make the one-hour commute to San Jose.

But despite all the success, there was still one big problem in West's life:

Her mother.

Christine was living with West, and West was paying all her mother's bills, buying her clothes, groceries and anything else Christine needed. The relationship was often strained, and West spent much of her time trying to make sure her mother didn't do anything crazy. The need to monitor her mother was evidenced by Christine's actions while the two shared a home in downtown San Jose in the early 1990s, just before West bought her home in Los Banos.

At that time, Christine, West said, was obsessed with a neighbor's dog who kept walking through the yard of their rental home. As a result, Christine bought a huge bag of cayenne pepper and spread it all over the neighbor's yard.

"She sprinkled it all over their lawn so this dog would get a snootful of cayenne pepper," West said. "The guy is right next door, working in his driveway, and he's out there wiping his eyes. My mother said, 'I told that son of a bitch last week, keep that dog off my lawn.'"

The pepper didn't solve the problem, and the German shepherd continued to annoy Christine by prancing through the yard and barking late at night. Christine decided she would fix the problem for good with gopher poison stuffed in raw hamburger meat.

"The guy's German shepherd ate it," West said. "The next day, the guy's pissed off because he finds his dog with his teeth through a wooden board. I guess it was from the spasms. So I went to my mother, and I said, 'Did you feed that dog that?' and she said, 'Yeah, I did. I hate that son of a bitch.' " I told her, 'If they ever found out you poisoned that dog, they'll put you in prison for that,' " West said. "She said she hated the guy, and she didn't like other people's dogs."

But while West and her mother were often at odds, they also loved each other. It was a complex mother-daughter relationship, and West said she was always looking out for her mother. There were plenty of times when they enjoyed each other's company, and one of their favorite hobbies involved frequenting Native American jewelry stores in the San Jose area, where they bought art, jewelry and other Native American artifacts for West's Los Banos home.

The mother and daughter became obsessed with Indian culture, and Christine claimed she was half Apache Indian. West claimed the Apache heritage as well, and the two women even started frequenting the Native American Indian Center in San Jose.

22

Tyla Knotchapone will never forget the day Brookey Lee West and her mother, Christine Smith, walked into her Alcoholics Anonymous meeting at the Native American Indian Center in late 1993. Knotchapone could tell the two women were bad news.

"The energy was real strong," Knotchapone said. "We could see it, and we could all feel it."

The bad vibes were particularly strong for West, who wore skintight clothing in a room full of Indian men, and she was strutting around like a hooker trolling for a date.

"She had jet-black hair and red fingernail polish, and her dress was very inappropriate," Knotchapone said. "Her cleavage was exposed, and her makeup was like Elvira's. She had her eyeliner way up, and she wore all black clothes.

"I could tell Brooke wasn't there for herself, her soul or her sobriety," Knotchapone said. "She was there to cause trouble. It was like she was a demon."

Another attendee of the meeting, Henry Murillo, took notice of West, too.

"She was, like, dressed in all black, she had bright red lipstick, bright red fingernails, bright red shoes," Murillo said in a statement to police. "I was, like, trying to avoid her, because I just got an eerie feeling."

"She was just like staring at me, checking me out, like she wanted to be picked up," Murillo said.

Virtually everyone who was present at the meeting wondered what the two white women were doing in a meeting designated for Native Americans. The mother and daughter said they were Apache Indian, but no one was buying it because their skin was white as snow.

"Who let these two in?" Knotchapone said.

"I pretty much knew something was up with this woman," Murillo said of West. "She was kinda just using the place as a pickup joint . . . she was fishing for someone."

After West and Christine made their entry, the twenty or so people in attendance gathered in a circle and, in a ritual dating back nearly seventy years, started to share with one another their troubles with alcohol. Christine was one of the first people to stand up, and she recounted for the group her years of substance abuse in Texas and California.

"The mom shared with us about being in prison, that she did time in the joint," Knotchapone said. "A real Bible-thumper. I told her that our purpose here was to share about alcohol, and we needed to limit it to that."

West sat quietly in the circle of recovering addicts, listening to their confessions. Everyone started to assume West was going to remain silent, but just when the meeting was about to conclude, West stood up and went off on a venomous tirade about her ex-husband.

She said he was a no-good bastard who deserved to be dead.

"She was talking about spitting on this guy's grave," Murillo said. "She went off for quite a while. I thought, jeez, she's kinda flipped out."

When the meeting was over, Knotchapone huddled with some of her Native American friends, and they all agreed West had frightened them. She was mean-spirited, she dressed like a whore, and no one could figure out what she was doing there.

"I went and huddled with some of my sisters, and I asked them, 'Are you experiencing what I'm experiencing?'" Knotchapone said. "One of my sister—her name was Linda—said, 'They are really strange, both of them. Don't talk to them.' They gave me the creeps, and we all agreed there was something wrong with these two."

Murillo discussed the women with his friends as well, and they made the same observations.

"Somebody mentioned she was the black widow," Murillo said.

23

The first month of sobriety is a miserable experience for most addicts. The party is over, the body is adjusting to a chemical-free existence and most find themselves grieving the loss of their best friend—drugs or alcohol.

Wayne Ike was going through such torture while living at the rehabilitation home for alcoholics on Rhodes Court in San Jose in 1993. The Shoshone Indian from Elko, Nevada, was at the Native American Indian Center because of extensive alcohol abuse, but despite his anxiety, he found some comfort in the camaraderie he shared with the eight other Indian men who were in rehab with him.

"It was really a nice house, and we all pretty much got along," Ike said. "All the food was paid for."

Ike was at the house for a little more than a month when something very strange happened. He was cleaning the kitchen of the residence in late 1993 when a fine-looking young woman in tight clothes strutted in. She walked up to Ike, introduced herself as Brookey Lee West, unbuttoned her blouse and showed Ike her breasts.

"She sees me, she walks up, she pops open her blouse,

and I'm looking right down at her titties," Ike recalled. "She said, 'I like a man who cleans house, and I'm horny as hell.' I was asked out for dinner," Ike said. "She was good-looking. She had nice, big green eyes and big red lips. She was well dressed. She had nice clothes and a nice car."

Ike went out on a series of dinner dates with West, and West always paid for their dinner and drinks. Within a few weeks, Ike was fucking West hard during overnight stays at San Jose area hotels, and sometimes they fucked in West's Toyota MR2 two-seater.

"She was wild in bed," Ike said. "We'd even do it while we were driving down the road, in a parking lot, wherever. She was just easy to latch on to," Ike said. "You just got to get to know her . . . and then just grab her, and you have her in your arms and stuff. That was no problem. She was really crazy about me. She was crazy about Indians. She wanted to marry an Indian guy."

But while the sex was good, Ike recognized there was something wrong with West. Something just wasn't right with this person. For example, he couldn't understand why West, an apparently well-off technical writer, was frequenting the rehabilitation home on Rhodes Court and looking for a companion in a home filled with recovering addicts.

"I really don't know what in the heck she was doing there for an intelligent woman," Ike said. "She needed a man or something. [It was a place] where nobody would . . . look, you know. Drunken Indians. She was a smart lady, she was good-looking . . . and I smelled a rat," Ike said.

Ike was bothered by West's comments about children. She said she wanted nothing to do with children, and the remarks turned Ike off. He had two kids and loved them both.

"She didn't like children," Ike said. "She [said she] gave her daughter away."

"She always talked about money, and it would get on your nerves," he said. "She always had money."

The monthlong relationship came to an end when, while sitting in West's car in front of the rehab home, West told Ike no man was ever going to cheat on her and get away with it. West reached into her purse, pulled out a .38-caliber revolver and pointed it at Ike.

" 'If I ever catch you messing around, I'll use this on you,' " he recalled West telling him. " 'If I catch you fucking around, I'll shoot your ass.' "

Having a firearm pointed at him was the final straw. Ike realized West was crazy, and he started hiding from West whenever she showed up at the rehab center. Slowly, West gave up on Ike, and she focused on another resident of the rehabilitation home—Howard Simon St. John.

"It was crazy," Ike said. "My friends were telling me to get away from her. To me, [the relationship] was kind of spooky. She was like a black widow type. She was like a lady who knows how to suck a man dry. She loved being in power."

Brookey Lee West had everything going for her in 1994. She had a lucrative job, a nice house in the rural community of Los Banos, California, and a Jaguar parked in her driveway. She seemed an unlikely match for Howard Simon St. John—a penniless, homeless drunk with rotting teeth.

But after her relationship with Wayne Ike faltered, West set her sights on St. John, and she asked him out to dinner despite their starkly different positions in life.

"When I first met Howard, he looked kind of bad," West said. "He was real overweight, and his hair was sort of long. Yet I could see that if he lost some weight, and if he got his hair cut, he would be really good-looking. He had a gentleman quality about him, and that part of him was unbelievable. I view life this way—people can be down. They can be sick, and they can have a lot of bad things happen, and they can pull themselves back up. That's the way I saw it."

St. John's friends, however, were at a loss to explain West's interest in him. West was an attractive, professional businesswoman, and she was hooking up with an obese, convicted felon in rehab.

"I was shocked," Thomas Gutierrez said. "I was like, what is this good-looking woman doing with Howard?"

Thomas and his wife, Dana, remember meeting West for the first time. She showed up with St. John at Dana's mother's house in 1994, and Thomas noticed St. John was no longer in his street clothes. He was well dressed, his hair was cut and he was groomed.

"When he came to the house, and brought her over for the first time, I said, 'Holy mackerel,' " Thomas Gutierrez said. "She looked like she was well put together, and she had her stuff together. Real responsible, and she was pretty."

Dana Gutierrez found the relationship extremely strange as well.

"The first time I ever saw her, I definitely got a bad feeling," she said. "I thought, this is not right."

Thomas Gutierrez was baffled by West's generosity, so he pulled his friend aside and politely expressed his misgivings about West.

"I had this bad feeling," Thomas Gutierrez said. "I told Howard, 'You know what? I'm glad for you, Howard. I'm glad you are getting straight. This might be what you need to get your feet on the ground.'

"But I said, 'Howard, what is she doing with you?' " he recalled. "Howard started laughing, and I started laughing, and I think he thought I was playing it off. But I said,

'Howard, look at you, and look at her. Is this really love, Howard?' And he goes, 'Yeah.'

"I said, 'Well, the best of luck to both of you, but if there's an insurance policy out there, you better be careful,'" Thomas Gutierrez said. "I was joking, but at the same time I wanted to put the thought in his head."

Tony Mercado was shocked by the relationship as well.

"I just said, 'Something is wrong here,'" he said.

Tyla Knotchapone was concerned, too. She was already wary of West due to her behavior at the AA meetings, and when she learned West was dating St. John, she literally feared for him.

"Howard had a potbelly, he had missing teeth, he had shabby hair, and she dressed him up," Knotchapone said. "I said, 'Howard, why is she doing this for you?'"

St. John told Knotchapone that West loved him and he loved her. He said he was especially captivated by West's sexuality—she was constantly teasing him with sex, and he loved it.

"Some of the statements Howard told me from Brooke were, 'Guess what I have on today? Fancy red lace underwear. It's pretty, like my nails,'" Knotchapone recalled. "That was what Brooke was saying to Howard, and we would tease Howard, saying, 'Geez, those words are hot for you?'

"But he was higher than a kite. He said, 'Oh, she is the woman of my life' and 'This is what I've been waiting for,'" Knotchapone recalled.

"I think the whole relationship revolved around sex," Knotchapone said. "There was no deep feeling from the heart. It was lust, sex and money. The Howard we used to know was never into that."

After about a month of dating, St. John told his friends he was taking West back to South Dakota to be married on the reservation. But when St. John called his father,

Sylvester told him not to bother—Howard was not welcome on the reservation. St. John and West then took a weekend trip to Reno and got married there. When they returned, the two told St. John's friends at the Native American Indian Center about the marriage, and West started showing off a huge diamond ring that she said St. John had paid $20,000 for.

Knotchapone laughed out loud at the idea of St. John's buying the ring. He, after all, was enrolled in the Four Winds program, and no one staying at the home on Rhodes Court could afford to pay their own rent, much less purchase a $20,000 wedding ring.

"The Four Winds program, that was the last stop," Knotchapone said. "The house they lived in, that was the last house on the block, as they say. Every Indian man you saw in there, they didn't have any kind of resources. Howard didn't have that kind of money.

"We used to tease Howard, and we'd tell him the ring was out of a bubble gum machine or a Cracker Jack box," Knotchapone said.

Knotchapone sensed a storm was brewing in Howard's life, and she repeatedly warned St. John that his new wife was no good for him. But there was no talking to St. John.

He was in love.

"We all told Howard, 'She scares us,'" Knotchapone said. "I was worried about Howard, and I told him, 'You are playing with fire, Howard. You are in the danger zone.'"

24

Mike Stoykovich and his wife, Crystal, are a couple of country bumpkins at heart. They each grew up in extremely rural areas—for Mike, it was Michigan's picturesque Upper Peninsula, and for Crystal, life began in the heart of Iowa. Their childhoods were spent in quiet, sleepy farming communities where everyone knew everyone, and their early years instilled in each a profound love of life in rural America.

But as is often the case, life rarely lets one pick and choose one's fate, and for the Stoykoviches, their time in the country was short-lived. The two married young, and a military career for Mike led him to Southern California. There, the couple had six children, and the economic demands of supporting such a large family mandated that the couple spend most of their time in the greater Los Angeles area, where Mike worked at the post office to pay the bills.

Yet Mike eighty-two, and Crystal, eighty, never gave up on their dream of returning to their rural roots, and in 1993 the Stoykoviches moved to the tiny farming community of Los Banos, California, on the western side of the San

Joaquin Valley. The Stoykoviches were charmed by the municipality of what was then 15,000 people.

"It is such a friendly town," Crystal Stoykovich said. "Everyone is nice, and no matter who you see, they wave to you. We felt like everyone was waiting for us with open arms."

The Stoykoviches were impressed by the natural beauty surrounding the city. There are flowing green farmlands, the Diablo mountain range and its ominous Pacheco Pass, which is a foggy, rocky escarpment travelers are forced to scale while driving to Los Banos on state Highway 152 from San Jose.

Los Banos is also adjacent to the pristine San Luis Reservoir. The series of lakes serves as a significant water source for the massive citrus, nut and cotton farms surrounding Los Banos.

The Stoykoviches scouted out new housing developments in Los Banos, and they settled on a planned community of one- and two-story houses on the outskirts of town called the Gardens. The Stoykoviches plunked down $125,000 for a new single-story home, and their residence was the first to be built on Fir Street.

"There was grass farmland in the back of our house, and we had jackrabbits running through our backyard," Crystal said. "It was beautiful."

But the Stoykoviches' return to the country came with one drawback. The neighbors from hell were about to move in across the street.

Brookey Lee West purchased a home on Fir Street in 1993, and at first the Stoykoviches were glad to have new neighbors. West moved in with her mother, Christine, and initially the two seemed like a normal, everyday mother and daughter. West was the first to introduce herself to the couple, explaining she was a technical writer in San Jose. West said she bought her house with a GI loan from her prior military service, and she told the Stoykoviches some fat lies about her nine-month military career.

"She told us she was a sergeant," Mike said.

"She told us she flew planes," Crystal recalled.

The Stoykoviches met Christine days later. She was thin and frail, and she always wore gray sweatpants and a gray sweatshirt. She had her hair wound in a long, dark braid stretching to the middle of her back, and the Stoykoviches—eager to make friends in their new neighborhood—invited Christine into their home.

"A very strange woman," Mike said. "She said, 'I'm Cherokee Indian, and I take no gump from nobody. I'll kill somebody if I have to, and we Cherokees don't stop at anything when we want revenge.' I didn't think she was Indian, but she claimed it."

Christine proceeded to tell the Stoykoviches a series of strange stories as she sat in their living room. She said she was born in Texas, and as a child growing up in rural Ennis, she spent time riding the rail lines with bums and hoboes.

"She said she used to ride the trains as a hobo, and she learned how to take care of herself in the boxcars," Mike Stoykovich said. "She said she was twelve, and when the bums got fresh with her, she would pull a knife out on them."

Christine said her nine-year-old granddaughter, Susie Alcantar, was kidnapped from a department store when she was five, and that West had hired a private investigator to find the child. Christine never discussed the real story behind West's separation from her daughter—that West gave the child away to her teachers at her Arizona boarding school.

"She had tears in her eyes when she was telling us this," Crystal said. "Christine still had a pair of the child's baby shoes, and she said, 'These were my granddaughter's shoes, and I miss her an awful lot.'"

The most shocking story Christine told the Stoykoviches, however, detailed her proudest moment in life. In her slow Texas drawl, she offered a grandiose, blow-by-blow account of blasting a hole in her lover with a shotgun in Bakersfield.

"She said, 'If I couldn't have him, neither could his wife,' so bang, she shot him," Crystal said. "You got the idea you'd better not cross Christine."

The Stoykoviches concluded Christine was certainly bizarre, and perhaps mentally ill, but she was also colorful and interesting. Christine was soon showing up every day at the Stoykoviches' front door, usually while the Stoykoviches were eating lunch or dinner. The Stoykoviches regularly invited Christine to eat with them out of pity. She was a very simple woman, and it seemed she was extremely lonely while her daughter was working in San Jose.

"She would make a point of showing up when we were eating, and I kind of felt sorry for her, really," Crystal Stoykovich said. "She was alone while her daughter was working, and I think she was really lonely."

"I don't think she was getting much to eat over there," Mike Stoykovich said. "She was very frail, and we didn't think she was eating at all."

Shortly before Christmas 1993, Christine invited Crystal over to her house to see a Christmas tree she had decorated. Crystal walked in West's home and noticed there was barely any furniture in the house, yet there were racks and racks of expensive clothing in West's bedroom, and the clothes still had the price tags on them. The amount of new clothing struck her as unusual.

"I started to wonder what kind of life they were leading," she said.

Christine brought Crystal a series of strange gifts in the coming weeks. One gift was an obnoxious, oversized scarf adorned with blue butterflies, and another was a pair of earrings carved out of a potato.

"She'd done it with a big potato," Crystal said. "She sliced it, carved the earrings, dried them and then she painted them. I said, 'Oh, how do you do that?' and she said, 'I'm not going to tell you the secret.' It was a nice thing to do, but people would look at you twice if they saw you wearing these potato earrings."

There came a time, however, when the Stoykoviches saw another side of Christine. The incident unfolded when Mike voiced an interest in buying a small Ford Tempo car owned by West. West and her mother offered the car for $6,500, but when Mike checked with the lender of the car, he found West owed only about $3,500 on the vehicle, and the car's book value was much less than the price West was asking.

"I said, 'Oh, boy, they're trying to double their money,' " Mike Stoykovich recalled.

He kindly told West he no longer wanted to buy the car, and Christine was enraged.

"The old lady was mad at us," Mike said. "She was furious."

Around the same time the car deal fell through, Christine delivered a pot of what she called "northern bean soup" to her neighbors. Mike Stoykovich took one taste of the soup and was aghast. The dish tasted like a bucket of salt.

"I tasted it, and it was all salt," Mike Stoykovich said. "I dumped it out in the garden."

Over time, the Stoykoviches recognized Christine was not normal, and they decided it was best to keep their distance.

"We were like, golly, who do we have living across the street?" Crystal said.

Sandy Corona has faced her fair share of obstacles in life. The pretty, sweet-natured Ohio native, now fifty-seven, was born with congenital progressive deafness, a disability that wasn't diagnosed until she was nine. But Corona's parents made it clear to their daughter that her disability was not going to hold her back in life, and as a child she faked several school-administered hearing tests to stay in a traditional school.

"My mom didn't want me to be abnormal, which she thought most deaf kids were because they were separated from so-called normal kids, so she instilled in me that I was a normal kid who couldn't hear well." It was the best thing she ever did for me, Corona said.

"I taught myself to lip-read well enough that I was actually the first handicapped student to integrate into the schools in Ohio," Corona said. "I remained in regular school, graduated with honors, and I was awarded several scholarships to Wright State University."

Corona completed three years of college before dropping out of Wright State to support her family. She eventually married her first husband, Dan, and Corona bore two lovely children. The relationship failed years later, and the marriage was dissolved.

Corona met her second husband, Al Corona, in Dayton, Ohio, in 1987. Al Corona was the love of Sandy's life, and the couple married, then moved to Gilroy, California, where Al Corona worked as a computer analyst. Life seemed to be going well for the Coronas, until tragedy shattered their world, in 1992, when Sandy's son, Gregory Douglas Turner, was brutally murdered in Ohio. Turner was shot and bludgeoned by a man jealous over a girl Turner was dating, and the loss of her only son devastated Sandy Corona. The killer was caught and sentenced to twenty years to life in prison, but the punishment was of little solace—life would never be the same again.

A year later, in June 1993, Sandy Corona felt it was time to move from Gilroy. The house she lived in reminded her of a visit her son made to California shortly before his death, and overwhelmed by grief, she felt it was time for a new environment.

"Prior to my son's death, he had visited us and stayed overnight at our house in Gilroy," Sandy Corona said. "The house had a lot of memories, I was distraught, and I didn't want to live there anymore."

The Coronas started looking for affordable new housing developments in rural California, and they found one in the Gardens community in Los Banos. The community offered quiet, peaceful country living in a neighborhood lined with farms and two-lane roads, and the Coronas were quickly sold on life in Los Banos. They purchased a two-story home on Fir Street, and they moved in the latter half of 1993, around the same time Brookey Lee West and her mother moved in to their home down the street.

Sandy Corona sensed Christine had experienced a lot of trials in her life.

"She was a thin, slightly built woman, and she had a lot of wrinkles," Sandy Corona said. "She looked like she had been through a lot. She was an older, weathered woman, and she told me she was part Indian."

Sandy Corona did share some similar interests with Christine. They both enjoyed crafts and making dolls, and Christine started to visit the Corona residence regularly.

"Chris said she didn't have a lot of friends, and she asked if she could come calling," Sandy Corona recalled. "My mother passed away when I was thirty-five, so I thought it would be nice to be friends with an older woman."

In turn, Christine invited Sandy over to her house, and during her single visit to West's residence, she noticed the racks of expensive clothing that Crystal Stoykovich had also observed.

"They had all this clothing, and I was shocked," Sandy said. "The clothing still had the plastic bags and the price tags on them, and there were boxes and boxes of shoes and hats. All sorts of brand-new things, like from Saks Fifth Avenue, Neiman Marcus—you know, all these really ritzy, expensive stores. All brand-new clothing."

After Christine visited the Corona residence on a few occasions, Sandy and Al Corona realized she was, well, strange. She told Sandy she could make a special potion to improve an individual's love life. On another occasion, Christine walked in the Corona home through a back door without ever knocking or letting her presence be known. When Sandy walked into her living room, she was startled to find Christine in her house, and the incident made Sandy Corona uneasy.

On yet another occasion, Sandy caught Christine secretly putting a note on the Coronas' front door.

"She'd written a note saying, 'Deaf woman lives here. Please call this number in order to get in the house,' and she'd written down her own phone number," Sandy said. "I told her I appreciated her concern, but such a note would endanger me rather than help. I told her I had taken care of myself for years, and I was capable of continuing to do so."

By late 1993, Christine was scaring Sandy Corona.

"Chris told me she had been on death row for a while," Sandy said. "I said, 'What in the world?' She said she married a police officer, had an affair with a married man and had gotten someone to kill her lover."

Strangely, Christine said the shooting unfolded in Texas—not Bakersfield—and she was spared from the execution chamber when the victim "came back to life," Al Corona said in a statement to police.

"Somehow he came back to life when he was in the morgue," Al Corona said. "It was real crazy talk . . . I just figured, you know, she is crazy. Nobody kills somebody, and all of a sudden the guy comes back to life in the morgue."

The Coronas questioned Christine how she could have ended up on death row for shooting a man who didn't die.

"That's Texas for you," Christine responded.

Christine seemed proud of her violent history, and her stories upset Sandy greatly. Her son had just been murdered two years earlier, and Sandy was keenly aware of the pain and misery caused by violent crime. She told Christine she was not impressed with her stories of violence and killing.

"I told her we were still going through some things [emotionally], and I was sorry, but I had serious problems about continuing a relationship with her if she'd been convicted of murder," Sandy said. "She said she believed in victims' rights, but she was being honest."

Christine, however, wasn't finished with her disturbing stories. She said her granddaughter was kidnapped from a department store when she was five, and that West had hired a private detective to find the girl.

"I was struck by the fact that this woman, who said she committed murder, had a missing grandchild," Sandy said. "She was frightening me, so I and my husband did not want her in the house anymore."

Sandy and Al Corona concluded Christine was someone they didn't want to associate with, and they started avoiding her like the plague.

The Stoykoviches and the Coronas weren't the only residents on Fir Street to realize they were living next to a couple of weirdoes. Laura Parra lived across the street from West and Christine, and she, too, was startled by her neighbors' strange habits.

"They were both weird," Laura Parra said. "Very odd."

Parra, forty-four, is an attractive, blond-haired mother of two children who moved to Los Banos in 1993 with her now ex-husband Fermin Parra. Laura is a vibrant, optimistic woman, and her glowing spirit gives no indication of her daily struggles with the potentially deadly disease of multiple sclerosis. She was diagnosed with MS as a young woman, and the disease has caused her an untold amount of pain and emotional difficulty. When her children were young, one of her hands frequently clenched up so tightly she had to change diapers with her teeth.

But with medication, her faith in God and a good attitude, she has persisted through the misery, and she now takes special pride in being an MS survivor.

"I have four friends, and their cause of death was MS," Laura said. "In my opinion, they gave in to the disease. They stopped fighting, and I believe God makes you stronger."

Laura Parra and her then-husband came to Los Banos from Gilroy, a city on the outskirts of San Jose, because the cost of living was much cheaper.

"We were paying $1,250 a month in rent in Gilroy, and this was ten years ago," Laura said. "Today, I'm paying about the same, I own my own home and I live in a very small, quiet town. I love it here."

Laura vividly remembers meeting West for the first time. West walked across Fir Street to introduce herself, and Parra sensed West was not quite normal.

"She was just a very different person," Laura said. "I thought she was a little creepy from the first moment I met her. She looked like she was on drugs or something. Odd."

Despite her first impression, though, Laura visited with West, and she, too, saw all the new clothing in West's home.

"I thought she might be a madam for a bunch of prostitutes," Laura said.

In her visits with West, Parra also recognized that West

and her mother were at odds with each other. On one occasion, Laura saw West screaming at her mother as they walked home from a grocery store.

"I was in front of my house one day, and Brooke and Christine were walking down the street," Laura recalled. "Brooke was just screaming at her. She was yelling at Christine in a way you'd never talk to your mother."

Days later, Laura was watering flowers in front of her home when she saw West yelling at her mother again.

"She called her a crazy bitch to her face," Laura said. "I was like, 'Oh, jeez, finish watering and get back in the house.'"

And on yet another occasion, West personally told Parra she disliked her mother.

"Brooke said her mom was a lunatic, she was driving her crazy and she didn't want her mom around," Laura said. "She was driving her crazy. She talked about what a pain in the ass her mother was, and her exact words were, 'She's a crazy bitch, and I can't wait to get her out.'"

25

On March 3, 1994, at 11:20 p.m., an anonymous caller dialed 911 in Milpitas, California, to report a car burning in an industrial area of the city's border with San Jose. A patrol officer with the Milpitas police department responded to the scene and found a 1989 Jaguar sedan smoldering on a dirt road just off Lundy Lane.

The car was a complete loss.

About fifty minutes later, the vehicle's owner, Brookey Lee West, called police in San Jose and reported the vehicle missing. West told the cops that on the night of March 3, she and her boyfriend—she did not identify him by name—went to dinner and a movie at a shopping complex at 3161 Olsen Drive in San Jose. After the Steven Seagal action flick was over, West and her boyfriend emerged from the theater near the city's historic Winchester Mystery House and discovered the Jaguar was gone. The vehicle, West said, had a common antitheft security device known as The Club on its steering wheel at the time it disappeared.

The white Jaguar, according to police records, was purchased by West just a month before it was stolen and torched. West bought the vehicle at a Buick dealership in Santa Clara in February 1994, by trading in a Toyota MR2 and putting down a $1,500 deposit. The deal required West pay a rather steep monthly payment of $554.

West's insurance company, AAA car insurance in California, cut a check of $18,897 to GMAC financing in Sunnyvale after the car was torched, and it must have seemed to West her financial liability for the car loan was over.

But unbeknown to West, the insurance company was suspicious. AAA directed the California Automobile Association to investigate, and the association, in turn, hired an investigative company called Lee S. Cole and Associates to conduct an inquiry. Cole and Associates investigator Dwight Bell, a retired thirty-year veteran of the California Highway Patrol, was assigned the case.

"We got this particular case . . . primarily because it was a Jaguar and because it was a vehicle fire, which is our area of expertise," Bell said in a statement to authorities.

Bell also found several aspects of the theft suspicious.

"In short, the 1989 Jaguar sedan was found on fire by the Milipitas police department before it was reported stolen," Bell wrote in a letter to the Automobile Association. "It was noted that the radio/stereo unit or speakers had not been removed from the Jaguar, and all wheels and tires were in place. . . . I thought it [also] interesting that the initial information came from an anonymous caller. I eliminated any mechanical, electrical or fuel source as the cause of the fire. In other words, there was no engine fire. There was no electrical fire, there wasn't a transmission fire, a battery fire, anything of that nature. The fire did not, in fact, start in the engine compartment. The fire pattern and the damage was definitely indicative of a fire starting in the passenger compartment. . . . I did not find a residue of flammable fluid, primarily because the fire had been set in the open, in the weather, so long before I got to it. [But] the metal distortion to the top of the doors definitely would indicate that the fire was from some type of flammable application."

Knowing the fire was not an accident, Bell then set out to contact the owner of the vehicle, but it took him multiple tries to get in touch with West, whose mailing address turned out to be a post office box in Santa Clara. Bell also called West's work phone number at the Syntex Pharmaceuticals building on Page Mill Road in Palo Alto, and he couldn't get in touch with her.

"My initial calls to the work number connected with an answering machine that disconnected before I could leave a message," Bell said.

Bell finally did get in touch with West, but he was calling from a pay phone, and a construction company happened to be running a jackhammer nearby. He said he would call West back, but he was never was able to get in touch with West again.

On May 9, 1994, Bell completed the first of two reports he prepared to summarize his investigation on the theft, and at the time he had few leads to work with.

But the investigation into West's burned-out car was about to heat up. Nearly three weeks later; on May 27, 1994, AAA insurance received a phone call from a man who claimed to be the arsonist, and his name was Howard Simon St. John.

26

Howard Simon St. John moved in to Brookey Lee West's Los Banos home in early 1994, and to his new neighbors it seemed as if the Tasmanian devil himself had just spun down Fir Street and invaded their peaceful community. St. John was drinking again, and the results were predictable—he was noisy and rude, and he was observed stumbling through the neighborhood drunk out of his mind on multiple occasions.

"He was basically a drunken Indian," Laura Parra said.

West introduced her new hubby to Parra shortly after St. John moved in, and Parra was astonished by West's choice for a husband.

"I thought, 'Wow, what a weird couple,'" Parra said. "He was a big guy who looked like an old-time biker. Sometimes he didn't wear a shirt, and he wore scraggily clothes. She had just met this guy, and then they got married, and I was like, 'What is she doing with this guy?'"

Sandy Corona said St. John had little regard for the sanctity of the neighborhood. "He yelled a lot, he always seemed to be slamming the front door, and he always

Brookey Lee West poses for a snapshot during interviews with the author at the Southern Nevada Women's Correctional Center in North Las Vegas. West is serving life in prison without the possibility of parole for the murder of her mother. *Photo by Ralph Fountain. Legal rights to photo owned by the author.*

Brookey Lee West talks with the author about the murder of her mother, Christine Smith. West claims her mother died a natural death, and was not murdered—a claim authorities say is implausible given the evidence in the case. *Photo by Ralph Fountain. Legal rights to photo owned by the author.*

LEFT: Brookey Lee West's husband, Howard Simon St. John, is pictured in this vacation snapshot. Weeks after marrying West, St. John was found shot to death and his corpse was dumped in rural Tulare County, California. *Photo courtesy of Wayne Ike.*

RIGHT: Daniel Haynes, formerly a homicide detective with the Tulare County Sheriff's Office, stands at the crime scene where Howard Simon St. John's body was found in the Sequoia National Forest. St. John, the husband of Brookey Lee West, was found murdered in Tulare County just weeks after surviving a domestic dispute with West in which he was shot in the neck. *Photo by the author.*

Brookey Lee West's brother, Travis Smith, is pictured in this Wanted poster issued by Las Vegas police. To this day, neither Travis nor his body has been located. *Photo courtesy of the Las Vegas Police Department.*

WANTED

MISSING PERSON

TRAVIS LEE SMITH

TRAVIS LEE SMITH
C.I.I. – A05560685
SEX: M HAIR:BRN EYES:GRN
HT:6-02 WT:200 DOB:08-29-56

THE ABOVE PHOTO IS TEN (10) YEARS OLD. SUBJECT WAS
ADJUDICATED CRIMINALLY INSANE. HE HAS SPENT TIME IN
THE ATASCADERO FACILITY IN CALIFORNIA.

SUBJECT IS ONLY A WITNESS OR MISSING PERSON

If contact is made, immediately contact the Clark County District Attorney's
Office, Las Vegas, Nevada - Investigator Joel Moskowitz at 702-455-5886
or Deputy District Attorney Frank Coumou at 702-455-4296.

Christine Smith is pictured as a young woman in Texas. *Photo courtesy of Billy Sands.*

Christine Smith was sixty-four when this photo was taken for a bus pass in Las Vegas. She was later found sealed in a garbage can in her daughter's storage shed. *Photo courtesy of the Clark County District Attorney's Office.*

The trash can containing Christine Smith's corpse is pictured at the Canyon Gate Mini-Storage shed, where Brookey Lee West stashed her mother's body in 1998. *Photo taken by Las Vegas police; courtesy of the Clark County District Attorney's Office.*

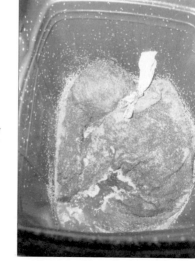

Christine Smith is pictured in death at the bottom of a trash can. On her body are insects that forensic scientists later used to show that Smith's murder was likely premeditated. *Photo courtesy of the Clark County District Attorney's Office.*

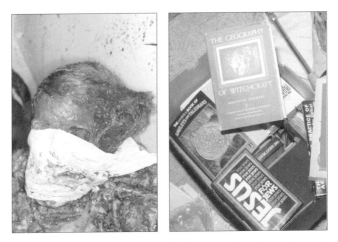

LEFT: Christine Smith's decomposed body had a plastic bag tied tightly over her face. Authorities believe the bag was likely a device used to hasten Smith's death after she was sealed in a garbage can. *Photo courtesy of the Clark County District Attorney's Office.*

RIGHT: Books found next to Christine Smith's remains in a storage shed are displayed in a Las Vegas police crime scene photo. The books include *The Satanic Bible* and *The Geography of Witchcraft*. *Photo courtesy of the Clark County District Attorney's Office.*

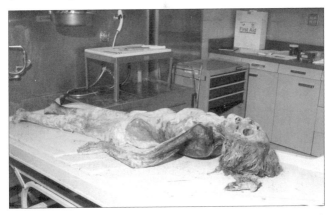

Christine Smith's decomposed body is displayed on a gurney at the Clark County coroner's office after the bag covering her face was removed. *Photo courtesy of the Clark County District Attorney's Office.*

Brookey Lee West's father, Leroy Smith, is pictured in this driver's license photo. *Photo obtained via an open records request.*

A skull that Brookey Lee West's father, Leroy Smith, likely wore around his neck during Satanic ceremonies is pictured along with its carrying pouch. *Photo by the author.*

Las Vegas homicide detective Dave Mesinar was the lead detective in the case against Brookey Lee West. Much of the evidence he gathered earned West a life sentence in prison. *Photo by the author.*

Clark County prosecutor Frank Coumou is pictured in his office. Coumou, along with prosecutor Scott Mitchell, secured Brookey Lee West's murder conviction. *Photo by the author.*

Clark County Deputy Public Defender Scott Coffee, who was Brookey Lee West's lead defense attorney. *Photo by the author.*

LEFT: Brookey Lee West is pictured in this grade school photo. *Photo courtesy of Billy Sands.*

RIGHT: Brookey Lee West is pictured in a Los Banos, California, mug shot. The photo was taken shortly after West shot her husband, Howard Simon St. John, in the neck. He survived the shooting, only to be found murdered weeks later. *Photo courtesy of the Los Banos Police Department.*

Brookey Lee West, a talented artist, stands next to a sketch she drew of Mona Lisa while incarcerated at the Southern Nevada Women's Correctional Center in North Las Vegas. *Photo by Ralph Fountain.*

looked a little disheveled," Corona said. "He was always acting like he was high, and it looked like he was drinking a lot. A lot of the neighbors on both sides of Brooke's house heard a lot of bottles breaking, and they heard cursing inside Brooke's house."

Mike Stoykovich met St. John in early 1994. At the time, St. John was working on a sleek white Corvette that Stoykovich had never seen parked in West's driveway before. Stoykovich, interested in making friends with his new neighbor, walked across the street and introduced himself.

"I walked over and I said, 'I'm Mike Stoykovich,' and he said, 'I'm Howard,'" Stoykovich recalled. "He didn't give me his last name. He said he had bought the car at a swap meet for $5,000, and I said, 'You know, that's a pretty good price.'"

About a week later, Stoykovich saw St. John in front of West's home again and yelled out a friendly hello. This time, St. John acted as if Stoykovich wasn't even there.

"He turned his back on me," Stoykovich said. "I told my wife, 'Howard's living with a wealthy woman, and he must be too good for us. If that's his way of living, we just won't bother with him. . . . I guess he thinks he's too good for the peons around here.'"

Days later, Stoykovich realized he hadn't seen West's new Jaguar in her driveway in weeks, so the next time he saw Christine, he asked about her daughter's car.

"I said, 'Where's the Jaguar?' and she says, 'Someone stole it, stripped it, and all they found was the burned shell,'" Stoykovich recalled.

Crystal Stoykovich said word soon surfaced that Christine and her new son-in-law were not getting along, and Christine's visits to the Stoykoviches' home were getting less and less frequent. And then, without any notice, Christine moved out of her daughter's house without telling anyone.

"The next thing we knew, she had moved back to Santa Clara," Crystal Stoykovich said. "She [Christine] really didn't say too much before then. All we heard from her was that she didn't think [the relationship between St. John and West] was going to work."

"Christine couldn't stand Howard," Parra said. "Brooke said the two fought like cats and dogs, and it was either her or him. She said one of them had to go."

West's stepmother Chloe Smith, said that when Christine moved out, West bought her mother a van and loaded up her belongings in it. West parked the van in the parking lot of a city park in Santa Clara, and left Christine there.

"She took the van, and she left it in a parking lot over in Palo Alto," Chloe Smith said. "She took her mother over there, dropped her off, and she said, 'This is yours, this is where you are living. Don't come see me anymore.' She just dropped her off and left her there. It was very strange."

Chloe questioned her husband, Leroy, about Christine's living in a van, and Leroy said West's decision to leave her mother in a van in a city park was consistent with the strained mother-daughter relationship.

"Leroy had always told me she hated her mother," Chloe said.

Christine's migration into homelessness coincided with a couple of other unusual events on Fir Street. Sandy Corona said a few homes on Fir Street were burglarized after St. John's arrival, and some started to wonder if West or St. John had anything to do with the break-ins.

"Whenever the houses were broken into, it was when the people were away, and it was as if somebody knew their habits," Corona said. "No one ever saw Howard go to work, and everyone seemed to think Brooke and him might have had something to do with it."

The break-ins prompted Corona to start a neighborhood watch program. She held a series of neighborhood watch meetings at her house, and the only residents of Fir Street who weren't invited were West and St. John. On May 21, 1994, Corona sponsored a particularly successful watch meeting attended by dozens of neighbors, and everyone present expressed optimism that the program would eventually deter the burglaries.

The next morning, Corona opened her front door and found a huge pile of ice on her front porch.

"It looked like someone had dumped a cooler of ice on the front porch," Corona said.

Corona looked down the street and saw St. John standing in front of West's residence. He was holding a drink in his hand, and he raised it toward Corona.

"He smiled, and I got the distinct impression he had done it," Corona said. "I didn't know what to make of it. The man just terrified me."

Her husband, Al, told his wife not to worry about the pile of ice on the front porch; but a neighbor later suggested the ice might be a warning to Sandy to mind her own business.

"This neighbor said, 'Don't you watch gangster movies?'" Sandy said. "When you ice someone, what you do is you murder them. This may be a warning. I was like, 'Oh, my God, we are having all these meetings at my house, and what are these people going to do next?'"

By far, though, the most concerning aspect of St. John's move to Fir Street was the increased police presence in the neighborhood. Beyond the watch program, residents noticed officers with the Los Banos police department regularly driving up and down their street, and Parra said the police were called to West's home multiple times during the early-morning hours of 1994.

"There were more than a few incidents," Laura Parra said. "The police started showing up, and I would say it was at least four times. Honestly, the first time I thought it was stolen goods, because I knew Brooke had all these new clothes coming into her house. Then I thought, well, maybe it's drugs. She's all weird and stuff, so I thought she was dealing drugs. Plus, her husband was always either loaded or drunk, so I decided I wanted to stay away from all of them."

27

Thomas Gutierrez and his wife, Dana, don't believe their friend, Howard Simon St. John, was the menace his neighbors on Fir Street perceived him to be. More likely, St. John was drinking heavily, which made him ornery and depressed, and he probably ended up rubbing people the wrong way in a mostly white, middle-class neighborhood where he was out of his element.

"Howard would make you feel comfortable no matter where it was," Thomas Gutierrez said. "He got along with everybody."

In the spring of 1994, Thomas and Dana Gutierrez visited St. John to see how he was doing. The couple made the hourlong drive from San Jose across Pacheco Pass to Los Banos, and when they arrived, they found St. John living in the nicest place of his life. West's residence was an extremely clean single-story house with large picture windows, and St. John's new existence seemed to be a world away from his prior life of homelessness and destitution on the streets of San Jose.

But once again, within a few minutes of watching St.

John and West interact, Thomas and Dana Gutierrez got an eerie feeling about the relationship.

"Usually my gut instinct is very good, and I was very uncomfortable around her," Dana Gutierrez said. "When we went to their house, I was like, 'We're here, okay, let's go.' You know how you feel when you meet someone, and you don't even want to socialize with them? I didn't want to socialize with her at all."

Thomas Gutierrez felt the same way.

"I was trying to get in and out, because I didn't feel comfortable, either," Thomas Gutierrez said. "I wasn't comfortable because I felt like she was going to hurt my friend. I didn't necessarily think she was going to kill him or anything, but I felt she was playing with his heart and toying with his feelings. I would look at her, and I would look at him, and I was thinking there is no way they could love each other. If she really loved Howard, I would have sensed it."

The visit to West's house lasted less than an hour, and shortly before the couple left, St. John said something that startled the couple.

"He told me she was into witchcraft and stuff, and I didn't believe him," Thomas Gutierrez said. "I said, *'Yeeaah, right.'*"

But then St. John walked Thomas Gutierrez through the house and showed him a series of bizarre objects that he said West used to practice witchcraft. Strange trinkets. Handmade dolls. A shrunken head. A voodoo doll.

"I saw all these objects, witchcraft objects, voodoo dolls, and he was telling me what they were," Thomas Gutierrez said. "Then he said, 'She can put a spell on you.' Brooke was in the kitchen, she heard us talking, and she looked over and said, "Yeah, I can. I can put a spell on you.' I said, 'That's okay. I'm already married.'"

Everyone laughed at the crack, and Thomas Gutierrez

felt the conversation was lighthearted in nature. But at the same time, the topic matter was a little unnerving.

"I don't know the difference between good or bad with that stuff," he said. "I just know it was there. Handmade dolls and shrunken heads. Little ones."

"By and large, she was joking," Dana Gutierrez said. "It wasn't a threat or anything . . . but it was weird."

A few weeks after the visit to Los Banos, St. John showed up at Thomas Gutierrez's house in San Jose, and the two started to talk again about West. Thomas said that during the conversation St. John revealed West wanted him to burn her Jaguar in an insurance scam.

"He started telling me she can't make the payments on the Jaguar," Thomas said. "So he wanted me to help him, and I said, 'No way, I ain't getting involved in this, Howard.' He was like asking me for permission," Thomas said. "It was like, 'Do you think I should do it?' I said, 'No man, don't get involved. These days, they can lift fingerprints off anything, and you don't know who could see you. Do you know what is going to happen if you get caught?' I told him, 'Don't even do it,' and he said, 'Okay.' "

St. John's friend Tony Mercado said he visited his house around the same time, and during the visit, Mercado saw him hovering in his garage over a sawhorse. St. John had a hacksaw in his hand, and he was using it to cut through The Club vehicle antitheft device.

"He was cutting The Club, and I was like, 'What you are you doing?' " Mercado said. "He wouldn't tell me what he was doing, but something was clearly wrong."

On March 3, 1994—just days after Mercado witnessed this spectacle—West's Jaguar was found burned in Milpitas. St. John later confided in Mercado that he was the arsonist, and he said West's insurance company was suspicious.

"He told me about the Jaguar," Mercado said. "The insurance company was calling, and she [West] was getting nervous."

St. John told Thomas Gutierrez the car had vanished, but at first he didn't confess to being involved.

"He just said, 'The car is gone,'" Gutierrez said. "Then, the next thing I know, Howard comes driving up in a Corvette. He said, 'Brooke bought it for me. It's a wedding gift.' And again, I'm thinking, 'What is she doing spending this kind of money on Howard?' It was real suspicious."

Later, however, St. John told Gutierrez the truth about the Jaguar, and Gutierrez sensed his friend was in deep trouble. He'd married a woman he barely knew, and within a few weeks of the marriage, he was allegedly committing felonies for his new wife.

"He told me the story," Gutierrez said. "He said, 'The investigators are coming around asking questions, and Brooke is panicking. She is going to put the blame on me.' And, I was like, 'I told you, Howard.' He said, 'Things are getting out of hand. It's getting wild, and they are getting close.'

"He was scared. He thought they were going to get popped for it, and he said Brooke was getting nervous, too."

28

May 21, 1994 was a quiet, peaceful spring day in Los Banos. The sun was out, the temperature was hot for May and a light breeze was whisking its way across the community's farmlands and into the Fir Street neighborhood.

For Mike and Crystal Stoykovich, this was a perfect day for a drive to nearby Morgan Hill to visit family. The two hopped in their car around midmorning, and as they pulled out of their driveway, they noticed Brookey Lee West and Howard St. John embracing across the street.

"They were lovey-dovey," Mike Stoykovich said. "When we left, they were hugging and kissing in the garage."

Laura Parra and her husband, Fermin, noticed West and her husband in the garage, too.

"I was going to mow my lawn as I normally do on Saturdays . . . I could hear music playing, and I could see them dancing with each other," Fermin Parra said in a statement to police. "They were in an embrace."

Fermin Parra went about mowing his lawn, and it seemed as if it was going to be a nice, quiet weekend day. But a short time later, Fermin Parra was approached by

St. John, and he noticed St. John was intoxicated.

"He said, 'My name is Howard. What's your name?' " Fermin Parra told police. "And I told him my name, and it took him several tries to remember it. He introduced himself to me at least four times during the conversation, which was very typical of talking to somebody who was under the influence. . . . He had no short-term memory."

Fermin Parra said St. John was not threatening, but he questioned why everyone in the neighborhood was avoiding him. St. John said it was obvious everyone on Fir Street didn't like him, and St. John speculated that perhaps his neighbors were keeping their distance from him because of West's mother, Christine.

"He said, 'I'm not poison, you know,' " Fermin Parra said. " 'Nobody never says anything to us. They pretend like we're not here.' I told him, 'Hey, I'm talking to you now.' He mentioned that he knew Brooke's mother didn't get along with a lot of neighbors."

St. John gave Fermin Parra a strange feeling, so he went back inside his residence and told his wife and children to stay away from the couple across the street. Later that day, Fermin Parra's neighbor Raymond Delgado rang the Parras' doorbell, and Fermin Parra stepped outside to talk to his friend.

The two were talking for about twenty minutes when Fermin Parra heard a loud cracking noise coming from West's house.

"I thought I heard a door slam," Fermin Parra said.

Laura Parra was working in her garage, and she heard the noise, too. The noise sounded like a firecracker.

"But I knew it wasn't a firecracker," she said. "You heard some noise, and you heard some yelling."

What happened next shocked the Parras to the core. Laura Parra looked across the street and saw St. John stumbling out of West's garage. He was covered in blood, he

was holding his neck and he was pacing back and forth like
a wounded animal, screeching in agony.

"He yelled, 'She shot me!'" Laura Parra recalled. "He
came out staggering with blood all over the place, and it
was like a movie. He had a lot of blood on him, and I'm
looking at him, thinking, 'No, that's not fake blood, she really did shoot him.'"

"What I remember him saying is, 'She's got a gun in
there! A .357,'" Fermin Parra told police. Someone ran inside the Parra house to call 911—the Parras don't remember
who. Almost simultaneously, Los Banos police officer Steve
Goeken arrived at the scene and approached St. John in the
driveway. Officer Goeken said St. John was bleeding badly,
and he recorded in a police report what happened next:

> I observed St. John walking out, bleeding from the right
> shoulder area. He immediately said, 'She's got a gun,' point-
> ing toward his wife, who was later identified as Brookey
> [West]. I immediately grabbed Brookey, I patted her down,
> and she did not have a weapon. But she pointed towards a
> table where there was a .32-caliber revolver, which I then
> recovered. Howard said, 'She shot me,' and I observed his
> neck area, which did appear to have an entry wound on the
> right lower portion of his neck. Brookey then said, 'I did
> shoot him, but it was an accident. I didn't mean to.'
>
> While waiting for my sergeant to arrive, I kept the two
> subjects separated. At one point, Howard stated, 'Bitch,
> you shot me. I'm going to kill you.' I then asked Brookey
> what happened, which she said, 'He was coming at me,' so
> she got a gun out of her purse and pointed it at him, but . . .
> it just went off. She said she set the gun down and she went
> and called 911.

Laura Parra, still standing in her driveway, watched
a team of paramedics load St. John into an ambulance,

and then West emerged flanked by two officers.

"They brought Brooke out in handcuffs, and I thought, 'Oh, shit,'" Laura Parra said.

Laura Parra was overwhelmed by the events across the street. She had moved to Los Banos get away from the trials of the greater San Jose area, and she was now living across the street from a bunch of lunatics. There was Christine—the ex-felon who talked regularly to her neighbors about shooting people. There was St. John—a drunk who looked like he just walked off the prison yard. And there was West—a woman who shot her husband in the neck.

"They were the neighbors from hell," Laura Parra said.

Brookey Lee West was transported in handcuffs to the tiny downtown headquarters of the Los Banos police department for questioning in her husband's shooting. Police were hopeful West would give a statement, and they got more than they ever hoped for when West decided to talk at length.

West told officer Goeken that St. John was drunk and was being extremely aggressive with her. She said the shooting was one of a series of domestic disputes initiated by St. John, and that the two had been cleaning the garage when St. John threatened to attack her.

The following are excerpts from West's interview with police:

GOEKEN: I just need you to basically go through and tell me just what happened between you and your husband, Howard St. John, tonight.

WEST: Well, I guess it started early this morning. He got mad at me because he thought that I washed his pants with his wallet in it. . . . He was real, real intense, and he took his fist, and he just banged the switch on the washer and broke the washer.

Later in the day, as the two were cleaning their garage, West said St. John seemed obsessed with the idea that she was going to leave him, and he snapped.

WEST: He grabbed a hold of me, and he was trying to kiss me and everything, and I said, 'Howard, I'm not leaving you. I don't know where you are getting this idea.' He said, 'Well, you said if I got drunk, that you would leave.' I said, 'I know how you are when you are drinking, okay,' but I said, 'I'm not leaving you.'

West said St. John then went off on a verbal tirade, calling West a "fucking cunt."

WEST: I was starting to shake because I knew what he was real capable of, and I didn't want to provoke him. I was just trying to be nice. I said, 'You need to calm down. I don't know how much you've had to drink, but you are pretty drunk.' He was real drunk, and so I walked away, and I started sweeping the floor.

So I started sweeping the floor . . . and he's like talking, like, 'No motherfucker is gonna get in my way.' Just talk like that. He wasn't even really addressing me, and I don't know what he was doing. I said, 'Look, Howard, what are you talking about? This is crazy, all right?' I kept sweeping, and he said, 'Come here and sit.' I said, 'Howard, I'm not a dog,' so then I sat on the side of him, and he was trying to kiss me and everything. He said, 'Take your clothes off. I want to make love to you.' I said, 'Howard, I don't want to. I don't want to take my clothes off here on the concrete. . . . I don't want to do it here.'

Then Howard got really, really nasty with me, and he says, 'You fucking bitch, you are trying to leave me.' He says, 'I know what you are going to do, Brooke.' I said, 'Look, Howard, I'm not going nowhere' [and] he sat up on the floor and he grabbed hold of my arm . . . and I twisted free of him, and I just said, 'Let go of me, dammit! Just leave me alone,' and he says, 'I'll show you, you fucking bitch. I'll show you exactly what I can do.' I said, 'Howard, don't do this, just don't,' and I guess I backed up into a corner because I had some things stacked there, and there were tables there.

My purse was sitting over there because I had sat it [there] earlier, on the table, and when he got up, I said, 'Howard, don't do this, get your control.' He said, 'I'll show you exactly what I'm fucking capable of, you fucking bitch!' He took [a] table and he just throws it. I mean, it just flips into the air. It's a pretty heavy table. He turns around, and he started for me, but when he threw the table, I just reached out and took the little thing where my purse is. I have this little thing that I carry that little pistol in, I just grabbed it, and I pointed it at him, and I said, 'Howard, you have to leave me alone. I'm not going to let you hurt me.' When he started at me, I just pulled the trigger. I didn't mean to hurt him. I didn't even mean to shoot him. But I wasn't going to let him beat me.

GOEKEN: Okay, has he ever beat you in the past?

WEST: I've never been with Howard when he's really been drunk. . . . He only did me that way one time, and he wasn't drinking.

GOEKEN: Do you normally carry your gun in your purse, or why was it in there?

WEST: Well, I had the gun in my purse. I had taken all of my guns to my dad's to be cleaned, and I put the big ones back in the closet. I have a small closet, and I had a locksmith put a deadbolt on there . . . because the law says you have to keep them locked up. Well, they are big, you know. One is a side-by-side shotgun and the other is a .357. I had put those up, but I hadn't put up the little gun. I don't know why. . . . The .32 is mine. They are all mine. I bought them legal, and they are all registered to me.

Goeken asked West what St. John said to her after he had been shot.

WEST: I said, 'Howard, just lay there. They'll be here in a few minutes.' He said, 'No, I know what you are doing. You're fucking trying to kill me. I know what you are trying to do.' I said, 'Howard, I'm not.'

Goeken asked West about St. John's history.

WEST: He has a long arrest record for assault, I know.

Police weren't necessarily buying West's account, and their investigation yielded a starkly different version of the shooting from St. John. Los Banos officer Terry Kirschman was dispatched to the emergency room of the Los Banos Community Hospital to try to get a statement from St. John. Luckily, the gravely wounded St. John was still conscious, and he gave a brief statement.

KIRSCHMAN: I asked St. John why he had gotten shot, and he stated that all she said was, 'I'm setting you up.' I asked St. John if there was any reason for this, and he stated, 'She's a crazy bitch.'

Upon reviewing the evidence in the case, Los Banos police and prosecutors felt there was enough evidence to file charges against West, and she was booked at the Merced County jail on charges of felony assault with a gun and corporal injury to a spouse. At first, it seemed to police like a pretty solid case. West admitted to the shooting; witnesses told police St. John emerged from the house screaming about his wife shooting him; the police had recovered the gun, which was a .32-caliber Colt revolver registered to West; and officers had a statement from the victim himself, and he was identifying West as the person who pulled the trigger.

29

Howard Simon St. John was one lucky son of a bitch on May 21, 1994. The .32-caliber projectile from his wife's gun shredded skin and tissue like a cannonball, tearing a huge, gaping hole in his neck. The bullet came to rest in his left shoulder, and it was the type of gunshot wound that would be deadly on ninety-nine out of one hundred occasions. But the Indian spirits must have been watching over St. John that night, because when he was flown by helicopter from Los Banos to Memorial Medical Center in Modesto, doctors discovered the bullet hadn't damaged any major arteries. The doctors decided to leave the bullet exactly where it was, giving St. John a lead token of his wife's love that he could keep with him forever.

The following day, on May 22, a still-groggy St. John picked up the phone in his room and called the AAA insurance office in San Jose. The company contacted its insurance fraud investigator, Dwight Bell, who called St. John at the hospital.

"I placed several telephone calls to Modesto, and the

hospital, and eventually, I got through to him," Bell said. "He was obviously under sedation, rather difficult to converse with, [but] at that time he said he had burned the car for her . . . for Brooke West, and she had bought a Corvette for him in payment."

It looked like a huge break for Bell's investigation. The investigator urged St. John to get some rest, and the two men agreed to meet in person once St. John got out of the hospital.

St. John was released from Memorial North hospital within the week, and he showed up at Tony Mercado's front doorstep in San Jose with a big bandage covering the opening in his neck. Teary eyed, St. John told Mercado and his mother, Angie Mercado, about the shooting and how West had ambushed him without warning in their garage.

"He said he was doing something in the yard, and she called him into the garage," Angie Mercado recalled. "She closed the garage door, and she said, 'I'm going to kill you because of the insurance. They are getting suspicious.'"

Thomas Gutierrez got the same story.

"Howard said he came inside the house. Brooke closed the door and said, 'Howard, I have to shoot you, and I'm going to burn the house down,'" Gutierrez recalled.

Meanwhile, in Los Banos, news about the shooting spread quickly through the community. A couple of days later, Mike and Crystal Stoykovich were in front of their home when a man in a pickup drove into West's driveway. The individual was an older, thin-framed gentleman with white hair and a thick, handlebar mustache. Mike Stoykovich walked over and introduced himself to the man, who said he was West's father, Leroy.

"Remember the book *Heidi*, with her grandpa in the Alps?" Crystal Stoykovich said. "That's what he looked like. He was an older man with a thick white beard."

Leroy talked to Mike Stoykovich about his daughter's troubles, and Leroy's voice seemed tinged with anguish as he talked about his disappointment over West's decision to marry St. John.

"He said he couldn't understand why a bright girl like Brooke would get involved with somebody who didn't have anything," Mike Stoykovich recalled. "He said, 'When Howard gets his Indian check [from the government] he probably buys a case of wine or something, and when it's gone, he waits for the next cheek.'"

Leroy said his daughter was housed at the Merced County jail on assault charges, and Leroy had no plans to get her out of jail until she calmed down.

"He said, 'A bail bondsman called me, and he wanted to know what I wanted to do about her bond,'" Mike Stoykovich said. "And [Leroy] says, 'Leave her there a couple of days until she cools off, and I'll go down and pick her up.'"

A couple of days later, West's neighbors watched in astonishment as Leroy dropped his daughter off at her house. She was released on her own recognizance by a Los Banos judge, and she was more than willing to tell the Stoykoviches and the Parras her version of the shooting. "The one thing she told us was Howard threw a table at her, a big banquet table with the folding legs," Stoykovich said. "She said when he threw that table, he was drunk, and she said, 'He probably would have killed me.' So she just pulled the gun out and winged him. She said, 'I didn't want to kill him, but I stopped him,' and then she went in and called the police.

"She said she had a restraining order because she didn't want him around the house, and she said she was going to keep a rottweiler in the house in case he'd come over, you know, and break in the house," Stoykovich said. "She was afraid of him. She was there all by herself, and her dad was gone."

"She was telling me it was completely self-defense, that he was coming after her," Laura Parra said. "I just kind of took it as, he was throwing all this stuff at her and she shot him. But I was wondering what she was doing with a loaded gun in her purse in the garage."

By all accounts, it appeared the relationship between West and St. John was over. West was talking about restraining orders, and St. John had reported his wife for insurance fraud. Everyone who lived on Fir Street suspected that their neighborhood would finally return to normal and that the volatile relationship between West and St. John had ended for good.

They were wrong.

Within a few weeks of St. John's shooting, the unthinkable happened—St. John was back at West's home on Fir Street.

"He said, 'She's trying to make it up to me, you know?'" Mike Stoykovich said.

His decision to return to West was a complete shock to those who knew him. "I said, 'Man, are you nuts?'" Thomas Gutierrez said. "'What is this?' I told him quite a few times, I said, 'Howard, I don't mean to break your heart, I don't mean to bust your balloon, but look at you and look at her. This woman is going to kill you.' And he said, 'Nah, we were just arguing and fighting.' He said, 'She just got a little scared.' I said, 'If that's how she acts when she's scared, I hate to see her when she's pissed off.'"

Tony Mercado warned his friend as well.

"I told him not to go back with her," Tony Mercado said. "I said, 'Otherwise, you are going to get killed, Howard.'"

But despite the hole in his neck, St. John wasn't listening. And to Dana Gutierrez, the decision was a sad commentary on St. John's status in life.

"I don't think Howard really had anyplace else to go," she said.

Angie Mercado said St. John told her West had promised to sign over all her worldly belongings if he came back.

"He said that she was going to sign over the Corvette to him because it was still in her name," Angie said. "And then I said, 'Howard, are you going to go back with her?' And he goes, 'Well, I don't know,' and right then I knew that he was. So then, I guess she contacted him again and said that she would sign over both cars and the house to him."

The couple was reunited even while felony assault charges were still pending against West. The reunion of St. John and West was a death knell for Dwight Bell's insurance fraud case. Bell repeatedly tried to contact St. John for more information about the burned-out Jaguar, but St. John was deliberately avoiding the private investigator.

Bell finally tracked down St. John outside the Valley Medical Center in San Jose on June 1, 1994. St. John was sitting on a park bench, waiting for a doctor's appointment to get treatment for his neck, when Bell approached. The investigator immediately realized St. John was very, very drunk.

"Well, as he sat down on a bench . . . he emptied a half pint, one of those small, half-pint bottles of tequila," Bell recalled. "I don't know how many of those little airline-type bottles he had in his pocket, but he drained one or two of those, and he followed that up with a can of Coke that he had in his hand."

St. John proceeded to recant everything he previously said about burning his wife's car, and he told Bell he made up the story about the insurance scam to get back at his wife because of his anger over the shooting.

The following is the tape-recorded statement St. John gave to Bell:

BELL: Howard, give me your full name.

ST. JOHN: Howard St. John.

BELL: Do you have a middle name?

ST. JOHN: Yeah.

BELL: What's that?

ST. JOHN: None of your business.

BELL: Okay, what's your date of birth?

ST. JOHN: 5/15/58.

BELL: And, ah, are you staying on Rhodes Court?

ST. JOHN: Not no more. I got kicked out.

BELL: Could I reach you at any of those telephone numbers?

ST. JOHN: Nope.

BELL: Okay, give me an idea about how much you've had to drink today?

ST. JOHN: About a pint. About six of those little bottles right there.

BELL: And that's tequila?

ST. JOHN: Yeah, tequila.

BELL: And what else have you taken?

ST. JOHN: Crank [crystal methamphetamine].

BELL: How much?'

ST. JOHN: Oh, about half a gram.

BELL: Do you smoke that?

ST. JOHN: No, snort it.

BELL: Snorted it . . . all right . . . tell me what happened on the night, ah, the Jaguar incident.

ST. JOHN: Well, all I know is, I and Brooke went out. She came by, and picked me up at home. At the Rhodes Court address.

BELL: Uh huh.

ST. JOHN: And when she picked me up, we went out to Flames, and from Flames we went to go see a movie. A movie, by uh—what's his name? Remember that there karate guy, Steven Seagal, or something like that.

BELL: Uh huh.

ST. JOHN: So we spent a total of time, oh, about four hours, five hours there, three hours—something like that. Hell, I got no idea. And then, and then when we came out of the movies, the whole fucking car was gone.

BELL: Okay. You, uh, you told, Mr. Vallejos of Triple A and also Mr. Walker that you had burned the car. Is that right?

ST. JOHN: No, I didn't burn it. The reason why I said that [was] 'cause I wanted to get back at her. The reason why I did that was because she fucking shot me, and I wanted to get back at her.

BELL: Okay, but let's not get ahead of ourselves. Okay, the car is gone from the parking lot that night?

ST. JOHN: Yeah.

BELL: And then what happened?

ST. JOHN: Then we, uh, we waited for the police for about a whole fucking hour it seemed like.

BELL: Well, you described over the telephone to me, a few days ago, the location where the car was burned. You said next to the railroad tracks.

ST. JOHN: Oh, yeah, because, uh, because . . . because . . . because the, uh, that there place that . . . towing . . . that the towing yard told us where exactly the car was picked up from. And then, and then, it was also written in the police report, so they, yeah, I fucking have it. Yeah, so, that's from reading the police report, and from what the towing company told us. So we went over there, and looked at the spot.

BELL: Oh, you went and found the spot?

ST. JOHN: Yeah.

BELL: All right.

ST. JOHN: Yeah, it was just obvious.

BELL: Uh huh.

ST. JOHN: You know.

BELL: You also told me over the telephone that you and Brooke got married?

ST. JOHN: Oh, yeah . . . in Reno, April thirtieth.

BELL: And, ah, where did you go live?

ST. JOHN: [I] went to go live with her [in] Los Banos. Fir. Sixteen-something. You know, I can't remember that fucking address.

BELL: Well, where does Brooke work?

ST. JOHN: She works at a company called [Syntex] . . . that's located off Page Mill Road.

BELL: Did you have a job?

ST. JOHN: No . . . because I got a hernia, so that stops me from my profession.

BELL: And, uh, the incident [the shooting] happened Saturday morning?

ST. JOHN: It happened Saturday night. I was drunk . . . I fucking tore up. I went over there and tore up her house. I slapped her around. And then, she was just . . . it was just common sense, you know? She didn't know what to do, you know. She panicked.

BELL: Uh huh.

ST. JOHN: You know, she fucking shot me, you know. Hey, you know, I deserve it. I mean, when somebody hits a woman, come on.

BELL: You're not supposed to do that?

ST. JOHN: I know that . . . I don't fucking blame her for fucking doing that shit.

BELL: She shot you in self-defense?

ST. JOHN: Yeah. I mean, it's fucking all there in the fucking police report. These fucking cops seen the house and everything. I'm just doing this so I can fucking try to get at her ass. The reason why I told you everything because I fucking seen the car, I read the police report, I seen where the car came from. I figured it out, put two and two together, and I was all fucking all high on fucking drugs anyway when I was in the hospital.

BELL: Uh huh.

ST. JOHN: So I just put two and two together. I mean, come on. Any fucking dummy can fucking make up something like that.

BELL: So you made up this story . . . of burning up the car?

ST. JOHN: Oh, yeah. Fuck, I had to, 'cause I'm trying to get her back.

BELL: Does she know that you called [us]?

ST. JOHN: No, no, She don't fucking know nothing.

BELL: Do you think she's contacted them about you?

ST. JOHN: I don't know. Probably . . . because she knows I'm crazy. Because, hey, I've been fucking put in the nut ward a few times.

BELL: Where?

ST. JOHN: South Dakota. Here.

BELL: What for?

ST. JOHN: 'Cause of my drinking, drugging problem. I got a whole fucking stack of fucking records.

BELL: Uh huh.

ST. JOHN: You can fucking go in there [to the hospital]. I almost died here, twice—no, three times—for overdose. Drugs . . . alcohol.

BELL: Okay, well, I appreciate your information.

30

Tyla Knotchapone learned of Howard Simon St. John's shooting and his miraculous survival from her friends at the Native American Indian Center in San Jose, and she was horrified. She wasn't, however, surprised. She had sensed a storm brewing in St. John's life two months earlier, and now that storm had come ashore with a fury.

In late May, Knotchapone sought out St. John, and she once again told her friend of her reservations about West.

"He mentioned he wanted a divorce, and that he felt very uncomfortable with her, and that he wanted his life back," Knotchapone said. "He said, 'You know, if I didn't meet her, this bullet wouldn't be in my neck.' He said, 'I just want to forget her. She is bad news. I think she is going to kill me.'

"He was in tears, actually," Knotchapone said. "He said, 'I can't believe I have this kind of problem in my life with a woman. This woman is dangerous, Tyla. I don't know how to go about divorcing her. It's like she's got me in a web, and I know the way out, but I'm scared. What could be next? I'm scared to find out.'"

Knotchapone wept during the conversation. She pleaded with St. John to leave his wife, and she offered him a bed in the small apartment she shared with her ten-year-old daughter in San Jose.

St. John didn't take up the offer.

" 'I don't want to put you and your daughter on the line, because she is a crazy lady, you know?' " St. John told Knotchapone.

St. John said he wasn't the only person who feared West—her mother did, too. He said West was abusive to Christine, and he actually witnessed acts of violence by West against her mother.

" 'She barely gets along with her mother,' " Knotchapone said, quoting St. John. " 'She even threatens her mother sometimes. The mother doesn't know how to even speak to her own daughter. She gets all scared because she's at the age where she's helpless.' He would hear [them] arguing," Knotchapone said, and West would tell her mother, " 'I wish you were dead, mother, you son of a bitch!' "

"She [West] would start throwing things around," Knotchapone said. "There goes her bottles of perfume all over the place. He [St. John] said she even picked her mother up and slammed her body against the dresser and told her, 'I wish you were dead. I'm so sick of you hanging around me. You're just getting old anyway. You should have just dropped dead when you were in prison. Why stay alive?'

"I mean, that is the way she talked to her mother when they were in a heated argument," Knotchapone said. "[That] is what he was telling me."

Knotchapone asked St. John why he had gone back to his wife, and St. John had no answer.

" 'I'm so stupid,' " St. John told Knotchapone. " 'I don't know why I went back with her.' "

31

Late on the night of June 2, several residents of Fir Street heard a commotion, looked out their front windows and saw something extremely strange. Brookey Lee West was running down the street like a commando carrying out a covert operation behind enemy lines.

"I looked out my window and I thought, 'Oh, my God,'" Laura Parra said. "Brooke was running around like a military person. She was crouching, hiding on the ground, going behind cars and stuff, and she was dressed in what looked like military clothes. I thought, 'What the hell is going on here?'"

West ran to the front doorstep of the home of Robert and Tara Fullington, who lived a few houses down on Fir Street. An officer wrote in a police report what the Fullingtons told authorities:

They were asleep at their residence when they heard someone beating on their front door. Robert Fullington opened the curtains next to the door, but he did not open the front door. At that time, he observed a female standing outside, who identified herself as Brookey West, who lives at an address down the street, and she requested that they call 911 immediately. She needed the police for immediate assistance. The Fullingtons advised that they would call the police, but they did not open the door to allow Brooke to enter their residence.

The Fullingtons then called 911 per Brooke's request, and they looked out the window as they waited for the police department's arrival. While looking out the window, they observed that Brooke took off running northbound down the street, and she hid in the front yards of several other residences.

Los Banos police arrived within a few minutes, and they located West standing in the middle of Fir Street. Officer Steve Goeken, who responded to the shooting that St. John had survived at West's house just thirteen days earlier, asked West what was going on, and she said St. John had threatened her because she'd misplaced a photo from their wedding in Reno.

She said she feared St. John was going to kill her.

Goeken memorialized the incident in a Los Banos police department report.

I responded to 1639 Fir Street on a report of a female requesting the neighbors call the police. When I arrived, I made contact with Brookey in the street. She advised me that she wanted me to go in the house to see if Howard was there. She said that he has been acting crazy because he is upset over a picture that he could not find of them when they got married in Reno. She said when they were coming down [Pacheco] Pass today, that he had slapped her twice because he was upset that he couldn't find it. She said when they got home, she was telling him that she was going to go look in the car to find it, but he did not want her to leave the house. She said that after she took a shower, she then went to the door, and he asked her what she was doing again. She told him she was going to the car to look for the picture, and he told her to shut the door. She said she then ran out the door and shut it behind her, and she hid until I got there. I then went in the house with Brookey, where I made contact with Howard, and I asked what the problem was. He said he was not angry anymore, and that he was mad about a picture of them together in Reno that they could not find. Brookey said she just wanted to leave, and that she went to get in her car, but Howard said it wasn't running. I asked him what was wrong, and he said he pulled the ignition wires off it. Brookey said she did not want me to have him removed from the house—that she would go stay with friends.

At West's request, Officer Cindy Hoskins gave West a ride to an all-night coffee shop in Los Banos, and West told the officer she wasn't going back home. She planned to divorce her husband.

Neighbors saw St. John coming and going from the residence in a panic the following morning, and he told neighbors West left the home the night prior and had not returned. Several times throughout the day, he jumped in West's car, peeled out of the driveway and then returned several hours later. He was frantically looking for West, and his search continued throughout Friday and into Saturday, June 4.

"We saw Howard driving Brooke's car wildly," Laura Parra said. "He would leave the house and speed somewhere, then come back speeding to the house. He was there by himself."

By Saturday afternoon, St. John concluded West had been kidnapped, so he called the Los Banos police department to report West missing. An officer filed a missing persons report for West that afternoon:

On June 4, 1994, at approximately 12 p.m., I contacted Howard St. John in regards to a missing persons report. Howard St. John stated that his wife, Brookey Lee, was missing from their residence, and she was last seen on June 2, 1994, at approximately 11 p.m. Howard St. John stated that on June 3, 1994, sometime in the evening, his wife, Brookey Lee, contacted him stating she was at a local motel, and she had gotten beat up, and she possibly broke her arm. Mr. St. John stated he did not feel she was missing voluntarily.

The missing person is Brookey Lee St. John, also known as Brookey Lee West. [She is] a white female, approximately 40, with hazel eyes. She is also known to wear contacts, and she has brown, shoulder-length, straight hair. Date of birth is June 28, 1953.

Mrs. West is missing from 1639 Fir Street. No possible destinations known. I note Mrs. West possibly has a mental condition, and she might be suicidal. Mrs. West has a brown birthmark on her right forearm, and she has two gold-capped teeth in the bottom left side of her mouth. Mrs. St. John was seen leaving the area in an unknown direction wearing a pink sweat top, pink sweatpants, black Reebok shoes, and a black purse.

I note that this couple has had a couple of serious altercations in the past few weeks where this department has had to respond for assistance. Brookey Lee West was seen on June 2, 1994, by officer Cindy Hoskins of the Los Banos Police Department, at which time Brookey Lee West stated to Officer Hoskins that she was not planning on returning. This would be an indication that Brookey Lee West is missing voluntarily.

Howard St. John gave me Brookey Lee West's father's phone number in the Bay area. Her father's name is Leroy Smith, and I [could not contact him]. At approximately 1:10 p.m. on June 4, 1994, Leroy Smith's wife, [Chloe], contacted me at the department and gave me information stating that she knew for a fact that Brookey Lee West was not in the Los Banos area—that she is in the Bay area. Santa Clara to be exact, staying at a motel for the time being. Leroy Smith's wife was unable to give me a number to contact Brookey Lee West, but she stated she would talk to her husband. She would have him try and get in contact with Brookey and have her contact the department to clear up this matter. Given the circumstances of the past few weeks regarding different cases, in this officer's opinion, Brookey Lee West is voluntarily missing, and it is possible she is leaving her husband.

That night, on Saturday, June 4, St. John called West's father, and Leroy could tell St. John was stone-cold drunk. He slurred his words as he asked Leroy where his wife was, and Leroy assured St. John that West was okay. But despite the assurances, St. John kept calling Leroy Smith throughout the night, and the phone calls became so persistent, Leroy finally unhooked his phone so he could get some sleep.

That night, St. John also called Tony Mercado's mother, Angie.

"He didn't know where she was, and the dad [Leroy] had told him not to worry—that she was okay," Angie Mercado said. "I think right after that, Howard started drinking, and then he called me back, and he said that the dad had said that she was there [at Leroy's]."

St. John made one other call on what would prove to be the last night of his life. He phoned the Four Winds rehabilitation center on Rhodes Court, and he got in touch with an old friend named Ernie Turtle. Turtle, a Native American man who was a member of the Four Winds program, said St. John relayed how he and his wife were having problems, and in a drunken rant St. John told Turtle he was going to get even with his wife for running off on him.

"Well, he mentioned something about wanting to kill her, you know, and getting even," Turtle told authorities. "He was drunk, you know."

Sometime during the next twenty-four hours, someone shot St. John in the back, and his corpse was driven several hours away to Tulare County, where his killer dumped the remains like a piece of trash alongside the Tule River in Sequoia National Forest.

It was a sad, degrading end to a mostly sad existence for the Sioux Indian from South Dakota.

32

Where a crime is coolly premeditated, then the means of covering it are coolly premeditated also. I hope, therefore, that we are in the presence of a serious misconception.

—Sherlock Holmes, in Sir Arthur Cohan Doyle's "The Problem of Thor Bridge"

In the days following the discovery of Howard Simon St. John's corpse in the Sequoia National Forest, Tulare County homicide detective Daniel Haynes went into bulldog mode. He was dead-set on solving St. John's murder, and he wasn't going to let go of the case until St. John's killer was arrested, convicted and locked away in the California prison system for life.

The first lead of any significance came when St. John's father, Sylvester, told Haynes his son's wife had shot St. John in the neck just thirteen days earlier.

"He told me there had been some problems that landed Howard in the hospital," Haynes said. "We were on the road then to Los Banos. It was our best lead at the time.

"You've heard, 'Where there's smoke, there's fire'?" Haynes said. "When you don't have anything outside of what was going on there in Los Banos, then that's where you look, and I looked hard."

Haynes and his partner, Herman Martinez, drove out to

Los Banos on June 9. "A real nice guy," Haynes said of Martinez. "A Vietnam vet, probably six feet two inches tall or so, and he's very, very professional. A fairly quiet guy, but he's someone you would definitely want on your side if you are in a fight.

"He's very meticulous," Haynes said. "All work, no play, and he comes in and does a straight, honest ten or twenty hours of work for the day, and then he goes home. He's a hard-core family man, and he has two sons who are also in law enforcement."

The detectives' first stop in Los Banos was the police department, where Sergeant Carey Reed briefed the Tulare County investigators on all the problems at West's house on Fir Street during the last two months: a shooting, a handful of domestic violence calls and an insurance fraud investigation in which her husband had reported her to the authorities for the burning of her Jaguar.

"Los Banos police were very helpful, and the district attorney's office there was extremely helpful, too," Haynes said. "It's very difficult to work a case out of town like that when you are on strange turf, when you don't have the resources and when you don't have the knowledge of the area. It's nice to find [a police department] that rolls out the red carpet for you, and they did."

After the briefing from Los Banos police, Martinez and Haynes drove a little more than two miles from Los Banos police headquarters to West's home on Fir Street. They noticed in the driveway a small Chevrolet sedan belonging to West and a white Corvette belonging to St. John. The detectives obtained a description of the residence, and they returned to downtown Los Banos, where they met Merced County deputy district attorney William C. Hunter at his office. The detectives asked Hunter to pursue a search warrant for West's home, and the warrant was later signed by local judge Phillip Castellucci.

The Tulare County detectives, accompanied by Sergeant Reed from Los Banos, then returned to West's home. The trio of investigators knocked on the door, and they were greeted by a frail, sweet-looking sixty-two-year-old woman with long, braided hair. Christine Smith introduced herself, invited the detectives inside and agreed to give the three men a taped statement.

"A little old lady," Haynes said. "Very nice. It was like talking to your grandma in her living room. She was friendly, and she'd answer any of your questions. How truthful? I don't know. You wouldn't immediately suspect her of being involved. It wasn't until much later on in the investigation when I got a different opinion of her."

The senior spoke in a thick Texas accent, and she proved to be a wealth of information for Martinez and Haynes. The Caucasian woman started off by claiming she was "part" Apache Indian and her daughter was "about 15 percent" Indian. She said she never did like St. John, a violent, temperamental drunk.

"He's a very violent man," she said in a taped statement. "He's got a record from here to Kansas City and back. Armed robbery and everything else. She really picked a thug . . . a hooter and a tooter. Crazier than a bedbug."

Christine frowned on the relationship between West and St. John, she said, in large part because St. John moved into West's house before they were married.

"I'm pretty churchly, and I don't go for the ways of modern young people," she said. "I don't go for that. I'm a Christian, and I don't go for it. To me, my home is sacred ground, and that's the way it is. I couldn't compromise, in other words."

The detectives asked Christine whether her daughter was a gun owner, and she said her daughter was fond of firearms.

"She takes her guns to her father [for cleaning], because, you know, it's like a collection," Christine said.

Christine also confirmed her daughter had shot her husband in the neck nearly two weeks earlier.

"She plugged him through the neck," she said.
"Shootin'. 'Plug' is a Texas slang for it. I know that they
were having trouble, and she was supposed to have shot
him," Christine said. "He was insane drunk. He would have
killed her if she hadn't of shot him with that little pistol. . . . He was a huge man, and compared to her, it'd be
like a pissant coming up against an elephant. He was crazy.
He was trying to get at her to kill her. She had no intentions
of killing him. . . . She just wanted to stop him. He's a big,
huge man, and when they get drunk, they go insane."

"So when you say 'they,' you're talking about a person
like Howard?" Martinez asked.

"Indians," Christine said. "Indian people. All of them
go crazy when they drink. I'm sure you heard the
history. . . . Well, I know when I drink I ain't got no sense,
so I don't drink. . . . Indians do that. They just go crazy
when they drink that firewater. Just crazier than a loon."

But by far the most valuable information Christine provided to detectives was West's whereabouts on the weekend of St. John's shooting. On the evening of Thursday,
June 2, Christine said St. John threatened her daughter's
life in an argument over a missing photo from the couple's
Reno wedding, and the threat prompted West to run to the
neighbors, who called the police.

During the dispute, Christine said St. John tore the distributor out of West's car to prevent her from leaving.

"He didn't want her to go," Christine said. "He wanted
her to stay here so he could beat the living hell out of
her . . . he was souped de gooped . . . and no way was she
going to buy that. She went to the people down here across
the street, she banged on their door and she asked them to
call the police."

Christine said the Los Banos police drove West to an

all-night coffee shop downtown to get her away from St. John on the night of June 2, and while at the coffee shop West met a truck driver. According to Christine, the truck driver gave West a ride over Pacheco Pass to San Jose, and the next morning, on Friday, June 3, West rented a car and got a hotel room there. That day, Christine said, her daughter went to work at Syntex Pharmaceuticals in nearby Palo Alto, where West was working on a freelance technical writing project.

After she was done working, West went to a do-it-yourself legal advice business in the San Jose area and filled out paperwork for a divorce. West then returned to her hotel room to get a good night's sleep.

The next day, Saturday, June 4, West picked up her mother from her van at a city park in Santa Clara, and the two went shopping all day. That night—the night authorities suspect St. John was slain—West dropped her mother off at the van, and West went back to work at Syntex Pharmaceuticals, where she worked all night. Christine told the Tulare County investigators that while her daughter was at work West received a call from St. John, and St. John cursed his wife for leaving him in Los Banos. During the phone call, St. John said his Corvette was in the shop for repairs, and he wanted West to go pay for the repairs, then get the Corvette back to the house immediately.

"See, I'm going to have to use some profanity, and it just hurts me," Christine said. "[But he said], 'Get your fuckin' ass over and pick up . . . the Corvette'."

Christine said her daughter also told her St. John had stumbled across about $3,000 in cash West had hidden in a kitchen drawer of her home before fleeing Los Banos in the domestic dispute. St. John told his wife over the phone he was taking the money and going to Reno with his "hometown boys."

"Who are you going with?" West supposedly asked her

husband, according to Christine. " 'None of your fucking business,' " she said St. John responded. " 'When I get back from Reno, that son of a bitchin' car, bitch, better be in the driveway.' That's what he said to her."

The next day, on Sunday, June 5, Christine told the detectives she and her daughter returned to Los Banos because they believed St. John had left for Reno. When they returned to the home on Fir Street, they found her house in shambles. "The whole house was completely turned upside down. Beer cans, tequila bottles," Christine said.

Christine and her daughter found two different types of cigarette butts in the home, which indicated to Christine someone else had been in the house with St. John prior to his departure to Reno. She said she and West cleaned the house all day Sunday, and West didn't learn of her husband's murder until a phone call came from St. John's mother, who had been in touch with the Tulare County authorities, which told her St. John had been murdered.

"She says, 'Well, you know, Howard's dead,' " Christine quoted St. John's mother as saying. "And Brookey said, 'No. Howard went to Reno, and he took $3,000,' which was her full income tax check."

St. John's father called a short time later and asked West to authorize the release of his son's body from the Tulare County coroner's office. Sylvester St. John told West he wanted his son's body returned to South Dakota for a proper burial on the Indian reservation.

"The father called and wanted to know if Brookey would sign the release papers to him so they could carry him back to the Dakotas to be buried on Indian ground in Indian style," Christine said. "And, uh, Brookey said, 'Well, I don't know how much money that would cost me to do that,' and he said, 'You don't have to pay. I'll do the paying through the Indians.' "

"And, uh, he thanked her," Christine said. "He's a very nice person, and the mother's a very nice person, too. But, uh, Brookey said, 'It can't be, because Howard went to Reno, and I haven't heard from him.'"

St. John's father supposedly said to West during the phone conversation, "Well, he's had these type of things. He'll leave. We haven't seen him in fifteen years, and he'll leave and be gone maybe sometimes five years. We never knew where he was."

Christine then made a point of telling the detectives West should have receipts to prove her whereabouts in San Jose on the weekend of the shooting. When asked about her daughter's rental car, Christine said, "She had a rental car and, uh, I can't keep the story like it's supposed to be."

Moments later, during the middle of the interview with Christine, the phone rang. West was on the line. West said she was in nearby Gilroy, but she would hurry home to meet with the investigators. West arrived at the Los Banos residence shortly after six p.m., and she, too, agreed to give a taped statement to the Tulare County investigators.

Haynes' first impression of West was that she was a normal woman.

"Nothing out of the ordinary," Haynes said. "Quiet. Soft-spoken. Ordinary in appearance. She answered all of our questions."

Haynes is prevented from discussing specifically what West said to police, but her seventy-two-page taped statement documents her alibi for the murder. The following are excerpts.

MARTINEZ: This taped interview is being conducted at 1639 Fir Street in Los Banos. Today's date is 6/9/94. The time is 6:32 p.m. Present at this taped interview are myself, Detective Herman Martinez, Detective Daniel Haynes, Detective Carey

Reed of the Los Banos police department, and the subject is Brookey Lee West.

MARTINEZ: Brooke, for the purpose of this interview, what is your full name?

WEST: My full given name on my birth certificate is Brookey Lee Smith.

MARTINEZ: And you were married to whom on April 30?

WEST: Howard Simon St. John.

MARTINEZ: This individual's [body] was located in Tulare County. Are you familiar with Tulare County?

WEST: No. I've heard of it, you know, but I'm not like familiar . . . I couldn't say I've been there.

MARTINEZ: How have you heard about Tulare County?

WEST: Well, the Tule Indian Reservation is in Tulare County.

MARTINEZ: Have you ever been to Tulare County?

WEST: I've probably passed through it going to Los Angeles or something.

MARTINEZ: Do you know if Howard had gone specifically to the Tule Indian Reservation?

WEST: I don't know if he had ever been there . . .

MARTINEZ: Do you know of any specific person or persons that Howard associated with, who were from any of these reservations that we talked about?

WEST: No. He knows many full-bloods. My husband is Dakota Sioux. . . . There are six nations of Sioux.

MARTINEZ: Do you know which reservation in Dakota his Sioux tribe is from?

WEST: He's Wompton Saxton Sioux, but I'm not sure of the name of his reservation. He had showed me his papers, and he says he is registered Wompton Saxton.

MARTINEZ: Okay. Do you have any Indian heritage?

WEST: We're Mescalero Apache. I met Howard at the Four Winds Lodge. The Four Winds Lodge is a rehab center for Native Americans in San Jose. It's on Rhodes Court. Right around the corner from that is the Native American Indian Center in

San Jose. I used to [take my mother] there to the Four Winds
Lodge on Friday evenings, mainly because they had open AA
meetings. Open to the public. Even though . . . these are all
male participants that go through rehab.

MARTINEZ: What was the reason for you going there?

WEST: My mother is an alcoholic, and I took her to meetings because she couldn't drive at the time.

MARTINEZ: When was it when you first met Howard St. John?

WEST: I didn't actually talk to Howard or meet Howard because
Howard didn't want to meet me. [He] just wanted to watch me
for maybe three or four months. When they [Indians] first see
somebody they want, they are not like white people. They
don't just introduce themselves. They have to watch you for a
while, then they have to decide if, you know, what their approach is going to be.

MARTINEZ: So that's how you became acquainted with Howard?
You saw him speaking at that AA meeting. And then?

WEST: Yes. I took my mom to the meetings on Friday, and . . .
Howard was just there. He just turned around, I just turned
around, and he was just right in front of me. And then he
shook hands with me, and I said [unintelligible], and he said,
"My name is Howard."

MARTINEZ: You spoke to him first?

WEST: Yeah. He was right in my face. I didn't know what else to
do. I had asked him about that later, and he said, "Well, I decided that it was time to meet you." I had wanted to meet him.

MARTINEZ: So, basically, the people that were [at these meetings]
were Indians?

WEST: Most of the time. I would say that it is very rare [for] white
people . . . I don't know why. It just seems to be that way. You
rarely see any white people there without [them] being married to [an Indian] or to have a half-breed . . .

MARTINEZ: So you and Howard eventually met. How did the relationship start with you guys as far as starting to socialize
and that sort of thing?

WEST: Well, Howard had a problem. He had a hernia, and he was unable to work. Howard was an excellent mechanic, and he was unable to work because he couldn't lift, and he was very depressed. I spoke with him many times, and I thought I could help Howard because I had helped other Indians there. I would do things for them—get them shampoo for their hair. Especially the ones who wore their hair very long.

MARTINEZ: Where did he live at the time since he didn't have any money? How did he support himself?

WEST: Well, he was in the program. The Four Winds Lodge Native American program.

MARTINEZ: You guys eventually became girlfriend/boyfriend?

WEST: Well, I worked with Howard for a long time. I wanted him to be around me before anything happened like that because the way that American Indian males look at women is not the way white people [do]. You know, it's like they kind of have a [possessive] attitude. "Well, that's mine." Like a car, and so you have to have an attitude with him, that you [let them] know it's either this way or that way. So, for a long time, many months, we were just friends, and I helped him, and I bought the right groceries for him, and the right herbs, and the right teas, so he could start taking the weight off, and he did very well. He went from 304 pounds to 240.

MARTINEZ: How long did this go on?

WEST: Few months.

MARTINEZ: So how long did you guys go together, I mean—how long?

WEST: I did not change my relationship with Howard until about last year in October. I started seeing him as a man instead of just a friend.

MARTINEZ: Okay, who initiated that? That change of relationship, from being a friend where you were nurturing him to a relationship where you were seeing him as a man?

WEST: I think both of us did.

MARTINEZ: And whose house is this?

WEST: It's my house . . . I closed on September 30, 1993.

MARTINEZ: And you say in October was when your relationship changed with Howard?

WEST: Yeah.

MARTINEZ: So your house came first, and then Howard?

WEST: Yeah. I moved here, and my relationship with Howard changed.

MARTINEZ: Did Howard move in to the house then?

WEST: Yes.

MARTINEZ: I'm going to ask you some personal questions. Before February or March, did you and Howard have any sexual relationships?

WEST: Yes.

MARTINEZ: Did your family know about your relationship? That he was living here?

WEST: They didn't know anything about Howard until he moved in.

MARTINEZ: Did your family—I'm talking about your mother, your father—did they accept that relationship?

WEST: My father, you know, he just says, "You are an adult. You can make your own decisions." My mother was not happy about it because she felt he was trying to use me. We had originally planned to go back to the Sioux reservation in South Dakota [to get married]. Actually, we were supposed to leave tomorrow.

MARTINEZ: Did you guys go to South Dakota to get married?

WEST: No. We got married in Reno. He was very insistent, and he said, "Well, we can get married in Reno, and [then] we can get married on the reservation, too." We were going to go back [to South Dakota] and get married anyway, because he hadn't gone home in a number of years. I basically wanted to do the trip so he could see his family. And . . . he wanted a Corvette. I bought him his Corvette. The white one. I bought it after he moved in. Uh, I needed a second car, [and] he wanted to restore [it].

MARTINEZ: You guys came back from Reno. What was the atmosphere? What type of home life did you have?

WEST: After we came back from Reno, I think [he was] a different man than before . . . I don't understand what happened to him. He had a real attitude change. All I can say is that his attitude became nasty to me, like, I would ask him questions, [and] he'd say, "Shut up. It's none of your fucking business." Stuff like that . . . he just changed. Before, he treated me respectfully. He didn't cuss at me.

MARTINEZ: Was he physical with you? By that I mean, did he assault you? Did he hit you?

WEST: Just recently, he did do that. The very first time he actually hit me physically was when I had picked him up [after] he had gotten out of the hospital. This was on a Tuesday evening when I picked him up.

MARTINEZ: Why was he in the hospital?

WEST: Because he had a gunshot wound to his shoulder.

MARTINEZ: How did—how did he get shot?

WEST: I shot him.

MARTINEZ: Why is that?

WEST: Well, it wasn't deliberate. He got mad because he thought that I had washed his pants with his wallet in it—he was drunk. . . . I've had so much happen to me, but this is to the best of my recollection. I was sweeping [the garage], he laid down in the dog's bed, and he says, "Come here and sit." I looked at him, and I said, "Howard, I'm not the family dog, okay?" He said, "I know you're not the family dog. I told you, fucking bitch, get over here and sit down."

He went crazy, and he started calling me all kinds of names. He says, "You don't have nothing. You think you've got something? You fucking whore. You don't have nothing." And he got up off the floor, and he says, "I'm going to kick your ass."

He was screaming and ranting at me, and he got up, and he took this big, long table, and he just flipped it like it was a quarter. Just turned it in the air. He says, "I'm going to beat your ass." I couldn't run, and I knew I couldn't get away from him, and I seen my purse sitting there. I just reached out. I just unzipped [it]. I grabbed the pistol, and I was backing up, and he came at me. He said, "I'm going to beat your ass," and I said, "Howard, don't," and I was shaking.

I drew [the gun]. I wanted to run, but I couldn't. I didn't have enough room. I don't know why. I just grabbed it, and see, I thought maybe he would stop. I didn't want him to beat me. I didn't really even want to hurt him. I was shaking, you know, and he just kept coming at me, and I said, "Stop," I'm backed up against the wall, and I was shaking. I just shut my eyes. I said, "Stop," and I just pulled the trigger. I wasn't really trying to hurt him. I guess it caught him in the shoulder, or something, and he looked at me. He fell on the garage floor.

He said, "You fucking bitch, you just tried to kill me!" I said, "Howard, I didn't try to kill you. Let me call 911. Just lay back. I don't know how bad you are hurt." He kept reaching for me, and I wouldn't let him get ahold of me. I came in to call 911, and then I seen him run past me.

MARTINEZ: Did the police arrive?

WEST: Yeah, they did . . . [Howard] was in the driveway, and he's screaming, "That fucking bitch! Lock her up. She tried to kill me!" The officer asked me if I was armed, and I said, "No, sir." [He asked] where the gun was, and I said, "It's over there on the table," so he took it. He spoke with me for a few minutes, and he says, "Well, I have to arrest you." They put [Howard] on a stretcher, and they took him to the hospital.

MARTINEZ: So that was the incident that we're talking about where you shot him, and that's why you shot him. Did you guys ever go to court over that issue?

WEST: Well, I was in jail and everything, and then I'm supposed to go back on the twenty-fourth which I will do. I don't know what will happen. I gave a statement to the officer, and he taped it.

MARTINEZ: That's one incident. How long was he in the hospital?

WEST: He was in the hospital for a week, and I was in jail for a few days. I had asked to be released on the date of my arraignment, which was the following Monday, and the judge wasn't very sympathetic to me. I don't think the judge really realized I was the victim at that point. . . .

MARTINEZ: Who got out first? Your husband or you?

WEST: I did. And the judge . . . it took him a while to figure out if they were going to let me go, on [my own recognizance]. I told the judge, I said, "I'm the only one working. There is nobody to care for him," which was a fact. I said, "I have property . . . I need to be out working, if it's at all possible."

He [the judge] said, "I was unaware that your husband [was] very, very intoxicated, and he has a very long record for assault. . . . Based on these facts, if you promise me that you will not do anything to harass him or have any weapons, and show up in court, I will release you on [your] own recognizance."

MARTINEZ: Did they give you the gun back?

WEST: No.

MARTINEZ: Okay. What about the other guns? The .357, and a shotgun. What happened to them?

WEST: My father has them.

MARTINEZ: Did he own guns? Howard?

WEST: Howard told me he had a .38. He said he gave it to a [friend]. I had never seen Howard with a gun, okay? I never saw the gun, so I don't know if he was fabricating or not. Howard always told me that he carried a gun in his sleeve—in a jacket. But I never saw it. . . . I had [also] begun to suspect over the last couple of weeks that he had given the house keys to other people.

MARTINEZ: And who would that be?

WEST: I don't know. The reason is because he made a strange remark to me. He said, "I've got friends, and they are going to keep checking on me . . . they can come up here and check this place out at any time." I didn't understand. I said, "What do you mean, check it out?" And he wouldn't answer me.

MARTINEZ: Where did he say his friends were from?

WEST: He didn't.

MARTINEZ: You suspected he may have given the keys to somebody else?

WEST: Yeah. He became that secretive.

MARTINEZ: Did you notice if, in fact, there were any occasions that somebody else was coming into the house?

WEST: I didn't ever really know. Howard got to where he wouldn't let me have the car. Throughout the day, he was checking on me, and he would be very, very, very mad at me if I wasn't there [at work] to answer my phone.'

MARTINEZ: After Howard got out of the hospital, did he come straight to the house?

WEST: I didn't go to Howard, because I wasn't sure of his frame of mind. I wasn't sure of the medication he was taking. I wanted to give him a little bit of time before I made any contact with him. So I was released later in the evening, sometime on a Wednesday. Howard, I guess, was released on a Sunday. He went to a powwow. . . . I didn't know what to do. I didn't have anybody to talk to. I wasn't sure. I didn't know if he would retaliate against me.

MARTINEZ: When did you see Howard again?

WEST: I saw him the following Tuesday evening. He called me at my office, and he wanted to see me. I didn't know what he wanted in terms of, you know, like divorce. He seemed okay. He wanted to talk to me. I went to [Four Winds] at 109 Rhodes Court. . . . I seen him out on the street, and I stopped the car. I was driving the little Chevy. The other car was still in the shop. He just looked at me really strange and he took off running. And I thought, "What the hell is he running from?"

[He was] running away from me like he was afraid of me or something. So I . . . drove around the corner, which would have put me on East Santa Clara Street. It's just like a little corner, and I saw Howard coming across the street. I stopped, and I said, "Howard," and . . . he turned around, and he ran back into a liquor store. I thought, "Well, I'm not going to mess with this because I don't need to be arrested for something when I'm not really trying to harass him." So I just drove off, and then I went to a phone booth in Santa Clara. I called him there [at the Four Winds] and I said, "Howard, you called me. You had to see me. I would like to see you. I know we have so many problems. I don't know—I'm a nervous wreck. I'd like to talk to you." He said, "Well, come over here and pick me up on the corner where you just seen me fifteen minutes ago."

So I drove up over there on the corner. He came out and said, "Get out of the fucking car. I want to search you." He was real belligerent.

MARTINEZ: He said he wanted to search you?

WEST: Yeah. He said, "Give me your fucking purse," so he took my purse, and he searched me and checked my purse.

MARTINEZ: Did he say why he was searching you?

WEST: Who knows? He thought I wanted to hurt him. I didn't want to hurt him to start with. I said, "Howard, I'm not armed," and he said, "Get in the fucking car. I'm driving." So we get into the car—we wanted to be able to talk privately— and we went to a motel, and I rented a motel room at the Days Inn there in Santa Clara in the name of Brooke West. He had bought a six-pack of beer. We went into the room. He wasn't really violent to me, and I didn't really know what to expect. I just sat down in a chair, and . . . he was calm at first. He took out a beer, and he just drank it down, and then he got another one out, and just drank that down. I said, "Howard, you shouldn't be drinking, you know?" I didn't know what type of medicine he was taking. I didn't know what to think. He took another [beer] out, and he picked it up like he was going to hit me in the head with it, and I flinched, you know? I jumped. I thought, "Well, I had better get out of here." And, he says, "Honey, I'm not going to hurt you." He put his arms around me, and he said, "I know what I did. I know I caused this." And he drank another beer.

I asked Howard at the motel, "Would you be willing to go for counseling?" I didn't know what to think. I didn't really want to leave him, even though in some ways I was really scared of him. He said, "Yeah, you know, I'll do it." And then he got very, very mad at me. He pulled open his shirt [showing the gunshot wound to his neck], and he said, "You see what you did to me?" I said, "Howard, I didn't do it on purpose. I didn't mean to hurt you."

MARTINEZ: Was there a physical confrontation between you and Howard there at the motel room?

WEST: Yeah. He slapped me twice.

MARTINEZ: How come?

WEST: He was mad at me . . . he said that I was bragging that I hurt him.

MARTINEZ: So he slapped you a couple of times. Did he hurt you in any other way?

WEST: No. He could have really hurt me, you know, but he didn't. He just slapped me.

MARTINEZ: Where did you guys go?

WEST: I brought him here. . . . Now, before I go any further, I want to tell you that that day, on that Tuesday, I cashed my tax-return check for about $3,400, and I had all $100 bills. I still have a little paper from [the bank] because I guess they roll up $1,000 in division of $100 bills. I had cashed it, and I didn't make the deposit because I was anticipating going to go get the Corvette [out of the shop]. But Howard didn't know at that moment that I had all that money.

[Two days later, on], June 2, he dropped me off [at work] in the morning. He seemed okay. [Then] he called me up. He seemed really down and really depressed, and I said, "You don't sound like you feel very good."

MARTINEZ: Where was the [tax-return] money?

WEST: I hid it here in the house.

MARTINEZ: Where?

WEST: In a drawer in here, in the kitchen. . . . So he picked me up, and it was in the middle of the afternoon, and his attitude was very, very different. I smelled alcohol. I said to him, "You've been drinking," and he said, "No, that's cough syrup."

MARTINEZ: What are your normal working hours?

WEST: They are whatever I want. I have [a] twenty-four seven schedule. I have an access card that lets me in.

MARTINEZ: And by the way, where do you work?

WEST: Well, I'm a contractor. A job shop will hire me, and then they will send me to a job site, so I'll usually work at that job site even though I don't work for those people. . . . I write books. I can write anything, but my main living has been from the high-tech industry. I write manuals for their computers, and for their software. For example, if they want me to write a book that tells a person how to sit down and use their software application, I go there.

MARTINEZ: How long have you been doing this?

WEST: Thirteen years.

MARTINEZ: So Howard picked you up [on June 2] at work. Where did you guys go?

WEST: We went to a Walgreens pharmacy in Santa Clara to fill his painkiller prescription. [The pharmacist] said it was Vicodin, and that it was a very strong prescription. She said, "I want you to understand, Howard. You do not drink with this and you do not drive."

I wrote them a check for it, and we left. He drove part of the way [back to Los Banos]. There is a Chevron station at 152 East, so we stopped there, and we got a couple of sodas, and he said, "You drive because I need to take a couple of pain pills." So he took two of them, and I said, "You know, you really don't have to take two of them." And he said, "It's none of your fucking business how many I take, all right? I can take half this fucking bottle and I'd never even feel it." So I drove home.

MARTINEZ: What time did you get home?

WEST: I don't know. It was in the evening. Maybe six p.m. or seven p.m.

MARTINEZ: Anything happen when you got home?

WEST: He was just sort of laid-back. I don't remember . . . I think we rented a couple of movies . . . [and then] I was seriously thinking that this was all a mistake. He seemed fine, and he said, "Let's take a shower." I said, "Okay," so we went in and took a shower in the master shower. All of a sudden, he turns around and he looks at me rather strangely, and he gets this strange look across his face. He says, "Where is that fucking picture?"

I looked at him, and I said, "What? What picture?" I got out of the shower, and I thought, "Uh oh. Tantrum." There was a snapshot taken of us when we got married in Reno. That's the one he was looking for. I didn't know where the picture [was].

He says, "If I don't get that fucking picture by midnight, I'm going to tear this whole fucking house up, and I'm going to beat your ass." So I came in here, in the kitchen, and I went through some drawers and everything, and I made sure that the money [from the tax returns] was stuffed back there.

I said, "I know where I put it [the photo]. It's in the car. Let me go out there and look." What I was really trying to do was get away from him. So I went and I opened up the garage door, and I had my purse and my keys. I picked [them] up on the way out, and he didn't even notice, and he wasn't fully dressed. He had on his underwear and a T-shirt. He didn't even have his shoes or anything. He was tearing up things in the bedroom. . . . I just reached up, and I just grabbed the garage door, and I took off running. I hid in a field over here for a long time. I was just shaking. I didn't know what to do. I just shook. I just sat there until I could get my composure, and then I went to some neighbors over here on the corner. . . . I banged and banged on their door. The guy answered. He didn't open his door. He just peeked out of his blinds, and he said, "Yeah, what can I do for you?" I said, "My name is St. John, please call the police for me." He says, "I've got it." I was just shaking. It wasn't very long after that a police officer drove up, and then there was another lady [officer] who followed him up like three minutes or something. . . . And Howard [told the police] "Well, I was looking for this picture, you know, and she's just freaking out, and there's nothing wrong." And . . . I said to this lady [officer], "I want to get the car. I need the car."

MARTINEZ: Which car are you talking about?

WEST: The little Chevy. And Howard spoke up. He said, "Well, you can't take it because I took the distributor out of it, and I don't know what happened to it." And so the officer asked him, "Why did you take the distributor out?" and Howard said, "Because I didn't want her to leave. I wanted to keep her."

MARTINEZ: Did you suggest that you stay here or go or what? What was the agreement?

WEST: I just said, "Look, Howard, you can stay, okay? I don't know what I'm going to do right now." I was just a wreck. I left with the police officer, and I asked the officer, "Is there an all-night restaurant I can stay at?"

MARTINEZ: What's it called?

WEST: I don't know the name. . . . It starts with a B . . . but it's down on Pacheco Boulevard.

REED: Grandy's.

WEST: Uh, [the officer] took me there.

MARTINEZ: To Grandy's?

WEST: Yeah. This little restaurant. And I had a cup of tea, and I sat for a while. I didn't know what the hell to do. . . . I didn't call my dad . . . I had some money on me, but . . .

MARTINEZ: How long were you there?

WEST: Maybe an hour.

MARTINEZ: Did you meet anybody there?

WEST: No.

MARTINEZ: Okay. What did you do? Did you stay there?

WEST: Uh, no. I stayed for a while. I just had a cup of tea, and then I got out, and [I] started walking . . . toward the Pacheco Pass.

MARTINEZ: Where were you going?

WEST: Um, I hitched a ride with a trucker.

MARTINEZ: You were walking at the time, and then you hitched a ride? Where was the trucker at when you hitched a ride?

WEST: Um, down here near this Shell station. I was just getting to that point.

MARTINEZ: Do you know who the trucker was?

WEST: He—he owned his own truck. The name of the truck was Delgado Trucking. He was from Fresno. Uh, he said his name was John, and, uh, he asked me, "Could I give you a lift?"

MARTINEZ: Oh. He asked you?

WEST: Yeah, and you see, he had gotten gas or something, and [he] pulled out, and he was checking his truck, and he noticed I was walking toward [Pacheco] Pass. I said, "Are you going to San Jose?" And he says, "Yeah, this is my regular route." He hauled paper . . . cardboard boxes.

MARTINEZ: Uh huh.

MARTINEZ: What date was this on?

WEST: This was on the evening of June 2 going into the morning of June 3. Thursday [night] to Friday morning. He took me all the way into San Jose, and he left me there where the Denny's is, near the airport. And I asked him to leave me there, because I went and rented a car from Dollar Rent A Car. I had to have transportation. I had to go to work. So I went to work that morning on Friday—about six or seven a.m. I was there very early.

MARTINEZ: Did you have any clothes with you?

WEST: All that I had was what I had on. I didn't even have any good clothes on.

MARTINEZ: And where did you stay?

WEST: Well, before I tell you where I stayed at . . . I had made several phone calls. I didn't know what to do. I thought, "I'm going to have to leave him, because I don't think I could deal with this fear." So I contacted a company—they go by the name of C&C Paralegals—I have their card. I can give it to you, show it to you. I went over there immediately, and I had them fill out papers for a restraining order and a divorce.

MARTINEZ: Who did you talk to there?

WEST: Um . . . I'll have to look his name up.

MARTINEZ: About what time was it when you were there?

WEST: In the morning time. Maybe ten or eleven a.m . . . something like that. I wrote them a check. $425. [They said we] have to have cash before we can start the process on the paperwork, so I went to the bank, and I cashed my payroll check that I've had from a couple of weeks ago.

MARTINEZ: Where was the $3,400?

WEST: Still here.

MARTINEZ: With Howard back at the house?

WEST: Yeah, still.

MARTINEZ: But Howard didn't know [about the money]?

WEST: No.

MARTINEZ: Then you went to work after that?

WEST: Um, I went to work. Yes. I went to work.

MARTINEZ: What happened after work?

WEST: I went shopping that evening way over on the East Bay. Um, I'll give you the receipts to what I got. I just bought some clothes and some personal things so I could take a shower, and then I came back to Santa Clara, and I checked into a place called the Budget Inn."

MARTINEZ: These items—were they purchased with cash, or were they purchased with a credit card?

WEST: I wrote a check for them.

MARTINEZ: Did they take your ID?

WEST: Yeah. They accepted them . . . I have the receipt. I

can show you. I think it was Mervyn's, and then I know I stopped at Wal-Mart drugstore to buy a blow dryer.

MARTINEZ: This would have been on Friday?

WEST: Friday afternoon. Actually, I didn't do the shopping until that evening.

MARTINEZ: About what time?

WEST: During the evening time. Maybe seven or eight p.m. Something like that.

MARTINEZ: Okay. You did some shopping. What happened then?

WEST: I came back to Santa Clara, and I checked into a place called the Budget Inn. Address is 2499 El Camino Real in Santa Clara. That was Friday evening when I checked in there.

MARTINEZ: How did you pay for that?

WEST: On the credit card. My Mastercard.

MARTINEZ: How long did you stay there?

WEST: Just that night.

MARTINEZ: What time did you check out?

WEST: Uh, at eleven a.m., Saturday.

MARTINEZ: Where did you go then?

WEST: I picked up my mom, and we did some errands . . . probably till about seven p.m., and then I took her back to her van, and I went back to work.

MARTINEZ: Seven . . . ?

WEST: In the evening. I stayed up with coffee.

MARTINEZ: Who works with you?

WEST: Oh, there's many people coming and going.

MARTINEZ: Where is that located?

WEST: Um, the assignment is at Syntex Pharmaceuticals company in Palo Alto . . . it's on [Hillview].

MARTINEZ: And who else works with you there in that office?

WEST: Oh, there are lots of people who come and go.

MARTINEZ: At seven p.m. at night?

WEST: Oh, there isn't anybody there. You have to use your card key to get in.

MARTINEZ: Is there some type of record that, when you use your card, there is some type of recording that would show that you were checked in that time?

WEST: Yeah. The computer logs in.

MARTINEZ: Who would have that?

WEST: Their security department, I suppose.

MARTINEZ: And that works merely by you running your card through it, so it can show them that you were there?

WEST: I guess so.

MARTINEZ: Even if you didn't go inside the building?

WEST: Um, yeah . . . think it would do that.

MARTINEZ: What time did you go in there?

WEST: During the evening.

MARTINEZ: So you checked in. How long were you there?

WEST: A long time. Several hours. I had lots of phone messages, and I had one from an officer at the police department here in Los Banos.

MARTINEZ: They called you there?

WEST: They said that my husband put a missing persons report on me. . . . Then I had messages from my father, and I called my father, and he said that Howard had been on the phone like every ten minutes. All night.

MARTINEZ: Howard was calling your father?

WEST: Yeah.

MARTINEZ: What was he saying when he was calling your father?

WEST: I don't really know. He was just real, real drunk . . . he just said it was a lot of drunk talk. You know, like, "I love her" and "She's just left." You know. That kind of stuff.

MARTINEZ: You said you made other phone calls or somebody talked to you [at work] on the phone besides the officer?

WEST: Howard called me.

MARTINEZ: What did he say?

WEST: He asked me to come home. He was sorry that he scared me. I said, "No Howard, I'm not coming home. I know you are drunk, and this is not a good idea right now."

MARTINEZ: Did he call collect, or did he call direct?

WEST: He just called. He called from home.

MARTINEZ: Okay. So that call would be recorded then as far as the bill? How long did you talk to him?

WEST: Just for a few minutes. I said, "Howard, no. I'm not coming home," and then he got real mad. He said, "Fuck you. You can come home if you want [because] I ain't going to be here when you get home." And I said, "Well, what are you going to do?" He says, "I'm leaving. I am going to Reno . . . I got the $3,400."

MARTINEZ: Did he say how he found it?

WEST: Probably just digging through the drawers, looking for something else, and he probably accidentally found it, which I was hoping he wouldn't, but he found it.

MARTINEZ: Was there anybody else in the house with him?

WEST: I don't know, because I haven't been here. These were his exact words: "I'm going to Reno. . . . One of my hometown boys is picking me up." I said, "With who?" He says, "It's none of your fucking business." But he didn't say when he was leaving, and he hung up on me. . . . All he said was, "One of my hometown boys is picking me up." That's all he said.

MARTINEZ: If he took the $3,400, why wouldn't he take the car also?

WEST: I don't know.

MARTINEZ: Did you come home?

WEST: I didn't come home until the next day [Sunday, June 5] around eleven a.m. I called my father, I brought my mom. I stopped and I picked her up.

MARTINEZ: Weren't you afraid that Howard was going to be home?

WEST: Not with the $3,400. No, because he liked to gamble.

MARTINEZ: And you were coming home to see if, in fact, he'd taken the money?

WEST: Uh, I knew he had the money. He [hadn't] known about the money, so I knew he had found it. I came home, and I asked my mom to wait outside.

MARTINEZ: What did you find?

WEST: The house was a complete pigsty with bottles. You know, tequila bottles, and a lot of beer cans. There's still beer in the refrigerator.

MARTINEZ: Did it look like just Howard [had been] here at the house?

WEST: There was somebody else here, too, because there were [two types of] cigarettes—a brand he did not smoke. Howard smoked Camel. There were Camels, and then there was a pack of Marlboro. There were cigarette butts put out in beer cans. There were empty brandy bottles. Empty tequila bottles. I just sacked it all.

MARTINEZ: Where did you take it?

WEST: I took it over there, and [I] threw it in a Dumpster.

HAYNES: What Dumpster was that?

WEST: Just a Dumpster behind one of those places over there, and I just threw it out. I didn't want to leave it here.

MARTINEZ: Would it still be there?

WEST: I don't know. I just tossed it.

MARTINEZ: So this would have been on . . . ?

WEST: Monday afternoon.

MARTINEZ: Uh, you got back . . . ?

WEST: Sunday afternoon [June] 5.

MARTINEZ: You picked up your mother at her home at about eleven a.m. at her van?

WEST: Yeah . . . I got here about eleven a.m.

MARTINEZ: What day was that?

WEST: Sunday.

MARTINEZ: Sunday. And then, uh, so you cleaned up all day Sunday, and then Monday you got rid of all that stuff?

WEST: I still had more to clean up. . . . There were drawers dragged. There was paper all over. I told my mom. "We'll just stuff everything back in the drawers," and we left midday, and then we went to the valley.

MARTINEZ: The valley. Where at?

WEST: Over in San Jose. And I took my mom to the bank. She withdrew some money for me. I had to borrow some money from her to pay for the Corvette. And I picked up my mail, because I have a mail drop there, and then we had dinner at Denny's. And I called my dad.

MARTINEZ: Did you go to Tulare County yesterday?

WEST: No. I didn't.

MARTINEZ: What do you think might have happened to Howard?

WEST: I don't know. I have no idea what happened that day. I can tell you based on what I've been told, he was very belligerent. I don't know what happened to Howard. I don't know where he went. I know he had money. . . . But I was getting ready to have papers for the restraining order and the divorce.

He said, "One of my hometown boys is picking me up." I said, "Who?" And he said, "It's none of your fucking business."

MARTINEZ: I don't have any other questions.

WEST: Wait. Wait. Can you please tell me what happened?

MARTINEZ: He died as a result of gunshot wounds, and that's all we'll talk about the case—as a result of gunshot wounds. This will be the end of the taped interview.

Once the interview with West was complete, Haynes and Martinez told West they wanted to search her home and vehicles, and she consented to the search. The detectives scoured through the house for more than an hour, and they collected a number of items. They included a twelve-pack of Budweiser beer left behind by St. John; a box of white plastic garbage bags; a cigarette lighter with the words DAKOTA CASINO SIOUX on it; a roll of plastic tape; a bottle of carpet stain cleaner; a box for a Savage shotgun; a leather handbag containing 12-gauge shotgun shells; and two letters to West from Christine and St. John.

The letter from Christine to her daughter read:

Dear Brooke:
I wish you would come and see me. I love you Brooke, no matter what you do or did . . . You need me, and I need you . . . I will always love you . . . You [are] the only one in this world who loves me, and it doesn't matter . . . know I'm with you. Love you.

Your mother.

The second letter was from St. John. It read:

To my baby.
Wish this would have never happened tonight. Sweetheart. I told you that I will never hurt you, and I mean that . . . What I say, I mean. Haven't I always kept my word to you? I know what we are going through is hard. I always thought that my shit don't stink, but, when it comes to you, I hurt so hard. Like, right now, I don't know what to do . . . I don't know if I should just cash in my chips and let you go on with life, and leave you alone. Brookey, my baby, I love you. I wish I could always be with [you] forever. You know, when I was in the hospital, all I ever thought of was you. What I'm trying to say is, I love you. What has happened between us? I hope we can always be together forever. Well, if you leave me, there is only one way out. I have 20 of them. You know what I mean, so good bye. I love you.

Haynes, Martinez and Reed left West's house around midnight, and the two agreed that portions of West's story weren't adding up. She said that on June 2—the night of the domestic dispute—she had gotten a ride from the police to an all-night coffee shop, and then she started hitch-hiking toward San Jose. The very premise of her hitchhiking late at night over the ominous Pacheco Pass, a remote stretch of mountainous, winding highway, seemed preposterous. No one in her right mind would try to cross the pass on foot in the middle of the night.

Also, West seemed to be deliberately trying to document her whereabouts during the entire weekend in which St. John was slain. It seemed as if she was going out of her way to formulate an alibi.

"I can't talk about anything she actually said, but I think there were things probably said in her statements that didn't make sense in my mind," Haynes said.

Still, Martinez and Haynes were not going to jump to any conclusions. St. John, after all, was no saint, and there were plenty of possible scenarios in which he could have been murdered. Maybe he did leave the house with friends and with West's tax money and was then murdered and transported to Tulare County by some unknown suspect.

"We have to approach it with the idea that every stone needs to be overturned," Haynes said. "Howard had been around. He had been in rehab. There were too many unanswered questions at that point to form any opinion."

But the detectives were suspicious of West. She had shot her husband nearly two weeks earlier. There was an insurance fraud inquiry pending, and her husband had ratted her out to the insurance investigator.

There was certainly a potential motive to want St. John dead.

"I would not have eliminated her as a lead when I left her house," Haynes said.

33

Laura Parra was driving down Fir Street a few weeks after Howard Simon St. John's murder when she witnessed one of the strangest sights of her life. Brookey Lee West was walking on the side the road, and she was dressed like a witch. Her hair, her pants, her shirt and her shoes were all black.

"She had a thick white powder caked all over her face," Parra said. "There was no color in any of her hair or clothing. I didn't even know it was her. It was very, very weird, and she looked like a forty-year-old lady trying to be goth. It was like she thought she was a witch."

On June 10, 1994, Daniel Haynes and Herman Martinez drove to San Jose to contact West's father. They met Leroy and his wife, Chloe Smith, at their front doorstep, and the couple invited the Tulare County detectives inside.

During their interview of Leroy, it quickly became apparent to the detectives that Leroy was the person West sought out whenever she was in a bind. He was the one who picked his daughter up from the Merced County jail after she shot her husband in the neck, he was the one who took possession of his daughter's guns to prevent her from violating a judge's order not to possess weapons and he was the person West called in San Jose on the weekend of St. John's murder.

"My impression was that Brooke's contact with her father took place when Brooke was in trouble, and daddy had to help her get out of it," Haynes said.

In a taped statement, Leroy told the detectives his daughter's alibi for the slaying. The detectives then asked Leroy if he had any guns, and Leroy produced an arsenal of firearms. There was a loaded gun behind a couch, another in a nightstand, and other firearms in a locked cabinet. The guns included a .38-caliber Smith & Wesson revolver, a German Mauser pistol, a .38-caliber Derringer, several rifles, a Ruger pistol and a 12-gauge shotgun.

The detectives took the guns to the Tulare County crime lab to be examined by a forensics firearms expert. The weapons could not be linked to St. John's murder.

The crime lab was, however, able to examine the bullets plucked from St. John's body during autopsy, and the ballistics indicated a .38-caliber handgun was probably the murder weapon. The gun used to kill St. John was likely a Colt or a Miroku make, and the description was similar to the weapon Wayne Ike saw in West's possession the night West threatened to shoot him.

The actual murder weapon was never found.

After their interview with Leroy, Haynes and Martinez spent the next several days in Los Banos talking to West's neighbors. The neighbors recounted the bizarre events at 1639 Fir Street, and they gave the detectives a far different picture of West's mother, noting that Christine Smith bragged about killing a man and being on death row.

"The neighbors all took Christine in," Haynes said. "She was the sweet little old lady who lived around the corner. They welcomed her into their home, and in very short order they had to run her off their property.

"I suspect anyone who was around Christine or Brooke had similar experiences. They couldn't keep friends, and these people saw something in these two they didn't want around. I got to know the whole neighborhood," Haynes said. "That was an interesting street. My impression was they were all scared."

Mike Stoykovich provided a valuable clue to the detectives. He told police that on the night of the slaying he never saw anyone other than St. John at West's house, and there were no loud parties. The account contradicted West's claim that someone else was at the house partying with St. John the night he was slain.

Armed with the witness accounts of Christine bragging about shooting someone, the detectives ran a background check and learned of her assault conviction from Bakersfield in 1961. The detectives then returned to West's home to interview Christine about her criminal history.

SMITH: Assault with a deadly weapon with intent to commit murder is what they booked me on. I shot him. He was a man I was going with, and, uh, it was one of those triangles you get involved in. I'll admit, it was premeditated. . . . He was a boyfriend. Maybe you all better listen to this because you might learn something. He handled the breakup from me in the wrong manner. Are you with me?

MARTINEZ: So you were intending to . . . ?

SMITH: Kill him. Do [I] have any sympathy? Am [I] feeling sorry? Hell, no.

"I was quite surprised," Haynes said. "You wouldn't see it by looking at her. Of course, the shooting had been many, many years before, but when asked, she had nothing to hide."

Next, the detectives spent weeks interviewing St. John's friends at the Native American Indian Center and the Four Winds Lodge.

"That was not the friendliest setting," Haynes said. "They don't welcome you. When you go into a rehab center like that, it's like you are still on the frontier, and you are the white man. Their [attitude is] 'I can't talk to you.' It took some time convincing some of those people I was there to avenge Howard's death. I had to tell them, 'You know, if Howard were here, he'd tell you to talk to me.' "

Gradually, St. John's friends warmed up to Haynes and Martinez. One especially helpful witness was Knotchapone, who told the detectives about West's spewing venom about her ex-husband at the AA meetings. Knotchapone also relayed how St. John once told her he feared West might kill him.

"She was very open," Haynes said. "She was a wealth of information. She was extremely close to Howard emotionally, and his death really tore at her. More than anyone else, she wanted to see justice."

Thomas Gutierrez and Anthony Mercado told the detectives West hired St. John to burn her Jaguar. Interviews with officials from AAA insurance and investigator Dwight Bell revealed West collected more than $18,000 in insurance for the burned-out Jaguar, and Bell told the detectives St. John had revealed the insurance fraud scheme to him, then recanted.

The detectives also learned St. John's white Corvette was in a Milpitas repair shop at the time of the slaying. The owner of the auto shop, Mark Morales, said that one or two days after St. John was found dead, West showed up at his auto shop in Milpitas to pick up the Corvette.

West appeared disheveled and extremely exhausted.

"On that day, he noticed Brooke was extremely un-kempt," Haynes wrote in a police report. "She was out of it, as though she had been up all night or had not slept. . . . She was having a lot of trouble, and he assumed she was having trouble because she had not slept in quite some time."

The account of West's exhaustion coincided with the detectives' theory of the case—that West had killed her husband on the evening of June 4 and drove all night to Tulare County to dump the body. The scenario of West's being up all night might account for West's sleep-deprived state at the auto repair shop a day or two later.

Haynes and Martinez tracked down the rental car West drove on the weekend St. John disappeared. West told the detectives she drove the car from San Jose to Los Banos, but paperwork from the rental car company showed West racked up more than 1,000 miles on the vehicle. The mileage was hundreds more than what should have been on the rental car's odometer, according to police reports. The detectives suspected it was possible West accumulated the mileage driving to the Sequoia National Forest in Tulare County to dispose of St. John's corpse.

But by the time the detectives tracked down the rental car, it had already been rented twice by other customers. The vehicle had been cleaned each time it was rented, and there were no valuable clues inside. No bloodstains. No fibers. No bullet holes.

The Tulare County investigators spent several more months checking West's alibi, including West's claim that two nights before the slaying a trucker gave her ride from Los Banos to San Jose as she hitchhiked over Pacheco Pass. West said the truck driver, named John, worked for a company called Delgado Trucking, so with the help of the California Highway Patrol, the detectives obtained a list of every Delgado Trucking in the state. None had drivers in

Los Banos or surrounding areas that night, according to police reports.

West provided receipts to the detectives showing a number of purchases in San Jose on the weekend of the murder. The receipts placed her in San Jose on the actual day of the slaying, but they did not, however, account for her exact whereabouts on the evening of June 4 or the early morning hours of June 5.

To check West's alibi further, Haynes and Martinez contacted a security supervisor for Syntex Pharmaceuticals. West said she was at the business working on the night of June 4, and the detectives were told by the supervisor that time cards filled out by West placed her at the business that evening. A computer security system also showed West used her company-issued identification badge to access the business that night, but there was no way of documenting exactly when West left Syntex. This meant West was unaccounted for the entire night of the slaying and the morning hours of June 5.

"Her coworkers knew exactly nothing about her," Haynes said.

Haynes and Martinez sought out West's brother, Travis, for questioning, but they couldn't find him. The detectives knew Travis was once committed to the Atascadero state prison for the criminally insane, and they knew Travis lived on the streets of San Jose, but an extensive, days-long search for Travis at homeless shelters and on the streets of San Jose turned up nothing.

"To this day, the brother exists by name only," Haynes said. "The information I was given back then was he was homeless. He was living under bridges. No one had seen him for some time. When they did see him, it was because someone [in West's family] was driving by, and they happened to see him alongside the road, and they stopped. It wasn't like he was coming home and having Thanksgiving dinner.

"It seemed like, for the most part, he was pretty much written off," Haynes said. "I certainly never could find him, nor could anyone else find him."

Search warrants were served by Martinez and Haynes on West's bank records, phone records and credit card accounts. The records showed West was in San Jose on the weekend of the murder, and they confirmed the phone calls she said she made.

Gradually, Haynes and Martinez pieced together a portrait of a successful, intelligent businesswoman known by no one.

"Brooke gets close to no one," Haynes said. "She has no real friends—at least not anyone I could identify as someone she buddied around with. Brookey would never list an address other than a drop box or a post office box. I don't care if it's the vehicle registration or the phone or water bill—you'll never find a physical mailing address for her.

"Your average, reasonable, prudent individual wouldn't do something like that," Haynes said. "If you are out in the middle of nowhere and the corner store was the only place available for a drop box, okay. But she lived her life that way. Brooke never wanted to be found by anybody, ever, for any reason. I've never ran into someone like that. I've never ran into anyone else who lived a life like Brooke did. It's almost a life of cover—someone who doesn't want to be found."

Over time, the inconsistencies in West's statement made the detectives more and more suspicious. Her alibi could not be confirmed, and try as they might, the detectives could never identify any other suspects in the slaying of St. John.

"In my opinion, without going into any reason, I believe Brooke was responsible for his death," Haynes said. "She's the only suspect I ever developed. Often, in a case like this, you can have a multitude of suspects, and you have to figure out which one. Not only did things point to her as the best possible suspect—there was no one else."

Haynes also entertained the possibility West's mother and father were involved. Of Christine, he said, "She was capable of the crime. It was something to consider. It's not something that can be overlooked, as opposed to your grandma, who's never done anything wrong in her life. It's something that's got to be looked at."

Of Leroy, Haynes said, "There was absolutely nothing to lead to him as a potential suspect in this case, other than he's the father of Brooke West, which doesn't make him a murderer. Is he someone who may know what is going on? Yes. Looking back, is he someone who is capable of helping in the aftermath of an event like this? Yes.

"My personal opinion is this family was in and out of a lot of things, and I think more than one thing has been covered up in their lives," Haynes said. "I think any one of them is capable of getting into a mess, and the others would come in and bail them out. That's my impression. Brooke, her mother, her father, her long lost brother. . . . I think that was their life.

"If Brook was responsible, I think the mother could have been part of getting the body out there. Anyone can shoot somebody, and we know she [Christine Smith] can, because she's done it in the past. From interviews, she shows no remorse for it. That tells you a lot about a person," Haynes said.

Haynes, Martinez and their colleagues at the Tulare County sheriff's department spent nine years investigating West in the slaying of her husband. They interviewed every witness several times over, and they produced an investigative case file nearly 2,000 pages long.

The detectives consulted with the Tulare County district attorney's office to determine if West should be charged, but prosecutors felt they didn't have enough to go on. There was circumstantial evidence for sure—a questionable alibi for West, and she had shot her husband two weeks prior to his murder. She had a potential motive as well. Her husband reported her to authorities for insurance fraud, and if he was dead, any potential fraud charges would evaporate.

But the detectives were told by the Tulare County district attorney's office that if a prosecutor was going to stand in front of a Tulare County jury and ask them to convict West of murder, they had to have more evidence linking her to the crime.

The murder of Howard Simon St. John remains among the unsolved files at the Tulare County sheriff's office to this day.

"When you work something that hard for so long, it's hard to get rid of," Haynes said. "It's even harder to realize someone got away with it, whether it's Brooke or not. Somebody got away with it, and it just so happens, I believe Brooke's responsible.

"You never forget a case. I don't lie awake at night and worry about it anymore, but it's the type of case you'll think about the rest of your life. I don't really know what else I would do. We put in thousands of hours."

34

For much of their twenty-year marriage, Leroy Smith was a kind and loving husband to his wife Chloe. But in 1995, a series of events unfolded that caused Chloe Smith to realize she had married into a spider web.

The events started with tragedy. Leroy was diagnosed with terminal brain cancer in late 1995.

"He came home one night and he told me, 'This is the hardest thing I've ever done in my life, but I have to tell you, I'm dying,'" Chloe Smith said. "It was devastating."

Terribly distraught, Chloe Smith was forced to contemplate life without Leroy. He was the one who always took care of her, and he was the one who made sure she was safe in life. Leroy was also the one who paid the bills, and as Chloe Smith waded through her grief, she realized she had to begin to take control of the couple's finances. She started to look into her husband's management of their money, and she was mortified at what she found. Throughout 1995, Leroy had forged Chloe Smith's signature on about twenty-five credit card applications, and he took out nearly $250,000 in cash advances without ever telling her.

Chloe Smith suspects the money went to Leroy's daughter, but there is no proof this is true.

"Brookey told me he was gambling it all away," Chloe recalled. "I told her, 'That's bullshit.'"

Chloe Smith also started to question whether West was meddling in her father's finances to secure his belongings after his death. The suspicion was bolstered during a trip Chloe and West took to meet with a San Jose doctor about Leroy's prognosis in early 1996. During the drive, West said Leroy was financially destitute and owed thousands to Asian bookies. To pay off the debt, Leroy gave the bookies his prized gun collection.

"She said he owed these gambling debts to these Chinese bookies, they were threatening to do harm to Brooke, and who knew what they were going to do," Chloe Smith said. "She said, 'We had to come up with some money, so we gave them all the guns.' She put the guns in a big white cotton bag and dropped the guns off on some street corner."

West said the Asian bookies were threatening to make West "work in their whorehouse" if the debt wasn't paid.

"I told her, 'This is ridiculous,'" Chloe said. "I said, 'Brooke, what are they going to do? You are forty years old. All they'd have you do [in a whorehouse] is sweep the floors.'"

Simultaneous to the bizarre story, Chloe noticed Leroy was getting more and more distant. Leroy was spending all of his time with West—not Chloe—and when Leroy suffered a ministroke because of the cancer in 1996, Leroy forbid his wife from visiting him at a temporary inpatient care facility.

"Brookey spent day and night there," Chloe said. "He asked me to please not show up, and I'd show up anyway, and he really didn't like it. Finally, he got so mad at me that he just screamed and yelled at me for coming."

Still, Chloe loved her husband, and she assigned his

meanness to his disease. It wasn't until several weeks later, on February 26, 1996, that Leroy's dark side emerged in full fury.

On that day, Chloe was organizing the couple's finances, and she asked West about the whereabouts of six titles to vehicles owned by Leroy and Chloe Smith. West informed her the titles were probably at a San Jose apartment Leroy was using in between chemotherapy treatments. Chloe and West drove to the residence to get the titles, and they found Leroy resting in bed. Chloe and West then started looking for the vehicle titles, all the while trying not to wake Leroy.

"I was trying to get paperwork together," Chloe said. "I was trying to pay a couple of bills, and I was trying to get everything in line. So Brooke told me she thought her dad had brought some stuff to the apartment, and maybe it would be there. She said, 'I think I saw my dad sticking a box under the bed.'"

Chloe walked to the bed Leroy was sleeping on, got down on her knees to search under it, and within seconds heard a large crackling sound behind her. The noise sounded like a bug zapper.

"Brooke came up behind me with a stun gun," Chloe said. "I was under the bed, and she tried to hit me with it. It was one of those real powerful ones, like 200,000 volts or whatever. She tried to hit me on the side of the neck, but for some reason she didn't get me. She got the bed covers. I knew the sound, and I pulled out from under the bed. I turned around and said, 'What the hell are you doing?'"

Leroy sprang up in bed and started screaming in a bloodcurdling pitch.

"You troublemaking bitch!" he said. "This is all your fault!"

Chloe darted for the door like a deer. Her head spinning from fright, she scampered down a flight of stairs and into the apartment complex parking lot, where she called the police on her cell phone. West was trailing her, screaming at her in a rage.

"She had her hand behind her back, and I'm on the phone talking to 911, telling them, 'I think they are going to kill me,'" Chloe said. "Brookey's yelling at me, 'You troublemaking bitch! Get off that phone! You are nothing but a troublemaking bitch!' Just before the police got there, she [West] jumped in her car and drove off with the stun gun."

The San Jose police believed Chloe Smith's account, but they had no evidence to make an arrest. West and the stun gun were already gone, and Leroy told the police his wife was lying about the entire incident.

"Leroy came out and told the police it was all a big lie, and he said no one tried to hurt me," Chloe recalled.

"The police told me I ought to start carrying a gun," she said. "Can you imagine?"

To this day, Chloe Smith is convinced West was trying to murder her. West, she suspects, wanted to kill her so she would be able to take control of her father's assets after he died.

But there was a bigger prize, too. An insurance policy Chloe took out at work dictated that if she died before her husband, Leroy stood to inherit about $250,000.

"If I had predeceased him at that time, I had about a quarter million dollars worth of life insurance," Chloe said. "So if I died, she [West] would have been next in line for that, and Leroy knew this.

"I think she would have killed me," Chloe said. "What was she going to do, stun me, let me lie on the floor and say, 'Gee, I'm sorry, it was a mistake?'

"Just another body," she said. "I don't know what makes her tick."

Leroy Smith died from brain cancer in Los Banos two months later.

MOTHER

35

Las Vegas is a city of last chance—a place where the nation's rebels, misfits and downtrodden come for salvation from financial ruin, a broken marriage or a life filled with mistakes. Vegas offers a fresh start, a new beginning, a chance at being a born-again American.

At least that is what one is led to believe.

The reality of the city, however, is far different from the reputation. Vegas can be a cold, hard place for the undisciplined. Drinking, drugging and gambling can quickly lead to homelessness, and most who end up on the city's streets rarely escape its death grip.

There is no better demonstration of this than the leagues of homeless men who line Bonanza Road in the downtown corridor of the city every morning. Unshaven and dirty, they stand on the street corners and flag down pickups in the hope they can land a few hours of manual labor in the valley's construction industry. The jobs usually pay for another beer, another hit of methamphetamine, a nightly stay at a weekly rent motel, or a few more minutes on the gaming tables. America's city of last chance—a repetitive, des-

perate cycle of substance abuse, sin, poverty and lonely
death.

Christine Merle Smith got her last chance in life in 1997, at
the age of sixty-five, when her daughter, Brookey Lee
West, drove her to Las Vegas and set her up at an apartment
complex on Sahara Avenue known as the Orange Door
apartments. The two-story, low-income flats sit just west of
Interstate 15 in a once classic Vegas neighborhood long
ago destroyed by poverty and gangbangers. Christine,
however, had no reservations about living at the Orange
Door apartments. In fact, she thrived there, and she quickly
became close friends with several of her neighbors. One
was Alice Wilsey, a sweet-hearted, sixty-six-year-old Utah
native who worked as a bookkeeper at the 7-Eleven convenience store headquarters for Las Vegas. Out of kindness,
Wilsey served as Christine's caretaker at the Orange Door.
She made sure Christine had food, she took her to the bank
to use the ATM and she took her to run basic errands for
prescriptions or medical appointments.

"We were good friends, and I looked out for her when
her daughter Brooke was in California," Wilsey said.
"Christine had a very serious case of osteoporosis. She was
kind of bent over, and it caused her abdominal pain. Christine also had a hard time taking a shower. She had to have
a shower seat . . . and she couldn't remember my phone
number. She couldn't even remember her own address. I'm
pretty sure she was getting Alzheimer's."

Another woman who Christine befriended at the Orange Door apartments was Judy Chang, seventy-four. The
white-haired woman with a soft voice and an even softer
temperament was born in Illinois but lived much of her life
in Texas, and she became friends with Christine in short
order.

"Christine was a lot of fun," Chang said. "Our day would start at seven thirty to eight a.m. Christine would come and look in my apartment window, looking to see if I was up yet so I could come out and sit and talk. Her daughter would be out in California, and she would be in her little apartment all alone, and she would get bored. So we would go out by the pool (of the apartments) and we would have lunch out there, and we'd sit out there all day long."

Christine told Chang and Wilsey her daughter was a technical writer in San Jose, and her son, Travis, was homeless in the Bay Area.

"She told me that he was a street person, that he was an alcoholic, that he drank a lot, and he didn't have a place to live," Wilsey said. "He apparently took drugs, as well."

Christine was a conservative Pentecostal, she said, and she prayed daily to a wood-burned picture of Jesus on the wall of her apartment.

"Sometimes she would break into a strange voice, and she would talk in this thick tongue, and you couldn't understand what she was saying," Chang said. "It would go on for a few minutes, and then it would be over, and she'd say the Holy Ghost got her."

Christine also bragged to her friends about her Indian heritage—even though she was white—and she bragged that she was once on death row for shooting a man. She said she escaped the electric chair in Texas when her victim didn't die.

"It was one of the first things she told me," Wilsey said. "Chris loved to tell this story. It was a big thing in her life."

Chang recalled, "She told me she was on death row in the penitentiary, and I said, 'Well, what happened?' She said she had shot a man, and I said, 'You shot a man? What did you do that for?' And she said, 'Oh, well, he was acting the fool.' I was thinking, 'You don't get on death row unless the person died.'"

Around the same time that they met Christine, Wilsey and Chang also met Christine's daughter, and they both liked West. West stayed at her mother's apartment every few weeks in between her commutes to work in San Jose, and in late 1997 West moved into her mother's apartment.

"I understood they both loved each other very much," Wilsey said. "They showed me a picture of Brooke always taking care of her mother and giving her mother things. But later on, I discovered that wasn't true."

West often took Chang out to lunch or dinner, and she occasionally studied tarot cards with Wilsey.

"Brooke was very good at the tarot cards," Wilsey said. "Excellent. She was an excellent reader. And I know a little bit about it because I have tried some of it. I have a tarot card program on my computer, and every time Brooke would come over, she'd want me to read the cards for her. But I'm not really versed in it like Brooke was.

"Brooke is really psychic," Chang said. "She believed in it, and her mother told me Brooke once helped the cops in California find a little girl who was kidnapped and molested. This child was hidden away in some guy's garage, and Christine said Brooke helped the police find her."

Near the end of 1997, West and Wilsey took Christine to a pet store in Las Vegas to get a dog, and Christine picked out a little brown Chihuahua she named Chi Chi. Chi Chi followed Christine everywhere over the next several months, and the dog became the most cherished thing in Christine's existence.

"He was so sweet, and I know Christine loved that dog," Wilsey said.

But a couple of months later, sometime in January or February of 1998, Judy Chang visited Christine at her apartment, and when she arrived, she found Christine on the tail end of a bitter argument with her daughter over Chi Chi.

"Christine was on the couch, and she had her little bitsy

dog, and Brooke was [on the phone] trying to give her dog to somebody," Chang said. "Christine said, 'No! You are not giving my Chi Chi away!' And Brooke looked at her kind of funny. I said a few words to Chris, and then I said, 'Okay, Chris, I'm going to go ahead and go. I'll see you in a couple of days.'"

Alice Wilsey had a similar odd encounter with West and Christine around the same time. She stopped by Christine's apartment and found her in bed, and it appeared to Wilsey that Christine was very ill.

"She was not able to get out of bed alone by herself," Wilsey said. "She was sort of—, almost like she was drugged, or she was just extremely tired. I saw Brooke give her what she said was aspirin twice. Chris had to go to the restroom, and so I helped her to the restroom. It was an ordeal because she just couldn't [move] by herself. I have no idea what her illness was at that time, but she appeared to be ill."

Two days later, Chang went back to Christine's apartment, and West said her mother had suddenly moved to San Jose to live with her brother, Travis.

"I said, 'Hi, where's Chris?'" Chang recalled. "Brooke said, 'Oh, I took her to my brother's to stay.' Brooke said, 'I gave her three choices. She either goes to a home for older people, she goes to my brother's, or I'm leaving and I'm not coming back anymore.'"

West told Chang she gave her mother about an hour in the middle of the night to decide whether she wanted to live with her brother, reside in the old folks home or never see her again. According to West, Christine decided to go live with Travis, a person Chang and Wilsey knew to be a street person.

"So she [West] said, 'I just jumped up and got some bags and started throwing Christine's belongings in a bag,'" Chang said, quoting West.

West went on to say that she drove Christine to West's brother's house in San Jose in the middle of the night.

"She told her mother, 'We're going right now,' " Chang quoted West as saying.

" 'Well, can't we wait until the morning?' Christine said," Chang recalled.

" 'No, I don't want you to change your mind,' " West said she told her mother. "So she grabbed up the bags and things and left with her.

"She didn't even stop to say good-bye," Chang said. "That wasn't like Christine."

Wilsey got a similar story from West. Christine, West claimed, went to live with her homeless son.

"I saw Brooke, and she said that she had taken her mother in the middle of the night. She had packed up her mother and took her to San Jose," Wilsey said. "She said that her mother was staying with Christine's son, Travis, and he had a girlfriend. She moved Christine into the apartment with Travis and his girlfriend."

Christine Smith was never seen alive again.

Natalie Hanke was working as a technical writing supervisor for a Silicon Valley computer company called Hybrid Networks in 1997 when Brookey Lee West applied for a job at the company, and almost immediately Hanke was impressed with West's resume, intellect and talent.

"I hired Brooke, and I got to know her on a daily basis," Hanke said. "We worked together, and I enjoyed Brooke's company. She's very bright, and she's fun."

Hanke, an attractive forty-year-old woman with blond hair, struck up a casual friendship with West, and during the next three years Hanke became one of the few people who ever really got to know West. She and West occasionally went to dinner after work or talked once or twice a week on the phone, and during their conversations, West confided in Hanke some of the most intimate details of her life.

"She admitted to me that she was on some medication, that she was manic-depressive, and sometimes she got a little moody," Hanke said.

"Her mother was quite strange, from everything I heard at the time," Hanke said. "[West] was raised by people who walked around with shotguns."

"She said her mom was a Satan worshipper and that her mom was crazy," Hanke said. "Brooke had told me such horrific stories about her childhood that they just tore my heart out. It just made me think, 'Jeez, this is one of those times in your life where you meet someone who needs a hand, so you give them a hand.'"

Hanke sort of felt sorry for West given her turbulent childhood, and at the same time she saw West as an extremely talented woman. West was personable and clever, and she was very good at taking complex information about computers and condensing it into manuals people could understand. The talents landed West jobs at some of the Silicon Valley's highest-paying computer companies, including Cisco and Hybrid.

"She was so good at this job, and so many people are not," Hanke said. "You have to have a detail-oriented mind, a disciplined mind, and you have to be very bright. She is all that."

But despite West's talents, she never seemed to reach her potential. She wore worn-out clothes to work even though she was making $60 to $70 an hour, and she could be abrasive. Many of West's coworkers labeled her "strange," and they avoided her. In 1997, the workplace strangeness culminated in West disappearing from her job at Hybrid without calling anyone. Fearing the worst, Hanke filed a missing persons report with the sheriff's department in Santa Clara County.

"I had no idea where she was," Hanke said. "I didn't know if she'd been kidnapped or what."

The police called Hanke a few days later to let her know West was safe, and within a few more days Hanke learned West had checked herself into the psychiatric wing of the Veterans Administration hospital in Las Vegas.

"She had a problem with her medication, and I guess she had some sort of episodic event, which caused her to be in the hospital for a month or so," Hanke said. "We sent her a beautiful bouquet of flowers that said, 'Get well soon.' I told people at work she got in a car accident and she's in the hospital. I thought it was stress induced."

After West got out of the hospital, she seemed even more willing to talk to Hanke about her past, and she started to reveal her deepest, darkest secrets. She detailed for Hanke the shoplifting scams West carried out with her mother.

"She told me about this big burglary ring where you'd go and you'd steal a bunch of clothes professionally," Hanke said. "She said she had been arrested for over $100,000 worth of stealing in Los Angeles."

West told Hanke she possessed special psychic powers.

"She can hold an object and tell you who owned it or what have you," Hanke said. "And she actually did that for me once. She's never been to my parents' house, and yet she described my parents' living room and this china cabinet where this sugar bowl [was]. So, you know, it was something interesting to me. I make no judgment."

West said her dad was a witch, and he handed down the craft to his daughter.

"She said, 'It's historical—my family's been in witchcraft for generations,'" Hanke recalled.

"She said her dad was a very powerful warlock, and that he was the source of her psychic power. Her dad would do incantations, and her dad would put evil hexes on people.

She said he taught her spells, and he taught her hexes, and she also said he's extremely dangerous when crossed."

West went on to reveal that her husband, Howard Simon St. John, was a murder victim.

"I said, 'Oh, come on, Brooke. You didn't have anything to do with that,' " Hanke said. "And she said, 'Um, well, I won't say that I wouldn't have done it. Someone beat me to it.' "

But of all the strange things West told Hanke, the thing that stuck out in Hanke's mind was the way West talked about her own mother. West, it seemed, hated her mother. She constantly vented to Hanke during their phone calls about financial problems her mother was causing her, and she repeatedly said her mother was a "psychopath" who couldn't be trusted.

"Increasing problems with her mom," Hanke said. "It was a regular event. Every phone call . . . it was her mom was crazy, a sociopath, and all this stuff. And I said, 'Well, Brooke, you know, you moved into your mom's place. Why don't you just leave?' And she said, no, her mom should be the one to leave. She's crazy like her brother, [Travis]. She said her brother was a sociopath, and she was gonna send her mother to go live with her brother.

"It was a love-hate thing with her mother," Hanke said. "It seemed like a thing of dominance. There was a need to dominate her mother. Somewhere, psychologically along the way, she had been damaged by her mother."

36

In mid-February of 1998—just two days after Christine Smith disappeared from the Orange Door apartments—Alice Wilsey was walking through the courtyard of the apartments when she saw a homeless man pulling a blanket out of a Dumpster. It was a blanket Wilsey immediately recognized as Christine's, one she had given Christine as a gift.

"It was a green blanket that I had given to Christine, and I saw a street person take that very blanket out of our Dumpster and walk away," Wilsey said.

Seeing the blanket in the trash made Wilsey suspicious. It certainly didn't seem likely that Christine would have just thrown it in the trash before departing to San Jose, and Wilsey was starting to doubt Brookey Lee West's story that Christine had moved to live with West's homeless brother.

"A lot of what she told us just didn't make sense," Wilsey said. "I was thinking about the possibility of foul play."

That same day, Wilsey went to Christine's old apartment and encountered West cleaning. Wilsey noticed

Christine's white scarf was still in the apartment, her painting of Jesus still on the wall.

"She wore [the scarf] even in the summertime," Wilsey said. "The painting—she almost worshipped it. The face of Christ. Christine would have never left that picture behind."

West then offered to give Wilsey all her mother's groceries.

"I said, 'What if Chris comes back?' " Wilsey recalled. " 'Isn't she gonna want these things?' "

"Well, she's not gonna come back," West told Wilsey.

"How do you know?" Wilsey asked.

"Because I threatened to put her in a home if she comes back," West said.

Wilsey wasn't the only one suspicious of West's story. A few days after Christine's middle-of-the-night departure, Chang visited Christine's old apartment, and she, too, noticed Christine's most cherished possessions still in the apartment. Among them were Christine's arts and crafts and a set of handmade dolls Christine had showed off to her friends.

"I looked way up on a shelf, and I saw a little bitsy box, and there was a ring in that box," Chang said. "It was a ring that I saw Chris wear the first time I met her. It looked like an opal stone and a turquoise stone."

Chang asked why Christine's ring was still in the apartment if she'd moved to San Jose to live with her son.

"That wasn't my mother's ring," West said. "I asked her so many times where it was, and she couldn't remember where she put it."

Chang asked West how Christine was doing.

"She said, 'Oh, she's doing fine,' " Chang recalled. "She said they [Christine and Travis] were talking about moving to Bakersfield."

In the fall of 1998, another incident unfolded that made Wilsey even more suspicious. Wilsey and West were using

Wilsey's tarot card computer program, and Wilsey decided to call up tarot cards on the computer screen while she thought of Christine.

The first card?

Death card.

The second card?

Death card.

The third card?

Death card.

The fourth card?

Death card.

Four death cards in a row.

"I read the tarot cards in my computer for Chris, with Chris in mind when I did it, and every time, the death card came up," Wilsey said. "I told that to Brooke, and Brooke said, 'What?' She tried to show that she didn't believe it."

By November 11, 1998, Wilsey decided to tell the police about her suspicions that West had murdered her mother. Wilsey sat down at her computer and wrote a lengthy letter to police detailing all the odd circumstances surrounding Christine's supposed trip to San Jose to live with her homeless son. In it, she wrote:

I am concerned about the possible demise of Christine M. Smith, born Feb. 15, 1932, in El Paso, Texas. Christine and her wonderful dog are gone. I have many reasons to disbelieve the story that Christine is with her son:

1—Her son is an alcoholic, a heavy drug user and is a street person.

2—Since Christine has been gone, I have discovered that some of her treasured things are still with West.

3—Christine was heavy into religion and had a picture of Jesus Christ. That picture is now in the possession of West.

4—West threw away many of Christine's things.

5—*No one in the neighborhood has talked to Christine since the day she left.*

6—*West said that Christine has called her a few times and said to say hello to her friends. I don't believe her.*

I have discovered that West has times when she is violent in nature because of her mental disability. Since her doctor told her that she must get away from her mother, I feel that she killed her mother in a rage and left her someplace where she wouldn't be found.

Is it possible to check Christine's doctor and bank accounts to see if they are still being used? If her Social Security is still being deposited in her account, and if so, what location is the money being taken from? West has access to Christine's account as she helped her set it up. I believe it is with Nevada State Bank.

My name is Alice Kay Wilsey and I live at the Orange Door apartments. I would appreciate it if West would not be told about the possible investigation as she would know who is responsible for the inquiry. If she did dispose of her mother, my life would be in danger.

Wilsey printed out the letter and drove to the Las Vegas police substation on Fourth Street in downtown Las Vegas. Wilsey asked to see a detective, but the detectives were unavailable, and Wilsey was asked to return a few days later.

Wilsey left the police station with the letter in hand, but she never went back because she doubted whether the police would believe her. She also questioned whether her suspicions about West were accurate.

Christine spent the next twenty-seven months rotting in a garbage can at the Canyon Gate Mini Storage on West Sahara Avenue.

* * *

In 1998, Brookey Lee West announced to her friend Natalie Hanke that she had finally solved the biggest dilemma of her life—what to do with her pain-in-the-ass mother.

"She said she had sent her mother away to live with her brother," Hanke said. "She said, 'They deserve each other.'"

Over the next three years, West called Hanke on the phone several times, and during many of those calls West told Hanke her mother was living with her brother, Travis, in San Jose. In one call that Hanke remembers well, "She said she had just gotten off the phone with her mother, and her mother was driving her crazy," Hanke said. "Her mother needs some money, and she needs money a lot. She goes, 'Natalie, I can't visit them. I can't stand being around them.'"

Hanke said there was nothing in West's tone or demeanor to suggest what was really going on—that her mother was already dead.

"There was nothing at all," Hanke said. "She acted as if her mother was alive and well."

In 1998, West attended Hanke's fortieth birthday party at a local restaurant in Foster City, California, and during the party, West produced an expensive birthday present. It was a small box containing a diamond ring, and to Hanke, the ring looked like it had been worn before.

"She made a big speech about what a great friend I was," Hanke said. "The only person who ever gave anything to her without expecting anything in return. It was obviously a ring that had been worn, and it was just inappropriate all the way around.

"I tried to give the ring back to her the next day, and a week later, and a month later, and she said no each time," Hanke said.

Hanke started to suspect the ring belonged to West's mother, and she persisted in trying to give back the gift.

"Finally, she goes, 'Natalie, that ring is possessed. I don't want anything to do with it,'" Hanke said.

"I said, 'Well, why did you give me a ring that's possessed?' " Hanke said.

"Well, it's only possessed for me," West said.

Months later, in 1998, Hanke went on vacation in Las Vegas, and during the trip Hanke agreed to get together with West to see how she was doing. As soon as Hanke arrived, West insisted Hanke come visit her mother's old apartment at the Orange Door. The apartment was small and cramped, and Hanke immediately noticed the residence was decorated with dark, occult-themed artwork and statues.

There was a disturbing gargoyle statue inside, and a bloodied picture of Christ on the wall.

"There was a religious painting, and it looked like it had been stolen from a church or something," Hanke said. "Christ on the cross. And it looked to me like blood had been added to it. I remember animal bones being on a table there, and there was just this feeling of weirdness. Books on Satan [and] witchcraft. I said, 'That's a little weird, Brooke,' " Hanke recalled. " 'Why do you have animal bones in your living room?' "Oh, that's my mom," West responded. "She's crazy. She reads them or something."

Hanke felt like she needed to leave the apartment as soon as possible, so she faked illness and rushed back to her hotel room. She was freaked out by the incident and decided to slowly distance herself from West, but there was one more time when Hanke ran into her.

In 1999, Hanke happened to return to Las Vegas on another vacation, and she reluctantly agreed to meet with West again. But this time, she made it clear that she had no intentions of going back to West's apartment. Instead, she met West for lunch, and during the meal at a Strip casino, West told Hanke she had a new boyfriend named David.*

"She looked at me in this very strange way, which I've never forgotten, and [she said], 'David and I want you to come to the storage locker,' " Hanke recalled.

Hanke said the invitation seemed extremely strange. It was a hot summer day in Vegas, and no one in her right mind would head out to a storage shed unless they absolutely had to.

"It's like 110 degrees out, and she's trying to get me to go to the storage locker," Hanke said.

"My gut instinct was like, 'No, this isn't going to happen.'"

Hanke believes West was plotting to kill her and steal her identity.

"I don't know for certain that she was going to do me in, but nothing else seems to make sense given the patterns of behavior and given that she wanted me to go to the storage locker," Hanke said. "Especially now [it makes sense] because I know that her dead mother was in that storage locker. She had already been decomposing for a year or two."

37

Any professional gambler in Vegas will tell you that good luck comes in streaks. When the good luck comes, you ride it like a wave, but when the good luck goes bad, you never ride it out. You pocket your chips and run for the casino door as quickly as you can.

Up until 2001, Brookey Lee West's good luck streak was especially long. In 1985, she'd been in an explosive custody dispute that ended with her boyfriend's grandmother being shot in the chest.

No one ever suspected West or her father in the shooting.

That same year, she was arrested for felony theft in a shoplifting scam with her mother, and the two got off with probation.

In 1994, West was the prime suspect in the killing of her husband in Tulare County, but she was never charged.

And in 1996, she was suspected of using a stun gun on her mother in law in San Jose.

Again, she was never charged.

It was a hell of a run.

But on February 8, 2001, West's luck officially went

cold, and there was no more running away from her
mother's murder.

"We felt like we had a case, so I decided I was going to
go ahead and arrest her in the death of her mother," Las Vegas homicide detective Dave Mesinar said.

To Mesinar, the evidence supporting West's arrest on a
murder charge was overwhelming. Christine Smith's body
was in a garbage can in a storage shed rented in West's
name; a search of West's apartment had turned up a key
matching the lock on the storage shed on the door of unit
#317 at Canyon Gate; financial records from West's apart-
ment indicated West's mother was continuing to receive
Social Security checks long after she was dead; and the
checks were being direct deposited into an active bank account that West had access to.

But to arrest West, Mesinar had to find her. He started
his search by telling all of West's neighbors at the San
Croix condominiums—where West now lived—to be on
the lookout for her. One of West's neighbors there called
Mesinar on the night of February 8 and told him she was
back at her apartment. Mesinar raced back to the condo-
minium complex, but he was just minutes late. West had
apparently discovered a business card left by the homicide
detective on her front door, and she fled.

Mesinar started to drive back home, and within a mile
or two he got an extremely lucky break. He stumbled
across West's pickup in a convenience store parking lot on
Rainbow Boulevard.

"Dumb luck," Mesinar said. "We knew what kind of
truck she had, we had the license plate number, and there
it was, parked in front of a 7-Eleven at Rainbow Boulevard and Sahara Avenue. I was like, 'Oh, my god, I see
her in there. She's buying a cup of coffee.' I waited until
she came out, and then I called in the black-and-whites to
stop her."

Patrol units stopped West's pickup on Rainbow Boulevard in Las Vegas. West got out of her car, was handcuffed and was driven to the Las Vegas police Homicide Detail on West Charleston Boulevard.

Mesinar then called Sergeant Kevin Manning, and the two met up just before midnight at the office to confront West about killing her mother.

Manning quickly took notice of how normal looking their suspect was.

"Nothing unique about her, and nothing sinister," Manning said. "The type of person you'd pass on the street and you'd never even take notice of. She looked normal. But to us, that is not what matters. It is what you can't see that is significant. It's not the outward package.

"We brought her into an interview room. I had a tape recorder, and I told her about her Miranda rights," Mesinar said. "Sergeant Manning was there, along with myself, and she appeared calm. Very matter of fact. The first thing I did was tell her that her mother was dead. For all I know, I don't even know if she knew, but when I told her, all she said was, 'My mother died a natural death, and I want to talk to an attorney.' We were in the room just a minute."

West's response to the news that her mother was dead was very telling. West wasn't stunned with shock when told her mother was in a garbage can, she wasn't teary eyed, and she wasn't outraged. It was clear to the detectives that West already knew her mother was dead.

"There was never, ever any signs of grieving," Manning said. "There was never any kind of feeling of loss."

There would be no lengthy statement to police like the one given to Tulare County homicide detective Daniel Haynes in the slaying of Howard Simon St. John. This time, West was silent.

"I think she realized things were not good for her," Manning said.

West was led in handcuffs to Manning's sport utility vehicle and then driven to the Clark County Detention Center in downtown Las Vegas for booking on a murder charge. During the brief, ten-minute drive, West asked Manning how she could take care of an outstanding traffic ticket.

"She had a traffic ticket, she was going to court and she was worried about a warrant being issued for this traffic ticket," Manning said.

"I told her, 'That's the least of your worries,'" Manning said.

"I've got nothing to worry about," West said.

38

On February 9, 2001, the television news stations in Las Vegas were in a frenzy over the arrest of Brookey Lee West. All of the three local stations in Vegas led their broadcasts with stories about the woman charged with murdering her mother and stuffing her in a can to rot.

"Is it a murder mystery now solved, or the most bizarre sort of burial?" a gorgeous blond news anchor asked on television station KVBC Channel 3.

In the story dubbed "Mini Storage Murder," Channel 3 reporter Kim Capozzo aired the first interview with the suspected killer at the Clark County detention center. West looked pale and heavy on television—she was at least forty pounds overweight—and her brown hair was cut short at the shoulders.

"At most, I'm guilty of not reporting my mother's death," West told the reporter through a Plexiglas window at the jail.

"You put your mother in the storage shed?" Capozzo asked.

"I did," West said.

"But you did not murder her?" Capozzo asked.

"That's correct."

"My mother wasn't murdered at all," West told journalist Cindy Cesare of KLAS Channel 8 television station. "My mother died of natural causes."

"Why didn't you bury her?" Cesare asked.

"These are some very interesting answers that people would like to have," West said. "They will get them, but I can't give them to you in this particular filming because this is stuff I have to give to my attorney."

Las Vegas homicide detective Dave Mesinar watched the television interviews with glee. West was squawking before she'd been appointed an attorney, and in the interviews she admitted she put her mother in the storage shed. The admission made Mesinar's job much easier because he no longer had to investigate other possible suspects.

"She still never said, 'Oh, my god, my mother's dead,'" Mesinar said. "There was no emotion at all, and I'm thinking, 'This lady killed her mother.' It was valuable to me just to see her nonreactions and her nonemotions on TV. I honestly think she was enjoying the attention."

Hours later, Mesinar got another surprise. His phone rang, and on the line was former Tulare County homicide detective Daniel Haynes, who now worked for the Porterville, California, police department. Haynes heard about West's arrest from his former partner, Herman Martinez, and he called Mesinar to let him know about Howard Simon St. John's murder.

"My thoughts?" Haynes said. "I wasn't surprised, and honestly I was relieved. At least she was caught for something.

"They weren't aware of Howard's murder, so I said, 'Man, have I got a story to tell you,'" Haynes recalled. "I said, 'Here's the case number, here's your contacts, and you are going to be quite pleased to find a lot of your background work is already done for you.' "

St. John's murder, the shooting of Ray Alcantar's grandmother in Palo Alto, the stun gun attack on Chloe Smith, West's missing brother and the details of West's crazy family were all valuable facts for Mesinar because it reaffirmed his belief that West was capable of killing.

"It showed me Brooke has some deep-rooted psychological problems, and that she is unstable," Mesinar said. "She isn't all there."

One particular fact from St. John's murder captivated Mesinar. St. John was found in the Sequoia National Forest with a plastic bag partially on his face. Christine had a bag tied tightly on her face, and Mesinar was optimistic the details of the bag on St. John's face could be used against West in a Las Vegas courtroom.

"We had similarities with plastic bags around or near their heads," Mesinar said. "There has got to be some significance to that."

Mesinar and another homicide detective, Darlene Falvey, traveled to Los Banos and interviewed all of West's old neighbors. With the help of Nevada prosecutor Frank Coumou, they tracked down Natalie Hanke, they interviewed West's stepmother, Chloe Smith, and they tracked down Christine's neighbors at the Orange Door, Judy Chang and Alice Wilsey.

"Brooke told everyone her mom was in California living with her brother, so we decided we had to try and find her brother, Travis," Mesinar said.

Mesinar, Falvey and Clark County district attorney's office investigators Pat Malone and Pete Baldonado spent weeks looking for Travis Smith, but like Haynes, they never found him.

"We checked the welfare rolls in California," Mesinar said. "We got Travis' prints from the FBI, and we sent

them to all the coroner's offices with unidentified dead
bodies. We never found him. We put in hours and hours
looking for him, and all we came up with were dead ends
everywhere we looked."

There was, however, one fascinating clue uncovered
during the search for Travis. Around the time Travis was
last seen alive, West wrote a letter to the Social Security
Administration asking the agency to deposit her brother's
Social Security checks in a bank account West had access
to. Mesinar considered the possibility that West had murdered her mother, her husband and her brother, and if that
was true, he'd apprehended a female serial killer.

"The more we dig, the more people we find who are
shot, killed or missing," Mesinar said. "At some point, it
becomes more than a coincidence."

But despite the suspicions, Mesinar still had one major
problem with his case against West. West was claiming her
mother died a natural death, so Mesinar went to Clark
County medical examiner Gary Telgenhoff to affirm Telgenhoff's suspicions that Christine Smith was murdered.
Telgenhoff, however, shocked Mesinar, telling him the
cause of death for Christine was undetermined—not murder. The medical examiner decided Christine's body was
too decomposed to determine a cause of death.

"I didn't make the decision lightly," Telgenhoff said. "I
agonized over this. I stayed up at night, and I thought about
it a lot. But if I was going to say she was murdered, then I
could envision three other pathologists questioning the decision," Telgenhoff said. "They would say, 'On which basis
did you decide she was killed?'

"I could say she was in a garbage can and she had a
plastic bag around her mouth," Telgenhoff said. And then
they would say, 'Yeah, but what was the mechanism that
killed her? Demonstrate that to me.' And I couldn't. There
was nothing left of her body to see. No marks. No hemor-

rhages. No bruises were left. There were no bullets or stab wounds.

"I could see myself being on *60 Minutes* when it comes out later that somebody else killed her, and this woman [West] didn't know what had happened; then I'm out there with my dick in the wind," Telgenhoff said. "I didn't make a lot of friends in the police department that day."

Mesinar was mortified. The detective's seemingly solid case now had a huge, gaping hole in it, and if the county's medical examiner couldn't say Christine Smith was murdered, how could a jury?

39

Justice, and only justice, you shall pursue.

—The Bible

Clark County prosecutor Frank Coumou was taught early on in life that rules were made to be followed—not broken. He was born to an authoritative Dutch ship captain named Bram Coumou, who demanded his children always respect the rules.

"With my dad the captain of a ship, you just didn't question him," Coumou said.

A prosecutor in Las Vegas for thirteen years, Coumou was also taught another very important life lesson as a child—respect your mother. The lesson was driven home to Coumou as a child growing up in South America's Dutch Guiana, which is now called Suriname. Suriname and its dense jungle landscape was a stopping point on Bram Coumou's shipping route, and settling his family there allowed the cargo ship captain to see his wife and children once a week or so. But when Bram Coumou was out to sea, the Coumou family paid a price. The Coumous, who are white, were targeted by the country's black majority.

"My mom went through hell because, when my father was away, we had bad things happen to us," Coumou said. "Our house was totally burglarized. One time we came home, and someone had broken in and defecated inside the house. Another time, our car was turned over. They were trying to get us to leave."

The experience left Coumou with a profound respect for his mother's courage, and he never forgot how she got the family through those difficult times.

"Your mother is someone you treat with respect and dignity—not put in a garbage can," Coumou said.

Coumou was assigned to prosecute the case of Brookey Lee West in February of 2001, and he was horrified by the crime.

"I remember going back to my office with the case file, going through it, and then I got to the pictures," Coumou said. "When I saw the pictures of Christine in that can and how her body had liquefied, I was shocked. It was gross and nasty, and then there was a plastic bag tied over her face. It was like the night of the living dead. Who does that to her own mother?

"You are charging the daughter with killing the mom, stuffing her in the garbage can and taking great efforts to seal the garbage can with the duct tape," Coumou said. "Then the body is stored with all these books about Satanism and witchcraft, and I was like, 'Whoa, this is not the gangbanger shooting the gangbanger. This is something way different.'"

Coumou was assigned to prosecute West with veteran prosecutor Scott Mitchell of the Clark County district attorney's office. Mitchell is a quiet, reserved father of seven and a bishop in the Church of Jesus Christ of Latter-day Saints, and when he reviewed the contents of the West case file and the details of Howard Simon St. John's slaying, he saw an obvious pattern in West's behavior. Instead of just separating herself from the people who became problems in her life, West killed them like a black widow preying on her bloodline.

"Howard Simon St. John became inconvenient to Brookey West," Mitchell said. "He appeared to be a weight around her neck. He was someone who couldn't support her or himself, he was threatening to squeal on the insurance fraud, so it appeared to me that she took his life.

"It looked like that is what happened here in Las Vegas with her mother, too," Mitchell said. "Her mother became a weight around her neck. She didn't want to be making trips back and forth from Las Vegas to San Jose, so to rid her life of one more inconvenience, she took her life.

"And it appeared that she did the same thing with the brother, although we can't prove that because we never found the brother," Mitchell said. "But the suggestion was there that he met the same fate, and that he disappeared off the face of the earth.

"We are probably dealing with a serial killer, and we are only scratching the surface," Coumou said. "Everywhere she goes, people turn up dead or missing, and I think she got caught because she got sloppy. I think she got caught because she killed somebody who was too close to home, and she couldn't cover up for that one."

After receiving the case file, Coumou set out to determine whether Christine Smith's Social Security checks were a motive for her slaying. Social Security records showed that in December 1997, just two months before she disappeared, Christine asked the Social Security Administration to begin depositing her checks directly into a Nevada State Bank account. Although West was not named on the account, prosecutors learned from Christine's friends at the Orange Door that West helped her mother establish the account. This, the prosecutors believe, allowed West to learn the account's personal identification number.

Coumou charted the Social Security deposits to Christine's bank accounts after Christine was last seen alive, and he charted the withdrawals as well. The financial records showed $1,000-a-month deposits were being made from 1998, when Christine disappeared, until the discovery of her body in 2001, and throughout those years, more than two dozen withdrawals were repeatedly made at ATMs where no video surveillance was in place. Most of the withdrawals were made in San Jose or Las Vegas, and an examination of West's banking records showed withdrawals were often made from her accounts at the same time from the same ATM machines.

Coumou and Mesinar were unable to say definitely that West made the withdrawals from her mother's account, but such a scenario certainly seemed likely.

"This woman was decomposed and in a garbage can, so it's obviously impossible for Christine to be going to all these areas and withdrawing the money from her account," Coumou said. "I think Brooke thought she was entitled to the money. In her mind, she thinks, 'I still have mom, and nobody is ever going to find out about it.' She thought she was going to get away with it. No one was asking any questions for three years, and that money kept on getting deposited, so she kept spending it."

Coumou also pursued the possibility that the method of death for Christine was part of a Satanic ritual. The premise was based on the books found at the crime scene, and it was only furthered by the letter sent to Ray Alcantar by West's father days after Alcantar's grandmother was shot in Palo Alto.

Coumou meticulously scoured through *The Satanic Bible* and *The Geography of Witchcraft* in search of a reference to killing someone and tying a bag tightly over his face. He found vague reference to killing victims and keeping them from telling secrets in the afterlife. Coumou believes there was a connection between Satanism and the way Christine's body was disposed of.

"If you read *The Satanic Bible*, it talks a lot about doing things to people who have wronged you," Coumou said. "Maybe West thought in her mind, 'My mother has kept me trapped all my life.' I don't think it is too far-fetched."

Mitchell and Coumou ultimately decided, however, not to pursue the Satanic angle at West's murder trial, because they worried if they were to get a murder conviction of West, the Nevada Supreme Court would find the Satanism theory too inflammatory and overturn West's conviction.

"I stayed away from it because I didn't want the media spectacle, with headlines about Satanism and witchcraft, and then have it blow up in my face later," Coumou said. "Ultimately, that is not the only motivating factor as to why she killed her mother, either. She killed Christine because she hated her mom and she wanted to get rid of her."

The prosecutors felt they had a strong case. There was no disputing West put her mother in the can—she'd already admitted it; she had a financial motive to kill her mother; and witnesses told how Christine had become a burden to her daughter. To make their case even stronger, the prosecutors asked jail officials to monitor West's phone calls, and in a call West made to a male friend in Northern California, West said, "No one knows" where her brother is.

That would directly contradict what West told everyone—that she had sent her mother to live with her brother in 1998. If West walked into court and continued to maintain that she did, in fact, take Christine to live with her brother and then put her mother in the can at a later date, the jailhouse tape recording would destroy such a claim. To Mitchell, the tape showed West lied about the whereabouts of her mother from the very beginning, and the call also showed West likely knew no one was ever going to find her brother.

"She had to know Travis was not going to be found to be able to say that with confidence," Mitchell said.

But the prosecutors had one very big problem. There

was no cause of death for Christine, and without a medical examiner willing to say Christine was murdered, West could tell the jury her mother died a natural death, and the jury might just believe her.

Coumou decided to try something different. He consulted a forensic entomologist to see if an examination of the insects found on Christine's body could yield any clues about when she died and the circumstances surrounding the disposal of her corpse.

It was an extremely wise move.

40

On his rural farm in Rensselaer, Indiana, Dr. Neal Haskell gets up most mornings, cooks his breakfast, reads the paper and he heads out to his grassy farmlands to pluck bugs off decaying pig flesh.

"I enjoy collecting insects," said Haskell, a burly, bearded man with a big belly and even larger personality. "Entomology is like going on a treasure hunt. There are just so many different specimens collected, and every time you go to a different habitat, there is something new. Plus, it's been a damned good excuse to travel throughout my life. Hey, it's too cold, so I've got to go to Florida or the Yucatan Peninsula to collect bugs."

Haskell is a forensic entomologist and professor at St. Joseph's College in Rensselaer. He has spent decades studying insects, and he is an expert on the role bugs play in the decomposition process of bodies. The way bugs consume a corpse or animal is pretty much an exact science, he said. As soon as the body dies, there are certain insects that show up like clockwork, and the bugs on the body go through specific, discernible life cycles while feeding on the flesh.

By examining whether an insect is in egg form or is a maggot, cocoon or fly, Haskell can often make observations about the time of death for the victim.

"In certain cases, we may also be able to show the geographical location where a body has originated from based on a particular [insect] species," Haskell said. "We can also do drug testing on maggots and larvae that have been feeding on human remains. . . . And then there is a new application. It is the recovery of human DNA from the blood meals of insects that feed on humans such as lice, bed bugs, fleas and mosquitoes."

Haskell's understanding of the role insects play in the decomposition of the human body has led him to be a much-sought-after expert in criminal cases across the United States. He has testified in or consulted on five hundred different cases, and he is a consultant for numerous criminal forensics television shows, including HBO's *Autopsy.*

In 1999, he examined the bodies of four Anasazi Indians found in a grave in Farmington, New Mexico. The four Indians were bludgeoned to death, and forensic science determined the deaths unfolded sometime around A.D. 750. By examining the insect remains on the ancient corpses, Haskell could say the victims were likely killed in the summertime.

"It was most likely summer, and the individuals were held above ground before they were buried for a considerable period of time because they had a good amount of fly puparia or cocoon stage [on them]," Haskell said.

In the spring of 2001, Haskell was contacted by Clark County prosecutor Frank Coumou and Las Vegas homicide detective Dave Mesinar to see if he could determine a time of death for Christine Smith. He was also asked to see if he could make any findings about the circumstances in which Christine's corpse was stuffed into the garbage can.

Haskell examined the insect specimens collected at Christine's autopsy under a microscope, fully expecting to find a fly species that is commonly referred to as the blowfly. The blowfly is easily recognized by the metallic green and blue coloration of its body, and it is usually the first bug to find a body after an individual's death.

"I've seen [blowflies] find dead animals within fifteen to twenty seconds after death. . . . These blowflies can detect a dead animal from over a mile to a mile and a half away," Haskell said. "So they have very strong chemical receptors that will key in and then follow, primarily, upwind. They will fly upwind, trace the odors upwind and access the remains.

"The blowflies will be among the very first colonizers," he said. "The quicker [an insect] can get to that food and start utilizing it, the greater [its] chance for survivability."

But when Haskell examined the insects from Christine's body, he was shocked to find no blowflies at all, which told him Christine's body was placed in the garbage can almost immediately after death.

"The absence of any of these early colonizers [blowflies] tells me that this body, these remains, had to have been purposely placed in such a way as to exclude the early colonizers," Haskell said.

Instead of blowflies on Christine's body, Haskell found an insect species known as humpback flies. The gnatlike flies, also known as coffin flies, are notorious for being able to access dead bodies in confined spaces such as coffins or mausoleums.

"These flies are so tenacious, they've been found to burrow down three to four feet through soil to coffins," Haskell said. "They are very tenacious at getting into any small crack or opening, particularly when we have the remains in an advanced decompositional state. So a garbage can, I wouldn't think, would be much of an obstacle."

Haskell's findings were extremely important to Coumou because they showed Christine's murder was pre-meditated. Since there were no blowflies on the body, West must have already had the garbage can ready at the moment her mother died, and she immediately stuffed the body into the can, preventing the blowflies from finding the remains.

"If Christine was killed, then Brooke must have already had the tools ready—the garbage can, the cellophane, the duct tape, the wrap, the plastic bags," Coumou said. "Had mom died of natural causes, and then Brookey goes out and gets a garbage can, you are going to find blowflies. But we never found them. So that tells me she got all the tools she needed to put her mom's body in there.

"I think West probably drugged her mom, put the plastic bag over her face, and she realized the bag wasn't quite doing the trick, so she got the garbage can," Coumou said.

Haskell also raised a much more sinister possibility for the manner in which Christine was killed. Perhaps the blowflies never found Christine's remains because she was still breathing when she went into the can.

"It's possible West put her mom in there while she was still alive," Coumou said.

41

There are certain cases that are referred to as "bad fact" cases in the world of criminal defense attorneys. Your defendant's DNA is found at the crime scene, the victim's blood is found on your client's clothes, the assailant was captured committing the crime on videotape, or the suspect confessed on camera. They are the type of cases that beg for a plea deal—not a jury trial.

To Clark County deputy public defender Scott Coffee, Brookey Lee West's murder case was not a "bad fact" case. In fact, when Coffee was assigned to defend West in court in the spring of 2001, he was convinced West had a good chance of being acquitted of first-degree murder.

"I thought the case had potential," Coffee said. "It's not your normal case, of course. A daughter is charged with killing her mother. But you ask yourself, 'What can they prove?' And the fact that a body is in a shed someplace, even if it has been there a long time, doesn't prove murder to me."

Coffee is not your stereotypical defense attorney. He is tall, somewhat portly and down-to-earth. He has an aura of confidence but not arrogance. Adopted as a child to a logger and a stay-at-home mom in Red Bluff, California, Coffee worked his way through high school and then went on to college in Oregon for an undergraduate degree in philosophy.

"Where do you find a job in philosophy?" Coffee said. "Driving cabs."

Instead of driving a cab, Coffee cut firewood for a year with his dad after college. His first wife had family in Las Vegas, so Coffee moved to Southern Nevada and took a job managing a fast-food joint.

"Raley's Hamburgers," Coffee said. "A little fast-food place, seven hundred square feet, and we had up to twenty-eight people working there at a time. Hang and bang."

He quickly realized the burger business wasn't for him, so he enrolled in officer training school for the U.S. Marines. He dropped out of officer school just two days before he was commissioned.

"They didn't like me and I didn't like them," Coffee said. "They were probably going to drum me out anyway, and it just wasn't the right fit. I'm more the type to stick my thumb in authority's eye than follow their rules."

Coffee went to law school next, and it was there that Coffee found his calling. He hired on with the Clark County public defender's office in Southern Nevada in 1995, and he honed his skills as a trial lawyer over the next six years with a simple, down-home approach that connects with Las Vegas juries. At thirty-nine, Coffee is now recognized as a shining star in the public defender's office.

In 2004, Coffee won what many thought was an unwinnable case as the defense attorney for a slaying suspect named Michael Kane, who plunged a knife in another young man while on an LSD trip in Vegas. At Kane's trial, Coffee presented evidence that Kane was mentally ill and that he didn't know what he was doing at the time of the killing. A jury agreed and returned a verdict of not guilty by reason of insanity—the first jury verdict of its kind in Nevada in a decade.

"The jury recognized that Mike was mentally ill, and the best thing to do was to put him in a mental institution," Coffee said.

In West's case, Coffee knew he needed help in court because of the magnitude of the case and the media attention, so he asked fellow deputy public defender Lynn Avants to assist in crafting West's courtroom defense. Avants, the son of veteran Las Vegas police homicide investigator Beecher Avants, jumped at the chance.

"I was fascinated by the case," Avants said. "This whole garbage can thing in a storage shed was interesting. But as a defense attorney, I was thinking, 'How do you know she committed murder?' "

Coffee and Avants were impressed with West's intellect. Unlike many defendants, she was sharp, well spoken and logical.

"I like Brooke," Coffee said. "Brooke's very intelligent, she's a likeable person and, unlike a lot of defendants I encounter, she's bright. A lot of defendants have psychological problems or other issues such as a lack of education, but that's not the case with Brooke. She's self-taught."

West was adamant she was not guilty of murder. She told her attorneys her mother died a natural death, she panicked, and she put the body in a garbage can.

"She said she was traveling back from San Jose after picking her mother up [from her brother's], that her mother was sick, her mother had gotten the chills, and she died in bed," Coffee said. "She panicked. She had a garbage can full of books, so she dumped out the books, put her mother's body in the can, and then hid it because she was scared.

"Who put the body in the storage shed was never much of a question in this case," Coffee said. "The prints were on the plastic wrap, the name was on the storage shed rental sheet and there was no question who put the body there. She admitted it."

Coffee found West's account believable, and with the Clark County coroner's office labeling the cause of death for Christine Smith undetermined, Coffee liked his chances with a jury.

"No signs of a struggle," Coffee said. "Christine's nails weren't broken, her bones weren't broken. I know the body was badly decomposed, but there were a lot of good things Dr. Telgenhoff had to say from the defense perspective as to cause of death. There was no evidence of drugs in the system, no poisons, no gunshots, no stabbing. For all we know, Christine could have died of natural causes."

But Coffee and Avants are not dummies. They recognized that if West was going to be acquitted, they were going to have to overcome some huge obstacles in court.

"The problem is, you've got a daughter charged with killing her mother, and the mom is in a trash can, and she's rotted there for almost four years," Avants said. "People don't like that. And then you've got this theft problem with the mother's Social Security, so people were not going to be happy with Brooke. I was really concerned about that. The case doesn't have a lot of jury appeal because people are going to be fixated with the fact that the daughter is accused of killing mom."

Another huge problem were the books found at the crime scene. The news media learned of the books, *The Satanic Bible*, *The Geography of Witchcraft*, and *Necronomicon*, in April of 2001 during a preliminary hearing for West in the courtroom of Las Vegas justice of the peace William Jansen. Reporters grilled Coffee about the books afterward, and Coffee recognized the chum was in the water for the news media. West was no longer just a woman accused of killing her mother and stuffing her in a can. She was also a suspected Satanist and witch.

"We had witch hunts in Salem several hundred years ago," Coffee told the *Las Vegas Review-Journal*. "This shouldn't turn into one."

The next day, the *Review-Journal* ran a section-front story about the books at the crime scene and the suspicions that West was involved in witchcraft. Coffee knew if a jury heard about those books, West didn't stand a chance in hell of being acquitted.

"When we first heard about the case, we heard a lot about devil worship and things like that. That stuff really doesn't have a place in a court of law," Coffee said.

"There are all kinds of First Amendment problems as well," Coffee said. "Let's just say, for the sake of argument, she was a devil worshipper. Doesn't mean she's guilty of anything. Or lets say she is a witch. Doesn't mean she's guilty of anything.

"You want to talk about prejudicial," Coffee said. "Witches? Devil worshippers? You are automatically going to put the jury in the mind-set that she must be guilty, and it is not necessarily the truth. And Brooke's got a First Amendment right to practice whatever religions she wants."

Travis Smith's missing status was another big dilemma. They suspected prosecutors were going to imply Travis was murdered by his sister, and Coffee and Avants' hands were tied in diffusing those suspicions, because they didn't know where he was, either.

"I don't know how you prove a negative," Coffee said.

Perhaps the most troublesome aspect of West's case was her prior history. West was a suspect in her dead husband's shooting; she had a mother-in-law who was stun-gunned; she had an ex-boyfriend who believed West had shot his elderly grandmother; she had a felony grand larceny conviction; she had a missing brother; and she had a father who was a practicing devil worshipper.

"I know a lot about West," Coffee said. "I know she has been institutionalized, and I know the state is going to try to dig into that. I know they are going to try and dig into witchcraft, whether it is legitimate or not. I know they are searching San Francisco covens and things, trying to look for something to tie in the witchcraft, and they'll try to find anything and throw it against the wall to see if it will stick."

With this in mind, Coffee invoked West's right to a speedy trial, meaning prosecutors had to present their case to a jury within sixty days of arraignment or the charges would be dismissed.

"The whole idea was to push the state forward with what they had," Coffee said. "We wanted to try this case on the body in the storage facility and nothing else. The state was digging, and this was becoming more and more about West's past than it was what they had against her. The less time they had to scramble and investigate, the better off we were."

Coffee got his wish. West was arraigned on May 1 in the courtroom of District Judge Donald Mosley. She entered a not guilty plea, and her trial was scheduled for July 2, 2001.

Brookey Lee West's fate would soon be in the hands of a jury.

42

District Judge Donald Mosley is a man who presides over his courtroom with an iron fist. Known as one of the toughest sentencers at the Clark County courthouse in Las Vegas, he is admired as a judge willing to give a defendant every benefit of the doubt when it comes to making sure he or she gets a fair trial. But once you are convicted in Mosley's courtroom, look out. If you are a convicted murderer, rapist or child molester and you appear before Mosley for sentencing, you might as well kiss your ass good-bye and resign yourself to spending your remaining days looking out an eight-inch-wide window from a jail cell in the Nevada penitentiary.

"I know I have that reputation," Mosley said. "I'm a firm believer that you ought to work for what you get, and there ought to be consequences for what you do, right or wrong. You do something good, you ought to be rewarded. If you do something screwy, you ought to be punished."

The tall-wiry, cowboylike figure with grayish-brown hair hails from Tulsa originally, and he comes across as a mix between Midwestern cowboy and Southern good old boy. A sportsman to the core, he loves to talk about hunting buck, ducks or other wild game in Northern Nevada and other hunting hot spots across the United States.

"That's what I do," Mosley said. "I hunt and fish. Most people understand being outdoors, you know, like hikers and bird-watchers. But to me, to go to all that effort and all that time and not have a gun in your hand makes no sense to me at all."

Mosley, during the last quarter century as a judge in Las Vegas, has found himself to be a lightning rod for controversy. He says what he thinks, critics be damned.

"A lot of judges are spineless," he says without flinching.

He's not afraid to mix it up, either, if necessary. During one verbal exchange with a motorist in rural White Pine County, Nevada, Mosley punched a man out in the middle of the road like a prizefighter felling a tomato can has-been in the boxing ring.

"The fact of the matter is, he attacked me and I dropped him on his butt in the street," Mosley told the newspapers in Las Vegas at the time.

In 2002, Mosley got in hot water with state judicial regulators amid allegations that he used his position as a judge to gain an advantage in his own child custody dispute. The Nevada Commission on Judicial Discipline fined Mosley $5,000 and gave him a public censure, but Mosley has always said he did nothing wrong. Mosley denies the allegations to this day, and despite the professional setback, voters, reelected him to the bench overwhelmingly in 2003.

"Someone once said, 'Mosley never dodges a bullet,'" Mosley said as he puffs on a big fat cigar in his county office, where smoking is supposedly banned.

It was in Mosley's courtroom that Brookey Lee West found herself in the legal battle of her life on July 2, 2001. Upon her arrival in court for jury selection, onlookers noticed West looked much different from her prior court appearances. She had shed a lot of weight, and she was dressed like June Cleaver. She wore frilly tops, her hair was in a curly bob and she looked like a librarian. Prosecutor Frank Coumou would later label West a chameleon who was trying to invoke sympathy from the jury.

"West is so good at creating this aura of 'Poor me,' when she's really not," Coumou said. "She's a criminal."

"She had a bookworm look," Mosley said.

True to his reputation as a fair judge, Mosley did everything he could to make sure jurors in the West case heard only what they needed to—no inflammatory facts that might prejudice their ability to be fair. He ordered that prosecutors not present details of any of West's prior encounters with the police to the jury. This meant the jury would not hear about Howard Simon St. John's murder, the stun-gunning of Chloe Smith, the shooting of Ray Alcantar's grandmother or even West's prior felony conviction.

He limited the number of autopsy photos the jury would see of Christine's melted body in a can. And although prosecutors weren't going to pursue the issue anyway, Mosley ordered there was to be no mention of Satanism or witchcraft during the trial.

"To a large degree, most of the rulings by the judge leading up to the trial were in favor of the defense," Coumou said.

Mosley did, however, give prosecutors some leeway in presenting to the jury evidence about the missing status of West's brother, Travis Smith. To Mosley, the information was relevant because West had told so many witnesses she had taken her mother to live with her brother.

Throughout jury selection, Mosley took notice of how at ease the defendant was. West was on trial for charges that could land her in prison for life, yet she seemed completely at peace with her circumstance.

"She was confident—almost smug," Mosley said. "I actually think she deluded herself into thinking she was going to walk. . . . Nothing seemed to bother her. It looked to me like she was going down the pike here, and she didn't seem to care."

West's behavior seemed so cavalier, at one point during jury selection, Mosley warned her.

"There has been an indication that throughout at least a portion of this process, the defendant was making eye contact with prospective jurors, mouthing certain words, smiling," the judge said. "I want to admonish the defendant that we will not have any more of that kind of thing."

A jury of six men and six women was picked in four days. The jury was a slice of middle-class America. Two jurors were teachers. One was a salesman. Two others were retired. One juror was a stay-at-home mother with kids.

West remained optimistic she would be acquitted of murder because, she says, she didn't kill her mother. She admits, however, that she had visions of a guilty verdict.

"I knew something bad was coming," West said. "Prosecutors? That's their job. To prosecute. What was it someone told me? It doesn't have to be true. It just has to work."

The police?

"I hate police," West said. "I do not trust police at all. . . . My dad always told me, 'Brookey, never trust the cops. They are dirty.' "

Opening statements in West's trial unfolded on July 6 in front of a packed courtroom, and both Coumou and Coffee started out strong in their remarks to the jury. Coumou recounted the gruesome details of Christine Smith's fate and presented his case: the fact that her body was in a storage shed rented by her daughter; how the key to the storage shed lock was in West's apartment; the bevy of witnesses who said West said her mother was alive when she was dead; the financial motive of stealing her mother's Social

Security checks; the bag tied tightly over Christine's face; and the unabashed hatred West had for her mom.

"From the outside looking in, it appeared like it was a normal relationship between mother and daughter," Coumou told the jury. "When you actually start looking and hearing the testimony of people who were close to the defendant, you will find the relationship was far from normal. She would make statements, 'My mom is a sociopath. My brother is a sociopath. They should be happy together,' " Coumou said.

Coumou told the jury West's statement that her mother was with her brother was a three-year-long lie concocted to cover up a heinous murder.

"There is no record of Travis Smith Jr.," Coumou said. "The idea of saying mom is going to go live with the brother and then maintaining that story would turn out to be just a big deception. [The] motive for this killing was hatred," Coumou said. "In addition to that [there] is the finance from her mom's Social Security money. . . . These are classic reasons [to kill], and the state intends to prove the defendant is guilty of murder."

Coffee conceded in his opening remarks to the jury that West stuffed her mother in the can.

"The body of Ms. West's mother was placed inside a garbage can in a storage facility," Coffee told the jury. "Of that, there is no question."

But he said West didn't kill her mother, and she wasn't the monster prosecutors were painting her as. She took her mother to the doctor, she helped pay her bills and, most important, she loved her mother.

"Ms. West also took care of her mother," Coffee said. "The state didn't mention that. She helped pay the rent. She took her to the doctor. She did the normal things that a daughter would do for a mother."

Coffee told the jury Christine was sixty-five years old,

and given her age, it was certainly possible she died a natural death.

"I can with confidence say one thing—it's doubtful she [Christine] would like to see her daughter wrongfully prosecuted for a murder that didn't happen," Coffee said.

"Dr. Telgenhoff is going to tell you that a lot of things can't be ruled out," Coffee said. "A heart attack can't be ruled out as a possibility. A stroke can't be ruled out. Christine Smith was asthmatic. Her lung capacity was low. The day before she left [the Orange Door apartments] her friend Alice Wilsey said she was as sick as she had never seen her before," Coffee said. "She didn't feel well.

"The mother was taken to live with the brother," the defense attorney said. "At some point, the mother comes back to Las Vegas. She dies. She dies from what we will learn were likely natural causes."

Coffee said that after her mother's death West panicked and put the body in the garbage can.

"Brooke West did do some things wrong," Coffee said. "When her mother dies, Brooke panics. She doesn't handle stress very well, as you will hear from a number of witnesses. She puts her mother in a storage facility. At that point, a lot of things become too late," he said. "Too late to call the authorities. Too late to report the death. Too late to tell anybody where mom is because of fear. This is motivated by stress.

"I will concede that Ms. West misused her mother's Social Security. . . . There's no question. She probably figured, 'Who's going to know?' "

And with that, the trial of West was under way. Little did Coffee know he would soon be fighting off a bombshell of a development that threatened to sink his client before he'd even called a single witness.

43

It never fails. Everytime a high-profile murder case begins in Las Vegas, an inmate at Las Vegas' dungeon of a jail—the Clark County Detention Center—comes forward to say the defendant confessed to him while behind bars. Brookey Lee West's trial was no exception. The jailhouse snitch in West's case was a pretty young woman named Heather Hearall, and Hearall was in custody on allegations she'd violated her probation in the winter of 2001 when she met West.

Hearall told authorities she was talking to another inmate about West's case at the jail when West walked up and started volunteering information.

"Without provocation, she told us that whatever happened between her and her mother, that her mother had forgiven her, and God had forgiven her, too," Hearall said. "That was my first interaction with Brookey West."

In another instance, Hearall said she overheard West talking to another inmate about her brother, Travis, and that during the conversation West detailed the method she used to cash her brother's Social Security checks.

"She talked about impersonating her brother," Hearall said. "That's the only way she could cash the check. She talked about having to dress as her brother. 'That's the only way I can cash the checks.'"

Prosecutors were elated with the potential bombshell witness. In the middle of West's trial, Hearall was brought into Mosley's courtroom where she repeated the same information she had told authorities. Mitchell and Coumou both agreed that Hearall's testimony sounded true.

"She said, 'Oh, yeah, Brooke was telling me how she had tried to disguise herself as her brother to try and get the Social Security money, so we seized on that," Coumou said. "I thought, 'We've got it. We've got proof of financial motive.'"

But Coffee argued to the judge that Hearall was lying to curry favor in her pending probation revocation proceeding.

"She's a jailhouse snitch with every motivation in the world to better her position," Coffee said. "What she said wasn't credible."

With Mosley on the verge of deciding whether Hearall should testify, Coffee announced he would seek a delay in the trial if she was called to the witness stand. He told the judge he would need time to try to disprove what Hearall was saying. This, in turn, alarmed the prosecutors, because the state had already spent the money to take the case to trial, and if a delay was announced, the state would have to start over again. Feeling that they had a strong case already and slightly worried that the jury might view Hearall's testimony with skepticism anyway, they decided not to put her on the stand.

As a result, the jury never heard what Hearall had to say.

44

The Heather Hearall fire was quickly squelched by Scott Coffee, but a bigger blaze was starting to burn in Donald Mosley's courtroom. Namely, a parade of witnesses was walking into court and portraying West as an unstable lunatic.

When the first of these witnesses, George Burnett, arrived in Mosley's courtroom on the afternoon of July 6, it seemed as if the ghost of Howard Simon St. John had just walked through the courtroom doors. Burnett, a Native American with flowing black hair running down to the middle of his back, took the witness stand and told the jury he was West's fourth and final husband. He said he met West in November 1996 at the Stardust casino on the Las Vegas Strip when West walked up to him and started the conversation.

It was the same way West had met St. John in San Jose nearly three years earlier.

"She walked up to me and asked me a few questions about my [Indian] heritage, and we started speaking," Burnett said. "I told her generally I was a loner out here [in

Vegas]. I really didn't have anyone to spend Thanksgiving with."

Burnett ended up spending Thanksgiving day with West, and a passionate, whirlwind romance ensued. The two were married on January 5, 1997, in a little chapel on the Vegas Strip, and the two then headed to the San Jose area, where Burnett planned to spend the rest of his life with his new bride.

But within a day of arriving in San Jose, West suddenly said she had to go back to Las Vegas to be with her mother.

"She said she had a problem with her mother being sick, and as I recall, she said that her mother wouldn't let her go," Burnett said. "She said she had to go back immediately to Las Vegas to help her mother out. 'She's just really kind of fucking up my life more or less,' she said."

Stunned, Burnett asked her, "What is this? What is happening? We come all the way out here, and all of a sudden, it's just like a total change of mind? The next thing I knew, her car was gone, and she was no longer there," he said.

After West left him, Burnett decided he wasn't going to give up on his new bride so easily, so he drove all the way back to Vegas and stopped by West's mother's apartment at the Orange Door. He identified himself as West's new husband, and he was surprised to learn Christine knew nothing of her daughter's marriage.

Christine quickly ran to the phone and called West, who denied the marriage to her mother.

"She told her mother she didn't know what she was talking about, [that] she didn't get married," Burnett said.

The marriage was annulled within a few months, and that was the last Burnett heard from his bride until her arrest in Las Vegas on a murder charge. Burnett's testimony, however, should have been an omen for West and her defense team, because the painting of West as an oddball by witnesses would continue pretty much nonstop for the next two weeks.

Natalie Hanke took the witness stand, and in what was perhaps the most dramatic moment of the trial, she tearfully told how West repeatedly claimed her mother was alive when she was really dead.

" 'Mom's a bitch. A sociopath. All she wants is money,' " Hanke quoted West as saying. " 'She never did a thing for me in her whole life.

" 'She's got to go, Natalie. She's got to go,' " Hanke said West told her in late 1997 or early 1998.

Coffee questioned Hanke's value as a friend, but the damage was done. The aura surrounding West in the courtroom was one of strangeness—a freakish lady who was a liar and therefore capable of murder.

"They painted Brooke as an oddball," Coffee said. "The insinuation was, be scared. If she could do this to her mother, what could she do to you?"

Clark County prosecutor Frank Coumou strongly disagrees. He said portraying West as an oddball wasn't a strategy—it was a matter of fact detailed by witness testimony and evidence. And providing the jury witnesses who observed West's strange behavior wasn't the only thing prosecutors did well at trial. They also laid out a case for murder.

Dr. Gary Telgenhoff walked jurors through the autopsy and how Christine's body rolled out onto the autopsy gurney like a waxy, cheesy ball.

"The first thing that was most noteworthy other than the body being in a trash can—which is something you don't see everyday—[was] there was a white plastic bag around the nose and mouth tied tightly behind the head," Telgenhoff said. "It certainly must have been tight before decomposition occurred."

Telgenhoff told the jury the cause of death was undetermined, but he gave prosecutors a tidbit of optimism when asked about the cause of death.

"Would [the circumstances] be consistent with the be-lief that this victim died of suffocation?" Coumou asked.

"Yes," the medical examiner responded.

On cross-examination, Coffee and Avants fought back, getting Telgenhoff to concede the circumstances of Chris-tine's burial could also be consistent with a natural death.

Joe Matvay told the jury how the crime scene was pro-cessed and how West's fingerprint was recovered from the cellophane wrap on the can. He showed the jurors the grisly crime scene photos and the images of Christine up to her neck in a soupy mix of decomposition and insects.

"I observed a human form or human figure at the bot-tom of the can," Matvay said. "The human form was in an advanced state of decomposition, and I could discern there was a head with hair present."

Several jurors appeared aghast.

Dr. Neal Haskell told about the life cycle of blowflies. Using a large chart with a picture of a massive blowfly on it, he narrated for the jury how the flies lay their eggs on bodies, the eggs turn into maggots, and then eventually the maggots form a cocoon.

"And after a few days in this form, the adult flies will eventually hatch out both male and female," Haskell said. "It will take a few days to reach sexual maturity, they'll mate, then the fly is off doing the next generation."

"Landing on your hamburger?" Coumou asked.

"We hope not," Haskell said.

Haskell told the jury he believed the blowflies were pre-vented from finding Christine's body immediately after death, and that putting the body in a garbage can would ex-plain the lack of blowflies on the body.

"And within your findings, is it also consistent with the theory that the victim could have been placed alive into this garbage can?" Coumou asked.

"I suppose it would be possible shortly after death, but

definitely into the period after death," Haskell said. "It would be definitely possible for any of that to have occurred."

Coffee was angered by the jury hearing the premise that Christine went into the can while she was still breathing.

"That just scares the hell out of you, doesn't it?" Coffee said. "Isn't that what you want [as a prosecutor]. It scares the heebie-jeebies out of you. She could have been put in there alive. We don't have any evidence of it, but it could have happened. What the hell is that?"

But Coumou and Mitchell continued with the assault. Three different bank employees and Dave Mesinar offered testimony indicating that withdrawals were made from Christine's bank account after she was dead. A Social Security investigator said West had written a letter to the administration asking it to deposit her brother's Social Security checks in a bank account. The implication was clear—West wasn't just stealing her mother's money, but her brother's, too.

A Las Vegas Valley nurse practitioner, Judy Zito-Pry, said she treated Christine on numerous occasions for minor ailments ranging from toenail fungus to urinary tract infections, and that West once expressed to Zito-Pry concerns about Christine losing her mental facilities.

"She was concerned about her mother's memory," Zito-Pry said. "She thought she'd developed Alzheimer's. She was quite concerned."

Zito-Pry said Christine had a history of asthma, and a test showed her lungs were in bad shape. Christine's lungs had the efficiency of a 132-year-old, the nurse practitioner said, leading Coffee to say Christine could have died of lung failure, old age or an asthma-related reaction to her asthma inhalers.

"Her health was basically stable," Zito-Pry countered.

But the most powerful witnesses for the prosecution were Judy Chang and Alice Wilsey. The senior citizens shuffled into court, took the witness stand and proceeded to humanize Christine for the jury with their emotional testimony. They painted Christine as a sweet little old lady who didn't deserve what she got. Chang described the last time she saw Christine alive.

"I walked down to the apartment to see her, and she was lying on the couch with a little dog, the little Chihuahua we called Chi Chi," Chang said. "All of a sudden, I heard Chris say, 'You are not giving my Chi Chi away!' Brooke looked at her kind of hard and weird like."

Chang told the jury that after Christine disappeared, Christine's belongings were still in the apartment at the Orange Door.

" 'Oh, she will forget all about them,' " Chang quoted West as saying. " 'She won't even remember them.' "

Wilsey told the jury Christine was ill the night of her disappearance, and that West was giving her "so-called aspirin."

" 'Here, honey, take this. It's aspirin,' " Wilsey quoted West as saying to her mother. " 'It will make you feel better.' She came in several times. She [West] told me that she could no longer live with her mother, and that she found a way to make a place for her," Wilsey said. "That she wouldn't have to be bothered anymore."

Under cross-examination, Wilsey and Chang acknowledged they liked West, and they continued to associate with her after Christine's disappearance despite their suspicions. Once again, though, the damage was done. West was perceived as a coldhearted killer.

"Alice was golden," Coumou said, crediting Wilsey for her courage in describing for the jury what really happened. "Her mind was so sharp, and she remembered everything. Suddenly, Christine was gone, and Brooke is giving away all the stuff that belonged to her mom."

The defense case, in comparison, was quick. One witness, Steven Michael Cornett, was a resident of the Orange Door apartments, and he said he actually saw West moving her mother out of the apartments. The testimony seemed to contradict prosecutors' contention that West had murdered her mother the night Wilsey last saw Christine.

A medical expert, Dr. James Anthony, told the jury he had treated hundreds of asthma patients, and that 5,000 people a year die from asthma. His testimony furthered Coffee's premise that Christine could have died because of a rare reaction from an asthma inhaler, and he said Christine's lung age of 132 was a significant health concern.

"That's very bad," Anthony said. "That's severe lung disease."

Closing arguments were delivered on July 18, and both Mitchell and Coumou rehashed their evidence one more time for the jury. Coumou emphasized the most crucial piece of physical evidence—the bag tied tightly to Christine's face.

"It's the one piece of evidence that cannot be explained," Coumou said.

Coffee told the jury that perhaps the bag was placed over Christine's face to preserve her dignity in death.

"It's a shroud placed over the face," Coffee said. "When people are in the hospital [and die], they have sheets pulled over their faces."

But it was too late—the jury was convinced Christine was murdered. After just a couple of hours of deliberation, on July 19 the jury returned a unanimous guilty verdict on a charge of first-degree murder. West showed no reaction, but for Coumou, Mitchell and Mesinar, the guilty verdict was an incredibly rewarding moment. They'd taken off the street a stone-cold killer who left a trail of missing and dead people in her wake, and justice had been served for Christine Smith, regardless of all her faults in life.

"There has been no one here to speak for Christine

Smith," Mesinar told the *Las Vegas Review-Journal*. "This verdict speaks for her."

Two months later, during her sentencing hearing, Mosley hammered West. He committed her to life in prison without any chance of parole.

"Ms. West is not being sentenced this morning for anything other than what occurred to this elderly woman," Mosley said. "Since the jury has made the determination of guilty, I have thought about this case on many occasions. And in each instance, I am left with one very nagging point of confusion. How did this white, plastic, kitchen garbage bag ever find itself around the nose and mouth of the decedent?

"We've heard two possible explanations. One is that it was a shroud, a sort of a covering of the face in deference to the decedent's status. And of course, we've heard the other suggestion—that it was, in essence, what killed her by virtue of suffocating.

"I have to tell you, Ms. West, that the latter is more likely in my view. She was overpowered, this item placed around her face, tied tightly, and she was placed into this garbage container, presumably to suffocate her. Now that doesn't paint a very pleasant picture.

"And while I think everyone would agree putting someone's mother in a garbage can to bury her is bizarre, placing her in there conscious to suffocate her is not only bizarre—it's criminal. You are sentenced to life without the possibility of parole. That's all."

45

The Southern Nevada Women's Correctional Center is located on the outskirts of the Las Vegas Valley along Interstate 15. It is a maze of hallways, cells, bars and barbed wire expressly built to house Nevada's female lawbreakers. Everyone from murderers to ordinary thieves in Las Vegas call the women's correctional center home.

Brookey Lee West is scheduled to spend the rest of her life at the prison, yet by all accounts she is a model inmate. She leads a Bible study class, she teaches other inmates art and she is an advocate for raising money for Nevada's wild horses, which are becoming more and more scarce in the natural landscape surrounding Las Vegas.

"While I'm in here, I don't do anything bad," West said. "I've never even had any kind of disciplinary action. I teach other inmates. I do an art program. I collect all this money to get people to participate [in the wild horses benefit program]. It's my job, but I don't get money for it. When the money is raised for these horses, the ultimate good is for these animals. They are created, just like we are, and they have a place, and they are losing that place. They need medical care. They need a lot."

West, in fact, seems to be making the best of her predicament in prison. She said that throughout her life she has suffered from a serious mental health condition—she is bipolar—and in prison she has gotten the treatment she needs to be a stable, productive person.

"I don't even see myself in a bad situation," West said. "I see everything as a learning experience. I came here, and I wasn't in good shape. I'm in good shape now. I'm meditating again. My diet is right. I'm starting to lose the weight I need to lose to be the right size. The shrink they've got here is really, really good. I get my medication. I see my mental health person, and she said I have a borderline personality, but she said that is a learned behavior and that I've made so many changes that I'm not really sick.

"[Being in prison] has really gotten me back on track, and I've been able to get the rest I needed," West said.

But just because West is in prison doesn't mean she admits to murdering her mother or anyone else, and she denies committing any crime other than shoplifting.

She denies having anything to do with Howard Simon St. John's murder.

"We were only married for six weeks. West said. It wasn't like there was some reason that I would want him dead," West said, denying there was a plot to kill her husband in order to quell the insurance fraud investigation for her burned-out Jaguar.

"The car was stolen. I know that Howard got mad at me because I didn't go to the hospital [when he was shot the first time]. He didn't know that I was under a restraining order, so he got pissed off, he called up the insurance company and he made up this story. When he realized what he had done—after the asshole got sober and off his medication, he told me, 'Do you think they are going to lock me up for it? ' I said, 'Why? You didn't do anything.' So that's when he called them again. I guess he met them somewhere, and that's when he told them he made the story up.

"The second time he told the story, he told the truth," West said. "The first time, he made the story up, he fabricated it, and I had nothing to do with it. All of that happened before he was dead. Why would I have killed him over something that wasn't going anywhere?"

West said she cooperated with the police in Tulare County.

"You think I killed him?" West said. "Well, go ahead and charge me. Try it. That's the way I feel about it. The reason I wasn't charged is because I wasn't involved in it. I told these people the truth. I sat for hours with those two cops. No lawyers or nothing. . . . They asked me everything in the book. Short of asking me how I liked him in bed, they asked me everything else."

West denies stun-gunning Chloe Smith.

"No," West said. "She thought that if she could get me arrested and get me out of her hair as opposed to putting my father in a rest home, she could do what she wanted. And I was like, 'No, we'll go to court over this. I'm not going to allow it.' "

West said she had nothing to do with the shooting of Ray Alcantar's grandmother, although she acknowledges her father sent the Satanic letter to Alcantar after the shooting.

"He said, 'You pray to your God; I think my God is just as good as your God.' He [my father] had the seal of his cult club on it. He didn't give a damn. He said, 'That's my God,' and Ray was freaked out about it from then on. . . . He blamed me for things I really didn't have any control over. I don't know what happened."

West said she is not a practicing witch or Satanist, although she has studied all kinds of religions.

"Well, that sells," West said. "It sells papers. It sells news. Who wants to read, 'Well, she's a really nice person, she just has a few problems.' That's not interesting."

West said her brother, Travis, will eventually surface, and she will be vindicated from allegations that she somehow killed him.

"He'll turn up," West said. "Mark my words. He will."

And, perhaps most important, West denies killing her own mother.

She said she took her mother to live with her brother in San Jose in 1998, and in 1999 she went back to San Jose to bring her mother back to Las Vegas. On the drive home, she said, her mother died in a hotel room, West panicked, so she placed her mother in the garbage can.

"We were traveling, I'm not going to tell you where, what state, but she was complaining that she was feeling bad, she was real, real tired, and she wanted to get a place to stay," West said.

"She went to bed. I got up the next morning, and she was dead. But I wasn't coping, I wasn't handling things very well, and I just freaked out. I couldn't handle her death. This is too much, too many deaths, too close together. And not only that, I wasn't really medicated.

"I already had the can. It was full of books. . . . I stood there for a few minutes, and I had her purse, which was that sack [plastic bag] she carried. I grabbed it, I dumped everything out of it and I just tied it behind her head," West said.

"I kept her, and I had to have her in something," she said. "But once I set her there [in the storage shed], I never, ever moved her again. I did nothing to even touch that. I kept it nice and clean there for her.

"If I had of been then like I am now, I would have never've done that. When you have the kind of condition I have, people don't understand," she said.

"I look at it the same way I looked at Howard's death," West said. "I knew I hadn't killed her, but I did keep her, and that's why I said on the news that I did put her there. Maybe that was the wrong thing to do, but I did put her there. But I didn't kill her, and I said I didn't kill her. Nobody killed her. She just died. And that's the way that it was."

West said she is confident someday she'll get out of prison despite her sentence of life without parole.

"There are a lot of people who go to the pardons board," West said. "They were all sentenced to life without parole."

In 2003, the Nevada Supreme Court denied Brookey Lee West's appeal on her murder conviction. She is still vowing to pursue the matter in both state and federal courts, claiming she is innocent. Nevada police and prosecutors say she is a dangerous woman who was convicted of a horrifying murder, and she deserves to remain in prison until she dies.

In the fall of 2004, West got a glimmer of hope for her appeals. A man identifying himself as Travis Smith went into a medical clinic in San Jose for treatment, and he used the same name and Social Security number as West's brother. The development sent a shock wave through Las Vegas—West's brother may actually be alive.

Defense attorney Scott Coffee sent an investigator to San Jose to see if Travis Smith could be found, but the investigator was unable to track him down. There were rumors that the individual identifying himself as Travis was becoming a nuisance in a well-to-do neighborhood in San

Jose, so the cops bought the homeless man a bus ticket to Florida to get him out of the city for good.

To this day, Travis Smith's whereabouts remain a mystery.

Glenn Puit, thirty-five, is an award-winning journalist and investigative reporter for the *Las Vegas Review-Journal* in Las Vegas, Nevada. He has spent his entire career writing about the criminal justice system, and he now covers the district court beat for the *Review-Journal*, which is Nevada's largest newspaper.

Previously, Puit worked at the Florence, South Carolina, *Morning News*, where he was the first reporter in the nation to document the federal government's theory regarding the identity of John Doe #2 in the Oklahoma City bombing. Puit also worked at the *Leader-Herald* in Gloversville, New York, and has a degree in journalism from Indiana State University in Terre Haute, Indiana.

A native of Lansing, New York, Puit lives in Las Vegas with his wife, Tina, and their two sons, Garrison and Glenn Jr.

TRUE CRIME FROM BERKLEY BOOKS

A BEAUTIFUL CHILD

*A True Story of Hope, Horror, and an
Enduring Human Spirit*
by Matt Birkbeck
0-425-20440-5
**The tragic, true story of the girl-next-door's
secret life.**

UNBRIDLED RAGE

*A True Story of Organized Crime, Corruption,
and Murder in Chicago*
by Gene O'Shea
0-425-20526-2
**Two cold case agents solve the mystery of the
40-year-old murder of three boys in Chicago.**

ON THE HOUSE

The Bizarre Killing of Michael Malloy
by Simon Read
0-425-20678-5
**The true story of the murder of a New York City
drunk at the hands of thugs who had taken out
an insurance policy on his life.**

HUNTING ERIC RUDOLPH

*An Insider's Account of the Five-Year Search for the
Olympic Bomber*
by Henry Schuster with Charles Stone
0-425-20857-5
**The definitive story of the hunt for the elusive
suspect in the 1996 Atlanta Olympic bombing.**

The Definitive History of the Phenomenon of Serial Murder

SERIAL KILLERS
THE METHOD AND MADNESS OF MONSTERS

PETER VRONSKY

NOW AVAILABLE

BERKLEY

—1—

Molly had come to view her New Year's Day ritual as something approaching a divine rite, and, as Papa had always done, she repaired to her office immediately following midday dinner. After closing the door behind her, she plucked a new leather-bound ledger from one of the towering bookshelves and laid it atop her writing table beside last year's ledger, which she had balanced the day before. She sank into the worn armchair behind the desk, withdrew her quill pen from the inkstand, and carefully inscribed the year—1816—on the front and spine of the new ledger. She then opened the old volume and reverently removed the document tucked behind the frontispiece.

"I owe Stephen Trevor five pounds," the document stated in an immature and faded hand. "To be repaid December 31, 1778, with six shillings' interest. Roger Beckwith."

"That was the beginning, Molly," Papa would invariably say as he transferred the yellowing note from the old ledger to the new. "It was a deuced easy way to earn six shillings, and young as I was, I found myself calculating the profit if I had a hundred pounds to lend rather than five. Or a thousand. Or ten thousand. And what else was I to do?"

As the years passed, Molly grew to recognize this as a rhetorical question.

"Recollect that I was the fourth son of a mere

baronet," Papa would continue. "Ambrose inherited the title, Cuthbert entered the church, Simon purchased a commission in the army; what was left for me? Indeed, as it happened, my course was dictated by fate. I was but a few days down from Cambridge when I chanced to win five hundred pounds at Newmarket. I thought to hide my winnings in the trunk I'd brought from school, and when I opened it, I discovered Beckwith's note at the very top. He had repaid the loan long since, of course, but both of us had quite forgotten the document he signed. I judged the combined circumstances a signal from heaven and used my winnings to establish myself as a moneylender."

Molly had been five when she first heard this story— it was just after Mama's death, she recalled—and several years elapsed before she detected a peculiarity in Papa's narrative.

"If you have brothers," she said, "are they not my uncles?"

Papa nodded, rather reluctantly, she thought.

"Then why do we never see them?" Mrs. Mulvaney, Molly's governess, was forever chattering of her multitudinous uncles and aunts and cousins, and Molly was enchanted by the notion of a large family of her own.

Papa's blue eyes clouded a bit. "I fear that moneylending has its disadvantages, Molly. There are many who regard it as a highly unsuitable profession—not good *ton* as they might say."

Molly was unfamiliar with this term, but if something wasn't *good*, she could only assume it was *bad*.

"My family were monstrous overset by my choice of career," Papa went on, "and vowed not to associate with me any further. I was in hopes they would eventually come round, but they have not."

"Umm." Molly mulled this information over a moment. "Was Mama's family overset as well?" she asked at last. Now she thought on it, she could remember no uncles or aunts or cousins prior to her mother's death either.

"I am sorry to say they were." Papa nodded. "In point

of fact, your mother's parents refused to consent to our marriage, and we were compelled to elope."

"Elope?" Molly repeated. It was a day for strange new words.

"We had to run away and be wed in secret," Papa elaborated.

"Umm," Molly said again. Eloping did not strike her as a very interesting subject, and for perhaps the thousandth time she asked Papa if she might have a pony of her very own. For the thousandth time, Papa said no.

With the passage of years—and the reading of numerous romantic novels, which Mrs. Mulvaney had strictly forbidden—Molly began to find men and marriage considerably more fascinating than horses. Many of the books she read featured star-crossed lovers required to overcome all manner of seemingly insurmountable obstacles in their quest for happiness, and she was inevitably reminded of Papa and Mama.

"Shall I also be compelled to elope?" she blurted out one New Year's Day. She was twelve or thirteen at the time, she reckoned, and she had interrupted Papa's annual recounting of his fortuitous start as a money-lender.

"Surely you don't think to marry just yet." Papa's tone was light, but there was a wary set to his lean jaws and rather pointed chin.

"No," Molly agreed, "but I shall be grown before long. Maybe I shall have to run away with a pirate." The heroine in the romance she had just finished had eloped with a pirate, though he had ultimately proved to be a marquis in disguise.

"You will not have to run away with anyone, Molly," Papa assured her. "When the time comes, as you put it, I shall . . . I shall make an appropriate arrangement."

Molly sighed, placed Roger Beckwith's note behind the frontispiece of the new ledger, and closed both the volumes on her desk. She often wondered if Papa had had a specific "appropriate arrangement" in mind or had merely been playing for time; often wondered what turn her life might have taken had Stephen Trevor not been spilled from his carriage and nearly crushed to death beneath it.

Mr. Trevor was excessively fortunate to have escaped the accident with his life, Dr. Dalton said, and *particularly* fortunate not to have lost his right hand, which had been trampled by one of his terrified horses. Fortunate or no, Papa was confined to bed for upward of a month, and when he first regained his senses—almost eight-and-forty hours after the mishap—he instructed his secretary, Gresham, to operate the business in his stead until he was fully recovered.

Gresham was a tall, cadaverous, dour man some ten years Papa's senior, but despite his forbidding appearance and demeanor, Molly was quite fond of him. And she noticed, before Papa's indisposition was a week old, that Gresham was fairly tottering with exhaustion.

"I well comprehend *how* to manage the enterprise," Gresham said defensively when Molly remarked his condition aloud at dinner. "However, I must now devote the business day to Mr. Trevor's normal responsibilities—interviewing clients, investigating delinquencies, conferring with our solicitors. I can discharge my own duties only at night, and the time available is insufficient for the task. The correspondence lags, as does the bookkeeping, and I have not filed a single paper since Mr. Trevor's accident." He shook his bald head, looking even more doleful than usual.

"I could discharge your duties!" Molly said eagerly. "I fancy Mrs. Mulvaney will attest that my handwriting is excellent, and I'm very good at sums."

"Your handwriting is barely acceptable," Mrs. Mulvaney corrected, "and arithmetic is your *only* academic accomplishment."

Mrs. Mulvaney had ever lamented Molly's lack of scholarly dedication, and on her charge's sixteenth birthday, two months since, she had informed Papa that any further attempts at education were likely to prove fruitless. Not coincidentally, or so Molly suspected, Papa was at the point of pensioning off their ancient housekeeper, and Mrs. Mulvaney had speedily assumed the post.

"My handwriting is acceptable enough," Molly insisted. "I could certainly fill Gresham's position for a few weeks."

"I daresay you could," the secretary concurred, "but I doubt Mr. Trevor would approve any such endeavor."

"But Papa need never know!" Molly could not have explained why she was suddenly so anxious to take Gresham's place; she had previously entertained only the vaguest interest in her father's profession. Whatever the reason—a desire to aid Papa in his hour of need, sheer boredom, a deeper motive she couldn't identify—she was determined to have her way. "We shan't say a thing to Papa; I shall simply do it. And then, when he is well, I shall stop, and Papa will never be the wiser."

Molly fully intended to adhere to these conditions when she seated herself at Papa's desk the following morning, but she had reckoned without two factors. The first was that she fell immediately and passionately in love with Trevor and Company the instant Gresham opened the ledger and began to explain the various entries. Molly was not content to know that an interest payment was recorded here while a payment to principal went there; she must understand how the interest rate was determined and when collateral was required and precisely what an annuity was. The same was true of the correspondence Gresham dictated: Molly soon demanded to know why this client was being threatened with legal proceedings while that one was to receive only the mildest reminder of a tardy payment. She shortly started to revise Gresham's letters—she, whose essays had been the bane of Mrs. Mulvaney's existence—and within a week's time he was giving her merely the substance of the message and permitting her to proceed without additional direction.

The second factor to alter Molly's initial plan was that Papa never really recovered from his injuries. On the day he left his bed and returned to his office, Molly loitered about under the pretext of seeing to his physical comfort. And watched, blinking back tears, as the pale, wasted figure behind the desk discovered that his right hand had been rendered virtually useless.

"Gresham!" Papa bellowed after an hour of agonizing effort.

The secretary rushed in from his own office across the hall.

"I can't write a damned word." Papa sounded perilously close to tears himself. "And I must draft a letter to Davies, denying his request for another annuity. Sit down, and I shall tell you what I wish to say."

Gresham hesitated a moment. "Actually I am rather occupied just now, Mr. Trevor," he said at length. "Perhaps Miss Molly could assist you." He hesitated again. "She was a great help to me during your illness, sir."

"Indeed?" It was surely a mark of Papa's debility that he offered no protest. "Very well, Gresham. Go back to your duties; Molly will serve as my right hand."

Papa returned wearily to his bedchamber just after noon, and for the remainder of his life, his working day seldom extended beyond the morning. Indeed, as the years passed and his health increasingly failed, his hours grew shorter and shorter, eventually degenerating to little more than a brief, largely symbolic appearance. By the time Molly celebrated her eighteenth birthday, she and Gresham were operating the business almost entirely alone, consulting Papa in only the most unusual of circumstances.

One of Papa's lungs had been permanently damaged by his accident, and Dr. Dalton had long predicted that his final illness would take the form of a cold worsening to pneumonia. However, since her father developed and survived several colds each winter, Molly succeeded in putting the physician's dire prognosis out of her mind; and the end, when it came, caught her dreadfully unprepared. Papa woke one Tuesday morning with a stuffy nose and streaming eyes, and by midday Wednesday he could scarcely breathe. Molly sent for Dr. Dalton, but he had no magical remedy in his medical bag and departed within half an hour, declaring there was no hope. Molly went to her father's bedside, essaying a cheerful smile, but Papa was not deceived.

"I have no will, Molly," he wheezed as she perched on the bed and took his hand.

"Well, do not tease yourself about it," she said brightly, struggling to keep the tremor from her voice. "We shall compose a will when you are up and about again—"

"Don't pretend," he interposed, gasping for every ragged breath. "There is no time to pretend. I advise you to sell the business and pension Gresham off; a thousand pounds will suffice. Invest the rest of the proceeds and then go to my brother Ambrose. I daresay he will find it in his heart to forgive the transgressions of a dead man." He managed a shaky smile. "Persuade Ambrose and his wife to pass you off as a distant relative and give you a proper come-out."

Molly wondered if this was the "appropriate arrangement" he had mentioned long ago or a last, desperate attempt to resolve her future.

"I should have sent you to Ambrose when you were eighteen"—Papa might have been reading her mind—"but I couldn't bear to let you go."

"Oh, Papa . . ."

But she could no longer control her voice, and she sat in silence and held his hand until she realized, some hours later, that it had grown quite cold.

Molly notified Papa's three brothers of his death, but none of them appeared at the funeral, and this circumstance seemed to sanction the course she had decided to follow. On the day after the service, which only she and the staff had attended, she summoned Gresham and Mrs. Mulvaney to her father's office and related their final conversation.

"However," she concluded, "I have determined to reject Papa's advice. I intend to keep Trevor and Company and operate it myself."

"But you cannot, Miss Molly," the secretary protested. "Our clients would not do business with a woman—"

"Our clients have done business with me these past three years," Molly interrupted. "Consider our methods, Gresham: you conduct the personal interviews, claim a need to confer with Papa, and actually confer with me. I perceive no reason we cannot continue to operate in precisely that fashion. No one knows of Papa's death except my uncles, and I judge it highly unlikely that any of them will come to seek a loan."

She could not repress a bitter smile, but Gresham did not respond.

"I shan't try to force you," Molly went on gently. "If you prefer, I shall abide by Papa's wishes in that respect; I shall pension you off and engage someone else to fill your place. But if you stay, I shall pay you ten percent of the profits in lieu of salary."

"Ten percent!" Gresham's mouth fell open, but he hastily snapped it shut again. "If you were to make it fifteen, Miss Molly—"

"Twelve," she said firmly. "Have we a bargain then?"

"Yes, indeed!" For the first time in Molly's memory, the dour secretary smiled sufficiently to display a tooth or two.

"But what of your come-out?" Mrs. Mulvaney wailed. "I am sure Mr. Trevor desired you to meet a fine gentleman and make a proper marriage, and he was well aware that no *respectable* man would wed a moneylender's daughter. To say nothing of a woman who *is* a moneylender." Tact had never been one of Mrs. Mulvaney's transcendent virtues.

"I am only one-and-twenty," Molly said. "I've ample time left to meet a 'fine gentleman,' and when I do, I'm confident he will find me quite respectable enough."

Mrs. Mulvaney appeared unconvinced, but a salary increase of one pound per month eased her apprehensions considerably, and both employees departed the office with a jaunty air of optimism.

Their optimism had been well-founded, Molly thought immodestly, gazing round the office this first day of 1816. In the three years since Papa's death, Trevor and Company had prospered beyond her wildest imaginings;

she was undeniably a wealthy woman, and Gresham was
well in the way of becoming a man of means himself.
Mrs. Mulvaney, for her part, seemed resigned to the fact
that Molly would never lead a "normal" existence and
devoted herself to cooking and tyrannizing the maids and
clucking over her charge. Indeed, Molly reflected, her
life had been altogether satisfactory until her recent
introduction to Viscount Ogilvie.

Well, she had not exactly been *introduced* to Lord
Ogilvie, Molly amended, and therein lay the first
problem. She had *seen* the viscount at Drury Lane, and
once she'd glimpsed the tall, handsome, dark-haired
figure in a nearby box, not even Edmund Kean's magnificent performance could divert her attention.

"Who is *that?*" she hissed to Gresham during the first
entr'acte.

The secretary didn't know, which Molly counted a
splendid sign since it indicated that the young man was
not one of their clients. Before the evening was over,
Gresham succeeded in learning that the gentleman's
name was Andrew Elting, Viscount Ogilvie; and as soon
as they returned from the theater, Molly rushed to Trevor
and Company's voluminous files. Papa's ambitious policy
had been to maintain records of "everyone in Britain who
is even a *potential* client," and Molly had instructed
Gresham to pursue this goal. Consequently, as she had
expected, she found two pages devoted to the Eltings,
and she studied them with mixed emotions.

The information on the first page was entirely to Lord
Ogilvie's credit. He was, Molly discovered, a bachelor of
eight-and-twenty who had succeeded to his title some six
years since. He spent the spring and fall Seasons in
London, where he owned a town house; the winter
months at his home in Brighton; and the remainder of the
year at his family seat in Warwickshire. He and his
widowed mother, with whom he resided, appeared to
live well if not luxuriously.

Another young woman would have judged the second
page of data equally commendatory, but Molly read it
with a sinking heart. From time immemorial, it seemed,

the Elting family had been untouched by any breath of scandal; the very blackest sheep had defied his father to enlist in the navy and had subsequently become an admiral. In the living generations, one of Lord Ogilvie's uncles was an admiral as well, one a bishop; and his younger brother was a rising curate. The viscount's own conduct was apparently irreproachable: he was not known to engage in excessive gaming or drinking or to consort with the demimonde.

In short, Lord Ogilvie was precisely the sort of "fine gentlemen" Mrs. Mulvaney had once referred to, and neither he nor his family was likely to find a moneylender sufficiently "respectable" to bear the Elting name. Molly briefly considered the possibility of appealing to Sir Ambrose Trevor after all, but she abandoned this notion almost at once. Even if Papa's eldest brother consented to forgive her association with Trevor and Company, which was by no means certain, he would undoubtedly insist that she give up the business before he agreed to bring her out. And Molly was too much the realist to burn all her proverbial boats without any assurance that Viscount Ogilvie would reciprocate her *tendre*.

Indeed, Molly was realist enough to recognize that she should put Lord Ogilvie altogether out of her mind, but she could not; and she began to cast about for a solution to her dilemma. While she would not sell Trevor and Company on sheer speculation, she sometimes entertained a vague dream of . . . of *escaping* it. Yes, she would think in those moments, she need only be "respectable" for the interval required to meet the viscount and secure his affections; she could then own to the truth, and he—hopelessly *bouleversé*—would count it a matter of no importance. At other times, she dreamed that Lord Ogilvie would catch a glimpse of her, much as she had of him, and be so smitten that he would quite overlook her background.

In fact, Molly reflected, idly fingering the new ledger, a "chance" encounter would not be difficult to arrange, for his lordship's town house in South Molton Street was but a short distance from Molly's quarters in Hanover

Street. The viscount was not presently in London, of course; he had gone to Brighton for the winter. But when he returned for the spring Season, Molly might well be able to bring herself to his attention. Lord Ogilvie would fall over head and ears in love with her and desperately set out to learn her identity. Not a whit daunted to discover that she was a moneylender, he would rush to Hanover Street and fairly batter down the door—

"Just what do you imagine you are at!"

Mrs. Mulvaney's shriek was punctuated by a resounding slam, and Molly's preoccupation was such that she briefly fancied her daydream had come to pass. She gazed at her office door, her heart hammering against her ribs, and when it swung open, she was nearly overcome by a foolish rush of disappointment.

"I told him he could not come in, Miss Molly!" Mrs. Mulvaney screeched. "I tried to stop him, but he walked right past me."

This did, indeed, appear to be the case, for even as she spoke, the housekeeper was clawing at one broad shoulder of the man who loomed in the doorway. Molly's disappointment swiftly turned to apprehension, for the intruder cut a most forbidding figure. He was well above the average height and, except for his shoulders, almost painfully thin. He had not always been so lean, Molly surmised, glancing at his attire; his waistcoat hung shapelessly round his ribs, and his buckskin breeches were decidedly drooping. Evidently his loss of weight was attributable to incipient starvation, for his ill-fitting clothes also suggested abject poverty: there was a great patch on one sleeve of his coat, numerous holes in his stockings, and a jagged rent in his neckcloth. His face was jagged as well—a collection of sharp bones and deep hollows—and it was topped by a thick, overlong, untidy shock of auburn hair.

"Shall I summon Mr. Gresham?" Mrs. Mulvaney was panting from her exertions. "Shall I desire Mr. Gresham to eject him from the premises?"

Molly privately doubted that Gresham's intervention would prove in the least effective: despite his excessive leanness, the stranger projected an unmistakable impression of physical strength. "I am sure that will not be necessary," she said as calmly as she could. "I fancy this . . . ah . . . gentleman has stumbled on the wrong house—"

"Oh, I fancy not." Molly thought he was attempting to mimic her tones, but she detected traces of an unidentifiable accent. "I fancy this is Trevor and Company, and I have come to negotiate a loan."

Had he not looked so ferocious, Molly would have laughed; as it was, she was hard put to keep her countenance. "Then you will have to speak with my father's secretary," she said. "If Gresham reckons you a satisfactory risk"—she gulped down another threat of laughter—"he will recommend you favorably to Papa."

"That must be an exceedingly interesting procedure." His normal inflection was a slight drawl. "Does Mr. Gresham merely pray to Mr. Trevor or does he conjure up his ghost?"

Molly felt her mouth drop open, and before she could recover herself, he went on.

"Your father has been dead above three years, I should guess, and I trust you will accept my belated condolences. And concur that as you are in charge of the operation, there is no need for us to waste Mr. Gresham's time. So if you will dismiss your servant . . ."

He inclined his auburn head toward Mrs. Mulvaney, who was still tugging at his ragged sleeve, and Molly hesitated. His disreputable appearance notwithstanding, he seemed an intelligent man of some education, and he had demonstrated no propensity for violent behavior. More to the point, he knew the truth about Trevor and Company, and Molly must determine the source of his information and the extent to which it had been circulated.

"Very well," she said. "You may go, Mrs. Mulvaney."

"Well, I shan't go far." Mrs. Mulvaney released the sleeve and stepped into the hall. "I shall stand just outside the door, and if I hear the _slightest_ untoward sound, I shall fetch the constable." This with a baleful glare at the intruder. "Remember that, Miss Molly; the tiniest *peep* from you, and I shall go for help."

She pulled the door to, leaving it a bit ajar, and the stranger pushed it firmly closed.

"Miss Molly?" he mused, turning back around. "Is your name Mary then?"

"My name is Miss Trevor to you," Molly snapped. "And who the devil might you be?"

"Ah." He nodded approvingly. "A woman who minces no words. May I sit down?"

To Molly's utter lack of surprise, he did not await a response but sauntered across the room, examining the bookshelves and the furnishings and the Axminster rug as he walked. When he stopped in front of the desk, he was illuminated by the winter sunlight streaming through the window, and Molly observed that his auburn hair was generously shot with gold and his eyes were an astonishingly pale shade of blue. And that, tempering his otherwise fearsome aspect, there was an incongruous splash of golden freckles across his cheeks and the bridge of his rather long nose.

He gazed at the ledgers a moment, then raised his pale eyes, and Molly willed herself not to look away. She had pondered her appearance at considerable length since her encounter with Lord Ogilvie and had decided that, if not beautiful, she was sufficiently handsome to garner the viscount's favor. Her face—like Papa's, like the stranger's —was a trifle too sharp, with high cheekbones and narrow jaws and a distinctly pointed chin. Nor was she entirely pleased with her hair: it was dead straight and an unremarkable blond in color. Her eyes, however, *were* remarkable—huge and thickly lashed and so deeply blue as to verge on violet—and she was blessed with fair and virtually flawless skin. Although, to say the truth, she often judged her complexion *too* fair because the slighest flush tended to set it quite aflame.

"Very nice," the intruder said.

His careless wave encompassed the sumptuous

appointments of the office, but his eyes had not left Molly's face; and she felt the onslaught of one of her infuriating blushes.

"Thank you," she muttered as he took the chair across the desk. "And now you've completed your inspection, perhaps you'd be kind enough to tell me your name."

"Would that I could, Miss Trevor, but if that were the case, I shouldn't be here. I am *known* as Jonathan Shelton."

His reply was most intriguing, but he had reminded Molly of her chief concern, and she elected to defer comment. "I should like you to explain, Mr. Shelton, precisely how you discovered my situation."

"It was really very simple." He flashed a smug smile, suggesting that it had not been simple at all. "As I indicated, I wish to negotiate a loan, and when I reached London, I began inquiring about the local moneylenders. I was consistently advised that Stephen Trevor was the finest of the lot, but I soon detected a curious circumstance: no one had actually *seen* Mr. Trevor for upward of three years. When I further learned he had been in ill health for some years prior to that, it was an easy matter to conclude that he had died."

"But how did you conclude that *I* was in control?" Molly demanded.

"My informants invariably reported that they had spoken with Mr. Trevor's secretary, who had subsequently conferred with Trevor himself. If there *was* no Trevor, I reasoned, the secretary must be conferring with someone else. I consequently took the liberty of interviewing one of your neighbors and established that Mr. Trevor had an adult daughter . . ." He stopped and sketched another self-satisfied smile.

"You then took the liberty of forcing your way into the house," Molly said severely, "and frightening Mrs. Mulvaney half out of her wits." To say nothing of myself, she silently added.

"I apologize if I alarmed *Mrs. Mulvaney*."

His tone was solemn, but there was a suspicious twitch

about his mouth. An oddly infectious twitch, and Molly sternly repressed a grin of her own.

"I hope you will forgive my impatience," he continued. "I am sure you understand that I wanted to pursue our discussion without delay."

"There will be no delay, Mr. Shelton," Molly said briskly. As always occurred when she turned her mind to business, she was totally serious, no longer the least amused. "I can tell you at once that I shall not lend you a single farthing."

"But—"

"But what if you expose me?" Molly interjected. "I anticipated that threat, and *you* should understand that I will not be intimidated. You will find it difficult to prove that Papa is not alive, and I shall simply take my chances."

"My, how you do run on," he said mildly. "I have no intention of exposing you; I merely wished to say that you have not heard my proposition."

"I am not interested in your proposition, Mr. Shelton. At the risk of offending you, I must point out that your appearance is scarcely designed to inspire the confidence of a prospective creditor. Indeed, I should as readily lend funds to a beggar in the street."

"How very harsh of you, Miss Trevor." He sighed and shook his red head. "I begin to believe that I should have remained in Canada."

"Canada?" Molly repeated. That accounted for his accent. "You have lived there all your life?"

"For all but two of my thirty years. I was in the fur trade."

"I have no desire to invest in the fur trade," Molly said firmly. "Particularly," she could not resist adding, "as you seem to have made scant success of it."

"Another harsh, unfounded judgment." He shook his head again. "In fact, I was *extremely* successful, but I . . . Never mind. I shall let you read it for yourself and then answer any questions you may have."

"It" was evidently the creased and soiled sheet of paper

he extracted from one pocket of his threadbare coat and
passed across the desk. Molly unfolded the letter, for such
it proved to be, and beheld a single paragraph written in
an exceedingly poor hand.

"Jon—" she deciphered, "I am sorry, but we need the
money much more than you. Before she died, Mama told
me that you are the son of a very rich English earl. She
couldn't tell me his name because she was deelerious."
Molly shuddered a bit in the absent Mrs. Mulvaney's
behalf. "I didn't tell you before because I was afraid you
would go to England and leave me. But now I have
Ralph, so you can go and find out who you are and be
rich. Nell."

Mr. Shelton's final remark notwithstanding, the letter
introduced nearly as many questions as it answered, and
after twice reviewing it, Molly passed it back. "I collect
that 'Nell,' whoever she is, stole some money from you,"
she said.

"Nell is my half sister, and she stole *all* my money," he
confirmed grimly, replacing the paper in his pocket. "She
and her fiancé, Ralph Grimes. All but a few pounds,
which, I presume, they fancied adequate to finance my
grand quest. Unfortunately, they reckoned without the
necessity for three daily meals. To my further misfortune, Ralph and I are the same size, or *were*"—he
plucked sardonically at his gaping waistcoat—"and he
helped himself to my clothes as well. All except for these,
which were literally upon my back. I estimate the total
booty at nearly seven thousand pounds."

"But how did they do it?" Molly gasped. "Did you keep
it in cash, just lying about?"

"No, but I might as well have done: Nell had free
access to my accounts. I daresay you find that hard to
comprehend, but I was sometimes in the wilderness for
months on end. And, frankly, I could never be certain I'd
come back."

"Were you in the . . . the wilderness when your mother
died?" Molly asked.

"Yes." His pale blue eyes briefly clouded; then he
slammed one fist into the palm of his opposite hand. "I

cannot *conceive* why she didn't tell me. Mama, that is. She did occasionally mention that I'd been born in England, but she never so much as hinted that Richard Shelton was my stepfather and Nell but my half sister. Indeed, I wonder if she intentionally told Nell. Perhaps, if she was delirious, it simply slipped out."

"Or perhaps," Molly said, "Nell fabricated the entire story. She and Ralph had an excellent motive for enticing you out of the country."

"Nell lacks the imagination to fabricate a shopping list," Mr. Shelton said dryly, "and Ralph is somewhat less creative than she. No, I am persuaded that her letter says the truth. And the most ironic aspect is that if she had told me two years since—when Mama died—I should have had no reason to abandon her and come to England. I was wealthy in my own right with every expectation of increasing my fortune . . ." His voice trailed off, and his lean jaws momentarily hardened. "But in the circumstances, I have everything to gain and nothing to lose, do I not, Miss Trevor? Even should I fail to establish my parentage, my situation will certainly be no *worse*."

"I suppose not," Molly agreed, "but I fear I cannot help you." She was sincerely sympathetic to his plight, genuinely regretful, but business was business. "You obviously wish a loan to meet your expenses while you conduct your search, and that could require considerable time. Nor is there any assurance that your quest will be successful. And however modestly you might live—"

"But I don't think to live modestly at all," he interposed. "To the contrary: if my search *is* to prove successful, I must be in a position to associate freely with the . . . the *ton*, I believe you call it. With those most likely to have been acquainted with my father. And in order to do so, I must represent myself as a wealthy entrepreneur from abroad. Which," he added darkly, "I recently *was*."

"So I am to provide vast sums of money for your wardrobe and your household and a carriage or two, no doubt," Molly said acidly. "Had you given any thought to the matter of repayment?"

"Considerable thought indeed. If, in fact, I discover myself the heir to a fortune, I shall give you ten percent of the value. If not, I shall establish myself in some sort of business and repay only the loan plus interest."

"I fear I cannot help you," Molly repeated. "In view of the very limited information you have, I judge it highly improbable that you will be able to learn your father's identity. Should you do so, it may well prove that you are not his legal heir. Indeed, if you will pardon me for pointing it out, you could well be illegitimate. In the interim, you would have lived like a fine gentleman at great expense to me . . ."

A fine gentleman! Molly caught her breath, overwhelmed by a sudden wild, wonderful notion. A wealthy entrepreneur from abroad with ties to the British peerage would be "respectable" in the extreme. And such a gentleman could easily have a female relative . . .

"I shall do it under one condition," she blurted out, before her customary common sense could intrude. "I shall do it if you permit me to pose as your sister."

She took some dim satisfaction in the realization that she had caught him entirely unawares: his pale eyes widened, and his brows shot into the fringes of his overlong hair. "Pose as my sister?" he said at last. "Whyever should you want to do that?"

"My motives need not concern you, Mr. Shelton."

"Ah." He grinned. "It has to do with a man, I'll warrant." Molly's cheeks blazed, and she hastily lowered her eyes. "Come now, Miss Trevor, if I am to assist you, I really must be apprised of the situation."

"His name is Viscount Ogilvie," Molly mumbled, tracing aimless designs on the cover of the new ledger. She described their encounter at the theater, related the background of the Elting family, and—judging her blush to have subsided—lifted her eyes again. "You may or may not be aware that moneylenders are not received in polite society," she went on. "But I fancy the Eltings would look with prodigious favor on the daughter of an earl."

"You would wed Lord Ogilvie under false pretenses?"

"Of course not!" Molly said indignantly. "Once I was confident of his affection, I should reveal the truth. If he loved me, it wouldn't signify a whit."

Her brave words sounded a trifle weak even in her own ears, and Mr. Shelton's pale eyes flickered briefly with an emotion she couldn't read.

"Very well," he said at length. "I shall allow you to pose as my sister. I do feel, however, that there should be a slight adjustment in the terms of our agreement. If your . . . er . . . suit is successful—"

"No," Molly interrupted firmly. "I daresay I could devise some other means of meeting Lord Ogilvie, but you would find no other moneylender in England willing to finance your scheme. No, the terms of our agreement stand."

"You're a hard woman, Miss Trevor." He heaved another dramatic sigh. "But I suspect you're right, so let us be about the planning. As your address is widely known, I fancy we must first locate a suitable house. You are no doubt familiar with London's various neighborhoods, so perhaps you have a suggestion."

"We shall not establish our household in London," Molly said. "It is not the Season, and the *ton* are presently in Brighton."

"Meaning that Lord Ogilvie is presently in Brighton."

"The *Regent* is presently in Brighton," Molly said stiffly, dismally aware that she was blushing again. "Or will be shortly, and where he goes, the *ton* follow. Furthermore, I chance to own a house there, and if I am not mistaken . . ."

She stood and walked to one of the bookshelves, removed a volume, opened it, found the pertinent entry.

"Yes." She looked up and discovered Mr. Shelton's pale eyes upon her, narrowed in keen appraisal, and, inexplicably, felt the threat of another flush. "Yes," she said again, her voice peculiarly unsteady, "the lease expired at the end of the year, and the house has not yet been relet. I daresay it will do very nicely, and I shall instruct Mrs. Mulvaney to begin hiring a staff."

"Is it a house upon which your father foreclosed?"

"It is a house upon which *I* foreclosed, Mr. Shelton."

"You're a hard woman," he repeated.

There was no mockery about the words this time, only those pale, speculative eyes, and to escape them, Molly hurriedly replaced the book on the shelf.

"While Mrs. Mulvaney is at her task," she said crisply, turning back around, "you must obtain a new wardrobe. I shall escort you to the various purveyors tomorrow."

"I am not quite the greenhead you fancy." He spoke, perversely, in an exaggerated drawl. "My current lamentable appearance notwithstanding, my taste in attire is generally excellent."

"And I daresay it would be excellent indeed if you had unlimited funds to expend," Molly said coolly. "I shall therefore accompany you so as to ensure that you exercise some restraint. I shall come for you at ten in the morning." She frowned. "Where, by the by, are you staying?"

"Staying," he echoed. "That brings up a rather awkward circumstance."

He rose and traversed the room and stopped beside her. They had not previously stood together, and Molly remarked how very tall he was: she was fully five and a half feet in height, and she reached barely to his chin. Perhaps it was that—his excessive height—that made him seem uncomfortably close; at any rate, she stepped a bit away.

"I am not staying anywhere at present," he said. "The bill for last night's lodging took my final shilling, I'm afraid. You appear to have ample space here—"

"No!" Molly protested. She was not yet ready to explain their odd arrangement to Mrs. Mulvaney. "No, I shall give you some money for room and board. Board especially, Mr. Shelton; you really must fatten yourself up. I shall expect receipts, of course."

His eyes flickered again—again unreadably.

"And do not call me a hard woman," Molly snapped. "I did not grow wealthy by dispensing charity, and I shan't impoverish myself in that fashion either. Now . . ."

She returned to her desk, opened the bottom right drawer, withdrew the cash box, and counted out twenty pounds. She crossed back to Mr. Shelton's side and laid the bank notes in his palm.

"That should keep you for some time," she said. "I recommend you engage a room at Limmer's; it is far from elegant, but they serve an abundance of good, plain food."

"Do you not wish a receipt for the money as well?" he inquired politely, placing the notes in his pocket.

"That won't be necessary." She was snapping again. "You may rest assured that I shall enter the amount in my ledger. Good day, Mr. Shelton; I shall see you at ten tomorrow."

He inclined his auburn head, went to the door, opened it, and Mrs. Mulvaney nearly tumbled across the threshold. Molly desired the housekeeper to show Mr. Shelton out, and when they had disappeared, she rushed to the door, slammed it shut, and collapsed against it, shuddering to contemplate Mrs. Mulvaney's reaction to the afternoon's events.

—2—

" . . . the most idiotish scheme I have ever heard of," Mrs. Mulvaney finished.

They were seated at the breakfast table, for Molly had decided to defer their discussion till the morning following Mr. Shelton's visit. She had rationalized that the delay would tend to dim Mrs. Mulvaney's memory of her confrontation with the bold intruder, but, in truth, Molly remained considerably in awe of the erstwhile governess. Her present demeanor would have inspired awe in any case: her black eyes glowed like angry coals, and her gray hair seemed fairly to bristle round her plump, flushed face. And after several hours of sober reflection and an extremely restless sleep, Molly was forced to own to some agreement with the housekeeper's assessment.

"The man is a barbarian." Mrs. Mulvaney was not finished after all. "Bursting in against my express instructions, behaving like a savage . . . *Dressed* a good deal like a savage, too, I might add."

"I explained that," Molly reminded her. "I explained how his sister stole his money—"

"Has it not occurred to you that he might well have invented that story so as to win your sympathy? So he could steal *your* money?"

In fact, this had occurred to Molly, and she bit her lip and gazed down at her plate. It was entirely possible that Mr. Shelton had told her one lie upon another, had written the letter from "Nell" himself, but did it really signify? He could provide the opportunity she'd dreamed of—the chance to escape Trevor and Company and be respectable and win Viscount Ogilvie's heart.

"Don't you see that it's my only chance, Mrs. Mulvaney?" Molly raised her eyes and spoke her thoughts aloud. "My only chance to meet a fine gentleman? Which," she added pointedly, "is what you have always wished for me, is it not?"

"My *wish* is that you could meet Lord Ogilvie without resort to . . ."

The housekeeper stopped and clapped one hand over her mouth, but it was, of course, too late. Molly had not advised Mrs. Mulvaney of her *tendre*, but Gresham clearly had, and Molly elected to turn the situation to her advantage.

"You know then," she said mournfully, lowering her eyes again. "Yes, Mrs. Mulvaney, I have quite set my cap at Viscount Ogilvie, and without him, I fear I may simply pine away." She ventured an upward peep through her lashes and observed, to her gratification, that the housekeeper's face had softened a bit. "Furthermore"—with a ragged sigh—"I feel I owe it to Papa." Mrs. Mulvaney had been utterly devoted to her late employer. "You will recollect that he desired me to have a come-out—"

"I do indeed recollect that," the housekeeper interposed severely. "Had you heeded his advice, you would not be in your present coil. And I am sure your father would *not* have desired you to embark upon a shameless plot with an uncivilized, unprincipled, un . . ."

But she had apparently exhausted her immediate store of "uns," and in the ensuing silence Molly squeezed her eyes tightly shut and set her mouth to trembling.

"Oh, very well," Mrs. Mulvaney said grudgingly. "Perhaps there would be no great harm in it. Though you must be exceedingly careful; you must not give him a farthing more than absolutely required."

"I shall be *very* careful," Molly promised, looking up, struggling to repress any hint of triumph. "And I am delighted to secure your approval, for I shall need your assistance in the matter of the house. Fortunately it is furnished, but I shall rely on you to engage a staff. Beginning with a butler, I fancy—"

"A butler?" Mrs. Mulvaney drew herself indignantly up. "I will not be ordered about by a butler."

"Nor did I anticipate you should," Molly said soothingly. "I planned for you to stay in London—"

"*Stay in London?* And permit you to be alone with that uncouth . . . uncouth . . ." She had found another "un" but evidently lacked a suitable noun to follow. "No, that is altogether out of the question, Miss Molly. I shall accompany you to Brighton and supervise the household as I have always done."

"Always," was not entirely accurate, but Molly chose not to issue a correction. "What of Gresham?" she asked instead.

"The maids can tend to Mr. Gresham very nicely. Although, without me to cook, I do wonder what the poor man is to eat. Well, I daresay Katie can improvise."

Katie was the chambermaid, and, as Mrs. Mulvaney was a perfectly wretched cook, Molly suspected Gresham would welcome the "improvisation." However, that did bring a delicate circumstance to mind: Mrs. Mulvaney could *not* be allowed to cook for the glittering guests Molly hoped to entertain in Brighton.

"I daresay you are right," she said. "In any event, I believe we shall need three or four maids and as many footmen, and I suppose Mr. Shelton, if he is to be properly attired, will require the services of a valet. And since you will be monstrous busy overseeing a staff of such size, perhaps you should also engage a cook."

"A cook?" The housekeeper's black eyes momentarily glittered with suspicion, but at length she bobbed her head. "Very good, Miss Molly; I shall begin the hiring at once."

"There is one other thing," Molly said as Mrs. Mulvaney rose. "You will have to address me publicly as Miss Shelton. Can you remember that?"

"I shall start practicing immediately, Miss M . . . Miss Shelton."

The name seemed to roll quite easily off her tongue, and Molly felt an odd shiver of fear, entertained an unsettling notion that she was losing her identity. "Excellent," she muttered. The corridor clock struck half-past nine, and she stood as well. "Please order out the carriage, Mrs. Mulvaney; I am to take Mr. Shelton to order a new wardrobe."

"I should certainly hope so." The housekeeper sniffed. "And after you have finished, you must go to the mantua-maker yourself."

"The mantua-maker?" Molly repeated. "But my clothes are quite adequate—"

"Your clothes are adequate for sitting behind a desk and attending the theater with Mr. Gresham," Mrs. Mulvaney corrected. "They are not in the *least* adequate for a respectable young woman of means who will be squired about Brighton by a *lord.*"

"I suppose not," Molly conceded. It was precisely what she wanted—to be respectable, to be courted by her handsome viscount—and she wondered why she should experience another little stab of dismay.

Mr. Shelton was waiting in front of Limmer's when the landau drew to a halt, presenting a most "uncouth" picture indeed, and Molly was thankful she could not see the expression of Lewis, the coachman, as the "barbarian" strode forward to join her in the carriage.

"What a splendid conveyance," he remarked, patting the leather squab beside him. "And your horses are magnificent; perfectly matched, I noticed."

"*So he could steal* your *money.*" Mrs. Mulvaney's words echoed ominously in Molly's ears, and she gazed coolly across at him. "Were *your* horses perfectly matched, Mr. Shelton? The ones your sister undoubtedly stole?"

"Oh, hardly," he said airily, "for I had no access to a fine institution like Tattersall's. No, I am happy to say that Nell made away with two miserable nags whose loss I do not regret in the slightest."

If he *was* lying, Molly thought, he lied prodigious cleverly.

"Speaking of sisters," he went on, "you really cannot continue to call me Mr. Shelton. You may recollect from Nell's letter that my nickname is Jon."

"Yes, Jon," she murmured.

"Now"—he settled comfortably against the seat—"to what tailor are you . . . ah . . . *escorting* me? Weston and Meyer are excellent, I'm told, and Guthrie as well."

He had obviously researched the city's male clothiers, and Molly felt her eyes narrow with renewed suspicion. "You were told aright," she said. "However, Papa patronized them both, and in his later years I often shopped in his stead. We shall therefore go to Schweitzer and Davidson. Permit me to assure you," she added frostily, "that their workmanship is quite the equal of those you mentioned."

"I do hope so. I am sure you will agree that if I am to pass as a wealthy man of business, I must fully look the part."

He broke into a jaunty, tuneless whistle, and Molly gazed stonily out the carriage window until they had reached the designated establishment in Cork Street. Lewis handed her out of the carriage, and she preceded Jon into the shop, where Mr. Schweitzer bustled forth to introduce himself and tender his assistance.

"We have come to order clothes for my . . . my brother," Molly said. She beckoned Jon forward, into the tailor's unobstructed view, and the latter's eyes widened with shock. "As I fancy you can see," she rushed on,"he has but recently returned to town."

"Returned from where?" Mr. Schweitzer's tone suggested that this dubious client might well have been a recent inmate of Bedlam.

"From Canada," Jon replied with an easy smile. "Jonathan Shelton at your service, sir"—he extended his hand—"and pray permit me to apologize for my lamentable appearance. The night before my ship sailed, the inn at which I was staying caught fire, and I was lucky to escape with my life. My life and my purse; the rest of my possessions were lost. Eager as I was to rejoin my dear sister in England, I elected to set out with only the clothes on my back, and I've scarcely had them off these past six weeks. An unfortunate decision, as it happened, because the food on the *Niagara* was virtually inedible, and I calculate I lost at least a stone." He plucked at his sagging breeches in confirmation. "Consequently, we shall have to tailor my new wardrobe to the size of the old, shall we not? And of course I quite realize that my present attire is altogether out of fashion; you will understand that life in the colonies is a trifle backward."

Molly found it most alarming that he could prevaricate with such glib facility, but Mr. Schweitzer seemed quite won over: he wrung the proffered hand at some length and, for good measure, clapped Jon on one broad shoulder.

"I do indeed understand," the tailor said jovially, "and we shall soon have you rigged out as befits a man of your position. Er . . . just what *is* your position, Mr. Shelton?"

"I was in the fur trade, sir. A dangerous and dirty profession, but, I am delighted to say, an extremely lucrative one."

"Indeed?"

Molly thought Mr. Schweitzer was at the point of rubbing his hands together in glee, but he managed to restrain himself. He propelled Jon on into the shop, chattering of coats and waistcoats and pantaloons, of smallclothes for evening and breeches for riding; and Molly trailed in their wake. She belatedly perceived that her presence was entirely gratuitous: as Jon's sister, presumably his financial ward, she could hardly attempt to limit his purchases. No, she could only stand in silence, inwardly seething with ever-growing rage, while the tailor displayed his patterns and fabrics and her darling "brother" ordered six of these and eight of those and a dozen of the other.

"Well, let me solicit your sister's opinion," Mr. Schweitzer said. "What do you think, Miss Shelton?"

Molly was by now so vexed that she had ceased to attend the proceedings, and the tailor's use of her assumed name served to exacerbate her distress. Miss

Shelton was not the woman Miss Trevor was; Miss Shelton was powerless, dependent . . .

"I . . . I'm afraid I wasn't listening," she mumbled.

"We were discussing the cloth for your brother's coats," Mr. Schweitzer said. "I advised him that the Prince wears superfine while Mr. Brummell prefers the Bath."

Based on the information in Trevor and Company's files, Molly suspected that Beau Brummell would shortly be bankrupt and could well be forced to flee the country. In the interim, however, he was the recognized arbiter of fashion. On the other hand, they might encounter the Regent in Brighton, and he and Mr. Brummell had altogether fallen out.

"Make up half of each," she snapped, regaining a bit of her normal aplomb.

"A decision in the tradition of Solomon himself."

The tailor beamed with approval, then ushered Jon to the rear of the shop, where he and his "lamentable" clothes were to be measured. They came back perhaps fifteen minutes later, both looking immensely cheerful, Mr. Schweitzer now prattling of when Mr. Shelton was to return for his initial fitting and when the order would be finished; and Molly discovered that she had developed a fearful headache. But the interminable ordeal was, blessedly, over: the tailor escorted them to the door of the shop and watched as they resumed their places in the carriage.

"Where do you want to go now, Miss Trevor?" Lewis inquired.

Molly peered nervously at the shop, but the door was closed, and Mr. Schweitzer had disappeared within. The coachman would have to be schooled in the use of her alias as well, she reflected, and her temples throbbed as if to protest the increasing complexity of her charade.

"Mr. Schweitzer recommeded Hoby the bootmaker," Jon said, "and Lock's for my hats—"

"Take your seat, Lewis," Molly interrupted. "Upon my signal, you will drive me to Dupré's."

The coachman bowed and strode to the box, and Jon's auburn brows met in a frown.

"Dupré's," he mused. "I do not believe Schweitzer mentioned them."

"I fancy not," Molly said icily, "for Madame Dupré is my mantua-maker. As it is abundantly clear that you've no intention of heeding my wishes in respect to your expenditures, *I* have no intention of skulking about while you fritter my money away."

"Insofar as I am concerned, I have not *frittered* a single farthing." His voice was quite as cold as hers. "Nor do I view myself as spending *your* money; one way or another, you will be repaid."

"I have only your word for that; I have no security for my loan. To the contrary: there is nothing to prevent you from absconding with your elegant new finery and manufacturing an elegant new tale for your next victim. Much like the excessively imaginative account you fabricated for Mr. Schweitzer."

"What would you have had me tell him? That my sister, which you presumably are, had stolen my fortune?"

"Of course not," Molly muttered.

"What is your point then?"

"My point is that you lie with monstrous ease, and I cannot but wonder . . ." She stopped and gnawed her lip.

"If I have lied to you?" he finished. "In that event, I daresay it would be best for us to terminate our agreement. I doubt Mr. Schweitzer has yet put scissors to cloth, so I shall rush right back and cancel the order. I shall return the balance of the funds you advanced me yesterday; I have it in my pocket. Unfortunately, I was compelled to spend eight shillings for bed and board, but I shall sign a note for that—"

"Stop it!" Molly hissed. "You are being absurd."

"*I* am being absurd? Permit me to remind you that my role in our little farce is essentially a legitimate one. I was, till very recently, a wealthy man, and I've every reason to believe myself the son of an earl. It is *you* who think to assume a false identity so as to deceive Viscount Ogilvie."

He had twisted the situation altogether to his advantage: since he could not prove himself honest, he had proved her *dis*honest. And, Molly realized dismally, he could utilize the same flawed logic anytime she dared to question his motives; he could invariably put her in the wrong.

"We can terminate our agreement at once," he reiterated. "If, however, you elect to proceed, I won't have you challenging each word I utter and every groat I spend." He might have been reading her mind. "I suspect you will choose to proceed even in those circumstances," he continued softly. "I suspect, your assertion notwithstanding, that you could *not* readily devise another means of meeting Lord Ogilvie."

Molly recollected her adolescent notion of stalking the viscount through the streets of London and grimly awarded Jon another score. But she could ill afford to let him know the magnitude of his victory, and she essayed a careless shrug.

"I suspect I could," she said, "but as we have already embarked upon our project, I shall, in fact, elect to proceed. You may go to the bootmaker and the hatter without me"—she tried to make this sound like a generous, nay, *regal* concession—"while Lewis drives me to Madame Dupré's."

"Very well." He clambered nimbly out of the landau, then gazed up at her from the footpath. "If I might tender an observation, the dull colors you favor really do not become you at all." His pale eyes swept from her brown Parisian bonnet to her brown pelisse to her brown kid shoes. "You should wear blue to emphasize your eyes. They're truly remarkable, you know."

"Thank . . . thank you," Molly stammered.

"You should also have your gowns cut to a better fit," he said. "The one you had on yesterday fairly hung about you."

"My dresses are designed for comfort," Molly said stiffly. "For working at a desk—"

"You won't be working at a desk in Brighton," he interposed. "I should guess you have an excellent form; don't hide it beneath all that drapery."

"Are you quite finished?" Molly choked, miserably aware that her cheeks were flaming.

"No, I am not. I find your blushes most appealing, but they do tend to betray your feelings rather too much. You could disguise them to a considerable extent if you used a bit of rouge. And you *must* do something about your hair."

"*I* must do something about *my* hair?" Molly cast a furious glare at his shaggy auburn mane.

"I shall naturally have mine cut before we set out," he said mildly, "and you should do the same. And it would be far handsomer if it were curly."

"That is entirely possible," Molly snapped. "However, my hair happens to be straight by nature."

"But nature can be improved upon. Nell's hair was dead straight too, but she had all manner of mysterious implements, and she was forever tying it up in rags . . . Well." He grinned. "Merely a few words of brotherly advice, which you may or may not decide to heed."

"I shall not heed them," Molly assured him warmly, "nor do I wish to hear any more of your advice. I believe Mr. Schweitzer stated that your clothes will be ready in two weeks' time. We shall therefore leave for Brighton in two weeks and a day, on the seventeenth. I shall come for you at Limmer's early that morning; eight o'clock, let us say."

"Should we not meet again prior to our departure? So as to discuss the details of our project?"

"We shall have ample opportunity to discuss the details en route," Molly said. "Indeed, I am sorry to say that we shall be confined together in the carriage for some eight hours."

"As you will."

His tone was expressionless, but his pale eyes briefly flickered in that unreadable fashion Molly had noticed the day before. She rapped smartly on the front window, the landau clattered to a start, and she granted Jon a curt nod of farewell. Brotherly advice indeed! she fumed as the carriage proceeded toward Leicester Square. He had sought only to humiliate her, to flaunt the advantage he had so unfortunately managed to attain.

But as Molly leafed through Madame Dupré's style-book, she found herself oddly drawn to the bolder, more revealing designs; and when she questioned Madame on this head, the mantau-maker declared that Miss Trevor would look *"très belle"* in a *"robe décolletée."* And when Molly went to the nearby linen draper to select the fabrics for her new ensembles, she discovered that in an astonishing number of cases, the perfect material chanced to be blue.

Molly was extremely busy during the ensuing week, conferring, on the one hand, with Mrs. Mulvaney, who was to go ahead to Brighton and ready the house; and, on the other, with Gresham, who was to direct Trevor and Company in her absence. In short, she had scant opportunity to ponder her appearance, but every time she passed a mirror, it seemed that her hair had grown longer and straighter and generally more odious. Consequently, when she returned to Madame Dupré for her initial fittings, she casually asked the mantua-maker to recommend a *coiffeur;* and, lest she change her mind, she scheduled an appointment at once.

Mr. Willingham came to Hanover Street the following morning, mere minutes after Mrs. Mulvaney's departure for Brighton; and Molly sat frozen in the chair before her dressing table, her eyes screwed firmly closed, while he pulled and snipped, pulled and twisted, combed and brushed, and pulled some more. At last he ordered her to open her eyes, and she could not repress a gasp when she beheld the arresting countenance in the glass. Mr. Willingham had cut her hair exceedingly short indeed— the hind hair was barely visible—but, with a profusion of curls spilling about her face, she somehow looked more feminine for all his drastic ministrations. Yes, she decided, he had rendered her *softer,* had made her pointed face seem delicate rather than sharp.

The hairdresser coughed, and Molly started, paid him

(tipping him far too much), and desired Katie to show him out. She then went back to studying her reflection, and a tiny smile of triumph tickled the corners of her mouth as she contemplated Jon's reaction. Not that she cared a deuce for *his* arrogant opinions. She observed, to her distress, that her mirrored image had developed a distinct flush, and she resolved to purchase a pot of rouge before she left for Brighton.

—3—

"Good afternoon, Miss Shelton." Mrs. Mulvaney pushed the front door fully open and beckoned them across the threshold. "And . . . and *Mr.* Shelton!" she gasped as Jon stepped into the vestibule. "How . . . how exceedingly handsome you look!"

"My observation precisely, Mrs. Mulvaney." Jon flashed his easy smile. "I told Molly earlier on that she's a sister any man could be proud of."

"I fancy so," the housekeeper agreed absently.

Molly noticed, with a flicker of irritation, that her eyes had never left Jon; but, upon reflection, she could well understand Mrs. Mulvaney's astonishment. To say the truth, she herself had scarcely recognized the transformed "barbarian" awaiting her outside of Limmer's that morning. As promised, he had been barbered, and his new coiffure bared all but the tops of his ears and revealed a goodly expanse of high, smooth forehead. He had apparently regained his lost weight—his new clothes fit him to perfection—but Molly thought he remained a trifle too lean. Well, perhaps not *too* lean, she conceded, for he did look prodigious well in the current styles: the immaculately tailored buff pantaloons flattered his long, straight legs; and the cutaway coat, of sapphire superfine, emphasized his broad shoulders and slender waist. His waistcoat was buff trimmed in sapphire, his neckcloth pale blue; and depending on one's perspective, his eyes looked now light, now darker . . . Molly suddenly realized that the eyes in question were returning her scrutiny, and—not entirely trusting her rouge—she gazed studiedly at the hem of her new midnight-blue pelisse.

"I believe you will find everything in order," Mrs. Mulvaney said.

Her remark was extremely well-timed, and Molly raised her eyes and peered about with elaborate interest. In point of fact, she *was* quite interested because she had not previously seen the house in Brighton; she had merely calculated, from its excellent location in Ship Street and an inventory of its furnishings, that it was of sufficient value to secure Lord Chudleigh's loan. She had observed from the street that it was a double bow-fronted structure faced with black mathematical tiles, and she now perceived that the bow windows fronted a dining room to the left of the foyer and a library to the right. As she had expected, the shelves in the latter were bare, for she had specified that Lord Chudleigh could retain his books and "any other items of sentimental significance." However, the entry hall seemed rather bare as well—it contained only a marble-topped console table—and Molly suspected his lordship had developed a sentimental fondness for various chairs and candlestands and other readily transportable pieces.

"Everything except the cook," Mrs. Mulvaney amended in a whisper. "I do not judge Mrs. Bradford's performance at all satisfactory. But," she added generously, "I shall permit you to decide for yourself. For the present, I shall instruct the footmen to bring in your luggage, and I shall then show you to your bedchambers."

"I daresay we can find the bedchambers without your assistance," Molly said. "We shall go on up, Mrs. Mulvaney; join us when you can."

The housekeeper nodded and tugged a bell cord near the solitary table, and Molly preceded Jon up the wide staircase to the first story. This floor comprised a large drawing room on one side, a parlor and music room on the other, but Molly—eager to rest from the journey—

paused only long enough to ascertain that the furniture was largely intact.

There were four bedrooms on the second story, and it was clear from the position of the doors that the one at the left-hand front was the master chamber. Molly opened the door, glanced around, and detected no major item missing here either. A wide canopied bed was centrally positioned against the rear wall, a pedestal cupboard beside it. A satinwood wardrobe and matching washstand shared the unbroken side wall, a dressing table and cheval mirror were situated near the door, and identical Adam chairs flanked the window in the front of the room. Evidently, Molly thought wryly, the chairs had been too cumbersome to inspire Lord Chudleigh's sentimental attachment.

"I fancy this will do very nicely," Jon remarked from his vantage point beside her.

"I fancy it will," Molly concurred. "We must now determine which of the other bedchambers Mrs. Mulvaney has taken so as to select a room for you."

"For me? I fear you misunderstood. I meant to say that *this* room will do very nicely for me; I am, after all, the master of the household."

As often happened, the sheer impudence of the man rendered Molly temporarily speechless, but at length she found her tongue. "You are exceedingly far from being the master of the household," she snapped. "It is *my* house—"

"But you must consider our imposture," he whispered, with a dramatic glance over his shoulder. "I daresay the servants would count it most odd if the younger sister were to occupy the master chamber while the older brother was relegated to one of the secondary rooms."

"I do not care a damn for the opinion of the servants," Molly hissed back.

"Molly, Molly." He smacked his tongue against his teeth. "If you wish to appear *respectable*, you really must look to your language. Insofar as the rooms are concerned, I am confident Mrs. Mulvaney would agree—".

"Confident I would agree to what?" the housekeeper demanded, materializing behind him.

"Molly and I were . . . ah . . . discussing the disposition of the bedrooms." Another winsome smile. "I pointed out that the servants would no doubt find it peculiar if she were to take the master chamber."

"And *I* pointed out—"

Molly was interrupted by a commotion on the stairs, and two footmen soon panted into view, bearing an unfamiliar trunk between them. It was an immense piece, fashioned of leather bound in brass, costing who-knew-how-many pounds; and she gritted her own teeth with rage.

"You may put Mr. Shelton's trunk in here," Mrs. Mulvaney said briskly, waving vaguely about the master bed-chamber. "And Miss Shelton's luggage"—she directed her attention to a second pair of footmen who had loomed up behind the first—"is to go in the green room across the corridor."

Molly ground her fingernails into her palms, but the circumstances quite precluded further argument. She spun around, stalked across the hall, threw the door open; and the second pair of footmen deposited her trunk in the middle of the green-and-white Axminster carpet. Molly had always loathed green, and a close examination of the room merely served to aggravate her already keen displeasure. It was far smaller than the master chamber and furnished with a plain, narrow bed, a scarred mahogany wardrobe, a painted washstand from which much of the paint had peeled, and a rickety rosewood dressing table. And, as if to heap insult upon injury, Lord Chudleigh had apparently absconded with the chair that should have stood before the latter.

During Molly's inspection, the footmen had disappeared and subsequently returned with the remainder of her baggage, and Mrs. Mulvaney met them at the door as they were bowing out again.

"Please summon Woodson to unpack Mr. Shelton's things," she instructed. "I myself shall assist Miss Shelton."

The senior of the pair—a tall bald man who looked astonishingly like Gresham—nodded his acknowledgment, the two stepped into the corridor, and Mrs. Mulvaney closed the door in their wake.

"How dare you take his part?" Molly said furiously when the tap of the footmen's steps had faded well away. "The master bedchamber should have been mine—"

"But it should not have," the housekeeper interposed. "Mr. Shelton was entirely right on that head: the servants would have judged such an arrangement most peculiar. And I've little doubt they would have babbled of it all about the town, for I find them rather too wide in the mouth. Indeed, I suspect they've already babbled of their mysterious Canadian employers, but perhaps that is all to the good."

"Mysterious?" Molly echoed. "Why mysterious?"

"Because they have pressed me for details about you and Mr. Shelton, and I had none to provide. I claimed I had met you only briefly myself, but that excuse will not continue to suffice."

"No, I fancy not."

Molly gazed longingly at the bed, but much as she wanted to rest prior to dinner, she recognized that Mrs. Mulvaney must be advised to the "details" she and Jon had concocted during the drive from London. She peered around for a place to sit, but *all* the chairs were gone, and she sank wearily on the bed and motioned the housekeeper to sit beside her.

"To begin with," Molly said, "there is a problem with our ages; as Jon is six years older than I, one would expect him to recollect our father. We shall therefore claim, should the subject arise, that he is only eight-and-twenty. In that circumstance, our father could have died when Jon was scarcely three, and it is possible Jon would not remember him."

"But will such a claim not make it more difficult for Mr. Shelton to learn his father's identity?" Mrs. Mulvaney objected. "Anyone familiar with his *true* circumstances would surely know his date of birth."

"We think not. No, it seems certain that there was

some . . . some secrecy surrounding Jon's birth: if he was the known, legitimate heir of an earl, his mother would not have taken him to Canada following his father's death."

"What if his father is not dead?" the housekeeper asked. "Mr. Shelton could be the illegitimate son of a *living* earl."

"In which event, it is most unlikely that his father would come forward to acknowledge him after all these years. No, Mrs. Mulvaney, we must proceed with the assumption that, whether Jon is legitimate or not, his father is deceased. At any rate, I believe he looks sufficiently youthful to pass for twenty-eight, do you not agree?"

"Yes. Though you might as readily claim that *you* are twenty-six."

Jon had pointed out precisely the same thing, and, as she had done then, Molly chose to ignore this horrid suggestion.

"We have determined to say that I have been in England these past six years," she went on instead. "We could conceive no other way to account for the difference in our accents."

"Six years." Mrs. Mulvaney nodded. "You would have been eighteen then, so I daresay you plan to explain that you came to England for your come-out. That you went to a relative—"

"No, not a relative," Molly interjected. "We cannot appear to have any English relatives—none we are acquainted with at least—because a relative would undoubtedly know our father's identity. We consequently intend to state that I was *brought* to England by a friend, a woman who had resided in Canada for some years herself. We shall call her Mrs. Alton."

"Why did your *mother* not bring you to England?" the housekeeper inquired.

"Because she could not leave our stepfather, whom we, of course, believed to be our father. Furthermore, poor Mama was not in the best of health."

"Yes, I fancy that will do." Mrs. Mulvaney nodded

again. "But if Mrs. Alton brought you to England for your come-out six years since, why have you not, in fact, come out?"

"Mrs. Alton fell ill while we were yet aboard the ship—"

"And died!" the housekeeper finished triumphantly.

"No, she did not die," Molly snapped. "If she had died, I should have returned at once to Canada, should I not? Pray permit me to finish, Mrs. Mulvaney. Mrs. Alton did not die, not then. Her final illness lasted for six long years, and in all that time she was never sufficiently well to bring me out." Molly heaved a great sigh; she was almost beginning to believe the sorrowful tale herself. "And I," she continued mournfully, "I was her faithful nurse and companion, scarcely leaving her bedside."

"How sad." The housekeeper actually sniffed a bit, and Molly hoped she could be half so persuasive when she repeated the story for real. "And then what happened?"

"Mrs. Alton expired at last, several months ago. I was at the point of arranging transportation back to Canada when I received a letter from my brother informing me that our dear mother had also died and he was en route to England. When he arrived, he related the most astonishing news: on her deathbed, Mama confessed that our natural father was a British earl. As she was delirious, she was unable to tell Jon our father's name . . . et cetera. Well, what do you think, Mrs. Mulvaney?"

"I think it will do," the housekeeper reiterated. "I shall ponder it and let you know if I detect any flaws, but for the present, I must see to dinner. Mrs. Bradford requires *constant* supervision."

She rose, and Molly stood as well. As she was still wearing her outdoor garments, she discovered herself uncomfortably warm, and she unfastened her cloak, tossed it on the bed, and proceeded to the dressing table to remove the matching bonnet. In the absence of a chair, she was compelled to bend half over in order to see into the mirror, and she recollected, with considerable annoyance, that there was a splendid cheval glass in the master bedchamber.

"You do look excessively well, by the by," Mrs. Mulvaney said. "Mr. Shelton was also right on that head. Blue quite becomes you"—she waved one hand the length of Molly's indigo carriage dress—"and I very much like your hair."

"I am delighted to hear it," Molly said dryly. "Katie has been tying it up for me, and I fear that task will now fall to you."

"You look excessively well indeed, and I daresay Lord Ogilvie will be altogether smitten. Though . . ."

"Though what?" Molly said.

"Never mind." Mrs. Mulvaney glanced at the clock on the mantel—an artifact Lord Chudleigh had miraculously overlooked. "I have desired dinner to be served in fifteen minutes, and I shall so inform Mr. Shelton."

"While you are about it, inform Mr. Shelton that I require one of his chairs." Molly indicated the vacant space before the dressing table. "And then please instruct one of the footmen to bring the chair to me."

"But there are other chairs," the housekeeper protested. "Chairs more suitable than his—"

"But I wish *Jon's* chair," Molly interrupted sweetly. "Pray see to it, Mrs. Mulvaney."

"Very well." She walked to the door, twisted the knob, turned back round. "As I doubt you would have the time to change for dinner, perhaps we could defer your unpacking till afterward. If that is satisfactory to you, Miss Shelton."

"Yes, that is satisfactory. And you needn't address me as Miss Shelton when we are alone. Indeed, I'd much prefer you to call me Miss Molly."

"No." The housekeeper shook her gray head. "No, it's best to use the same name at all times, lest I forget myself in public. I shall see you in the dining room, Miss Shelton."

She pulled the door open, stepped into the corridor, and closed the door behind her. Molly gazed after her, unable to repress the nagging little prickle of panic which had become all too familiar over the preceding

Even Mrs. Mulvaney, it seemed, was prepared to lay Molly Trevor forever to rest . . . She shook her own head, bent once more to the mirror, and hastily began to repair her hair.

The ensuing hours were in no way calculated to allay Molly's fears. When she ventured down to the dining room, she discovered that Mrs. Mulvaney had arrayed the entire staff in the vestibule for a formal presentation to their "mysterious" Canadian employers. Jon proceeded along the line, greeting them all with his easy smile, but Molly was keenly aware that this moment marked the final, irrevocable loss of her identity. Unlike Lewis and Mrs. Mulvaney and Jon himself, who were only playing a part, the servants assembled in the foyer would never know her as anyone but "Miss Shelton," would never know who she truly was. Neither would Mr. Schweitzer, of course, but Molly had been able to discount him, comforting herself with the reminder that she would not be compelled to see him again.

The introductions completed, Mrs. Mulvaney dismissed all but the footmen who were to serve at dinner and led the way into the dining room. Molly was initially heartened to find three places set; apparently, part or no, the housekeeper was not prepared to forgo the privilege of dining with her employers. However, Mrs. Mulvaney immediately explained to the startled footmen that, "by Canadian custom," the head of staff sat at table with the master of the household. And as the meal progressed, she managed to elicit a great deal of additional information for the footmen's benefit: inquiring about Miss Shelton's lack of a North American accent, lamenting her aborted come-out, sighing over Mrs. Alton's long illness and recent demise. Throughout this performance, Mrs. Mulvaney made a great show of sawing at her veal cutlet, as though it were exceedingly tough; chewing her boiled potatoes at great length, as if they were quite raw; and glowering from time to time at her plate. In truth, Molly judged Mrs. Bradford's cooking vastly superior to Mrs. Mulvaney's, but she had grown too overset to eat, and she merely toyed with her own food.

"And what brings you to England, Mr. Shelton?" the housekeeper eventually asked. Her numerous scowls notwithstanding, she had consumed every bite of her entrée and was busily at work on her lemon tart.

"I had become somewhat weary of the fur trade," Jon replied, "and I wished to see the land of my birth. But tell us, Mrs. Mulvaney, where is *your* home?"

The housekeeper frowned a bit, but it was clear that Jon did not want to mention his father, and she began to describe her early life in Norwich. She chattered on for some hours—or so it seemed to Molly—but at last she finished her tart, and the interminable meal was over. Mrs. Mulvaney excused the footmen and, when they had borne the final dish out of the dining room, closed the door and resumed her place.

"You should have told me of your father, Mr. Shelton," she hissed. "Told *them* of your father, I should have said." She gestured toward the door. "I stated to Miss Shelton that I would ponder your plan and advise you of any flaws, and I had found one."

"And what is that, Mrs. Mulvaney?" Jon said mildly.

"I judge your story quite credible, but how are you to bring it to attention in the proper quarters? How do you propose to mingle with the *ton?*"

This was a point they had not discussed en route from London, and Molly gazed down at her hands. Perhaps there was no way for her to be "respectable" after all, and she experienced an odd amalgam of emotions—a peculiar blend of disappointment and relief.

"That is why I prompted you to mention your father in the presence of the footmen," Mrs. Mulvaney went on. "Had you done so, I daresay all of Brighton would have known the tale by morning, and you'd have been fairly showered with cards of invitation. But it is not too late, is it? We shall talk of your father at breakfast tomorrow."

"I prefer a rather more direct approach," Jon said. "More direct and yet more subtle. Tomorrow Molly and I shall call on Lady Ogilvie."

"We shall do *what?*" Molly's eyes flew up, and her mouth fell open. "We cannot simply go to her house—

Lord Ogilvie's house, that is—and ring the bell . . ." But they could, of course, and though she could not have said why, she groped for another objection. "What . . . whatever would you say?"

"Frankly, I have not yet decided." He flashed his engaging grin. "But I shall certainly devise something before tomorrow."

"But . . . but . . ."

"You needn't tease yourself to thank me," he said solemnly. "After all, dear Molly, what are elder brothers for?"

He laid his napkin on the table, rose, bowed out of the dining room; and Molly stared imploringly at Mrs. Mulvaney. But the housekeeper was smiling as well, and Molly dropped her eyes again and fancied she could actually see her stomach beginning to churn with terror.

—4—

The peal of the doorbell reverberated through the house, sounding much like the proverbial knell of doom, and Molly clenched her hands. Though they were to ask for Lady Ogilvie, she counted it entirely possible that they would meet the viscount as well. Indeed, if his lordship was home, it was *likely* that his mother would desire him to join her guests. It was even conceivable, should Lord Ogilvie chance to be passing through the vestibule, that he would answer the bell . . .

Molly spun around and gazed desperately toward the landau, wondering if she might yet be able to escape. They could readily have walked to the viscount's house in West Street—it was under a quarter of a mile from Molly's own home—but Jon had felt that "our" carriage, splendid as it was, would enhance their story. So Molly had only to race down the shallow steps and leap inside—

"You've nothing to fear," Jon said softly. He had seemingly read her mind again, and Molly turned reluctantly back to face him. "If we do encounter Ogilvie, I've no doubt he'll judge you excessively fetching."

His pale eyes swept approvingly from the ostrich plume on her French bonnet to the toes of her blue satin shoes, and, as always, Molly found his scrutiny inexplicably unsettling. But perhaps, she thought optimistically, her rouge was serving its intended function, for he didn't appear to notice the maddening rush of blood into her cheeks.

49

"Yes?"

To Molly's unutterable relief, it was not Viscount Ogilvie who peered at them from across the threshold; it was a very short, very plump man who, despite his lack of height, managed to convey the impression that he was looking down at them.

"Good afternoon," Jon said pleasantly. "I am Jonathan Shelton and this is my sister Molly. We were in hopes of speaking with Lady Ogilvie."

"Shelton?" the butler echoed. "Ah, yes, the Canadians who have purchased Lord Chudleigh's home."

Evidently, Molly reflected wryly, the footmen had indeed circulated their tale round "all of Brighton."

"I shall take your card to her ladyship, Mr. Shelton."

The butler extended one hand, but his expression suggested that it was most improbable her ladyship would deign to see them. To make matters worse, Molly dismally recollected that they *had* no cards; she had quite forgotten this essential "respectable" accessory. She stole a sideward glance at Jon and discovered him energetically rummaging among his pockets.

"I'm afraid I've left my cards behind," he said sheepishly, his "search" completed. "Perhaps you might simply inform Lady Ogilvie we're here."

"Umm." The butler examined them with keen suspicion, as if contemplating the distinct possibility that anyone so bold as to call without a proper card might well be plotting some sort of criminal mischief.

"You might mention to her ladyship," Jon added, "that we have come at the urging of a mutual acquaintance. Countess Melnikoff."

"Umm."

The butler's mien was now one of agonized indecision: countesses were not to be trifled with, but, on the other hand . . . Jon stepped nimbly to one side, affording the butler a clear view of the landau, and he gave them a grudging nod.

"Very well," he said. "I shall advise Lady Ogilvie of your arrival. You may wait in . . ." Another grave decision; should they be shown to the main saloon or sent

round to the tradesmen's entrance? " . . . in the library,"
he finished, evidently gauging this a satisfactory compromise.

He beckoned them, though still rather grudgingly, into
the foyer, and Molly observed that the arrangement of
rooms was precisely the reverse of that in Lord Chudleigh's erstwhile home: the dining room was situated to
the right of the vestibule and the library to the left. The
butler waved them into the latter, hurried up the
staircase, and disappeared.

"Who the devil is Countess Melnikoff?" Molly hissed.

"Molly, please, your language." Jon affected a look of
fond exasperation. "There is no Countess Melnikoff, of
course."

"Then why . . . how . . ."

Jon moved away from the entry, sprawled on the
mahogany sofa in the middle of the room; and, lest
they be overheard, Molly was compelled to sit beside
him.

"If there is no Countess Melnikoff," she whispered
furiously, "Lady Ogilvie cannot possibly be acquainted
with her. So if, against all odds, she consents to see us,
what the d . . ."—she bit her lip—"what in the world
will you tell her?"

"We shall see," Jon said airily.

He began to gaze about the library, monstrous uncon-
cerned, and Molly looked stonily round as well. She
noted at once that the shelves were nearly as bare as those
in Ship Street; she doubted the entire room contained
above two dozen books. Which was not to say that the
shelves were actually *bare*, she amended, for there were
countless little ornaments scattered about. Unhappily,
most of these were of shellwork, which Molly quite
despised, and she tried to visualize the shelves with her
books, her own few ornaments . . .

"Is Ogilvie literate?" Jon frowned at the shelves with
elaborate puzzlement.

"I daresay he is considerably more literate than you,"
Molly said stiffly. "Lord Ogilvie was educated at Eton
and Oxford."

"Was he indeed? How fortunate that the experience did him no permanent harm."

Much as his sarcasm exacerbated her annoyance, Molly could not quell a stab of curiosity: she had not fancied him the kind to attach any importance to books or education either one. "Do you read?" she blurted out.

"Well, if I use my forefinger and mouth the words as I go—"

"I am attempting to be serious!" Molly snapped. "Do you *enjoy* reading?"

"Very much." He did, in fact, appear to be serious. "I daresay I read every book in York before I was done; that was *my* education."

"Your mother was not an educated woman?"

"She could read and write if that is your question, but . . ." His pale eyes narrowed, grew distant. "Mama struck me as rather . . . rather odd when I grew old enough to view her objectively. She spoke extremely well, nearly as well as you and Mrs. Mulvaney, but she had nothing to say. Nothing particularly learned or intelligent, I mean. So was she educated? I don't know; indeed, as I've recently come to realize, I know shockingly little about her." He returned his eyes to Molly. "At any rate, as I indicated, I obtained the bulk of my education from books. And I should never presume to imply that I am up to *Ogilvie's* weight in that regard; he is obviously a most distinguished scholar."

His voice was altogether solemn, but his lips were quivering at the corners, and Molly was momentarily relieved to detect the tap of footfalls on the stairs. Relieved until she unmistakably discerned two sets of footsteps rather than one, at which point she clenched her hands again and peered fearfully toward the door.

"Mr. Shelton! Miss Shelton!"

Lady Ogilvie sailed into the library, and Jon sprang to his feet. Molly attempted to rise as well, but she soon collected that she had suffered some sort of paralytic seizure, for she could not seem to move a single muscle. She was beginning to pray for immediate death when Jon tugged her, none too ceremoniously, up beside him.

"Good afternoon, Lady Ogilvie," he said. "How very kind of you to see us."

"Nonsense, Mr. Shelton; I am delighted to welcome friends of dear Countess Melnikoff. Whom I met several years since at the Regent's reception for the Allied Monarchs. She was, as I recall, in the party that accompanied the Czar to England." She hesitated a moment. "Er . . . the countess *did* indicate that that was where we met, did she not?"

"She did indeed," Jon assured her. "She has since immigrated to Canada, which is, of course, where *I* met her. And when she learned that I was returning to England, she insisted I seek you out. Of all the ladies she had encountered in Britain, the countess said, Lady Ogilvie was certainly best qualified to introduce us into society."

"Well, I daresay *that* is true."

Lady Ogilvie preened a bit, and Molly studied her as surreptitiously as she could. It was clear that the viscount had not inherited his height from his mother—she reached no further than Molly's earlobes—and it was impossible to determine whether her gray hair had originally been light or dark. Dark probably, for her ladyship had very fine brown eyes, and Molly wondered if Lord Ogilvie did as well. It somehow frightened her that she didn't know, that she had never been sufficiently close to see his eyes.

"I daresay that is true," Lady Ogilvie repeated. "May I see Countess Melnikoff's letter of introduction?"

"You could indeed if I had one"—Jon flashed his easy smile—"but I fear I do not."

"Umm." Her ladyship's eyes flickered with doubt.

"I fancy the countess did not realize you read Russian," Jon said.

"Read . . . ah . . . Russian?"

"You must have forgotten that the countess cannot write in English. Well, it is easy *to* forget," he added charitably, "since she *speaks* our tongue so very fluently."

"Yes, I had forgotten." Lady Ogilvie bobbed her head. "Yes, that quite explains it, so let us talk no more of

Countess Melnikoff." Molly thought this a prodigious good suggestion. "I cannot conceive why Higgins left you in the library, not even taking your wraps . . ." She cast the butler a look of keen vexation. "See to their things, Higgins, and then have tea brought to us in the drawing room."

The hapless butler assisted Molly and Jon out of their cloaks, took them and Jon's hat and walking stick, slunk away; and Lady Ogilvie led her guests up the staircase. Jon shot Molly a little smirk of triumph, which she elected studiedly to ignore, but his face was quite grave again by the time they had reached the top of the steps and entered the saloon. Lady Ogilvie waved them to a Hepplewhite sofa and herself took a nearby shield-back chair.

"Now," she said brightly, "I am given to understand that you have purchased Lord Chudleigh's home."

"So your butler mentioned." Jon nodded. "However, I was somewhat confused by his remark because we actually bought the house from a . . . Was his name not Trevor, Molly?"

"Yes," Molly muttered, passionately wishing she could strangle him without attracting her ladyship's attention.

"Ah, yes, Trevor." Lady Ogilvie pursed her lips most grimly. "Trevor, the moneylender. Yes, poor Chudleigh fell into Trevor's clutches some years ago, and that . . . that vulture snatched at the first opportunity to seize his lordship's possessions."

The first opportunity! Molly swallowed a furious inclination to inform Lady Ogilvie that "poor Chudleigh's" account had been fifteen months in arrears.

"What a shame," Jon clucked.

"Is it not? But let us speak no more of Trevor either." Another splendid suggestion. "Instead, Mr. Shelton, please do tell me about Canada; I've always thought it an excessively interesting country. I am particularly fascinated by the kangaroos."

Jon somehow managed to keep his countenance, regretfully advising her ladyship that he had never personally glimpsed a kangaroo. No, he was far more familiar with beaver, and as he recounted his many adventures in the fur trade (with, Molly suspected, substantial embroidery on the facts), tea was delivered, poured, and politely sipped.

"Canada *is* an interesting country," Jon concluded, "but, I am sorry to say, hardly a suitable home for a young woman. Which is why I have come to England, Lady Ogilvie: I am extremely eager to see my dear sister properly settled." He patted Molly's knee, and she repressed an ardent urge to bat his hand away.

"I fancy Miss Shelton would have been settled long since were it not for her misfortune," Lady Ogilvie said kindly. "I am also given to understand that she was to have been brought out some time ago . . ."

Her ladyship repeated the tale Mrs. Mulvaney had so carefully extracted for the benefit of the footmen, and Molly noticed that it had undergone several changes during the course of its rapid travels: Miss Shelton had now been in England for ten years rather than six, and her late mentor had become "Mrs. Walton." But perhaps, she decided, that was all for the best.

" . . . but perhaps that is all for the best," Lady Ogilvie finished. "At the risk of wounding your feelings, Miss Shelton"—she looked directly at Molly for the first time —"I must say that I have never heard of Mrs. Walton. And while I'm certain she was a *sweet* person, I daresay I am far better qualified to introduce you into society. However"—a delicate cough—"at the risk of giving further offense"—her eyes went back to Jon—"I must say that I am equally unfamiliar with the Shelton name. And as you were born in England . . ." Her voice trailed provocatively off.

"The Shelton name," Jon echoed heavily. He stared into his teacup, set it on the sofa table, reluctantly raised his eyes again. "In point of fact, Lady Ogilvie . . ." He stopped and wrung his hands, his face the very reflection of awful inner turmoil. "No," he muttered at last, "no, it doesn't signify. I'm sure there's no truth to the story—"

"No truth to *what* story?" her ladyship demanded, wriggling to the edge of her chair.

"No." Jon shook his auburn head with utter finality. "No, Molly and I have agreed not to divulge it—"

"Agreed not to divulge *what?*" Lady Ogilvie snapped. "If I am to assist you, Mr. Shelton, I really must know every detail of your background."

"Well . . ."

Jon gazed sorrowfully at Molly, as if to beg her indulgence in these exceedingly difficult circumstances, and then—once more wringing his hands, pausing at frequent intervals to regain his composure—described their mother's deathbed confession. Molly was compelled to own that he acquitted himself quite well: when, at last, he stumbled to a halt, she herself was half-persuaded that he had "held Mama's fevered hand" while she "raved" of the British peer who had sired her children.

"An earl!" Lady Ogilvie sucked in her breath. "Your father was an *earl.*" She sat back in her chair for a long moment of rumination, and eventually a tiny crease stole between her brows. "Though I am forced to wonder why your mother did not disclose your paternity until the very end."

"I expect she feared our stepfather," Jon said. "He was a violent man, insanely jealous . . . But what am I saying! You might well collect that I *believe* Mama's story, which, of course, I do not. Nor does Molly; that is why we agreed not to mention it to anyone. No, I daresay Mama, delirious as she was, resurrected some childhood fantasy . . ." He stopped again and assumed an expression of great alarm. "In any event, Lady Ogilvie, I implore you to keep our secret. Indeed, if you will forgive me, I must *insist* that you respect my confidence."

"I shouldn't betray your confidence for the world," her ladyship promised warmly. "In return, however, *I* must insist that you permit me to bring you out. Bring Miss Shelton out, that is. Please understand that we are not in London and it is not the Season, but I shall introduce you into society insofar as I can. Introduce Miss Shelton, that is. Indeed . . ."

She narrowed her brown eyes, tapped one forefinger thoughtfully against her teeth; and Molly's heart jumped into her throat. She distantly awarded Jon another score: he had cleverly enticed Lady Ogilvie herself to propose a meeting between his "dear sister" and her son.

"Indeed," her ladyship continued at last, "I should very much like you to meet my niece, Mr. Shelton."

This was so far from what Molly had expected to hear, had wanted to hear, that for a moment she thought she had *mis*heard altogether. But Lady Ogilvie chattered happily on, leaving no possible margin of doubt.

"My niece, Lady Ellen Palmer, a lovely girl." She beamed. "Though I fear you may find her a trifle . . . a trifle awkward, Mr. Shelton." Her face fell. "The poor child is scarcely out of black gloves, having lost her husband just above a year since. The inevitable tragedy of the woman who weds a man much older than herself." She sighed. "But with time"—she beamed again—"Ellen will be quite as gay and charming as she was in her youth, and I am *most* eager for you to make her acquaintance."

"And I am *most* eager to do so." Jon, now beaming himself, looked to Molly for concurrence, and she returned her *most* withering glare. "But, as I indicated earlier, Molly's welfare is my principal concern." A loving smile, another pat on the knee.

"Umm." Her ladyship frowned. "Well, I shall naturally present Miss Shelton to my son, and perhaps he—"

"Your son?" Jon interposed dubiously. "Molly *is* monstrous fond of children, but in the circumstances—I must once more ask your forgiveness, Lady Ogilvie—I shouldn't wish her to spend a great deal of time with a small boy."

"A small boy?" Lady Ogilvie giggled. "My son is eight-and-twenty years of age, Mr. Shelton."

"No!" Jon emitted an astonished gasp, then appeared to recover himself. "Surely you refer to your *step*son, Lady Ogilvie; you, too, must have married a vastly older man."

No, her ladyship trilled, no, despite her extremely youthful appearance, she really did have a twenty-eight-year-old son, a *natural* son of eight-and-twenty, difficult though everyone found that to credit. As it happened, her niece—the "lovely" Lady Palmer—was also eight-and-twenty, and Lady Ogilvie would be thrilled to introduce them both to the Sheltons.

"Well . . ." Jon's voice was again fraught with doubt. "Well, if it would prove no inconvenience—"

"It will prove no inconvenience whatever," Lady Ogilvie assured him. "I am conducting an assembly tomorrow evening, and I do not scruple to tell you that everyone of consequence in Brighton will be here. Everyone but the Prince," she amended with a moue of disappointment, "but he sent a *personal* note to advise me he's in the gout. The ball is to begin at nine, Mr. Shelton, and I shall look forward to seeing you then. And Miss Shelton too, of course," she added absently.

Her ladyship rose, marched to the bell cord beside the door, tugged it; and Higgins soon bounded into the room. Lady Ogilvie once more apologized for her butler's shoddy performance at the time of their arrival, then bade them good day, and Higgins escorted them out of the saloon and down the stairs. The poor butler was so distraught that he attempted to put Jon's cloak on Molly and her pelisse on him, but at length he sorted the various accessories out and—with a no doubt unprecedented show of remorse—accompanied them to the landau. Lewis assisted them into the carriage, clucked the horses to a start, and Jon favored Higgins with a parting wave of absolution.

"Well," he said cheerfully as the landau rounded the corner of Middle Street Lane, "I believe our meeting with Lady Ogilvie went very well. Do you not agree?"

He extended one long arm toward her knee, and Molly slapped his hand furiously away.

"If you try to pat me one more time," she hissed, "I shall knock you halfway to hell."

"Molly!" He affected another great gasp. "What would Lady Ogilvie say if she were to hear such horrifying language? I'm quite sure she would cancel your forthcoming introduction to her son—"

"I'm quite sure she would because Lady Ogilvie does not care a deuce about my introduction to her son. But she is *most eager* to present you to her niece . . ." To Molly's vague astonishment and abject dismay, she discovered herself dangerously near to tears, and she bit her lip and smashed her reticule between her fingers and her palm.

"She was merely attempting a bit of matchmaking." Jon's tone was mild, patient, which rendered the situation infinitely worse. "And I turned her attempt to your advantage, did I not?" Molly painstakingly inspected her crumpled reticule. "So why the devil should you be vexed with me?"

Why indeed? But vexed she was, and she cast about for some response which would enable her to salvage a shred of pride.

"Vexed?" she echoed at last. "I am vexed because you insisted that Lady Ogilvie not mention the matter of your father's identity. If your story is to be kept a secret, there is no hope at all you'll inherit a fortune, and my loan will *never* be repaid."

"Do not tease yourself about it," Jon said dryly. "Rest assured that Lady Ogilvie will circulate our tale with all possible speed; I shall be very much surprised if it fails to reach Ship Street by dinnertime. Lady Ogilvie possesses a combination of traits invaluable to our cause: she is a shameless social climber and inveterate gossip neatly enclosed in a single package."

To say the truth, Molly was rather inclined to concur in this assessment, but she felt compelled to defend her future mother-in-law. "*I* find Lady Ogilvie quite charming," she said frigidly.

"Do you indeed?" Jon's voice was at least as cold as hers. "Then I daresay you and your viscount will be enormously happy."

They proceeded to Ship Street in a silence considerably more frosty than the bone-chilling January day.

—5—

"*Will* you stop fidgeting!" Mrs. Mulvaney snapped. "I shall never finish your hair if you persist in squirming about."

The housekeeper's eyes met Molly's in the mirror, and Molly obediently stiffened, but she found it nearly impossible *not* to squirm about. To begin with, the Adam chair she had requisitioned from Jon's bedchamber was altogether unsuitable for use as a dressing chair—she was compelled to sit ramrod straight in order to see into the glass—but pride would not allow her to admit her error and secure a substitute. In the second place, her imminent introduction to Viscount Ogilvie had rendered her so nervous that she could actually see the pulses pounding in her throat and beneath the veins of her wrists.

"I am sure you are nervous about the ball," Mrs. Mulvaney said in a somewhat gentler tone. "But you needn't be, for I daresay you and Mr. Shelton will be the handsomest couple there. *If* you permit me to complete your hair," she added sternly as Molly started to relax her aching neck. "Yes, I fancy Lord Ogilvie and Lady Palmer will both be quite smitten."

Lady Palmer. Molly emitted an irritated sniff. Mrs. Mulvaney had, of course, been intensely curious about the outcome of their meeting with Lady Ogilvie; and after dinner, with the footmen dismissed and the dining-room door safely closed, Jon had related the afternoon's

events in vivid detail. Far from omitting her ladyship's
"bit of" matchmaking in his behalf, which was not in the
least germane to their endeavor, he had dwelt on it at
considerable length; and Molly's already keen vexation
had increased with his every word. She had consequently
declined to speak to him today—except, when absolutely
necessary, in monosyllables—but, to her further annoyance, he did not appear to care a deuce for her pointed
disregard.

"*I* do not fancy Lady Palmer will be smitten at all,"
Molly retorted, with another sniff. "Jon is not particularly well-looking—"

"Oh, but he is," Mrs. Mulvaney protested. "With that
splendid red hair and those remarkable eyes, such a very
pale blue—"

"He is far too thin," Molly interposed haughtily.

"He is a trifle on the lean side," the housekeeper conceded, "but my own husband was scarcely more than a
bag of bones. Cyrus always maintained that thin men
make the best lovers; proved it too."

"Mrs. Mulvaney!" Molly spun her head in shock,
winced with pain as the comb tangled in her hair, and
turned hastily back to the mirror.

"Be that as it may"—the housekeeper went unrepent-
antly on—"I am forced to own myself entirely mistaken
about Mr. Shelton. I have come to find him an exceedingly pleasant gentleman—"

"He is far from being a gentleman," Molly muttered.

"—and most intelligent and amusing as well. And, or
so says the chambermaid, he keeps his room excessively
neat." Mrs. Mulvaney cast a disapproving glance around
Molly's own bedchamber; among countless other
deficiencies, she had ever lamented her charge's inclination toward untidiness.

"Perhaps you should marry Jon yourself," Molly
snapped. "Barring that happy outcome, Lady Palmer is
welcome to have him."

"Oh, I daresay she *will* welcome him. Yes, if Lady
Palmer was wed to a much older man, she'll no doubt

find a strapping young fellow prodigious appealing—"

"That will be quite enough, Mrs. Mulvaney! I am thoroughly tired of discussing Lady Palmer."

"Very well."

The housekeeper seemed suspiciously tolerant of Molly's display of temper, and, in the glass, Molly thought she detected a slight twitch about her mouth. But there was no time to puzzle over her odd reaction, for Mrs. Mulvaney dropped her arms, nodded, and stood back.

"I have done as well as I can," she announced, "and if I do say it myself, I believe you look very taking. See what you think, Miss Shelton."

Molly rose, but she could see nothing except the area around her natural waistline, and with another stab of irritation she recollected the cheval mirror in the master bedchamber. She tugged the heavy chair aside and marched to the opposite wall, whirled back round, and narrowly repressed a gasp of shock. She had repeatedly tried on her evening gowns, of course, but that had been in the privacy of Madame Dupré's fitting room. The extent to which her flesh was exposed by the low, snug corsage of her dress now struck her as most alarming, nearly indecent, and she looked quickly downward. The body of the gown was plain from just below the bust to approximately the knee—an unadorned fall of pale blue lace over a matching satin slip. At knee level, there was a rouleau of the same satin, another round the bottom of the skirt, and, between them, a drapery of lace ornamented with satin roses. Molly's eyes crept fearfully back to the bodice—which seemed little more than a *strip* of deep blue satin, with only the *tiniest* sleeves—and she instinctively crossed her hands to cover her bare chest.

"Yes, it does require a necklace, doesn't it?" Mrs. Mulvaney mused.

She began searching through Molly's jewel box as though nothing whatever were amiss, and Molly cautiously lowered her hands. Mrs. Mulvaney was a devoted reader of *Ackermann's Repository*, so perhaps the daring dress was acceptable after all. The housekeeper hurried across the room and fastened Molly's pearl necklace round her throat and the matching earrings in her ears and once more stood away. The necklace did hide *some* of that frightful expanse of skin . . .

"Very taking," Mrs. Mulvaney said again. "Yes, Lord Ogilvie will be most smitten indeed."

Oddly enough, Molly had altogether forgotten the viscount during their conversation about Lady Palmer, and there was no time for a new attack of nerves: the mantel clock was striking a quarter before nine. Mrs. Mulvaney tugged on Molly's long kid gloves, draped a silk shawl over her shoulders, adjusted the shawl, and added an awkward little pat of encouragement. Molly bobbed her head in silent thanks, and the housekeeper accompanied her out of the room and down the stairs to the vestibule.

"Mr. Shelton!"

Mrs. Mulvaney clapped her hands, and Jon, who had been leaning against the newel post, drew himself erect and flashed his easy smile.

"How very taking *you* look!" the housekeeper proclaimed. "Did I not tell you, Miss Shelton? Did I not say that Lady Palmer will be utterly *bouleversée* when she sees him?"

Lady Palmer, Molly fumed; must Mrs. Mulvaney forever be chattering of Lady Palmer? She shot the housekeeper a quelling glare, then transferred her attention to Jon and was compelled to admit that he did look rather "taking." She had seen his long, shapely legs before, of course, but his satin smallclothes, his clinging silk hose, were considerably more flattering than the sagging breeches and darned stocking he had worn upon his arrival. His wasp-waisted coat emphasized his wide shoulders and slender waist even more than did his normal attire, and his snowy neckcloth was tied in a fashion so complicated as to defy the imagination. She raised her eyes to his face and observed that, perhaps in contrast to the neckcloth, his freckles seemed unusually pronounced. She attempted to persuade herself that this was a flaw, but, in fact, his freckles lent him an undeniable boyish appeal; and she dropped her eyes and peered studiedly around the foyer.

"Thank you, Mrs. Mulvaney," Jon said. "But I fear I'm scarcely fit to hold a candle to Molly. She looks quite . . . quite stunning, does she not?"

"Oh, she does indeed." The housekeeper clapped her hands again. "I'm sure Lord Ogilvie will be completely *bouleversé* as well."

"I'm sure he will." Jon sounded a trifle grim, but when Molly glanced toward him, she found his face expressionless, his own pale eyes blank. "However, no one can be *bouleversé* until we reach the assembly, and I daresay it is time to leave. Are you ready, Molly?"

To say the truth, she would much have preferred to slink back to her bedchamber, strip off her splendid new ensemble, and go to ground beneath the bedclothes, but she managed a nod. "Yes," she muttered, "yes, I am ready."

Mrs. Mulvaney rang for a footman to fetch their cloaks, and when he returned, they donned their outer garments and hurried to the landau, which was drawn up outside the house. Lewis assisted them into the carriage, took his place on the box, and—far too soon, it seemed to Molly—they were under way.

"You do look quite stunning, you know," Jon said as they rounded the corner of Ship Street Gardens. It was impossible to avoid his gaze—he was seated directly across from her—and even in the darkness, Molly could perceive that he was studying her most intently. "Did I not advise you that you would be monstrous becoming in blue?"

"Yes," Molly murmured.

"And in a gown which displays your . . . ah . . . form to advantage?"

"Y-yes," she choked.

"You're an uncommonly handsome woman, Molly."

His eyes were like pale, glittering lamps in the night, and Molly could bear his scrutiny no longer; she looked hastily down and began to pick imaginary threads from her pelisse.

"So I fancy we should be about the planning at once," Jon said briskly. "The planning of the wedding, that is, for I judge it quite likely that Ogilvie will offer for you within the week. Naturally I shall attend to all the legal requirements, and I daresay it would seem odd if I did not give you away—"

"Stop it!" Molly hissed. "Stop . . . stop mocking me!"

"I wasn't mocking you," Jon protested. "I was but jesting, trying to ease your nervousness a bit."

"I am not in the least nervous," Molly snapped, her teeth fairly chattering with terror. "So I should appreciate it if you would just . . . just hush until we get there."

His notion of a "hush" was his cheerful, off-key whistle, and Molly stared stonily out the window, affecting great interest in the King's Head inn as they passed it. Actually, she thought, the building—where Charles II had purportedly spent his last night in England before fleeing abroad—probably *was* interesting, but it was very poorly lighted and virtually invisible in the darkness.

Such was not the case with Viscount Ogilvie's house: it was ablaze from the understory to the roof, and though it was barely nine, a line of carriages already snaked well down West Street from the entrance. Jon ceased his whistling, and in the silence, Molly fancied she could now *hear* her heart drumming in her temples and thudding against her ribs. As they crept forward, she further realized that her breath was coming in great gasps which nevertheless seemed to furnish no air, and she stifled a keen inclination to leap out of the landau and, perhaps, throw herself beneath it.

"I should pat your knee," Jon whispered wickedly, "except that you have forbidden me to do so."

In point of fact, Molly would have welcomed one of his idiotish pats, would have welcomed any sign of support, but it was too late to say so: they had reached the head of the line, and two of the Ogilvies' footmen were handing them out of the landau. The servants escorted them to the door, and Molly searched eagerly for Higgins; his was, at least, a familiar face. But there was no sign of him, and while the footmen removed her and Jon's cloaks, Molly guiltily wondered if the hapless butler had been discharged for yesterday's "shoddy performance." Her fears were shortly laid to rest, for as she and Jon toiled up the staircase behind some two dozen other guests, Molly glimpsed Higgins at the entry of the saloon, announcing each arriving party as it reached him. Announcing Lord This and Lady That and the Honorable So-and-So until, at last, she and Jon were next . . .

"Mr. Shelton," the butler intoned. "Miss Shelton."

Molly cast a final desperate glance over her shoulder, but it truly was too late: Jon took her elbow, propelled her into the drawing room, and Lady Ogilvie bounded forward to greet them.

"Good evening, Mr. Shelton! How delighted I am that nothing prevented your attendance at my assembly. I have told Ellen all about you . . ."

Her ladyship rattled on, and Molly risked a tiny sideward peep. She could scarcely see the figure standing just behind Lady Ogilvie, but the viscount was clearly visible perhaps six feet away, at the end of what was obviously the receiving line. Well, he was not *clearly* visible, she amended; his back was turned to the entry, and he appeared to be conversing with a dark man approximately Jon's age. She somehow felt that he should *sense* her presence, should whirl about and rush to meet the woman of his dreams. But he did not, and Molly hastily returned her eyes to Lady Ogilvie.

" . . . and she is *exceedingly* eager to make your acquaintance," her ladyship concluded. She stepped aside, revealing the woman behind her. "Ellen, dear, *this* is Mr. Shelton. And this, Mr. Shelton, is my dear niece Lady Ellen Palmer."

Lady Palmer floated forward, gracefully extending one gloved hand, displaying not a hint of the "awkwardness" her aunt had warned them of. It was evident that Lady Palmer was Lady Ogilvie's blood niece: she was excessively slight in stature and had her ladyship's fine dark eyes. Lady Palmer's hair was very dark as well— nearly black—and her creamy skin tended toward olive.

Her coloring lent her a decidedly exotic aspect, Molly thought—the look of a Spaniard or a Gypsy—and this impression was in no way diminished by her daring emerald-green gown.

"Mr. Shelton." Lady Palmer's voice was girlish, rather breathy. "I must own Aunt Grace quite right on one head: I *was* exceedingly eager to meet you."

"Lady Palmer." Jon bowed over the outstretched hand, not quite kissing it; Molly would never have judged him capable of such gallantry. "I should like to present my sister Molly."

"Ah, yes, Miss Shelton," Lady Ogilvie said carelessly as Molly and Lady Palmer exchanged polite nods. "I am sure you are fairly *wild* to chat"—she beamed at Jon and Lady Palmer in turn—"but I wish to introduce Ellen to the remainder of my guests. So you will simply have to contain your impatience, Mr. Shelton; I fancy you can persuade Ellen to stand up with you after everyone has arrived. Meanwhile, you must meet my son. Andrew! Andrew, dear, you are neglecting your duties."

Lord Ogilvie nodded to the man with whom he'd been speaking, turned toward them, walked toward them, and Molly's heart crashed into her throat. The moment had nearly come, then the moment *had* come, and she heard the introductions only as distant snatches.

" . . . Mr. Shelton . . ." " . . . my son Andrew, Viscount Ogilvie . . ." " . . . Lord Ogilvie . . ." " . . . and his sister . . ."

"Miss Shelton."

The viscount's voice penetrated Molly's fog, and she gazed directly at him for the first time. And felt . . . and felt . . . She certainly did not feel *disappointed*, Molly assured herself; it was just that Lord Ogilvie looked somewhat different than she had imagined. To begin with, he was not so tall as she remembered, but that was probably in comparison to Jon, who was really *too* tall. And Viscount Ogilvie, while he could by no means be termed plump, seemed rather . . . rather *soft*; he had round, rosy cheeks and wide, somewhat fleshy jaws and a body that appeared to follow a straight line from his

shoulders to his hips. But that was merely in contrast to
Jon, of course, who was *far* too thin and had facial bones
fairly jutting through his flesh. The viscount did have
wonderful eyes, she observed—large and dark and
thickly lashed—and glossy dark brown hair. Though his
hairline was receding just the *smallest* bit at the
temples . . .

"Miss Shelton?" he repeated sharply. Sharply and
loudly, as if he had collected that she might be a trifle
hard of hearing.

"Lord Ogilvie," she murmured. "I . . . I am very
pleased to make your acquaintance."

"You do recollect, Andrew, that the Sheltons are
friends of Countess Melnikoff," Lady Ogilvie said.

"Yes, I do recollect that." The viscount smiled, and
Molly noted that his teeth were excellent. "The countess
is a charming woman, is she not?"

Jon emitted an elaborate cough, and Molly repressed
an urge to kick him soundly in one silken shin. Lady
Ogilvie had no doubt convinced her son that he *did* know
Countess Melnikoff.

"And now we all have met," Lady Ogilvie said
brightly, "I fear I must urge you on, for there are other
guests behind you. We shall talk again later in the
evening, Mr. Shelton."

Jon inclined his auburn head and ushered Molly on
into the saloon, and she could not quell a crushing sense
of anticlimax. She had not expected Lord Ogilvie to leave
the receiving line and grant her his undivided attention,
but, in truth, he had paid her *no* attention. Indeed, were
it not for the background information his mother had
clearly supplied, Molly doubted the viscount would have
noticed her at all. She bit her lip against a flush of
mortification, and Jon coughed again.

"If you say anything," Molly hissed, "I shall . . . I
shall . . ."

"Knock me halfway to hell?" he supplied, also in a
whisper. "That won't be necessary; I was merely going to
say that Ogilvie seems pleasant enough. And how

fortunate that he remembers our mutual friend Countess Melnikoff."

There was no point in responding; to the contrary, any response would but serve to titillate his perverse sense of humor. Molly contented herself with a brief frigid glare, then peered regally round the drawing room, observing that most of the furniture had been removed and an orchestra was seated in front of the window. As she watched, the musicians began tuning their instruments, and they soon struck up a waltz.

"Can you dance?" Jon inquired.

"Of course I can dance!" Molly snapped. She elected not to add that she could dance only because Mrs. Mulvaney—anticipating the come-out that had never come —had insisted she engage a dancing master.

"Then I daresay no one would judge it amiss if I were to stand up with my little sister."

Before Molly could demur, he seized her elbow, led her to the middle of the saloon, from which the Brussels carpet had been taken up, and gathered her into his arms. It belatedly occurred to Molly that she would not have supposed *he* could dance, but, in fact, he was far more accomplished than she, and for the first few minutes it required all her concentration simply to follow his lead. At length she grew comfortable with his rhythm, but her relief was short-lived, for she suddenly, inexplicably became most *un*comfortably aware of *him*. As she had surmised on the occasion of their initial meeting, he was extremely strong, and it must be that, she decided—that and his great height—which made him seem so appallingly close. His strength and his height and his breath against her temple and his hands, which, despite his gloves, were fearfully warm. Her heart began to race very oddly, and she drew a bit away.

"You . . . you dance quite well," she stammered.

"Thank you," he said gravely. "Countess Melnikoff kindly undertook to instruct me."

He must always be teasing her, Molly reflected furiously, must forever be tormenting her, and if she could have, she would have stalked immediately from the floor. As it was, she was compelled to endure the rest of the set, maintaining as much distance between them as she possibly could, and when the music finally stopped, she did indeed stalk away.

"Now," Jon said, catching her up, "shall we repair to the refreshment parlor or shall we—"

"*You* may do whatever you please," Molly interposed coldly. "I shall remain here and dance."

"Are you certain? I hate to leave you alone."

Molly thought he laid slight emphasis on the final word, as if to suggest the prodigious improbability that anyone *else* would seek her company, and she felt her eyes narrow with renewed rage.

"I am quite certain," she spat. "I am accustomed to being *alone*. Unlike Lady Palmer, I can do very nicely for myself."

"Lady Palmer?" he echoed quizzically. "What has she to do with you?"

What indeed? Molly could not conceive why she had said it, and she could only retreat with—or so she hoped —some degree of grace. "Nothing," she mumbled. "Lady Palmer merely struck me as the . . . the clinging sort."

"Really?" he said airily. "I hadn't noticed, but perhaps you're right. And if you are, she *is* much unlike you, isn't she? Not a hard woman of business . . ." He stopped, and his own pale eyes flickered in that maddening, unreadable way. "Are your feelings as hard as your clever little head, Molly? Because if they are not—"

"Please spare me your 'brotherly advice'; I fancy I can do very nicely without it as well. Go to the refreshment parlor, go dance with Lady Palmer, go to the devil for all I care. Just leave me *alone*."

"As you will."

He executed a perfectly splendid bow—he was mocking her again, of course—turned on his heel, and strode away. Molly spun about as well, proceeded in the opposite direction, and promply stumbled into an elderly gentleman who introduced himself as Lord Duke. Or possibly Lord Drake; he lacked most of his front teeth and did not speak very clearly. In any event, to make amends, Lord Duke/Drake asked Molly to stand up with him, and she slunk onto the floor, praying that Jon would not turn back and note her choice of partners.

Fortunately their quadrille so exhausted his ancient lordship that he pronounced himself quite unable to manage another set that evening, and, leaning heavily against her, he escorted Molly to the edge of the floor and tottered off. Relieved as she was to be rid of him, he had, in fact, left her entirely alone, and she gazed about, affecting great nonchalance and dismally wishing she had accompanied Jon to the refreshment parlor after all. Indeed, she was beginning to entertain the thoroughly unpalatable notion of skulking after him when she was approached by the young man she had seen with Lord Ogilvie upon her arrival.

"Miss Shelton?" He sounded rather breathless. "I trust you will not object if I take the liberty of introducing myself. I am the Earl of Durham."

"Lord Durham," she acknowledged politely.

She vaguely fancied he reminded her of someone, and she studied him a moment, attempting to determine who it was. Viscount Ogilvie, she soon decided: they were approximately the same age, and the earl was also dark, nearly as dark as Lady Palmer. On the other hand, Lord Durham was not built like the viscount at all; he was very tall and exceedingly lean . . . She became aware that he was returning her scrutiny, and she hastily dropped her eyes.

"I trust you will not object," he repeated, "but I was most eager to talk to you. Andrew has advised me of your . . . your situation."

As Mrs. Mulvaney had reported no gossip amongst the servants, Molly had come to believe that Jon's wry prediction was wrong, that Lady Ogilvie would not circulate their story "with all possible speed." However, it now appeared that her ladyship had merely saved her delicious *on-dit* for the ball, and Molly felt a stab of keen vexation for her "brother," who—in addition to his multitudinous other flaws—must invariably be *right*.

"Our situation?" she snapped, looking back at Lord Durham.

"Please do not be overset."

He obviously assumed himself to be the target of her wrath, for he flashed an apologetic smile. A familiar smile; he reminded her of *someone* . . .

"Andrew explained that the matter is a confidential one," the earl went on. "Lady Ogilvie told no one but him and Ellen, and Andrew has told only me, and *I* certainly shan't blab it about. No, you may be assured, Miss Shelton, that your secret is quite safe."

"Are you related to the Ogilvies?" Molly blurted out. "Forgive me for asking, but you bear some resemblance to the viscount and Lady Palmer."

"No." He shook his head, seeming peculiarly relieved. "No, Andrew and Ellen and I are but childhood friends."

"I see," Molly said dubiously. He could, of course, resemble Lord Ogilvie only by chance; that must be it.

"Let us return to your . . . ah . . . situation, Miss Shelton." He now appeared a bit impatient. "While I shall naturally respect your confidence, I should like to . . . to assist you insofar as I can."

Molly hesitated. Jon, she recalled, had informed Lady Ogilvie that neither of them credited their mother's deathbed confession. And though she realized that his protestation had been purely for dramatic effect, she judged it best, for the present at least, to adhere to his version of their circumstances.

"That is very kind of you, Lord Durham," she murmured. "However, Viscount Ogilvie must further have explained that Jon and I do not believe our mother's story. She was altogether delirious at the end . . ." She allowed her voice to trail mournfully off and, for good measure, heaved a great ragged sigh.

"But it could be true," the earl insisted, "and I am consequently prepared to pose some . . . some inquiries on your behalf. Very *discreet* inquiries, of course," he quickly added. "And in order to do so, I shall require additional information. How old are you, Miss Shelton?"

"Four . . . four-and-twenty," she stammered.

She had not anticipated the question, and she belatedly perceived that her confusion might well be construed as prevarication. Yes, Lord Durham *had* so construed it: his frown unmistakably implied that he had caught her in a vain little female lie about her age.

"And your brother?" he said. "How old is he?"

"Eight-and-twenty." Perversely enough, the *actual* lie emerged quite smoothly.

"Twenty-eight." He frowned again; maybe her response had not been so smooth as she thought. "And what did your mother look like?"

"Our . . . our *mother?*"

Molly had not expected this question either, and, far worse, she had no answer. She and Jon had not discussed his mother's appearance, and she distantly, frantically wondered how they could possibly have overlooked such a critical detail.

"Yes, your mother." The earl had ceased any effort to disguise his impatience. "I am particularly interested in her coloring; was it more similar to your brother's or to yours?"

"Her . . . her coloring." Molly licked her lips. "Well, it was actually *between*. Yes, M-Mama had blond hair. With a great deal of red in it," she speedily elaborated. "And her eyes were a . . . a medium shade of blue. And she was quite tall," she concluded eagerly. This seemed reasonably safe.

"Umm." Another frown. "That is most helpful, Miss Shelton, and as I indicated, I shall begin asking about at once. I shall naturally advise you if I learn anything of significance."

Lord Durham bowed and strode away, and Molly speculated as to precisely the sort of "asking about" he had in mind. Did he intend to inquire—"very discreetly," of course—if any earl in England might have fathered a son of eight-and-twenty, a daughter who *claimed* to be twenty-four? The mother of whom had blond hair with a great deal of red in it . . . It suddenly struck Molly as odd that Lord Durham should be "particularly interested" in their mother's coloring, and her brows knit in a frown of her own. But she was wasting precious time, she chided herself; Jon must be alerted to this unsettling new development.

She peered around the drawing room, seeking his auburn head, and observed that the receiving line had disbanded. The line had disbanded, and—her heart leapt into her throat again—Lord Ogilvie was walking toward her.

"Would you care for a glass of champagne, Miss Shelton?" the viscount said, reaching her side.

"In-indeed I should." Her mouth had gone entirely dry, and she feared she sounded much like Lord Duke/Drake.

"Then pray do help yourself. The refreshment parlor is just down the corridor, the first door to the right."

He gave her a pleasant nod, walked on, and Molly—her cheekbones quite frozen in a wide, vacuous smile—once more began to search for Jon. He was dancing with Lady Palmer, she soon discovered; apparently he had not delayed an instant when her ladyship was discharged from the line. And Lady Palmer definitely *was* the clinging sort: she was fairly coiled about him . . . Molly looked away, swallowing an infuriating lump in her throat, and, to her horror, beheld Lord Duke/Drake bearing down upon her. He fancied he *could* manage another set after all, he lisped through his remaining teeth, and he would be most honored if Miss Shelton would again stand up with him.

Molly squared her shoulders and marched onto the floor, persuading herself that she did not care a whit for Jon or Lady Palmer or even for Viscount Ogilvie. Nor for the fact that, at her full height, Lord Duke/Drake's bald scalp barely reached her nose.

—6—

Molly was awakened by the chime of the mantel clock,
and she lay still, her eyes closed, and attempted to count
the strokes. There were at least ten, she thought, possibly
eleven, and as she had surely missed the first, it might
well be noon. She briefly wondered why Mrs. Mulvaney
had not knocked her up long since; the erstwhile
governess subscribed to a theory that early rising was
essential to the maintenance of good health. But, Molly
recollected, she had instructed Mrs. Mulvaney not to
wait up for her, and the housekeeper no doubt fancied
she had remained at the assembly till dawn, having a perfectly splendid time.

In point of fact, Molly and Jon had left the ball just
after midnight, and Molly had had a perfectly *wretched*
time. She sat up in bed and glared about the room, but
the object of her intense displeasure was, of course, not
there. Indeed, she doubted he had yet risen, for his
strenuous evening must have rendered him quite
exhausted. Displaying an utter disregard for propriety,
he and Lady Palmer had stood up for every set. Well, not
every set: at one juncture, Jon and her ladyship had disappeared from the saloon and returned some fifteen
minutes later flushed wth jollity and champagne. At
least, Molly amended darkly, she *presumed* their happy,
rosy faces could be attributed to these innocuous factors.

Meanwhile, following their second set, Molly's aged
admirer almost literally collapsed and was compelled to

leave the assembly. Molly watched his departure with mingled guilt, relief, and—mostly—the awful fear that no one would attend her in his lordship's stead. However, this proved not to be the case: she stood up for *nearly* every set, and several young men even appeared to be rather smitten by her charms.

Several young men, but not Lord Ogilvie. No, far from being smitten, farther yet from *bouleversé*, the viscount seemed entirely oblivious of Miss Shelton's presence. Molly took some slight solace in the observation that he displayed no particular interest in any other woman at the ball; indeed, he led out a new partner for each set. At length she persuaded herself that Lord Ogilvie's formidable mother had commanded him, as host, to dance with *everyone*, and that, given time, he would have got round to Molly.

But it should have required no time, of course; Molly should have been the first. And the viscount should have been so enchanted, yes, so *bouleversé*, that he would quite forget Lady Ogilvie's instructions. Molly recalled her dream that his lordship would glimpse her in London, would fly to Hanover Street and fairly batter down her door, and could not repress a grim chuckle for her adolescent foolishness.

"Ah, you *are* having a good time then," Jon said cheerfully.

He had approached her from behind, and Molly started and spun around. Jon was, miraculously, alone, and she could only surmise that a call of nature, or some similarly urgent necessity, had forced Lady Palmer to uncoil her tentacles for a moment or two.

"We were wondering," Jon went on. "Lady Palmer feared that Burke would trap you; apparently the old rake has a keen eye for pretty ladies a third his age. But I collect he found you so enormously exciting that his lecherous old heart could not withstand the strain."

Lord Burke; not Duke or Drake, but Burke. And Jon and Lady Palmer had been merrily discussing the "old rake's" attentions to Molly, laughing quite uproariously, no doubt.

"But I daresay it was all for the best," Jon said, with a telltale tremor at the corners of his mouth. "I daresay Ogilvie was prodigious jealous . . . ." His voice trailed off, and his half-smile faded. "Er . . . you have danced with Ogilvie, have you not? I do not recall observing you together."

His pale eyes were serious, his expression one of unmistakable concern, and Molly found his sudden kindness far more distressing than his mockery.

"I had a glass of champagne with Lord Ogilvie," she replied stiffly.

She convinced herself that this was not exactly a lie: she and the viscount had, in fact, been in the refreshment parlor at the same time. But she could not continue to look at Jon while he evaluated her response, and as her eyes flew over his shoulder, she beheld Lady Palmer reentering the saloon.

"Indeed," Molly added shrilly, "I fear I had a trifle too much champagne, and I wish to leave."

"Leave?" Jon protested. "But it is scarcely midnight."

"Do not feel compelled to accompany me," Molly hissed. Lady Palmer had seen them and was bearing down upon them, a bright smile on her rather wide mouth. "I shall be happy to send Lewis back for you after he has driven me home."

"No; no, I shouldn't wish you to go alone."

And that, of course, was worse than if he *had* permitted her to depart alone. Jon tendered their excuses to Lady Ogilvie and Lady Palmer, making it sound as though Molly might well be at the brink of death, and one of the footmen ushered them downstairs, retrieved their cloaks, and summoned the landau. Molly remembered her conversation with Lord Durham, thought to advise Jon of what had occurred, but she discovered herself at the verge of idiotish tears and did not trust her voice. So she painstakingly studied her slippers all the way to Ship Street, noting that Lord Burke had deposited identical stains on either satin toe.

Molly sighed and glowered round the room again, but she shortly owned that she was behaving like a peevish child. Jon was in no way responsible for last night's debacle; Molly had only herself to blame. Obsessed by her cockleheaded notion that Lord Ogilvie would conceive a violent *tendre* the instant he glimpsed the alluring Miss Shelton, she had been far too . . . too reticent, she decided. She should have recognized and seized her opportunity when the viscount mentioned a glass of champagne, should have maneuvered him into escorting her to the refreshment parlor. No, her failure was hardly Jon's fault; she would simply have to be more clever the next time she encountered Lord Ogilvie.

But when, she wondered with a stab of panic, might that be? She recollected Mrs. Mulvaney's assertion that once the Sheltons' distinguished connections were known, they would be showered with cards of invitation; and she was inclined to rush to the vestibule at once to see whether any had arrived. But she dared not venture down in her dressing gown—she might stumble into a visiting footman or coachman—and she leapt out of bed, hurried to the wardrobe, and plucked out a morning dress of pale blue jaconet. She frowned at the bell cord a moment, but she was not ready for Mrs. Mulvaney's eager inquiries about the ball, and she donned the gown and dressed her own hair as best she could.

There were no envelopes on the console table in the foyer, but Molly comforted herself with the reminder that it was not yet one: those who *had* stayed at the assembly till dawn were probably still abed. She proceeded to the breakfast parlor just behind the dining room and was considerably less comforted to find Mrs. Mulvaney seated at the table, obviously awaiting her slothful charge.

"Ah, you are up at last, Miss Shelton." The housekeeper issued a disapproving sniff. "I do hope the food remains warm enough to eat."

She looked the attending footman a signal, and as Molly took her chair, he filled a plate from the dishes on the sideboard. Mrs. Mulvaney's dire intimation notwithstanding, the scrambled eggs were fairly steaming, as were the muffins, and the bacon was barely cool. In anticipation of a late supper at Lady Ogilvie's, Molly had eaten only sparingly at dinner, and, having left before the supper was served, she now discovered herself quite ravenous. Furthermore, she reasoned, shoving a great forkful of eggs into her mouth, if she was busily eating, she could not be expected to talk.

"*Mr.* Shelton rose hours since," Mrs. Mulvaney added with another sniff. "I asked him what time you left the ball, but he could not recall."

Molly granted him grudging thanks for not revealing the magnitude of her humiliation. "Where *is* Jon?" she said, anxious to shift the topic of conversation.

"He has gone for a drive with Lady Palmer."

"Lady Palmer!" Molly's fork slipped from her fingers and crashed to her plate, catapulting an unsightly glob of egg on the lace tablecloth. "Jon took *my* . . ." The house-keeper raised her brows in the direction of the hovering footman. " . . . took our carriage to . . . to gad about with Lady Palmer?"

"Oh, no, indeed. No, her ladyship came to fetch him in *her* carriage. A high-flier phaeton, I believe it is; in any event, it requires a ladder to reach the seat. I can hardly conceive how she manages it; she's such a *tiny* little thing."

"I collect you met her," Molly said grimly.

"Oh, yes, she came to the door herself to ask for Mr. Shelton. I . . ." Mrs. Mulvaney stopped and glanced at the footman, who was following the conversation with avid attention. "You may go, Reynolds," she said briskly.

He was clearly loath to do so: he carefully scraped the wayward eggs from the tablecloth, fussed at great length with the dishes on the sideboard, refilled Molly's coffee cup, which she had scarcely touched. But at last he shuffled out, closed the door, and Mrs. Mulvaney went on.

"I initially judged Lady Palmer's behavior rather bold. However, she explained that she merely wished to show Mr. Shelton round Brighton a bit, so perhaps there was no harm in it."

"I'm afraid I cannot concur," Molly snapped. "*I* judge her behavior shockingly bold."

"Do you?" Mrs. Mulvaney, who normally interpreted dissent as a grave personal insult, sounded astonishingly mild. "Well, I fancy we are all entitled to our opinions. I thought Lady Palmer quite charming, and she obviously *is* smitten with Mr. Shelton—"

"I advised you last evening that I do not care to discuss Lady Palmer," Molly interposed warmly. "And I have not altered *that* opinion one whit since making her acquaintance."

"Very well," the housekeeper said pleasantly. "Let us discuss Lord Ogilvie then. Mr. Shelton reported that you and he had a glass of champagne together. You and the viscount, that is."

"Yes," Molly muttered.

"And then what happened?" Mrs. Mulvaney pressed.

"He . . . he was monstrous occupied." Molly could not continue to meet the housekeeper's probing black eyes either, and she retrieved her fork and began spreading her remaining eggs about her plate. "In his role as host, I mean. Naturally he could not attend me to the exclusion of the other guests."

"Naturally not," Mrs. Mulvaney agreed. "And do not tease yourself about it; I daresay Viscount Ogilvie will soon come to call. Just as Lady—"

Molly looked up, prepared to cast an appropriately quelling scowl, but she was forestalled by the peal of the doorbell.

"Speak of the devil!" Mrs. Mulvaney hissed, jumping to her feet. "Well, not the devil, of course, but . . ." She wrung her hands a moment. "Maybe we should have engaged a butler after all; his lordship might feel we haven't a proper household—"

The bell pealed again, and with a small moan the housekeeper dashed across the room and out of the breakfast parlor, leaving the door wide open. Molly could clearly hear the tinkle of the dining-room chandelier as Mrs. Mulvaney pounded through, the tattoo of her footsteps in the vestibule, the creak of the front door.

"Lord Ogilvie?" the housekeeper said brightly.

The response was an indecipherable masculine mumble, and Molly's heart constricted most painfully.

"Lord *Durham*." To her credit, Mrs. Mulvaney sounded only moderately disappointed. "Do come in, and I shall see if Miss Shelton has finished breakfast."

Lord Durham. Molly gritted her teeth against a familiar wave of frustration and debated whether she should receive the earl. She was reluctant to submit to another series of questions without first consulting Jon, but, on the other hand, Lord Durham might have come to report that his "asking about" had borne some fruit. The prospect of the latter outweighed the hazard of the former, she decided, and when Mrs. Mulvaney appeared to announce his lordship, Molly trailed her back to the entry hall.

"Good afternoon, Lord Durham," she said.

"Good afternoon, Miss Shelton." He flashed a smile, that tantalizingly familiar smile. "I collect you were expecting Andrew?"

"No, I . . . I was not," Molly stammered. "No, I had been telling Mrs. Mulvaney about the assembly, and she had expressed her hope that we might be able to reciprocate Lord Ogilvie's hospitality. And I daresay that when the bell rang, she fancied—as all of us are wont to do . . ." But her explanation was growing far too long, far too frantic, and she ground to an abrupt halt.

"I do trust my call is not inconvenient?" the earl said politely.

"Oh, not at all," Molly assured him.

There was a brief, awkward silence, and it was left to Mrs. Mulvaney to suggest the need for a footman to take Lord Durham's cloak, the possibility that Miss Shelton might want to show her guest to the drawing room, the likelihood that his lordship might desire a cup of tea. Molly wryly wondered if the earl had guessed himself to be Miss Shelton's very first gentleman caller, but if he counted the housekeeper's intervention odd, his lean face betrayed no sign of it.

"Thank you," he said, "but I cannot stay. I wished to

beg but a few minutes of Miss Shelton's time, so perhaps we could"—his dark eyes darted swiftly about—"could simply step into the library?"

Molly nodded and preceded him into the designated room, where Lord Durham unfastened his cloak and tossed it on the gilded beechwood settee. He remained standing, eventually started tapping one of his highly polished hessians, and when Molly at last perceived that he was waiting for her to sit, she fairly collapsed on the settee, quite crushing his cloak in the process. The earl almost managed to repress his wince and emitted only a tiny sigh as he lowered himself to the mahogany sofa.

"No books," he remarked, peering idly about. "What a pity. I daresay Trevor sold them all the instant they fell into his greedy hands."

"I . . ." Molly began heatedly, but she recovered herself and bit her lip. "I daresay so," she murmured.

"Did you meet him?" the earl inquired. "Trevor, that is?"

Molly thought it improbable that she would have. "No, my brother dealt with Mr. Trevor."

"Of course," Lord Durham said. "Where *is* your brother, by the by?"

"He is out," Molly snapped.

"What a pity," his lordship repeated. "I was in hopes of speaking with him as well."

Molly entertained an inexplicable notion that he was lying, that he was, in fact, relieved to find Jon from home. But she could not conceive why this should be so, and she fancied her impersonation had rendered her altogether too wary.

"Well, he is out," she said again. It suddenly seemed best to tell him precisely where Jon was; he would learn of the drive soon enough for himself. "Lady Palmer very kindly undertook to show him round Brighton."

"Ah." He nodded. "Ellen *is* on the catch for him then. I surmised as much last evening, and it appears she has wasted no time." He stopped, frowned, nodded again. "Your brother is to be congratulated, Miss Shelton; it would be an excellent match."

"An excellent match," Molly echoed weakly.

"Excellent indeed, for Ellen is an exceedingly wealthy woman. Which is not to imply that Mr. Shelton needs her money," he added hastily. "No, it is clear you are quite comfortable." He waved his hand vaguely about. "But Palmer was one of the richest men in England, I'll warrant, and only a small portion of his estate was entailed. He settled a handsome sum on his daughter—his daughter from an earlier marriage—but the rest of it passed to Ellen. And she richly deserved it."

He chuckled at his little pun, and Molly essayed an appreciative giggle, but her throat seemed closed.

"Yes," Lord Durham went on, "Ellen deserved it; life with old Palmer could not have been easy. She earned every groat, and she can now afford to wed for love alone. To wed a man with no fortune, no title . . . Why, she could marry a beggar from the street if she chose," he concluded cheerfully.

Or a ragged Canadian adventurer without a farthing to his name; an impoverished fur trader with a fanciful claim to noble birth . . . Molly felt the dawning of a terrible suspicion, and she shook her head.

"She could not?" the earl asked quizzically.

"Yes, she could," Molly muttered. "I was but . . . but thinking—"

"That however handsomely your brother might be settled, you must consider your own future." Lord Durham gave her a kind smile. "You are quite right on that head, Miss Shelton, and I wish to assure you that I shall continue to assist you. Indeed, that is why I came."

"You have learned something?" Molly said eagerly. If he had, her suspicion was wrong; Jon's story was true.

"I fear not." He shook his own head. "To the contrary, my inquiries have failed to yield the slightest clue as to your identity, and it therefore occurred to me that you might have some . . . some evidence of your parentage."

"Evidence?" Molly realized that her tone was rather waspish, but he seemed to fancy her an utter sapskull. "If I had evidence, I should have produced it, should I not?"

"Of course you would," he said soothingly. "I refer to

evidence you may not have recognized. A box of letters, let us say; women are forever saving letters. Perhaps your mother had such a box?"

"Not to my knowledge." Surely Jon would have brought any relevant correspondence with him to England.

"Jewelry then," the earl pressed. "There might be a family heirloom of some sort. It could even be a piece of insignificant value."

"No, I think not." If there had been any jewelry, Jon's sister had undoubtedly appropriated it. If, indeed, he had ever had a sister . . .

"Possibly a souvenir." Lord Durham was beginning to sound a bit waspish himself. "People preserve the strangest things, Miss Shelton. Perhaps you have some item of your mother's which looks to be a meaningless childhood memento."

His prodding was growing increasingly dangerous, and, somewhat tardily, Molly glimpsed an avenue of escape. "I'm afraid I can't help you, Lord Durham. Apparently it slipped your mind that I have been in England for many years, and Jon brought our mother's things. Whatever things there might have been that he judged worth bringing," she quickly amended. "So I shall have to ask Jon about any . . . any evidence and let you know."

"Please do, Miss Shelton."

He rose and walked to the settee, and Molly leapt off his cloak. He snatched it up, shook it out, put it on; and she was gratified to observe that it was only a trifle wrinkled.

"Please do," he repeated, "for without evidence, I fear I can be of little assistance. I daresay I shall see you at Ellen's ball on Monday, and we shall discuss your progress then."

Molly knew nothing of an assembly at Lady Palmer's, nor did she have the remotest desire to attend one, but there was no opportunity to demur: the earl bowed and strode into the foyer, opened the front door, stepped outside, closed the door behind him. Molly sank back onto the settee, her mind whirling with the dreadful suspicion Lord Durham had aroused. She had barely begun to sort her thoughts when the door creaked open again, and she glanced up, assuming his lordship had left some article behind. But it was Jon who loomed up in the library entry, and Molly once more gritted her teeth.

"Sorry to disappoint you," he said, "but your suitor has departed. I met him on the doorstep, met him only briefly, I regret to say. I did not have a chance to inquire as to whether his intentions were thoroughly honorable, how he proposed to support you, et cetera. I promise to fulfill my brotherly obligations the next time I encounter Lord Durham."

Teasing, always teasing. Molly clenched her hands, determined not to rise to his fly. "Lord Durham is not my suitor," she said coolly.

"No? How unfortunate." Jon removed his cloak and tossed it carelessly on the sofa. "Would Durham's suit not represent a step upward? Let me see." He began to count upon his fingers, muttering under his breath. "Duke, marquis, earl . . . Yes, an earl definitely ranks above a viscount, so would Durham not be a better prospect than Ogilvie?"

"Stop mocking me!" Molly hissed, her resolve quite submerged in a flood of rage. "You are forever baiting me, forever at me like dogs at a bull."

"I wasn't mocking you, Molly; I was mocking *them*. Your so-called *ton*. Have you failed to see how shallow they are? How . . . how artificial? I daresay, given the opportunity, every person at Lady Ogilvie's ball would readily have claimed an acquaintance with Countess Melnikoff."

"Everyone except Lady Palmer," Molly suggested pointedly.

"Umm. Ellen does seem a bit less top-lofty than the rest."

"Ellen?" Molly echoed sharply. Apparently *he* had wasted no time either. "You are on Christian-name terms already?"

"It doesn't signify," he said airily. "I am accustomed to

Canadian ways, which are rather more casual than those here, and Ellen attaches no great importance to convention. But tell me, if Durham does not think to court you, why did he come?"

His eagerness to change the subject had by no means escaped Molly's attention. But this seemed as good a time as any to apprise him of the earl's interest in their situation; further discussion of "Ellen" could wait.

"It started at the assembly," she replied.

She proceeded to relate Lord Durham's offer of assistance, his inquiries concerning their background, and as she spoke, Jon crossed the room to the liquor cabinet beneath the window. He sniffed the contents of the various decanters, filled a glass from one of them, and turned back around just as she finished her description of their mother.

"You actually guessed quite well," he said. "Mama's hair had only a little red in it—she was mostly blond—but apart from that, you were remarkably accurate. And I must grant Durham some credit: it never occurred to me to attempt to establish *Mama's* family connections."

Molly narrowed her eyes, studied his angular face, but his expression was altogether innocent.

"And today?" he asked. "Did Durham fancy he had learned something?"

"No, today he came to see if we had any evidence of our parentage. He specifically mentioned letters and jewelry and souvenirs, but he was obviously seeking any item which might offer a clue to your father's identity." She hesitated a moment. "Do you have any such item, Jon?"

"Nothing." He shook his head, his hair gleaming red-gold in the winter sunlight streaming through the window. "Nothing but Mama's jewel box."

"Her jewel box?" Molly gasped.

"Empty." He shook his head again. "Nell took the jewelry, though I doubt it was of any value, but the box was too battered to suit her refined tastes." He flashed a wry grin. "Indeed, I'm not certain why *I* took it; perhaps because it is my only memento of Mama." His smile faded, and he took a long sip of his drink. "At any rate, I know Mama purchased the box in Canada—I well recollect that her first one fell to the floor and broke—so it could have no possible bearing on my father."

How exceedingly convenient, Molly thought, but she gazed at her hands and said nothing.

"Have you not wondered, Molly, *why* Durham is so anxious to abet our search?"

Jon's voice was very soft, as if the question far transcended the casual, and Molly's eyes flew up.

"I . . . I suppose he is merely trying to be kind," she said.

"I think not."

Jon walked back across the library, stopped beside the settee, looked down at her; and, as so often happened, Molly found his proximity oddly unnerving.

"I think Durham *does* wish to court you," he went on, "but he would much prefer to court the daughter of an earl. A woman of appropriate standing, of rank as exalted as his own."

There was no trace of derision in his pale eyes; they were gentle, sympathetic, and Molly once more clenched her hands.

"That is what I attempted to tell you last night." His voice had dropped so low she could scarcely hear him. "They will never accept you for what you are, Molly— not Durham nor Ogilvie nor any of them. One of them might well fall in love with the comely daughter of an earl, even the *unproved* daughter of an earl, but he— whoever he is—will never wed a moneylender. And your feelings will have to be hard indeed if you are to live a lie for the remainder of your life."

She could not bear it; she could not bear his pity a moment longer. "How fortunate that you have no such problem," she hissed. "That Lady Palmer attaches scant importance to convention."

"I daresay it would be if I had any particular interest in Ellen."

"That you met Lady Palmer at your *very first ball*." Molly flew heedlessly, relentlessly on. "She is an excessively wealthy woman, is she not? Precisely the sort of woman you set out to entrap. That was your intention from the start, wasn't it? You wished to pose as a man of means, as the possible son of an earl, so as to marry a rich woman."

"If I had sought only to wed a rich woman, I could have wed *you.*"

His voice was ice, his implication clear: he would not have a moneylender either. Molly felt as though he had struck her a physical blow, and she leapt to her feet and stumbled past him toward the door. But his lean fingers snaked around her elbow and drew her up.

"Whatever my feelings for Ellen, or lack thereof, she can be of substantial help to both of us." He was speaking in a hiss as well. "She is conducting an assembly Monday evening—"

"I do not want Lady Palmer's *help!*" Molly interposed furiously.

"Then you may sit at home and brood to your hard little heart's content. However, I count it most unlikely that Ogilvie or Durham will come to share your mopes."

He dropped her arm so abruptly that she stumbled again, and when she regained her balance, she raced out of the library and up the stairs without a backward glance. Raced away as if the devil himself were pursuing her as, indeed, she thought he might.

—7.—

Though Molly was far from suffering the mopes (or so she assured herself), she fully intended not to go to Lady Palmer's ball. It was not a question of "brooding," as Jon had so nastily suggested; she had said the simple truth when she advised him that she did not want her ladyship's help. No, her feelings on this head were strong —albeit, she owned, irrational—and she was determined to remain away from the assembly.

However, no other cards of invitation arrived on Saturday afternoon, nor on Sunday, and by Monday morning Molly was forced to concede Jon a telling point: Lord Ogilvie was most unlikely to keep her company in Ship Street during his cousin's ball. And she could ill afford to squander an opportunity to see the viscount again; she could scarcely render him *bouleversé* from a distance.

Molly sighed, adjusted the last of her curls, and slumped in the Adam chair. She had attempted to put Jon's dire prediction out of her mind, but it had lurked there, nagging at the edges of her thoughts, and she could no longer keep it at bay. Was he right in that regard as well? she wondered. Right to say that Viscount Ogilvie would never accept her for what she was? She recollected his mother's grim reference to Trevor the "vulture," recalled Lord Durham's odious remarks, and suspected that Jon's analysis was prodigious accurate indeed.

But did it really signify? She had, it was true, lamented

the loss of her identity, but what had she actually surrendered? What *would* she surrender if it was "Miss
Shelton" who ultimately wed Lord Ogilvie? She would
lose her name in any case; she would become Molly
Elting, Viscountess Ogilvie. The business then? She could
discreetly sell Trevor and Company and invest the
proceeds, and the Ogilvies would never question her
income; they would assume that the very wealthy Mr.
Shelton had provided his sister a splendid dowry. Or she
could retain the business, permit Gresham to operate it
and forward her share of the proceeds, and the result
would be the same. She could even visit Gresham from
time to time; she would be in town several months of the
year. And Mrs. Mulvaney would go with her, of course,
to London and everywhere else; if she objected to being
"ordered about" by a butler, she could serve as Molly's
abigail.

That left only Jon and the painful prospect that if he
wed Lady Palmer, Molly would see him from time to
time too. But why should the prospect be painful? Why,
indeed, should Molly care a whit if he *had* deceived her,
if he had invented his tale and borrowed her money so as
to win a rich wife? In point of fact, it would be to Molly's
advantage if he did marry her ladyship: he would be able
to repay his loan without delay.

But that thought *was* painful, though Molly could not
conceive why, and she drew herself hastily up and
examined her reflection again. Yes, she would go to Lady
Palmer's assembly after all, and she would approach
Lord Ogilvie quite boldly, and he would be altogether
smitten, and Jon could dally with their hostess as much as
he liked. Yes, it would work out excessively well, and
Molly wondered why her mirrored image looked so very
unhappy.

Following their quarrel, Molly had resolved to avoid
Jon insofar as possible and to treat him with only the
barest, coolest civility when they were compelled to be
together. As it happened, the latter endeavor proved unnecessary because Jon spent virtually every waking hour

with Lady Palmer: he dined with her on Saturday evening, accompanied her to church on Sunday and stayed for midday dinner, returned to her house Monday morning to assist in the preparations for the ball. Mrs. Mulvaney, who eagerly reported these activities to Molly, declared that she could positively *smell* a match in the making.

"Indeed," she added as she dressed Molly's hair for the assembly, "I should guess that Mr. Shelton and Lady Palmer, you and Lord Ogilvie, could well have a double wedding!"

Molly judged this an exceedingly poor idea and so advised the housekeeper in no uncertain terms.

In any event, by the time Molly descended the stairs Monday evening, she had not seen Jon for above two days, and her heart started to race most oddly when he glanced up at her from the vestibule. However, she managed to greet him with the chilly courtesy she had planned, and he reciprocated in kind, not even remarking on her sapphire net-and-satin gown, which was rather more daring than the one she had worn to Lady Ogilvie's. They donned their cloaks in silence, stalked to the landau in silence, set out in silence. Molly was beginning to speculate that they might never exchange another word, however frosty, when Jon cleared his throat.

"Do you not think it would be best to call a truce?" he said. "We can scarcely appear to be compatible siblings if we decline to speak to one another."

"Umm," Molly muttered.

"I daresay you expect an apology." He heaved a sigh, and Molly could not determine whether it was genuine or not. "Very well: I am sorry my comments overset you."

"From which I infer that you are not sorry for the *comments*," she snapped. "Not sorry for what you said."

"What did I say, Molly?" He had assumed his gentle tone, his patient tone, the tone she always found so unsettling. "I said that none of your lofty *ton* would accept you, and I shan't apologize for that because it is true. I said you would discover it damnably difficult to live a lie for the rest of your life. Perhaps I was wrong on that head, but I shan't apologize for having said it. So what did I say that you would have me retract?"

You said you wouldn't wed me, no matter how much money I had . . . "Nothing," she mumbled aloud. "It is just that you *were* wrong about the . . . the lie. I puzzled it through this morning, and I even perceived a way to keep Trevor and Company. Should I choose to do so."

"Did you indeed?" His new tone was utterly noncommittal. "Then you *would* marry Ogilvie under false pretenses. Ogilvie or Durham either one."

"My pretenses would be no more false than yours," Molly retorted warmly. "Or do you propose to bare your soul to Lady Palmer prior to the nuptials? To confess that you posed as the son of an earl in order to meet a rich woman? A rich *respectable* woman, I might add."

"Ah," he said softly, "I rather fancied *you* would apologize for that. For accusing me of trickery. But if you're quite persuaded I deceived you . . ."

His voice trailed provocatively off, leaving Molly to surmise his conclusion. Which she could, of course: he no doubt intended to suggest that they might yet terminate their agreement. But it would no longer be a suggestion, she realized dismally; it would now be a threat. Jon had unquestionably gained the advantage in their precarious charade: Lady Palmer might tolerate the truth, but Lord Ogilvie assuredly would not.

"I am prepared to accept your . . . your truce, Jon," she said as levelly as she could. "It doesn't much signify whether you deceived me or not; I daresay I need you as much as you need me."

"Oh, I daresay you need me rather more." He was speaking very softly again, but Molly detected an underlying tinge of danger. "So abide by our *truce* very carefully, Molly; do not think to try my patience too far."

Molly could conceive no dignified response to this, but fortunately she was not compelled to offer one: the carriage slowed, and she made a great show of peering out the window. They were obviously in the line approaching Lady Palmer's, and when Molly caught her

first full glimpse of the house, she willed her mouth not to
drop open. She had guessed—from its splendid location
in Pavilion Parade, immediately across from the Regent's
residence—that Lady Palmer's home would be quite
grand. But, in fact, the "house" was a veritable mansion
—an enormous brick structure, rectangular in shape,
with four full stories above the ground. She wondered
Jon's reaction when he had first seen it, had first
imagined himself its master, but she didn't really wish to
know.

Valiantly as she strove not to be impressed, Molly
could not but marvel at the number of Lady Palmer's
servants: there were some half-dozen footmen assisting
the guests from their carriages, perhaps a dozen taking
cloaks in the entry hall, and at least a dozen more ushering the arrivals up the staircase. Up the stairs to a real
ballroom, it shortly proved; the guests were whisked
round the first-floor landing, Molly gaining only a peep
at the magnificent saloon, and on to the second story.
There was an inevitable delay at the ballroom entrance,
and as soon as Molly was sufficiently close to see inside,
she looked past the receiving line and began searching for
Lord Ogilvie. She spotted his mother soon enough, chatting with Lord Durham, but the viscount was not in
sight. Molly contemplated the horrid possibility that
something had prevented his attendance at the ball, that
her sacrifice had been in vain, but as she dragged her eyes
back, she glimpsed his lordship in the receiving line.

Well, he was not actually *in* the line, she amended, as
she and Jon moved forward and her view improved. Lord
Ogilvie was situated just *behind* the line, behind the
young woman who stood next to Lady Palmer. A woman
of about her own age, Molly calculated, with pleasant
features and very light coloring. Indeed, were it not for
her coloring, the girl would have been quite handsome;
as it was, her fair hair and brows, her pale skin seemed to
run all together. But handsome or no, the viscount was
attending his companion most devotedly: whenever there
was a lull between introductions, the two of them broke
into animated conversation. And there were a goodly

number of lulls, Molly observed grimly, for Lady Palmer seemed to be debating the world's weightiest problems with every arriving guest—

"Molly!" Jon hissed.

She had missed the announcement of their names, and she tripped a bit as Jon urged her forward. Not, she reflected darkly, that Lord Ogilvie was likely to notice.

"Jon!" Lady Palmer seized his hand; for one dreadful moment Molly fancied she would bring it to her lips. "I am so delighted you can meet Maria at last." Her words suggested that she and Jon had been acquainted for months. Perhaps years. "My dear stepdaughter, Miss Maria Baird."

Miss Baird greeted Jon, Lady Palmer greeted Molly, Miss Baird greeted Molly, and they began discussing Miss Baird's harrowing journey to Brighton. Dear Maria had been three full days on the road from Bedfordshire, Lady Palmer lamented, having encountered one misfortune upon another, all of which her ladyship described in excruciating detail. Molly stole several glances at Viscount Ogilvie during the course of this interminable accounting, but his eyes remained riveted to "dear Maria."

At length Miss Baird's remarkable story was told, or so Molly collected because Jon was prodding her ahead again. By some inexplicable oversight, Lord Ogilvie looked directly at them as they passed him, and Molly recalled the necessity of capturing his interest.

"Good . . . good evening, Lord Ogilvie," she stammered.

"Good evening, Lady . . . er . . . Miss . . ." But it was clear that he did not remember her name, and he gave her a polite, apologetic smile.

Molly trailed Jon on into the ballroom, absently nodding to the faces she recollected from Lady Ogilvie's assembly, miserably pondering this latest and most distressing development. She had inferred from the viscount's previous behavior that at least she had no specific rival to contend with, and she was woefully unprepared to battle Miss Baird for his lordship's affection. But maybe, she thought optimistically, she had misread the situation. Perhaps Lord Ogilvie's attentions to Miss Baird were merely those of courtesy; perhaps Lady Palmer had even asked him to serve as her stepdaughter's escort. In the event of the latter, her ladyship might have mentioned her request to Jon, and Molly glanced up at him, thinking to inquire. But when his pale eyes met hers, they briefly flickered with sympathy, and she could bear no more humiliation. She looked back down and painstakingly inspected her ivory fan.

"Would you . . . ah . . . care for a glass of champagne?" Jon said.

To say the truth, Molly cared only to leave, to slink as far from the assembly as she could; had interstellar travel been available, she would eagerly have embarked on the next vessel. Barring any such dramatic flight, an escape to the refreshment parlor would have to suffice, but before she could assent, Jon tapped her shoulder.

"Never mind," he whispered. "Your other suitor is bustling this way. Durham. I shall permit you to be alone with him if you promise to conduct yourself in respectable fashion."

Molly wasn't certain she wanted to be alone with Lord Durham, but when she raised her eyes and started to say so, she saw Jon's auburn head already bobbing through the crowd. She peered about and soon beheld the earl, still some distance away but unmistakably "bustling" in her direction. She had lent no credence to Jon's theory that Lord Durham was investigating her suitability as a wife, but she suddenly recollected her odd impression that he had lied during his call in Ship Street, that he had been pleased to find Jon from home. Perhaps she could use Lord Durham to spark Lord Ogilvie's interest. Without wounding the earl, of course, for he did seem a sweet person.

"Good evening, Miss Shelton." His lordship's bustling had rendered him rather breathless. "I've been prodigious anxious to talk with you. Did you speak to your brother? Does he have any evidence of your parentage?"

"I fear not." Molly sighed, hoping to shatter his dreams

as gently as possible. "No, Jon brought only Mama's jewel box, and she purchased that in Canada. And it was empty."

"Empty?" He frowned. "Why would your mother own a jewel box if she had no jewels?"

Why indeed? "I . . . I did not mean to suggest that the box was *always* empty," Molly gulped. "When Jon brought the box, it held Mama's jewels, which she had willed to me." She vaguely indicated her sapphire necklace, the matching earrings, and Lord Durham studied them most intently. "But she purchased all the jewelry in Canada too," Molly rushed on. "That is to say, our stepfather purchased it *for* her—one piece every Christmas, one for each birthday—"

"Your stepfather must have been an excessively prosperous man," the earl interposed.

Good God. Would he next ask Richard Shelton's occupation, demand to know *his* appearance? Molly gazed desperately over his shoulder and spotted Lord Ogilvie and Miss Baird immersed in one of their merry little chats.

"Yes, he was," she concurred quickly, "and your reference to prosperity brings Miss Baird to mind. I collect she is the daughter of Lord Palmer? The one you mentioned Saturday? The one he settled so handsomely?"

"Yes." He sounded a trifle impatient. "Yes, and as Ellen is but a few years older than she, they have always been quite close."

That explained it, Molly thought, with a great inward shudder of relief. "And as you and Lord Ogilvie are quite close to Lady Palmer," she said eagerly, "you are *all* quite close to Miss Baird."

"No, that is not the case at all." He had grown decidedly impatient. "No, Palmer kept them both well cooped up in Bedfordshire, and I scarcely know the girl. Nor does Andrew though I daresay he soon will, for Lady Ogilvie intends him to marry her."

"Marry her!" Molly screeched.

"Well, why not?" Fortunately Lord Durham had

interpreted her abject horror as mere surprise. "It would be an excellent match for him. As I indicated Saturday, Miss Baird is extremely well-fixed, but I suspect Lady Ogilvie attaches more importance to her . . . to her standing, let us say. Palmer was a favorite of the Prince, and his highness has been monstrous kind to Ellen and Miss Baird since his death. And I am sure Lady Ogilvie calculates that the Regent would also look kindly on Palmer's son-in-law."

"But . . . but . . ."

"You think Andrew would not be Palmer's son-in-law?" He frowned again. "Perhaps not, in view of the fact that Palmer is dead. But the effect would be the same, and Lady Ogilvie is much concerned with effect. I mean her no insult, of course," he added hastily, "but she is a very ambitious woman."

"Yes, she is," Molly muttered.

"But let us return to you," the earl said firmly. "As I stated on Saturday . . ."

His lordship rattled on, and Molly tried to listen, but her eyes remained fastened to the viscount and Miss Baird. It was scarcely a wonder that Lady Ogilvie had displayed such scant interest in Miss Shelton, she thought bitterly. No, a wealthy Canadian with unproved ties to the peerage would do very well for her niece, who was securely established in society; but her son must have a wife of indisputable, impeccable background. At length she tore her eyes from the distressing scene across the room and forced herself to look at Lord Durham. But he had ceased his discourse, and he regarded her a moment in silence, his own dark eyes narrowed in speculation.

"Ah, I believe I see the way of it, Miss Shelton," he said at last. "You were not *expecting* Andrew Saturday; you were *hoping* he would call. You have quite set your cap at him, have you not?"

"I . . . I . . ." Molly dismally suspected that the entire world supply of rouge would not have disguised her blush; her cheeks felt like two small blazing fires.

"Pray do not be embarrassed," the earl said kindly.

"Have we not all conceived a violent *tendre* at one time or another? And I wish to assure you that yours is far from hopeless."

"It . . . it is?"

"It is indeed. As I explained, Andrew hardly knows Miss Baird, and, if I may be permitted to say so, you are much handsomer than she. Yes, if you could substantiate your connection . . . Well, I am sure I needn't remind you that an earl does rank above a viscount. And it might well prove that your family is also high in the Prince's favor. However"—he heaved a deep sigh—"*nothing* can be proved until you locate some evidence of your parentage, can it? I really must urge you, urge you most strongly, to speak to your brother again."

But he isn't my brother, and there is every possibility that he fabricated the whole tale . . .

"You might even wish to search among your brother's things," Lord Durham continued. "We men do tend to some carelessness in matters of detail."

He flashed a winsome smile, and for an instant Molly almost had it, almost apprehended who it was he resembled. Then his smile faded as quickly as it had come, and the similarity once more escaped her.

"Yes, Miss Shelton, talk to your brother, look through his possessions, and notify me *immediately* if you discover anything of interest. Much as I regret to point it out, time is of the essence."

He tossed his head toward the entry, gave her another smile—a kind, unrecognizable smile—bowed, and strode away. Molly gazed after him, both relieved and mortified that he was not a *parti* after all. Indeed, she reflected grimly, it appeared increasingly unlikely she would have *any* suitors until she established her alleged parentage. And if there was no evidence, if it was all a lie . . . One of the young men she dimly recollected from Lady Ogilvie's assembly approached and asked her to stand up for the boulanger, and Molly trailed him miserably onto the floor.

By Molly's reckoning, the ball went on forever. She allowed herself a tiny flicker of hope when the receiving line disbanded, but it soon became apparent that Lord Ogilvie would spend the remainder of the evening with Miss Baird as well. Lady Palmer, for her part, evidently felt that duty compelled her to distribute her favors among her guests, for she stood up with Jon only every *second* set. However, he did not choose to partner his "sister" during any of the alternate dances; he stood up with a series of elderly dowagers and exceedingly homely young women. At her ladyship's request, no doubt, Molly thought darkly; she had probably asked him to serve as unofficial host. So as to practice for the happy day when he *was* her host. The single bright spot in the entire wretched evening was that Lord Burke was not present; rumor had it that he was still recovering from his excesses at Lady Ogilvie's.

To Molly's utter astonishment and inexpressible joy, it was Lady Palmer herself who suggested that the Sheltons leave her assembly shortly after one in the morning. A young female guest, whose name Molly never did catch, had taken ill, and the remainder of her party greatly desired to stay at the assembly. And as Miss Whatever lived in Ship Street Gardens, just around the corner from the Sheltons, could Lady Palmer *possibly* prevail upon them to drive her home? Molly would cheerfully have driven Satan himself to his home in hell for a chance to flee the ball, and the nameless young woman's presence in the carriage had the additional advantage of prohibiting any private conversation between her and Jon. He did seize the opportunity to announce that he and Molly were to be invited to the Pavilion Saturday night—by "Ellen's" request, of course—and Molly could hardly issue an objection in front of their anonymous passenger. And perhaps, she conceded, she should not object, for Miss Whatever appeared fairly green with envy, though that could have been merely a symptom of her illness.

—8—

Breakfast the following morning was a rather frenetic affair, interrupted three times by the peal of the doorbell. Mrs. Mulvaney responded to these summonses and returned to the breakfast parlor on each occasion with a heavy ivory envelope in her hand and a triumphant smile on her plump face. To Molly's considerable annoyance, the housekeeper laid the envelopes beside Jon's plate, and he—to Molly's further irritation—continued placidly to eat, as though the Sheltons were, indeed, showered with cards of invitation every day in the week. When he had at last finished his meal, he rose, plucked up the still-unopened envelopes, and left the room. In hopes of appearing quite as nonchalant as he, Molly continued to eat *her* breakfast, but she was shortly overcome by curiosity, and she fairly wolfed down the final bites and set out in search of her maddening "brother." She found him in the library, sprawled on the scroll-ended sofa and reading, not the invitations, but a recent issue of the *Brighton Herald*.

"Are you *never* going to open them?" she demanded.

"Umm?" He glanced up from the newspaper. "Ah, the envelopes, you mean. You may open them if you like; I already know their contents."

"From which I collect that Lady Palmer has kindly arranged for us to be invited to other entertainments. In addition to our glorious evening at the Regent's."

"Surely you aren't overset about that." Jon laid the

paper aside. "What could be more *respectable* than a night at the Pavilion?"

It was a rhetorical question, and Molly looked away and affected great interest in the barren shelves.

"And Ellen did not arrange the other entertainments," Jon went on. "Not directly, at any rate. Are you not aware that word of our situation has begun to spread?"

In point of fact, Molly was aware of this: several of her partners at Lady Palmer's ball had made oblique references to her supposed father. But she did not care to own that Jon had been, as always, right, and she said nothing.

"So Ellen was responsible only insofar as she provided us further exposure," he said. "When I danced with Lady Bridger last night, she expressed her hope that we would be able to attend her musicale this evening, and Mrs. Mansfield mentioned her assembly tomorrow, and Lady Hampton alluded to a dinner party on Thursday. I fancy these are the confirming invitations."

He indicated the envelopes on the sofa table, and Molly said nothing.

"I should think you would be delighted, Molly." His tone was one of keen exasperation. "With every event, your credibility is enhanced; I daresay all of Brighton will soon be persuaded that you *are* the daughter of an earl."

"But it doesn't signify," Molly hissed, transferring her eyes to him. "It doesn't signify unless you can *prove* your father's identity. Lord Durham was pointing that out again last night, reminding me that we must locate some evidence."

"Durham!" Jon sounded a trifle peevish. "Why are you so concerned with Durham? I thought you had set your cap at Ogilvie."

He had used Lord Durham's precise words, and Molly briefly pondered the notion of relating her entire conversation with the earl. But pride would not allow her to confess the depth of her humiliation, and she cast about for a satisfactory dissimulation.

"I fancy Lord Ogilvie quite shares Lord Durham's

sentiments," she said. "Why should he court me when he can have Miss Baird? The *proven* daughter of a viscount."

"Ah." Jon nodded. "You know then."

"*I* know?" Molly gasped. "That would seem to imply that . . ." Her voice trailed off. Of course he would know of Lord Ogilvie's budding courtship; Lady Palmer had probably advised him well before the ball. "Why didn't you tell me?" she whispered.

"Why didn't I tell you?" He spoke almost as if he were posing the inquiry to himself. "I did not tell you because I didn't wish to discourage you. You must realize that matters between them—between Ogilvie and Maria—are far from settled."

Maria, Molly noted; it appeared that Lady Palmer already regarded him as a member of the family.

"The matter is far from settled," Jon reiterated, "and it is far too early for you to abandon your endeavor. Particularly in view of the fact that you now have ample opportunity to see Ogilvie again." He once more gestured toward the envelopes. "However"—he hesitated—"if I may be permitted another morsel of brotherly advice—"

"No, you may not," Molly snapped. "No, I have had quite enough of your advice." She spun around, started to stalk from the room, turned back. "What . . . what were you going to advise?" she muttered.

"You must put forth an effort to capture Ogilvie's attention."

"I well understand that!" She was snapping again. "Do you judge me an utter muttonhead? I quite recognize that he does not even recollect my *name*, but I can scarcely stroll up to him and initiate a conversation—"

"Why not?" Jon interposed mildly.

"What . . . whatever would I say?"

"Good God, Molly, you could say anything. For example, there is an item in the news"—he tapped the paper—"about three Lapland Eskimo en route to London with frozen game. Now that is a novelty, is it not? Frozen meat? Or you could adopt a more serious approach. Yes, I presume Ogilvie sits in the House of

Lords. Solicit his opinion of the Corn Laws; ask whether he fears a recurrence of last year's rioting."

"And then? What could I say after that?"

"Good God, Molly!" he repeated. "Do you fancy you'd suddenly be struck dumb? You find it monstrous easy to talk to *me*. Frequently to my regret, I might add."

"Very well," she said stiffly. "Let us assume that Lord Ogilvie and I are happily chatting together. What would happen next?"

"Next you would ask him to stand up with you."

"*Ask him to stand up with me!*"

"Naturally you would do so in subtle fashion, and it is imperative that you choose a waltz. As soon as you'd heard the first bars, you would begin tapping your feet, and then you would say, 'Forgive me, Lord Ogilvie, but I simply cannot stand still when they play a waltz.' At which point he would say, 'Then we must certainly stand up for this one, Miss Shelton.' "

Jon did, in fact, stand up, take Molly in his arms, and start to whirl her round the library, only slightly impeded by the Aubusson carpet underfoot. She surmised that he was holding her rather too tightly, for she discovered it prodigious difficult to breathe. And they must be moving somewhat too rapidly because her heart was drumming quite madly against her ribs.

"It is excessively important," Jon said, "that you look at him all the time you are dancing." Yes, they must be moving too fast, for he seemed a bit breathless as well. "He cannot fail to succumb to your beautiful eyes."

Molly dutifully gazed into his face and observed that his own eyes had changed, seemed wider, darker. Her knees grew alarmingly weak, and she dug her fingers into his back. "And . . . and then?" she croaked.

"And then you would remark that the room had become altogether too warm." His voice was nearly as hoarse as hers. "And Ogilvie would gallantly offer to escort you outside for a breath of air."

To say the truth, Molly *was* too warm, fearfully warm, and she did not object when Jon led her to the rear door and into the back garden. She inhaled a great lungful of fresh air, but it helped precious little because he was still holding her hand, and his bare fingers were terribly warm indeed. He drew her to a halt, stared down at her, and Molly shivered.

"Excellent," he said softly. "You are learning, for that is the next step. Yes, after a suitable interval, you would report that you now find yourself a trifle too *cool.*"

"Too . . . cool." Molly fancied he had mesmerized her; she could not tear her eyes from his, could not move, could hardly breathe.

"Too cool, and as Ogilvie would have left his cloak inside, he would place an arm about you to keep you warm." Jon demonstrated this procedure. "And then, if you continued to look at him like that, he would . . . would . . ."

Jon's other arm slipped round her, and he gazed down at her a moment, his eyes ablaze, two pale blue flames above the sharp bones of his face. He lowered his head, and Molly's stomach lurched, and she twisted out of his grasp.

"That . . . that will be sufficient," she choked. "I . . . I believe I have the idea."

She turned and raced back into the house—her legs trembling, her temples pounding—and dashed across the library and through the vestibule. She heard the slam of the garden door as she started up the staircase, and she paused, expecting a peal of mocking laughter. But there was only silence behind her, only the rasp of her own breath in her ears, and she rushed on up the steps.

The afternoon brought no more cards of invitation, but there was other confirmation of the Sheltons' advancement in society: Molly received two gentleman callers. The first of these was the Honorable Roger Sloane, whom she vaguely recollected as one of her recent dancing partners. She would not have remembered Mr. Sloane's name except for the calling card he supplied, but he soon gave her to understand that he would not be "Mr. Sloane" much longer in any case. No, he said, sipping tea in the drawing room, it was his sad duty to report that his father, Viscount Trowbridge, was mortally ill. Which meant, of course, that he himself would shortly be Viscount Trowbridge.

"I mention this only because I quite recognize your position, Miss Shelton," he added. "I quite recognize your desire to . . . er . . . associate with men of suitable rank."

Which meant, of course, that *he* desired to associate with *women* of "suitable rank." Molly managed a polite smile but did not proffer a second cup of tea, and Mr. Sloane speedily departed.

The second caller was Mr. Francis Crawford, whom Molly well recalled for having trod on her slippers sixteen times by actual count. She was initially heartened to learn that Mr. Crawford had no hope of a title; his closest connection to the peerage was a second cousin, and he was but a baron. However, as Mr. Crawford sipped *his* tea, he undertook a careful inspection of the saloon and soon began to estimate the cost of the various accouterments.

"Is that not a Savonnerie?" he remarked, indicating the carpet. "It would fetch a few pounds, I'll warrant. And"—with a gasp—"the window seats! The ones with the dolphin arms. I daresay *they* would fetch a fortune. But why should I be astonished?" he concluded after perhaps half a dozen similar observations. "*On dit* that your brother was immensely successful in the fur trade."

"Yes, he was," Molly concurred. "Unfortunately, like so many self-made men, Jon is obsessed with fears of fortune hunters. Really somewhat . . . somewhat unbalanced on the subject, I'm afraid. He has repeatedly advised me that I shan't have a farthing of his money if I take a poor husband. A man with an income under two thousand a year."

Mr. Crawford paled, clucked a bit in sympathy, and swiftly took his leave.

Molly sighed, returned to her bedchamber, and sank into the wretchedly uncomfortable Adam chair, the worth of which Mr. Crawford could no doubt have stated to the penny. She would not have judged either him or Mr. Sloane appealing in any circumstances; their conduct had merely reinforced her indifference. She *had* set her cap at Viscount Ogilvie, and she could not but wonder why, why she continued to pursue him when he had displayed not a flicker of interest. Perhaps there was an element of pride involved, she owned; she could scarcely bear the notion that he might objectively prefer Miss Baird to Miss Shelton.

But it was far too early to think in such terms, she chided herself; far too soon to admit defeat. She had met Lord Ogilvie just four days since, had put forth no real effort to capture his attention. Now, armed with Jon's instruction . . .

Jon's instruction. Molly's face grew warm, and when she stole a glance at her reflection, she was unsurprised to find her cheeks flaming even through her rouge. She was quite certain he had intended to kiss her, would have kissed her had she not dodged away. Had he sought only to mock her then, to tease and torment her in especially odious fashion? Or had he conceived a kiss as merely the climax of his "lesson"? She never had been kissed—that was true—but she had always assumed it was a perfectly natural function. Always assumed that when one was kissing the right person, one would sense what to do.

And so she would, she assured her mirrored image, when she had the opportunity to kiss Viscount Ogilvie. She would begin implementing Jon's techniques at once, this very night, and within a few days she would have that opportunity. Although—she frowned—she did not believe one was supposed to kiss a man before he had offered, so it might require several weeks. In the interim, she would put Jon's last, shameless bit of "instruction" altogether out of her mind.

Lady Bridger's musicale was scheduled for eight, and by seven, when Mrs. Mulvaney came to help her dress, Molly had nearly memorized the *Herald* article about the Lapland Eskimo, having decided that this was the proper, light approach to Lord Ogilvie. As the housekeeper arranged her hair, Molly practiced her opening comments and immodestly deemed her narrative quite sparkling.

"Is that not fascinating, Mrs. Mulvaney?" she finished. "Just imagine: frozen meat."

"Humph," the housekeeper snorted. "I daresay Mrs. Bradford would *serve* it frozen."

So much for practice, Molly thought wryly; she could only hope the viscount had a rather broader view of current events.

As it happened, Molly was not to learn Lord Ogilvie's opinion of the Lapland Eskimo—not that night, nor the next, nor the one after that. She had realized that she would be unable to speak with his lordship during the concert portion of Lady Bridger's entertainment, and she squirmed impatiently in her chair while a singularly untalented string quartet sawed and screeched their way through perhaps a dozen selections. After many hours, or so it seemed, the musicians were excused, and Lady Bridger announced that a buffet supper awaited her guests' pleasure in the dining room. Molly bounded down the stairs and lurked in the dining-room entry, intending to accost the viscount immediately upon his arrival. However, when he did arrive, Miss Baird was on his arm, and Molly dismally reflected that she should have foreseen this complication. She had little time to dwell on the latest frustration of her plans, for Mr. Sloane soon accosted *her* and offered himself as her supper partner. Between bites of collared veal and mutton casserole, he described his father's terminal symptoms in vivid detail, and Molly nodded and "ummed" and assured herself that she would have ample opportunity to captivate Lord Ogilvie at Mrs. Mansfield's assembly.

This phase of her project went substantially awry when the viscount failed to appear the following evening. Molly initially viewed his absence as divine retribution, exacted in specific opposition to her endeavor; but it soon turned out that Lord Ogilvie was only one of many invited guests who had tendered last-minute regrets,

citing the onset of a sudden illness. As those present
debated the nature of this mysterious plague, it further
proved that everyone stricken had consumed a largish
portion of Lady Bridger's pigeon pie while those spared
had not. Her ladyship was so overset that she departed
the ball at ten, vowing to discharge her cook forthwith.
The incident was a splendid recommendation for frozen
meat, Molly thought, and she jotted a mental note to add
that remark to her repertoire when she was granted the
chance to bring the subject to Viscount Ogilvie's attention.

His lordship was sufficiently recovered to come to
Lady Hampton's dinner party on Thursday, but Molly
swiftly abandoned any hope of private conversation. The
dinner was a formal one—there were thirty-six places
laid at the dining-room table—and she and the viscount
were seated diagonally across from one another. "Diagonally" in the respect that he was at the very opposite end
of the table; he could as easily have been in London for
all the personal contact so afforded. Molly was not a whit
cheered to observe that Miss Baird had been assigned the
chair beside his, that Jon was seated next to Lady Palmer,
and that she herself had been situated between Mr.
Sloane and Lord Durham.

"Well?" the latter hissed between the mulligatawny
and the entrée. "Did you heed my advice, Miss Shelton?
Have you talked to your brother again? Have you gone
through his things?"

"No, I . . ." But she could hardly confess that she
believed Jon a rank impostor, judged any pursuit of
"evidence" utterly gratuitous. " . . . I have not had an
opportunity," she finished lamely.

"No opportunity." His lean face hardened a moment;
then he sighed. "Well, it is scarcely my place to direct
your course," he said. "However, I must remind you that
time grows increasingly critical."

He tossed his head ominously toward Lord Ogilvie and
Miss Baird—chatting most vivaciously far, far down the
table—and Molly took refuge in a sip of wine.

"Was it not dreadful about the pigeon pie?" Mr. Sloane

put in brightly from Molly's other side. "*On dit* that it was overripe, but I am wondering. My father is monstrous fond of pigeon, and I am wondering if that contributed to his malady. I received word just today, by the by, that his condition has worsened . . ."

The future Viscount Trowbridge rattled on, and when Molly's beefsteak pie arrived, she was unable to eat a single morsel.

Molly did not remember dreaming of her conversation with Lord Durham, but when she woke the next morning, his words were ringing in her ears. "Have you talked to your brother again? *Have you gone through his things?*"

Molly sat slowly up in bed. She was persuaded that any further discussion with Jon would prove futile: if he was lying, he would continue to do so; if he had been honest, he had surely told her everything he knew. But much as the notion repelled her, she recognized that a search of his possessions might prove very useful indeed. In the unlikely event Jon had said the truth about his parentage, he might, in fact, have some scrap of evidence he had overlooked; as the earl had previously pointed out, men did tend to some carelessness in matters of detail. Given the far more probable circumstance that Jon had manufactured his story, his possessions might well yield incontrovertible proof of his deception.

His handwriting, for instance, Molly thought, her eyes narrowing. If Jon had composed the note from "Nell," he had probably made little—if any—effort to disguise his hand; neither Molly nor any other potential victim would have had occasion to compare the message to a sample of his normal script. However, if Molly could locate such a sample in his room—a memorandum, a shopping list—and additionally find the communication from "Nell," she could study the two together. And should the search for documents fail, she might yet be able to discover some other evidence of Jon's deceit.

The notion remained distinctly repugnant, but even as Molly tried to thrust it from her mind, she perceived its greatest benefit. If she could prove, prove beyond doubt, that Jon had lied to her, she would regain the advantage in their charade. Well, perhaps not the advantage, she conceded—Jon would gleefully remind her that her deception was quite as grave as his—but she would regain an equal footing. Jon could no longer tease and torment her, could no longer threaten the most dire consequences if she "tried his patience." No, if she had evidence of his imposture, evidence that would enable her to expose him at any time, the devious Mr. Shelton would have to deal with his "sister" in considerably more gracious fashion.

Molly rose and dressed with excessive care, realizing that she was postponing the ultimate moment of decision. Her recent conduct notwithstanding, she was not, by nature, a dishonest person, and she could scarcely bear the prospect of rummaging furtively among Jon's things. On the other hand, inaction could only lead to further mockery, further humiliation . . . The mantel clock struck noon, and she sighed, inspected her finished reflection, and crept into the corridor.

Molly's stomach rumbled as she proceeded down the hall, and she seized upon this as another excuse to delay: she would have breakfast and *then* she would determine her course. She paused at the door of the master bed-chamber, wondering if she could ever summon the nerve to venture inside, and when the door suddenly opened, her knees went weak with alarm.

"Ah, good morning, Miss Shelton." It was Woodson, Jon's young valet. "Looking for your brother, are you?"

"Y-yes, I am," Molly stammered.

"Well, he ain't here. He was going out with Lady Palmer, he told me. Left about two hours since, I fancy."

"I see," Molly murmured. "Thank you, Woodson."

He bowed and retreated down the stairs, leaving the door open, and Molly peered into the room. It was the perfect opportunity: the chambermaid had clearly come and gone—the bed was made up—and Woodson had completed his tasks. And if Jon was with Lady Palmer, he was likely to be away for some time more . . . Molly slipped through the door and eased it to behind her.

She gazed swiftly around the room, refreshing her memory of the furniture, and perceived at once that there were no documents lying conveniently about. As Mrs. Mulvaney had indicated, Jon was prodigious neat: not a single scrap of paper littered the dressing table, the washstand, or the bedside cupboard. Molly scurried to each of the pieces in turn, examining all the surfaces, opening the various drawers and doors, but found nothing of interest. Nothing but a tidy stack of receipts from Limmer's in the center drawer of the dressing table, and she repressed an inclination to remove them and calculate the total.

There was no clock in the master bedchamber—it had been one of Lord Chudleigh's sentimental favorites, no doubt—but Molly heard a chime from her own room and hurried to the wardrobe. It was fairly bulging with Jon's new finery, leaving no space for anything else, and her heart sank. She wondered if she had the time to check every pocket of every coat, every toe of every boot; feared she did not; suspected she would discover nothing if she did. She started to close the door, prepared to admit defeat, when she observed that the beaver hat in the center of the upper shalf was protruding a bit over the edge. She snatched it out and beheld a box resting on the shelf behind it.

The box, of course; Jon's mother's jewel box. Molly set the hat on the corner of the washstand and withdrew the box from the wardrobe. It was far from prepossessing, she noted, hardly the jewel box of an erstwhile countess: it was fashioned of pine, adorned with but a single rosette on either side, and it had been clumsily painted a hideous shade of green. Unpromising though it was, Molly tugged the lid up and caught her breath as she glimpsed a folded sheet of paper inside.

She placed the box next to the hat on the washstand, removed the paper, unfolded it, and her heart sank again. It was Jon's letter from "Nell," and Molly reviewed it fully half a dozen times, hoping to spot some tenuous clue. But there was nothing—no evidence of truth or deceit either one. Or was there? Molly pondered the ill-written missive, frowned, shook her head. She was confident by now that Jon could compose a considerably more literate message, could spell the word "delirious"; but if he *had* set out to deceive her, he might well have employed these very errors to disguise his authorship of the note.

No, the letter alone proved nothing, and it was time to end her fruitless search. Indeed—the clock across the corridor struck twice—it was well *past* time to leave Jon's room, and Molly's stomach began to flutter with panic. She grabbed for the jewel box, but it was precariously balanced on the edge of the washstand, and it began to slip from her hand. She brought her other hand up to catch it, dropping the note to the floor, and as her thumb smashed into the rosette on the right side of the box, she felt a definite depression and heard a slight click. She stared down at the box, marveling that she had saved it, and saw that the right-hand side had opened to reveal a small compartment. She groped inside, her fingers met something cold, metallic, and she pulled out a ring.

A ring! Molly slammed the jewel box back on the washstand and rushed toward the window to study her find in the sunlight. It was surely a signet ring, she thought, and with any luck, it would prove Jon's paternity the instant it was displayed. She reached the window, ground to a halt, held the ring eagerly up to the light, and made out a . . . a . . . A frog? Molly could scarcely believe her eyes, and, upon closer inspection, she owned that the creature on the ring could have been almost anything. The ring was obviously very old, the gold worn nearly smooth, but the vague design certainly *suggested* a frog—

"What the *devil* are you doing?"

Molly had not heard Jon's footsteps on the stairs, had not heard the door open, and she spun around and smashed the ring into her palm.

"Do . . . doing?" she echoed.

"Never mind." His pale eyes darted about, returned to her, froze with fury. "I see quite well what you were doing: you were searching among my things. So perhaps you might have the courtesy to tell me *why*."

"I . . . I . . ." But she could offer no remotely acceptable excuse, and, at any rate, an explanation no longer signified. She dashed across the room and dramatically opened her fist. "Look at what I found, Jon!" she hissed. "Evidence! The very sort of evidence Lord Durham asked about."

Jon plucked the ring from her outstretched hand and twisted it this way and that in the light. "Found it where?" he said at last.

As Molly described her discovery of the hidden compartment, his mood seemed to moderate a bit, and she decided to tender an excuse after all. "Lord Durham mentioned that you might have missed some clue," she concluded, "and advised me to look through your possessions. And I was certain, in the circumstances, you would not object—"

"I object very strenuously indeed," he interposed frigidly. So much for moderation. "Furthermore, I cannot suppose the ring has any bearing on my father. I cannot suppose any noble house in England would include a . . . a *frog* in its coat of arms."

"You do think it's a frog then?"

"What did you fancy it was?"

"A frog."

"Then we appear to have stumbled upon one small point of agreement." He strode to the washstand, examined the box a moment, replaced the ring in the hidden compartment. "Now if you will take your leave, I shall tidy up behind you, and we shall forget this entire unfortunate incident."

"Forget it?" Molly said incredulously. "Has it not occurred to you . . ."

She stopped and walked to the washstand, withdrew the ring again, and tried it on her third right finger. It was much too large; as she had surmised, it was a man's ring.

"Has it not occurred to you," she went on, "that it must have *some* significance? Why else would your

mother have hidden it? You must wear it to the Regent's
party tomorrow; you'll never have a better chance. You
must wear it to the party and show it around."

"Good God, Molly!" He stripped the ring from her
finger. "Would you have me prancing about, waving my
hand under every available nose, inquiring if anyone
recognizes this magnificent frog? I'm quite sure it is some
silly memento of Mama's."

He dropped the ring disdainfully back in the box; too
disdainfully by half, Molly thought.

"I find that very interesting, Jon," she said slowly,
coldly. "I find it monstrous interesting that you utterly
dismiss the possibility that the ring could have any
connection to your father. I can only collect that you
know for a fact there is no connection because you
fabricated your tale from the beginning to the end."

She waited for him to threaten her again, but he
merely watched her, his eyes narrowed to pale blue slits.
Now, she realized; if she was ever to regain the
advantage, it must be now.

"If I am wrong," she said, "I expect you to wear the
ring tomorrow evening. You needn't wave it about, you
need only wear it; I am certain it will be noticed."

"And if I do not?" he inquired politely. "Wear the
ring, that is?"

"If you do not, I shall assume you have lied to me and
reconsider our agreement in that light."

"You're a hard woman, Molly."

His voice was toneless, his face blank, his pale eyes unreadable. Molly whirled around, stalked into the
corridor, and crashed the door resoundingly closed
behind her.

Despite the circumstance that Lady Palmer had
engineered their invitation, Molly could not quell a rising
tide of excitement as the hour of the Regent's party
approached. She could scarcely conceive that Molly
Trevor, moneylender and daughter of a moneylender,
was to be admitted to the home of the most respectable
man in England. Well, hardly *respectable*, she amended,
recollecting his highness's rakeshame reputation, but he
was definitely the most *important* figure in the realm.
She briefly wondered Papa's reaction if he were alive to
witness her dramatic elevation in society, But that
speculation led her to the unsettling suspicion that Papa
would not entirely approve the ruse that had brought her
literally to the Prince's doorstep, and she hastily turned
her thoughts to the ring.

On that head, her initial excitement had waned a bit,
for she was forced to concur in Jon's opinion that the ring
was singularly unimpressive. Indeed, she might further
have agreed that it was a childhood memento of his
mother's, a ring she had worn as a girl, except that it was
sized for a man's finger. Perhaps it had no significance at
all, she conceded; it certainly had none if Jon had fabricated his story. But if he had not, if he had said the truth,
there remained the slender hope that the ring was a
peculiar family heirloom which someone would
recognize.

If he wore it, and when Molly reached the vestibule

Saturday evening, she looked immediately at his hands. However—another complication she had failed to foresee —he had already donned his gloves, and she lifted her eyes and pointedly raised her brows.

"It is here," he said politely, indicating a slight bulge on his third right finger.

"*What* is there?" Mrs. Mulvaney demanded, peering at his hand.

"That may be so," Molly snapped, "but it will do little good if it is covered."

"Surely you don't expect me to appear at the Regent's without proper gloves."

"No, I do not," Molly said coolly, "but neither do I expect you to wear your gloves throughout the evening. At the first opportunity, you must remove them."

"If such an opportunity presents itself, I surely shall."

"Whatever are you talking about?" Mrs. Mulvaney wailed.

"A . . ." But Molly feared that a discussion of the ring would perforate Jon's courteous facade, would stir the seething anger she sensed just below the surface. "Never mind," she said. "Please call for our cloaks, Mrs. Mulvaney; we should be off."

The housekeeper, who dearly hated unshared secrets, performed this task with exceedingly poor grace indeed, but at length Molly and Jon were suitably bundled and seated in the landau. In point of fact, Molly realized, as the carriage clattered to a start, their cloaks were barely necessary, for the night was unseasonably warm.

"It . . . it is quite pleasant this evening, is it not?" she remarked.

"Umm," Jon muttered.

He obviously did not intend to speak to her about the weather or anything else, and Molly gazed out the window and contemplated the festivities ahead. The invitation was for eight o'clock, but it was unclear just what sort of entertainment was planned. Lady Palmer had advised Jon that the atmosphere would be quite casual, and Molly had accordingly selected a simple white muslin gown, trimmed with only a rose ribbon below the bust. It now occurred to her that "casual," in court parlance, might be very formal indeed, and when she glimpsed the grounds of the Pavilion, her stomach churned with apprehension.

The landau stopped, and Molly craned her neck, anticipating a long line of carriages before them. However, she could see nothing but a liveried servant, apparently speaking to Lewis, and the coachman shortly left the box, walked to the side of the landau, and opened the door.

"We can't go no farther, Miss Shelton," he reported. "There's some kind of construction in the drive, I'm told. You're to walk on up, and I'm to wait for you here."

Molly was not in the least surprised by the coachman's intelligence: the Regent's constant renovation of his seaside retreat was an abiding scandal. "I perceive no need of that, Lewis," she said. "No need for you to wait, that is. The weather is excessively pleasant, and I daresay we can walk back to Ship Street as well. If Mr. Shelton has no objection."

"Umm."

Molly chose to interpret this latest grunt as one of assent, and after Lewis had handed her from the carriage, after Jon had clambered out the other door, the coachman turned the horses around, and the landau rattled away. Molly and Jon strode up the drive, she marveling anew that she was truly *here*, and eventually reached the domed Indian canopy of the *porte-cochère*. Another liveried servant admitted them to the octagonal entry hall and led them through a second entrance hall to the gallery.

Molly had thought herself prepared for the magnificence of the Pavilion, but she was not; she stumbled to a halt and frankly gaped. The gallery was at least a hundred and fifty feet in length, she estimated, and lit along its entirety by a muliplicity of flickering chandeliers and wall lanterns. It was done in vivid pinks and reds, ambers and blues, and the decor was distinctly Oriental: there were several bamboo armchairs, two great Chinese pedestals flanking the fireplace, a set of bamboo cabinets with red silk panels. She glanced up and observed that the ceiling comprised a series of skylights; she doubted a single candle would be required on even the darkest day.

The most astonishing aspect of the whole astonishing scene, Molly decided, looking back down, was that the atmosphere did, indeed, seem prodigious casual. The gallery was furnished from end to end with chairs and tables and settees, and many of the guests were seated— chatting and laughing and sipping from glasses provided by a band of circulating footmen. The rest of the party evidently preferred to stroll up and down the immense corridor, pausing from time to time to greet acquaintances. Molly spotted a small orchestra at one end of the gallery, but no one was dancing, and, in truth, the music was scarcely audible above the buzz of conversation.

Molly peered about for a receiving line, but, to her further astonishment, there was none. She surmised that they were simply to step on in, to mingle with the crowd, but before she could move, she heard a familiar and most unwelcome voice.

"Jon! Miss Shelton!" Lady Palmer bounded up beside them, wearing her wide smile and a shocking dress of pale pink satin. "Did I not promise you would be *enchanté*?"

This inquiry was, of course, directed to Jon, but lest there be any question, her ladyship patted his arm and gave him the full benefit of her great dark eyes. Jon patted the hand which was patting his arm and smiled down at her.

"You did indeed," he said, "but you did not do the subject justice." He waved his free hand vaguely about. "And I am sure I speak for Molly as well as myself when I tender sincere thanks for having arranged our invitation." The mockery, that terrible mockery, had returned to his voice, and his pale eyes darted briefly to his "sister."

"I was delighted to assist you," Lady Palmer said warmly. "But come; you must meet our host."

She took Jon's arm and propelled him toward a knot of

people perhaps halfway down the gallery. Molly did not suppose either of them would notice if she vanished into one of the marble baseboards, but she trudged miserably in their wake. As they approached the group, Lady Palmer raised her hand, and the Prince Regent of England emerged from the circle and lumbered forth to greet them.

Molly had fancied herself prepared for his highness as well, but, again, she discovered herself mistaken. She had been aware that he was a large man; it was common knowledge that a mechanical contrivance was used to lift and lower him into his saddle. It was even rumored that the Regent needed four attendants and a chair attached to ropes to maneuver him into and out of his bath. But she had not expected him to be so *very* large: an enormously fat man with multiple chins, a monstrous belly that must render his feet forever invisible except in a glass, legs like sturdy young trees. She could only gape at him, as she had at his incredible home, until she detected a pregnant silence and realized that the Prince was staring rather irritably at *her*.

"Your . . . your highness," she stammered. She dropped the first curtsy of her life and dismally suspected she would have fallen had Jon's hand not snaked out to tug her up.

"Miss Shelton." He nodded, his chins catching in his neckcloth.

"And this is Mr. Shelton," Lady Palmer said.

"Your highness." Jon's bow was quite smooth, as if he had consorted with royalty all his days.

"Shelton," the Regent mused. "Are you not the one who has some pretension to an earldom?"

It was the perfect opening, and Molly held her breath. Jon had only to remove his glove and display the ring; he could even make a small jest about the undignified froglike device.

"No real pretension," he replied, with his easy smile. "No, I daresay Mama was reliving some childhood fantasy; I am given to understand that such a thing is not uncommon."

Molly shot him a furious glare, but no one seemed to notice. And, at any rate, the moment was lost: the Prince began to describe his and Mr. Nash's grandiose plans for the future improvement of the Pavilion. Molly entertained herself by calculating the cost of the multitudinous projected adornments, and eventually his highness excused himself to greet another contingent of guests.

As soon as the Regent had disappeared (insofar as a man of such remarkable size could do so), Lady Palmer once more took Jon's arm, and they joined the throng strolling up and down the gallery. Molly had little choice except to follow, assuming her brightest smile each time her ladyship stopped to chat with another party of acquaintances. They reached one end of the corridor, turned at the cast-iron staircase, and had traversed perhaps half the length of the gallery again when they encountered Lord Ogilvie and Miss Baird.

"Good evening, Ellen," the viscount said. "Mr. Shelton. Miss Shelton."

Molly judged it an excellent sign that he had at least recollected her name, though she was forced to own that he might have inferred her identity merely in context. In any event, after the group had exchanged notes about the exceedingly pleasant weather, there was a lull in the conversation, and Molly felt sufficiently confident to address a comment directly to his lordship.

"Have you quite recovered from your attack of food poisoning, Lord Ogilvie?" she asked. She feared her voice was a trifle shrill, hoped this was only her imagination.

"Fully so, I am happy to say, for I was prodigious ill indeed."

"How unfortunate that Lady Bridger could not have served frozen meat," Molly said. Lady Palmer, the viscount, and Miss Baird looked at her most oddly, and Jon emitted a strangled cough. "Not meat *served* frozen, of course," Molly rushed on, "but meat *preserved* by freezing. There was a fascinating article on that very subject in a recent issue of the *Herald.*"

"Was there?" his lordship said politely. He did not

appear in the least fascinated. "Well, if you will pardon us, we have yet to greet his highness."

He and Miss Baird wandered away, and Molly trailed Jon and Lady Palmer as they continued in the opposite direction. Perhaps, she thought optimistically, Lord Ogilvie's wretched experience had temporarily extinguished his interest in food. At the next opportunity, she would mention the Corn Laws.

By the time the pagoda-shaped clock on the mantel struck half-past nine, Molly's excitement had turned to fretful exhaustion. Her cheekbones ached from smiling, her feet throbbed from walking, and she was bored to the point of stupefaction. Were they to do nothing but parade interminably up and down the gallery? she wondered with a stab of keen vexation. If so, Jon would never remove his gloves, and there would be no hope, however slight, that the ring would be recognized. She was beginning to *wish* she might vanish through one of the elaborately embellished walls when she detected a general rustling and observed a sudden blossoming of playing cards and gaming pieces.

"Ah, the queen has sat down to play," Lady Palmer said.

She indicated a small woman some way down the corridor, and Molly briefly regretted not having been presented to her majesty. However, upon reflection, she doubted her second curtsy would have proved any more successful than her first, and—as the queen spoke very limited English—Molly could not suppose their conversation would have been particularly enlightening.

"Which means," Lady Palmer went on, "that we are now free to play as well. I have promised Lord and Lady Reeves a rubber of casino, Jon . . ." She hestitated, and they both glanced at Molly. " . . . and Miss Shelton can watch," her ladyship concluded brightly.

Molly plodded behind them to a nearby table, biting her lip against a flush of mortification. She might have been a child whose nanny had taken ill, a small girl whose awkward presence must be tolerated as graciously as possible. But the only alternative was to become—quite literally—a wallflower, and she greeted Lord and Lady Reeves with as much dignity as she could muster and drew a chair to one corner of the table.

Lady Reeves won the deal, and as she shuffled the deck, Molly belatedly perceived the significance of the game: Jon must remove his gloves to play. She watched, rigid in her chair, scarcely daring to breathe, as he stripped them off and laid them on the table beside him. She watched as, the deal completed, he reached for his hand and arranged it, the ring glinting from time to time in the glow of the wall lamp above him. He began to play, and at one juncture the ring clattered against the table when he laid his card. Molly was certain it had been noticed—Lady Reeves even frowned a bit at the distraction—but no one displayed the slightest flicker of interest.

It was, of course, foolish to expect that *everyone* would recognize the ring, Molly reminded herself, and there were but three people at the table. However, as the game progressed, those guests not themselves engaged in play drifted up, paused to observe the proceedings a moment, drifted away; and within the space of half an hour, Molly estimated that fully fifty people had seen the odd, distinctive ring. Fifty had seen it, not one had remarked it, and at length she slumped back in her chair. Her search, her quarrel with Jon, had clearly been in vain: at best, the ring was meaningless; at worst, Jon had lied from the instant he burst into her office.

Molly had long since lost any desultory interest in the game, and she gazed around, hoping to discover some other form of entertainment. But there did not appear to be any; the Regent's guests were gaming or walking about or watching the play. She shifted her eyes back toward the table, resigned to an excessively dull evening indeed, and glimpsed Lord Durham near the corridor entry. Evidently the earl had just arrived; she had not encountered him before . . . Lord Durham! She leapt out of her chair, murmured an excuse, and hurried to the entry.

"Miss Shelton," the earl snapped when she reached his side. "What a damned nuisance about the drive. I should have been late in any case, but I was driving my curricle, and I hesitated to leave it unattended. I was consequently compelled to drive home and walk back . . ." His explanation expired in a sniff of annoyance.

"I am sorry for your trouble," Molly said breathlessly, "but monstrous glad you're here because I . . ." She peered around and dropped her voice. "I have found something," she hissed.

"Found something? Found what?" He was squinting distractedly over her head; Molly wondererd if he intended to rip the Prince up for his inconvenient walk.

"Evidence," she whispered. "At least it may be evidence. I found a ring, Lord Durham."

"A ring?" he said sharply, staring down at her. "What sort of ring?"

"Not a signet ring, I'm afraid." His dark eyes were so intense that she heaved an apologetic sigh. "Indeed, the ring is excessively strange. It looks to be a . . . a frog."

"A . . . frog."

His dismay was manifest, and Molly dismally conceded that Jon had been right again. The question of his honesty apart, how could she have conceived that a frog would have any connection to a noble English house?

"It might not be a frog, of course," she amended weakly. "The ring appears to be very old, and it's difficult to tell."

"Where is this ring now?" the earl demanded.

"Jon is wearing it." She nodded toward the game table. "But pray do not tease yourself about it, Lord Durham. I'm sure you're quite right to suppose it has no significance."

"No, I fancy it does not, but I shall be happy to have a look."

He started to step away, and Molly grasped his arm.

"Please be . . . be discreet about it," she said. "Jon does not believe it has any significance either; indeed, he didn't wish to wear it. I fear he would fly altogether into the boughs if you were to draw attention to it."

"Rest assured that I shall not."

He sounded rather grim; perhaps she had painted too drastic a picture of Jon's potential displeasure. Be that as it might, he ambled down the gallery, and Molly shrank against the wall and watched as he approached the table. He stood at Jon's side a moment, affecting keen interest in the fall of the cards, then strolled back to the corridor entry.

"It is certainly nothing I recognize, Miss Shelton." In view of his sedate pace, he seemed oddly short of breath; Molly wondered if he suffered some sort of lung disorder. "To say the truth, I do not even think it a frog."

"No? What *do* you think it is?"

"As you pointed out, it is difficult to tell. Nor does it signify, for I am confident the ring has no bearing on your parentage. No, my advice to you, Miss Shelton, is to put it entirely out of your mind."

"Very well," Molly murmured. Though she had entertained but the smallest hope that the ring might prove Jon's honesty, she could not repress a flood of bitter disappointment. "I shall try to locate additional evidence then."

"Yes, you do that," he said absently. He hesitated, briefly narrowed his eyes, went on. "Did you leave your carriage at the gate?"

"No, we did not; it is such a pleasant evening that we decided to walk home. So I'm afraid we cannot take you up, Lord Durham."

"I see." He drew a deep breath. "I daresay I shall have to arrange other transportation then, eh, Miss Shelton? If you will excuse me . . ."

He bowed and hurried away, and Molly frowned in his wake. He appeared monstrous eager to arrange transportation home when he had only just arrived, but maybe, if he had a lung infirmity, he dared not undertake another walk. She trudged back to the table, sank into her chair, and pretended to watch the game until she suspected her eyes had quite glazed over.

At half-past eleven, the orchestra stopped playing, and

the queen and Prince ceased their respective activities and left the gallery. Molly assumed, nay, *prayed*, that the evening was over, but it was not to be: a regiment of footmen marched in and began depositing trays of sandwiches throughout the corridor. Molly was not in the least hungry, and she looked imploringly at Jon, but he was cheerfully collecting bank notes from his fellow players. He tucked the money in his coat pocket, and it soon appeared that victory had whetted his appetite, for he must consume two great sandwiches before they could depart. At interminable length, or so it seemed to Molly, they retrieved their cloaks and stepped out of the Pavilion and into the night. They were still not rid of Lady Palmer, whose home lay in their direction, and she and Jon conducted a final endless conversation on her doorstep. At last, however, her ladyship disappeared inside her great brick mansion, and Molly and Jon proceeded along North Street toward Ship. They walked in silence for a time; then Jon stopped and drew her to a halt beside him.

"What are we to do now, Molly?" he said levelly.

"Do?" she echoed.

"Are we to have another truce or do you wish to terminate our agreement?" There was no threat in his voice; he was utterly calm. "I trust you observed that I followed your instructions; the ring was on display above two hours. I calculate that half a hundred people saw it, and it inspired no comment whatever."

Except Lord Durham's, Molly thought. She wondered if she should tell Jon that the situation was even graver than he fancied, that their staunchest supporter had pronounced the ring quite meaningless. But, upon consideration, she feared he might, indeed, fly into the boughs if he knew she had solicited the earl's assistance, and she said nothing.

"In short," Jon went on, "the ring cannot prove my veracity. And I will not have you searching my room again, Molly. If you do and I learn of it, I shall leave in an instant."

A definite threat now, but one of a different sort: he spoke still with that eerie calm, and his pale eyes were deadly serious.

"If you prefer, I shall leave at once," he said.

"Where . . . where would you go?" She could not bear it if he went to Lady Palmer, but if he left Brighton, left England, if she were never to see him again . . . She felt as though a great fist had plowed into her stomach; she could scarcely catch her breath.

"Frankly, I don't know," he replied. "Frankly, as I believe you once predicted, I have come to judge it highly improbable that I shall be able to learn my father's identity. But that leaves your project, does it not? And on that head, only you can decide, Molly. What is it worth to you to pursue your acquaintance with Ogilvie? Is it worth your continued alliance with a man you believe a liar?"

His eyes were blazing down at her—she could see them even in the darkness—and she sensed that he was asking some other question as well, something far beyond his words. But she could not conceive what it might be, and she was too tired to puzzle it out.

"Frankly, I don't know." She borrowed his phrase because it reflected her own confusion. "I shall consider it and—"

She heard a footfall just behind them; she had forgotten they were in a public street. It was no place to hold such a critical discussion, and she started to say so, started to take Jon's arm and nudge him on. But before she could speak, before she could move, the footfall became a pounding tattoo, and she spun around.

"That's him, mates!"

There were four of them, Molly noted, four of them racing out of Bond Street, racing toward them. They looked like sailors, smelled like animals; she was later to marvel that she had registered these details. She even observed that the first one to reach them had blue eyes; she could clearly see them as he seized her shoulders and shoved her roughly aside.

Molly stumbled, reeled halfway about, would have

fallen had she not crashed into an iron fence fronting the nearest house. She clung to the fence a moment, temporarily stunned, and when she managed to turn back round, Jon was prone on the footpath, the assailants crouched about him.

"Dear God!" she screamed. "What the devil are you at!"

In fact, it was impossible to tell, but she thought they were tearing at his clothes. She also thought Jon was giving as good as he got: at several junctures, one of the attackers fell back, grunting with pain. But four must inevitably best one, and at length three of them stood up, panting from their exertions. The last remained crouched an instant more, and Molly glimpsed a glitter of metal; he must be lifting Jon's watch. Then he sprang up as well, and they were gone as quickly as they'd come, their footsteps pounding back up Bond Street. It had required no more than half a minute, Molly estimated, and, still dazed, she waited for Jon to rise. But he did not, and eventually she staggered away from the fence, tottered to him, dropped to her knees beside him.

"Jon," she whispered. "It is all right, Jon; they have gone."

He made no sound, did not stir, did not open his eyes. Molly's head began to swim, and she reached out for support, laid her hand on his chest. It was damp and warm, and when she drew her hand away, her palm was dark with blood.

—10—

Molly stared at her hand, combating another wave of dizziness, then looked back at Jon. She supposed she should feel his chest again, should ascertain whether he was . . . But she could not finish, even in thought, and she struggled to her feet and peered desperately about. Incredible though it seemed, there was no sign of activity in any of the surrounding houses; apparently her scream had not been heard. However, an interior light burned in the house behind the fence, suggesting that someone within was awake, and Molly dashed toward it. She had just mounted the first step when she heard the clatter of a carriage in the street, and she whirled around and raced into its path.

"Stop!" she shrieked, wildly waving her hands. "Please stop!"

The driver frantically jerked the reins, and one of the horses reared in protest, his hooves crashing to the cobblestones not six feet in front of Molly. The driver gazed incredulously down at her, muttering a curse under his breath, but before Molly could speak, one of the carriage doors opened and a man leapt out.

"What the deuce!" The passenger strode cautiously forward. "I say! Is that you, Miss Shelton?"

"Lord Reeves!" She stumbled ahead to meet him. "Thank God it is you, Lord Reeves. My . . . my brother has been attacked." She suddenly recollected the final gleam of metal. "Stabbed, I think."

"Good God!" He rushed to Jon's recumbent form, stooped a moment, hastily straightened. "He's breathing," he announced, and Molly's knees went watery with relief. "Carver! Alice!"

Molly passionately wished to help, but she discovered that she could scarcely stand, and she staggered to the carriage and collapsed against it. Her vision was beginning to blur, her mind to cloud, and she was but distantly aware of the frenetic proceedings. Lord Reeves asked their direction—she did remember that—and she believed he dispatched Lady Reeves to summon a physician. Sometime after that—it could have been a minute or an hour—his lordship assisted Molly into the carriage and eased Jon's head onto her lap. They—Lord Reeves and the coachman, she presumed—had laid Jon as prone as possible: his feet were at the opposite side of the carriage, on the rear-facing seat, his knees bent only so far as required to fit him in. Unfortunately, they had been compelled to cross his arms over his chest, lending him a distinct resemblance to a corpse, and Molly swallowed a threat of nausea.

"Now I shall drive us to Ship Street, Miss Shelton," Lord Reeves said. She dimly wondered what had happened to the coachman. "Do not be alarmed; I often sat up with the mail driver when I was young. I shall go very slowly, but you must try to keep him from bouncing about."

Molly nodded, Lord Reeves closed the door, and she detected a creak as he mounted the box. Evidently his driving skills had deteriorated since his youth, for there was a fearful lurch as the carriage lumbered to a start, and Molly reached across Jon's chest and grasped his opposite shoulder. As his lordship had promised, they proceeded very slowly, and she could hear the shallow rasp of Jon's breathing above the rumble of the wheels, the jingle of the harness. She peered at his chest, as though she could will him to draw the next breath, the one after that, and as the carriage made a slight turn, he was bathed in a flood of moonlight. The assailants had torn open his cloak and waistcoat, Molly saw, and the front of his shirt was soaked with blood. She quelled another surge of nausea and hastily looked at his hands. The robbers had stripped off his right glove as well, and she was not surprised to observe that they had taken the ring.

"It doesn't signify, Jon," she whispered fiercely. "It doesn't signify whether you lied to me or not."

But he couldn't hear her, of course, and she choked back a sob and clutched his shoulder until she fancied her fingers would break.

When they reached Ship Street, it became clear that Lord Reeves had sent his coachman ahead to alert the household to their arrival: the house was ablaze, the front door open, and all the Sheltons' male servants were milling in the street, still wearing nightshirts over their pantaloons. Lewis yanked the carriage door open even as the vehicle rolled to a stop and began yelling instructions to the motley crew: this one was to take Mr. Shelton's ankles, that one to support his left shoulder . . . The ensuing procedure created a good deal more "bouncing about" than the carriage ride, Molly feared, but she could only follow as they bore Jon through the front door and toward the stairs.

"Mr. Shelton!" Mrs. Mulvaney stared at Jon's scarlet shirtfront, her eyes wide with horror. "Miss Shelton!" She sprinted forward and seized Molly's hands. "Whatever has happened?"

"A robbery," Molly panted. "Jon was stabbed."

She looked at the staircase, watched as the bearers toiled toward the first landing. Jon seemed limp, horribly limp, and she squeezed the housekeeper's hands till Mrs. Mulvaney winced with pain.

"I cannot bear it," Molly croaked. "If he dies—"

"Mr. Shelton is not going to die," Mrs. Mulvaney interposed firmly. "A great, strapping young man like that . . . No, we shall be lucky to keep him abed till the doctor arrives, and he, I am told, is on his way. Here now; let me have your cloak, Miss Shelton."

Molly suspected that the housekeeper's optimism was

largely artificial, but she desperately wanted to believe the cheering words, and she offered no argument. Mrs. Mulvaney tugged off her pelisse, and Molly observed that the sapphire velvet was marked in half a dozen places with spots and streaks of blood. She gazed down at her dress and surmised that she had wiped her hand on the lower part of her skirt, for there was a great bloodstain there as well. She shuddered, once more feeling faint, and stood dumbly in the vestibule as Mrs. Mulvaney disappeared, returned, and extended a glass.

"Brandy," the housekeeper explained, shoving the glass in Molly's hand. "Drink it down, Miss Shelton; it will do you good."

The strong spirits burned Molly's mouth and throat, left her gasping for breath, but, in truth, she did feel somewhat better after she had drained the glass. She set it on the console table and, beckoning Mrs. Mulvaney to follow, hurried up the stairs.

They overtook Lewis' contingent at the door of the master bedchamber, where the coachman began shouting directions for the placement of Mr. Shelton in his bed. When this task was completed, Lewis announced that they were now to remove Mr. Shelton's clothes, and it soon became clear that he meant to divest Jon of *all* his clothing. Molly fancied that even the modesty of a sister was sufficient to permit her retirement from the scene, and she quickly closed the door and leaned against the wall beside it.

"Those *fiends!*" Mrs. Mulvaney wailed. "You must tell me precisely what happened, Miss Shelton."

Molly would have judged the housekeeper's curiosity a trifle indelicate in the circumstances had she not collected that Mrs. Mulvaney wished chiefly to distract her attention from the wounded man behind the door. She consequently described the robbery from the moment the assailants pounded out of Bond Street till the moment they raced away, the housekeeper clucking and sighing at appropriate intervals. Molly had just begun to recount their rescue by Lord and Lady Reeves when the bedchamber door opened and one of the footmen emerged.

"Mr. Shelton's clothes," he said gratuitously, indicating the bundle of garments in his arms. "I'm in hopes his waistcoat can be cleaned, miss, but I fear the shirt is ruined."

Molly recollected her fury at the vast sums of money Jon had expended on his wardrobe and gulped down a burgeoning new lump in her throat. "That is all right," she murmured. She had quite forgotten the footman's name. "I am sure you will do your best."

"That I will, miss. And here; they overlooked his money."

He proffered the roll of bank notes Jon had won at the Pavilion, and Molly absently deposited it in her skirt pocket. How ironic, she thought bitterly. The robbers had half-killed Jon for his watch and his ring, which could not be worth five pounds together, and had missed his cash—

There was a sudden rustle on the stairs, and Lady Reeves hove into view, a black-clad man of middle years hard on her heels.

"Miss Shelton," her ladyship wheezed. "Is your brother . . . ah . . ."

Molly believed the footman would have advised them if Jon had expired. "He is still alive," she said. "But please hurry."

The physician inclined his head and bustled into the bedchamber, closing the door behind him. If anyone could save Mr. Shelton, it was Dr. Dunn, Lady Reeves assured Molly. Dr. Dunn was generally recognized as the foremost physician in Brighton; indeed, he was frequently called upon to treat the Regent's gout. In view of the fact that his highness' gout was known to be worsening all the time, Molly counted this a rather dubious recommendation, but she merely nodded her gratitude for Lady Reeves's efforts. As she did so, the door opened, and Molly glanced sharply up, fearing the worst. But it was only the servants trooping out, still winded from their travail, and they bowed in turn to the three women in the hall and retreated down the steps. Lord Reeves was the last to leave the room, and Molly looked him a question as he pulled the door to.

"Dunn has just begun the examination," his lordship reported. "But be assured, Miss Shelton, that your brother is in excellent hands. Dunn even numbers the *Prince* among his patients."

"So I am given to understand," Molly muttered.

"While we are waiting," Lady Reeves said, "you *must* tell us precisely what occurred."

Molly suspected her ladyship's inquiry *was* one of sheer curiosity. However, there seemed no better way to pass the time, and Molly supposed the Reeveses—as Good Samaritans of the hour—were entitled to an *on-dit* for their assistance. So she related the story once more, to another appreciative chorus of clucks and gasps, and when she had finished, the Reeveses rewarded her narrative with deep, simultaneous sighs.

"How fortunate *you* were not harmed, Miss Shelton," his lordship said. "Indeed, it is fairly miraculous that the robbers failed to lift your jewelry."

He expansively waved one hand, and Molly remembered that she had worn her best pieces to the Pavilion—a diamond choker, matching earrings, and a gold-and-diamond brooch.

"Perhaps they fancied themselves short of time," she said. "They failed to lift Jon's money as well."

"Yet they took the time to knife him." Lord Reeves shook his head. "Well, you have my personal word, Miss Shelton, that I shall bring the matter up in the House. Our streets must somehow be cleansed of the cowardly scum who prey upon honest citizens . . ."

Lord Reeves warmed to his theme, began to expound on the urgent necessity of municipal police forces throughout the land. In other circumstances, Molly would have found his discourse quite interesting; as it was, she could only watch the door, her heart and stomach seeming to freeze together in a single great knot of terror. At last the door opened, Dr. Dunn stepped into the corridor, and Lord Reeves fell abruptly silent.

"I daresay the young man will be fully recovered in a few days' time," the physician said brightly.

Molly's knees went weak again, and she sagged against Mrs. Mulvaney.

"The knife was aimed for his heart," Dr. Dunn went on. "Aimed, at least, where the assailant *thought* his heart was located." He issued a small sniff of disdain for the attacker's lack of anatomical expertise. "In any event, it appears to have glanced off a rib and traveled harmlessly downward. He did lose a good deal of blood, and I fear he'll bear a nasty scar for the remainder of his days, but no vital organs were affected. I should add that he also sustained a blow to the head—it was that which rendered him unconscious—and he may be a bit fuzzy for some hours to come. But on the whole, he was excessively fortunate." The physician beamed, suggesting that Jon had been *especially* fortunate to secure his superior services.

"May . . . may I see him?" Molly asked.

"He is not yet awake, but it would do no harm if you wished to sit with him a moment. I shall return tomorrow to evaluate his progress."

Molly nodded, thanked Dr. Dunn, thanked the Reeveses, desired Mrs. Mulvaney to show the group out. She then slipped through the door, pushed it carefully to behind her, and crept to the bed.

Dr. Dunn's cheerful prognosis notwithstanding, Jon's appearance was sufficient to set Molly's knees to wobbling again, and she sank on the bed beside him. He was clad in a clean white nightshirt, but it had been left open at the neck, and she could clearly see the great bandage which swathed his left side, the bandage already flecked with a few spots of blood. She peered fearfully at his face and sucked in her breath. His skin was nearly as pale as his nightshirt, his freckles seeming so dark as to resemble drops of blood themselves. She looked on up and glimpsed the "blow to the head" the physician had referred to—a bruise at Jon's harline the size of a small

egg. And Dr. Dunn had *not* mentioned half a dozen other
wounds: additional bruises on both cheeks and one jaw, a
small cut in the vicinity of his right ear . . .

"Oh, Jon." She drew a deep, tremulous breath and
took his left hand in both of hers. "I am sorry for every
wicked thing I ever said to you, every wicked thing I ever
did." She realized he couldn't hear her; she could not
have spoken so if he could. "I didn't perceive until
tonight how . . . how monstrous fond of you I am, and it
doesn't matter a deuce if you *did* deceive me. You may be
my brother for the rest of your life if you like, and I shall
never utter another word about your father—"

"Umm." He emitted a low groan, and Molly anxiously
patted his hand. "K-Kitty?"

Kitty? Oddly enough, Molly had never considered the
women in Jon's previous life, but there would have been
women, of course. And if it comforted him to imagine
that she was one of them . . .

"Yes," she whispered. "I am here."

He raised his right hand and clasped it round the nape
of her neck, pulled her head down and . . . Molly had
often dreamed of kissing—of kissing the heroes in her
adolescent romances, of kissing Lord Ogilvie—but she
was totally unprepared for the reality of kissing Jon.
Unprepared for the softness, the incredible warmth, of
his mouth on hers. Unprepared for the jolt to her mid-
section, the terrible, wonderful stab that threatened to
drive the breath from her body. Unprepared for the sensation that she had somehow turned to liquid, that even
her bones had melted. But she had been right on one
head, she reflected distantly; she had been right to think
that she would instinctively know how to respond. She
opened her lips against his, moaned as he teased them
open yet further. He drew a bit away, then took her
mouth again; she could feel his tongue, feel his teeth—

"Miss Shelton?"

The door creaked, and Molly leapt off the bed,
tripping over her skirt.

"Is he all right, Miss Shelton?" Mrs. Mulvaney was peering over the threshold.

"Yes, he is fine," Molly choked. "I shall therefore retire, so if you would please extinguish the candles . . ."

She rushed across the room and through the door, barely aware that she had trod on the housekeeper's foot, and fled to the safety of her bedchamber.

When Molly woke, she fancied she had contracted some sort of dreadful illness: there was a brilliant light behind her eyelids, and she ached in every joint and muscle of her body. However, when she dared to crack one eye, she perceived that the light was sunshine streaming through the window and that her discomfort was due to the circumstance that she was lying crosswise on the bed, her legs and one arm dangling over the edge. She remembered that she had collapsed on the bed fully clothed, thinking to rest a moment before she disrobed and donned her nightdress; obviously she had fallen asleep in that torturous position.

She struggled upright, wincing with pain, and began to reconstruct the astonishing events of the previous evening. Not surprisingly, her mind turned first to the matter she had been pondering when she fell asleep, and her cheeks flamed in recollection of the shocking, shameless scene in Jon's bedchamber. She was compelled to own that there was one aspect of kissing she had not anticipated: she had not expected it would prove so very pleasurable to kiss a person of whom one was but mildly fond. Well, she was more than "mildly" fond of Jon, she conceded; she had said the truth when she'd whispered that she was *monstrous* fond of him. But her fondness was, of course, merely that of a sister for a brother; it in no way resembled a *tendre*. So she could only suppose that kissing created a purely physical response, could only be grateful that Jon himself would not recollect the scene at all. If he did retain some fuzzy memory, he would no doubt assume he had dreamed of "Kitty," whoever *she* might be.

Molly stood, her muscles shrieking another protest, and stripped off her bloodstained dress. As was the case with Jon's shirt, she feared it was soiled beyond salvation, but it would do no harm to instruct one of the maids to *try* to clean it. She folded it, started to toss it on the bed, felt a lump in the pocket, and withdrew Jon's wad of bank notes. Now that it was clear he would survive the attack, she could almost laugh at the prodigious incompetence of the robbers. They had overlooked her jewels, missed Jon's cash, and Molly now wondered if they had even taken his watch. The glitter she had thought to be the watch had actually been the knife. Indeed, upon reflection, she did not believe Jon *had* a watch; she had never seen him use one. So the robbers had lifted only a ring, a ring of excessively modest value . . .

Molly felt the blood drain from her face, and she sank back on the bed. Could it be that the robbers had *intended* only to take the ring? She reviewed the attack and recalled a detail she had failed to relate to Mrs. Mulvaney and the Reeveses: as the robbers rushed out of Bond Street, one of them had shouted, "That's him, mates!" "Him" was an exceedingly odd word to employ if they had been plotting to rob the next prosperous-looking pedestrian who happened along. No, they had been waiting for Jon, *specifically* for Jon. Waiting to steal the ring on his right hand—they had not removed his left glove—and to . . . to . . . *"The knife was aimed for his heart."* Dr. Dunn's words echoed in Molly's ears, and her stomach churned. The violence had not been random either; the assailants had planned from the beginning to kill their victim.

Good God! Molly's head started to spin, but at length the pieces fell into place. Someone at the Regent's party had recognized the ring after all, had additionally realized that it posed a grave threat. He had consequently ventured to the pier and engaged four sailors to remove the threat without delay, to take the ring and—for good measure—murder the man who wore it.

But who? Molly wondered frantically. As she had estimated, as Jon had pointed out, fully fifty of his highness' guests had had an opportunity to view the ring; any one of them could have commissioned the attack. Except Lord Reeves, she amended. Had he been responsible, he would surely have conceived some way to finish the job; he would not have summoned a physician and whisked Jon home. Lord Reeves and Lord Durham, for the earl had definitely not recognized the ring . . .

No, the earl had *said* he did not recognize the ring. Scraps of memory raced through Molly's mind, and her heart crashed into her throat. Why had Lord Durham taken such keen interest in the Sheltons' background? Jon had asked that question, had insisted the earl was courting Molly; she had even believed that for a time. But when it grew apparent that he was *not* a suitor? Why had Lord Durham been so eager to promote her relationship with Lord Ogilvie, to see his childhood friend connected to a young woman neither of them knew? He had not, of course; he had conveniently seized upon Molly's *tendre* to inspire an exhaustive search for "evidence."

And last night? The earl had been enormously dismayed to learn of the froglike device on the ring; Molly had foolishly interpreted his reaction as one of disappointment. He could not be certain the ring was what he suspected, what he feared, until he studied it, after which he hastened to inform Molly that it was meaningless. To inform her, in fact, that it was not even a frog; it wouldn't do for her to babble that intelligence to the wrong person. Lord Durham had then hurried away, allegedly to arrange transportation home, actually to arrange the disposal of his . . .

Of his what? Molly narrowed her eyes a moment, sucked in her breath. Of his rival, of course—the true Earl of Durham. There was no other explanation, no other conceivable circumstance that could impel his lordship to murder.

Molly sprang up, her heart now pounding with excitement, then collapsed on the bed again. Where was she to proceed from here? It seemed clear that Jon and Lord Durham's mutual situation, whatever it was, was not widely known; if it were, she or Jon would surely have heard some rumor of his possible identity. On the other hand, it seemed equally certain that *someone* might acknowledge Jon as Earl of Durham; otherwise the present earl would not have cared a whit about Jon's parentage. It remained, then, to locate that someone, and to do so, Molly would require considerable information about Lord Durham's family.

The kind of information in Trevor and Company's files. Molly felt another brief surge of excitement but shortly abandoned the notion of a drive to London. Thorough as the company's records were, there were inevitable gaps; she could spend two precious days on the road and learn nothing. Or, more likely, she would discover a few dry facts about the Durham earldom, and there would be no way to pursue her inquiries any further. No, what she really needed was to speak with a person who could supply gossip and innuendo as well as mere fact. A person of middle age, someone who had attained adulthood thirty or more years since. A person who would be eager to talk, who frankly enjoyed meddling in the affairs of others.

In short, what she needed was to speak with Lady Ogilvie.

—11—

Since the weather remained unseasonably warm, Molly
elected to walk to West Street—an unfortunate decision,
it proved, because with every step, she perceived an
additional obstacle in her path. To begin with, she
reflected, hurrying along Ship Street Gardens, she could
hardly burst into Lady Ogilvie's home and accuse Lord
Durham of attempted murder. No, she would have to
devise some excuse for her inquiries, and at this juncture,
she had no notion what it might be.

The excuse would have to be very credible indeed, she
further realized, turning into Middle Street, for Lady
Ogilvie would almost certainly repeat their conversation
to the earl. Unless Molly could manufacture a monstrous
good reason to pledge her ladyship to silence, and her
mind was blank on that head as well.

As she entered Middle Street Lane, Molly apprehended
the gravest complication of all: in view of his friendship
with the viscount, Lord Durham might well be at the
Ogilvies'. Should that be the case, her ladyship would no
doubt insist they all take tea together, and Molly would
be compelled to describe the "robbery" as if it were, in
fact, no more than that. And she would have to be excessively careful lest the earl suspect she had deduced his
role in the attack.

Molly reached West Street and stumbled to a halt, a
prickle at the base of her scalp. If Lord Durham did
suspect what she was at, she would be in considerable

danger; he had clearly demonstrated that he would stop at nothing to preserve his title. Which introduced the frightening possibility that the earl might come to West Street *after* Molly's own arrival, might overhear her discussion with Lady Ogilvie and readily discern her motives. That would be a dangerous circumstance indeed, Molly thought grimly, because no one knew her present whereabouts or her intentions.

She had planned to determine whether Jon was sufficiently sensible to conduct a conversation and, if so, to advise him of her conclusions and her projected call on Lady Ogilvie. However, as she lifted her hand to tap on his bedchamber door, she heard voices within and collected that Dr. Dunn had returned to examine his patient. She was hesitating, wondering how long the physician might stay, when Mrs. Mulvaney appeared at the top of the stairs, a tray in her hands.

"Ah, good morning, Miss Shelton. How lucky I am to find you here; you can open the door for me."

"You are serving tea to Jon and Dr. Dunn?" Molly said absently, noting the pot, the two cups and saucers, the various condiments on the tray.

"Oh, no, not to Dr. Dunn; to Mr. Shelton and Lady Palmer." The housekeeper frowned. "I must own that I was somewhat reluctant to admit her ladyship to Mr. Shelton's bedchamber; I fancied it might not be altogether proper. But she insisted that company would do him good, and I daresay she was right, for he seemed *enormously* cheered to see her."

Even as Mrs. Mulvaney beamed, her opinion was confirmed by a rich masculine laugh and a girlish giggle floating through the door. Jon was unlikely to mistake *Lady Palmer* for "Kitty," Molly reflected furiously.

"Would you care to join them?" Mrs. Mulvaney asked. "I shall be happy to bring another cup—"

"No, I would not care to join them," Molly interposed stiffly. "I am in the way of taking a walk."

"As you will," the housekeeper said brightly. "If you could but open the door then . . ."

Molly twisted the knob, barely cracked the door—

leaving Mrs. Mulvaney to kick it on open—and stalked down the stairs and out of the house.

So no one knew of her suspicions, Molly reiterated, peering at Lord Ogilvie's house, and if she were to meet with an "accident" en route back to Ship Street . . . But she was being prodigious melodramatic, she chided herself; it was broad daylight, and there was every chance the earl would not appear at all. Furthermore, she owed it to Jon to pursue her investigation: it was she who had forced him to wear the ring, she who had put his life at risk. She squared her shoulders, strode boldly ahead to the house, marched up the front steps, and rang the bell.

"Miss Shelton!" Higgins seized her hand and fairly dragged her across the threshold. "We learned a few hours since of your brother's *terrible* mishap. Is he . . . is he . . ."

"The doctor judges it only a matter of days," Molly said. The butler's eyes widened. "A matter of days until Jon is recovered," she hastily elaborated. "He is mending very nicely."

"What splendid news!" Higgins clapped his hands but could not entirely hide a small moue of disappointment: a murder just a quarter-mile away would have been a delicious *on-dit* to take back to Warwickshire. "Permit me to show you to the drawing room, Miss Shelton; I am sure her ladyship will be most eager to see you."

The butler took her cloak, escorted her to the first floor, and hurried up the next flight of stairs. Molly sank onto the Hepplewhite sofa, casting desperately about for a suitable opening, but nothing came to mind. She recollected her first visit to this room, remembered Jon's masterful manipulation of Lady Ogilvie, and wished she were half so clever, half so glib. But she was not, and all too soon there was a tattoo of footfalls on the steps, in the corridor, and her ladyship rushed into the saloon.

"No, do not get up, Miss Shelton. Oh, my poor dear child! What a perfectly *dreadful* experience; I am given to understand you were actually *there*. Do not lounge about, Higgins!" she snapped. "Bring us some tea; I am certain poor Miss Shelton could well use a strong cup of tea."

The butler scurried away, and Lady Ogilvie perched on the edge of the shield-back chair.

"Now, you must tell me all about it," she said, "not omitting a *single* detail. Oh, if only Andrew were here! But he has gone to commiserate with James."

"James?" Molly echoed politely.

"Lord Durham."

Molly could scarcely believe her luck; Lady Ogilvie herself had provided an opening. "What . . . what is wrong with Lord Durham?" she asked.

"He is ill, or so Higgins heard from Lady Bridger's housekeeper, who got it from James's valet." Molly heaved a great inward sign of relief. "It is nothing serious, I fancy, but Andrew dropped by to see. But enough of James, Miss Shelton; I *must* hear about the robbery."

It was clear that her ladyship would not be diverted, but Molly jotted a mental note of the earl's illness; it might prove useful after she had told her story. This she now proceeded to do, and—since Lady Ogilvie was such an attentive audience, since Molly was thoroughly tired of repeating the tale—she found herself adding several embellishments. The robbers had been quite rough with her, she reported, leaving a painful bruise on one shoulder; she was able to wince most convincingly because she had twisted said shoulder during the course of her contorted sleep. Indeed, they had been *so* rough that Molly briefly lost consciousness while clinging to the fence. When she regained her senses, Jon's cloak and coat were already lying in the street, torn altogether to shreds. And the more she thought on it, and with all due respect for Dr. Dunn's opinion, she believed the assailants had stabbed Jon repeatedly rather than merely once. Lady Ogilvie remained poised on the very edge of her chair throughout this colorful narrative and, when she poured the tea, sloshed fully half a cup on the sofa table.

"And that is all," Molly finished. "Lord Reeves and I

brought Jon home, and the doctor came shortly thereafter."

"But Mr. Shelton *will* recover?" Her ladyship seemed a trifle disappointed as well. "Prior to your arrival, we had learned only that he survived the attack and was in the care of Dr. Dunn."

Molly suddenly wondererd if this was also what Lord Durham had learned, if it was Jon's survival and allegedly excellent medical care that had rendered the earl "ill." "Yes," she murmured aloud, "yes, he will be fine."

"Well." Lady Ogilvie set her cup and saucer on the sofa table. "It was very kind of you to come, Miss Shelton; very kind of you to inform me *personally* of your brother's condition. Be assured that I shan't keep you; I daresay you are quite exhausted."

Her ladyship rose, and Molly surmised that she had already ordered out her carriage. Within mere seconds of Molly's departure, Lady Ogilvie would be racing through the streets of Brighton, circulating the *true* and *complete* story of Mr. Shelton's brush with death. And Molly herself would have discovered nothing unless she spoke, spoke now, spoke this very instant. She groped about again, keenly aware that her ladyship was tapping one foot with impatience, and at last glimpsed the perfect excuse for her inquiries. Perfect, but her approach must be exceedingly subtle . . .

"I *am* exhausted," she said, essaying a tremulous sigh, "but I felt it imperative to seek your advice without delay. The fact is, Lady Ogilvie, that Jon's narrow escape served to remind me of my tenuous position in the world. If anything *were* to happen to him . . ." She allowed her voice to trail off and heaved another deep sigh. "Well, as Jon mentioned during our initial meeting, we came to England in hopes of settling my future."

"Yes, I recollect that." Her ladyship's tone unmistakably implied that this was hardly a convenient time to be discussing Miss Shelton's ultimate destiny.

"Of course my . . . my interest may be entirely misdirected," Molly said. "If Lord Durham *is* seriously ill—

and I have questioned the state of his health in the past . . ."

She stopped again, permitted her mouth to quiver a moment, bravely bit her lip. Lady Ogilvie frowned in puzzlement, and Molly feared she had been *too* subtle. She counted it wretchedly unfair that after a lifetime of humiliating blushes, she could not will her cheeks to flame at this critical juncture. But she could not, and she dropped her eyes as though in an agony of embarrassment.

"Miss Shelton!" Lady Ogilvie gasped. "I do believe you have conceived a *tendre* for James." Evidently she judged this *on-dit* nearly as magnificent as that of the robbery, for she sank back in her chair. "Do not deny it dear; your sentiments are clearly written on your face. And I am delighted to assure you that James's health is *excellent*. Indeed, I cannot but wonder why you concluded otherwise."

Molly raised her eyes, affecting great reluctance to do so. "I . . . I thought I had observed some slight difficulty in his breathing," she mumbled.

"My dear Miss Shelton." Lady Ogilvie shook her head with fond exasperation. "Has it not occurred to you that that is a splendid sign? If James reciprocates your affection, he would naturally be quite breathless whenever you're about. So, flattered as I am that you should seek my counsel, I collect you have made adequate progress without it. You need but exercise some patience, dear, and I am sure James will soon be hopelessly *bouleversé*."

Her ladyship's beam was one of finality, and Molly's mind churned. She belatedly perceived that she had painted herself into a corner: it would not do for Lady Ogilvie to suppose that Molly, too, was "hopelessly *bouleversée*." No, if her investigation proved successful, she must be in a position to entertain the viscount's courtship; she must not appear a flighty girl who tumbled in and out of love several times in the week.

"May I be frank, Lady Ogilvie?" she said.

As she had calculated, these were precisely the right

words to rekindle her ladyship's waning interest: she nodded and wriggled once more to the edge of her chair.

"I do, it is true, find Lord Durham quite . . . quite pleasant, but I should by no means term my emotion a *tendre*. Indeed, if emotion were the only factor to be considered, there are other men I might prefer." Lady Ogilvie's mouth opened, and Molly rushed on before she could ask the inevitable question. "However, emotion is *not* the only factor; as I stated earlier, I well recognize the tenuous nature of my situation. I well understand that there are many families—and quite rightly—who would not welcome a connection with a young woman of unknown parentage."

"Many such families." Lady Ogilvie sagely inclined her head. "Whether James's is numbered among them, I'm afraid I couldn't say. His only living relative is his paternal grandfather, and the man is virtually a recluse."

"His grandfather." Molly moistened her lips. "And who . . . who is he?"

"Why, the Marquis of Andover, dear; were you not aware of that? Oh, yes, the woman who weds James will be fortunate indeed. To say the truth, I attempted to encourage Ellen in that direction, but she and James have been friends from childhood, and she could not view him as a prospective husband. Which is lucky for your brother, of course."

Her ladyship beamed again, and Molly gritted her teeth.

"In any event," Lady Ogilvie went on, "James has wonderful expectations. Which is not to suggest that his *present* circumstances are in any way undesirable; I daresay his income is in excess of five thousand a year. But when Andover dies—and it can't be long; he must be close to eighty—James will be one of the wealthiest men in England."

"I see," Molly murmured. Her mouth had gone entirely dry, and she once more licked her lips. "Where does Lord Andover live?" she asked as casually as she could.

"In Hampshire, near Eastleigh. But I doubt James would take you to meet him; I do not believe they get on."

"Oh?" Molly's mind churned again. There was one further inquiry she wished to pose, and it seemed unlikely she would be granted a better opportunity. "Yes, Lord Durham once indicated that he had come into his inheritance in rather unusual circumstances."

"Unusual? Merely because his father was Andover's second son?" Molly's heart crashed into her throat. "Perhaps James meant to say that his late uncle was rather unusual."

"You . . . you knew him?" Molly said.

"Oh, yes. Durham—that Durham—was only a few years older than I, and I saw a good deal of him during the Season of my come-out. He did not strike me as unusual at the time, but shortly afterward he left Oxford and literally dropped from sight. There were all manner of rumors surrounding his disappearance, but my guess is that he had discovered himself mortally ill. At any rate, I later heard that he had died; the poor man could not have been above five-and-twenty."

"Was one of the rumors that he had married?" Molly asked.

"Probably so; there was every other conceivable *on-dit*. But I am persuaded he was not, for no one ever encountered his wife or widow either one."

She had learned all she could, Molly decided, more than she'd hoped, and she rose, prepared to take her leave. Lady Ogilvie sprang eagerly to her own feet, and Molly was reminded of her earlier surmise.

"I do most earnestly implore you not to repeat our conversation," she said. "You can well imagine my mortification if Lord Durham were to hear of my interest."

"I shan't breathe a word of it," her ladyship promised. She gave Molly a kind smile, bounded to the bell cord, tugged it, and Molly detected Higgins' footfalls on the stairs. "And pray do extend your brother my warmest regards and best wishes for a speedy recovery. Er . . .

you did say there were *four* robbers, did you not?"

Molly nodded, and even as Higgins escorted her to the
vestibule, she heard Lady Ogilvie pounding up the staircase
to the second floor. The butler assisted her into her pelisse,
bowed her out the front door, and—pretending not to
notice her ladyship's carriage drawn up outside the
house—Molly scurried into Middle Street Lane. She strode
briskly back toward Middle Street, her feet buoyant with
triumph, but by the time she reached the intersection, she
realized that her discoveries proved nothing.

No, she reflected, slowing her pace as she proceeded up
Middle Street, while she had learned a great deal about
Lord Durham's family, there was not a shred of evidence
that he and Jon were related. If they were, it seemed
most likely that Jon was the son of the earl's late uncle,
Lord Andover's elder son. In which case, it further
appeared that Jon was illegitimate after all: Lady Ogilvie
was persuaded that the young man had not married prior
to his death. But if Jon was illegitimate, the ring posed no
threat to Lord Durham; it was, at worst, proof that his
uncle had sired a child on some barque of frailty. Why,
then, had the earl been so desperate to steal it, so frantic
to dispose of the man who possessed it?

The logical answer to that, of course, was that he had
not. Molly turned into Ship Street Gardens and stopped.
It was entirely possible that the robbery had been just
that—a vicious, albeit clumsy, crime randomly perpe-
trated by unknown assailants. Then why, a voice inside
her whispered, had one of the attackers referred to
"him"? And why had they taken only the ring?

Molly gnawed her lip a moment and perceived but one
way to resolve the matter: Jon must travel to Hampshire,
introduce himself to Lord Andover, and explain the
situation to the marquis. She hurried on, eager to present
this proposal to Jon, but within the space of a few houses
she halted again. Jon might well insist that she had
allowed her imagination to run amok, berate her most
furiously for involving Lady Ogilvie, and adamantly
refuse to pursue the investigation any further. If he did

agree that her suspicions were valid, did agree to go to Hampshire, he would be unable to undertake the journey for some days. And Molly did not believe for an instant that Lady Ogilvie would keep their conversation in confidence. At the very least, she would provide her son a full report when he returned, and the viscount would relay the information to Lord Durham at the earliest opportunity. And if Molly's suspicions *were* valid, the earl would ensure that neither Jon nor she reached Hampshire alive.

So if anyone was to confront Lord Andover, it must be Molly, and she must leave today, leave at once, before Lord Durham could discover what she was at. But there was no "if" about it, she amended, drawing her cloak against a shiver: as soon as the earl learned of her inquiries, he would move to silence her. She raced to Ship Street—praying Lord Ogilvie would remain at his friend's a few hours more, praying Lady Ogilvie would not elect to join them—and ordered out the carriage.

Sometime during the night, the weather had turned foul, and when the house loomed into view, it was shrouded in mist and fog, the higher rooftops barely visible in the gloom. "Andover Castle," the innkeeper had called it, and Molly could see sufficiently to own that for all practical intent it was: a great, sprawling, asymmetrical structure with a square turret at one end, another in the center, and an enormous hexagonal tower just to the left of center. In normal circumstances, she fancied she would have been quite overwhelmed; as it was, she was so tired she could scarcely focus her eyes.

To begin with, she had had a fearful row with Mrs. Mulvaney.

"Going to London?" the housekeeper gasped. Molly had judged this the only credible explanation of her precipitate departure. "With poor Mr. Shelton on his deathbed?"

"Jon is hardly on his deathbed." Molly jerked her valise open and jammed in her nightclothes, several changes of

underwear, an extra dress. "You yourself just told me
that Dr. Dunn has pronounced him well on the way to
recovery."

"Well, it required me to tell you, didn't it?" Mrs.
Mulvaney sniffed. "You can't spare even a moment to
look in on him, can you? No, you must be gadding about
town while Mr. Shelton suffers."

In point of fact, the housekeeper had also reported that
Jon was "quite comfortable," but Molly deemed it best
not to argue. "I . . . I was busy," she said. "And as Jon is
confined to bed, it seemed a good opportunity to travel
up to London and check on the business."

"You and your business." Mrs. Mulvaney emitted
another sniff. "I hope your money will prove a comfort in
your old age, Miss Shelton."

Molly was utterly unable to fathom how her journey
might bear upon her "old age," but she elected not to
debate this either.

"At least go in and bid him good-bye," the housekeeper
said.

But that Molly had firmly determined not to do: she
didn't want to lie to Jon, and she was not at all certain she
could. "No," she said briskly, "no, I haven't the time."
Which, she reflected grimly, was all too true.

"It is fortunate *Lady Palmer* has the time to keep him
company, isn't it?" Mrs. Mulvaney snapped.

"Yes, it is." Molly slammed her case closed with
considerably more force than necessary. "Well, good-
bye, Mrs. Mulvaney. I'm not sure when I shall be back;
Tuesday, most likely."

"I frankly do not care," the housekeeper said haughtily. "I find your conduct altogether reprehensible, and
I'm sorry to own I had any part in your upbringing."

Molly cast her a warning look—one never knew who
might be on the listen at the door—but Mrs. Mulvaney
had already opened said door and was stalking out. Molly
hurried down the stairs, carrying her own valise, and
leapt into the landau.

In her eagerness to escape Brighton, Molly had given

inadequate thought to the trip as a whole, and as darkness fell, as they approached the Hampshire border, she realized she was in a bit of a hobble. If she continued to Eastleigh without stopping, it would be approximately midnight when she arrived, well after midnight by the time she inquired the location of Lord Andover's estate and proceeded to it. She doubted the marquis would appreciate being knocked up in the small hours of the morning, doubted he would be inclined to extend his hospitality to the strange young woman who had thus disturbed him. She could, of course, stop at an inn anywhere along the road, but if Lord Durham had learned of her journey and set out to overtake her, such a stop would render her an easy target. Were it not so cold (for the temperature had already begun to drop), she could proceed to Lord Andover's home and wait in the carriage till morning, but in the circumstances, that option was out of the question.

Eventually Molly decided to continue to Eastleigh and stop nearby for the night—a decision Lewis greeted with a notable lack of enthusiasm. The coachman was even less receptive when—at Eastleigh's largest, most luxurious inn—Molly was struck by a perfectly brilliant notion.

"The landlord informs me that Lord Andover's estate is some two miles behind us," she advised him. "Consequently, we shall drive a mile or two *ahead* and stay nearer to Romsey."

"Whyever should we want to do that, Miss Trevor?" he asked wearily.

In his exhaustion and impatience, he had obviously forgotten her alias, but if all went well, it would no longer signify.

"Because . . ." Molly stopped and bit her lip. She had told Lewis as little as possible about their trip, certainly hadn't told him they might be pursued, and she perceived no reason to alarm him at this juncture. "Never mind; just drive on. And," she added as he handed her back into the carriage, "we may not stop at the first inn we see. I

shall be seeking a rather . . . rather dilapidated place."
Should Lord Durham possess the wit to follow her past
Eastleigh, he would not expect to find her in a small,
crumbling roadside establishment.

Well, the inn had been small and crumbling in the
extreme, Molly reflected as the landau stopped; indeed,
she had spent much of the night in terror that the ceiling
would collapse upon her head. Not that she could have
obtained much rest in any case, for she truly believed the
mattress had been stuffed with rocks. Furthermore, her
rare moments of sleep had invariably been terminated by
a sharp pinprick beneath the bedclothes; she preferred
not to speculate as to the probable source of these inter-
ruptions.

Lewis opened the carriage door, and Molly observed
that the poor man was literally staggering; she shuddered
to contemplate the nature of *his* accommodations. He
assisted her out—though Molly would have been hard
pressed to say who was supporting whom—and she
peered fearfully at the great front door of Lord Andover's
castle. The very worst aspect of her terrible pilgrimage
was that she had yet to determine precisely how she
should approach the marquis; her fear of Lord Durham,
her wretched discomfort at the inn, and her exhaustion
during the drive back this morning had quite clouded her
mind. Whatever her words, she must introduce her
subject gradually, obliquely: if she was wrong after all,
she didn't wish to make a dreadful cake of herself.

Molly ascended the three shallow steps to the door,
rang the bell with trembling fingers, and at interminable
length, the door creaked open. The man on the opposite
side of the threshold was scarcely calculated to put her at
ease: he was nearly as large as the Prince Regent and
was glowering down at her over a veritable mountain of
chins, shirt-points, and lavishly starched neckcloth.

"Yes?" he intoned.

"I . . . I wish to see Lord Andover," Molly stammered.

"His lordship does not receive callers."

The butler (or so Molly presumed) started to close the

door, and she thrust one foot between it and the jamb, wincing a bit as her toes were pinched between them.

"Please," she begged, "please advise him I am here. It is excessively important. Indeed, I do not scruple to tell you it may be a matter of life and death." His eyes narrowed, and Molly wondered if he would be impressed by a reference to Countess Melnikoff. Probably not. *"Please,"* she repeated. "Just tell him I am here; that is all I ask. If he declines to see me, I shall go at once."

"Very well."

Molly suspected his acquiescence was primarily due to the fact that the frigid winter wind was turning his fleshy face quite scarlet. But it was hardly the time to look a gift horse in the mouth, and when he eased the door away from her foot, she bounded into the entry hall.

"Your name?" His voice was rather more frosty than the weather.

"Miss Trevor." This was the one point she had firmly decided: she could not lie to Lord Andover. "Miss Molly Trevor."

"Very well," he said again.

He strode out of the hall, and Molly noted several ominous signs: he had failed to bow, failed to take her pelisse, and he had left her most unceremoniously in the foyer. She had no intention of slinking away if the marquis initially refused to receive her, but she was too tired to consider what she would do in that event. To say the truth, she was too tired even to stand—her head was starting to swim—and she tottered toward the Egyptian sofa in the middle of the hall. She was halfway to her objective when she heard the tap of footsteps and stopped: she was far too tired to think and walk at the same time.

"Well, Miss Trevor," the butler said imperiously, reappearing in the archway, "his lordship has very kindly consented to see you . . ."

His words faded to an incomprehensible buzz as Molly obtained a clear view of the man behind him. Dear God, it was all true; every bit of it was true.

"Dear God, Lord Andover," she moaned. "I have found your grandson."

She felt herself swaying, felt her knees begin to buckle, and everything went black.

—12—

"Come now, Miss Trevor, open your eyes and have a sip. Please, Miss Trevor, a bit of brandy will do you good."

Brandy again, Molly thought groggily. And evidently Mrs. Mulvaney was so distraught as to have entirely forgotten her role: she was not to call Molly even "Miss Molly" and certainly not "Miss Trevor." But Molly fancied a bit of brandy *would* do her good, and she forced her eyes open.

She entertained a brief, wild notion that it was Jon hovering over her, Jon gazing down at her, but at length she recollected where she was and the nature of the shock that had rendered her insensible. She had been laid on the Egyptian sofa, she saw, and the man seated beside her, the man she had glimpsed in the archway, looked exactly like Jonathan Shelton. No, she amended, Lord Andover looked as Jon *would* if he survived to his lordship's advanced age: a few pale red strands threaded his thick white hair, and his eyes had faded to light blue-gray. But the sharp bones, the hollow cheeks, the longish nose were precisely the same, and Molly further realized why Lord Durham had always seemed so tantalizingly familiar. The earl had his grandfather's face, Jon's face, and Molly had been deceived by his coloring, had not looked sufficiently beyond his dark hair and eyes. She marveled a moment that no one had noted the remarkable resemblance between Jon and the marquis, then remembered Lady Ogilvie's reference to Lord Andover's reclusive habits.

"Splendid; you are not going to die on me after all." His lordship flashed a smile—it was Jon's easy smile—tugged Molly upright, and extended a glass. "Here now, drink this down, and then we shall have some tea."

Lord Andover's brandy was, if possible, slightly stronger than that in Ship Street, and when Molly had drained the glass, she feared she might well succumb to the fit of coughing that ensued. Eventually, however, she regained her breath, and the marquis rose and pulled her to her feet beside him. He was exactly Jon's height, she observed, not in the least bent by his years, and she gazed apologetically up at him.

"I am sorry to have caused you such trouble," she said. "But if I may impose a trifle more, my coachman—"

"Your man is warm and comfortable in the kitchen," his lordship interposed. "I propose that we ourselves repair to the drawing room; with any luck, Tanner will shortly bring our tea."

Molly nodded, and Lord Andover escorted her through the archway, across the small hall on the other side, and into the saloon. It was an enormous six-sided room, clearly situated at the base of the main tower, but Molly had scarcely begun to register the brilliantly painted ceiling, the glittering crystal chandeliers, the view of the manor park beyond the windows, when Tanner bustled in with a great silver tea tray. Molly thought the butler's expression rather guilty, as though he judged himself partially responsible for her swoon, and as soon as he had deposited the tray on a Pembroke table, he bowed and slunk away. The marquis seated Molly in one of the chairs beside the table, occupying the second himself, and poured two cups of tea.

"Sugar? Lemon? Milk?" he asked.

Even his voice was like Jon's, and in the flickering light of the candles above him, Molly could see a sprinkling of red-gold freckles across his cheeks and nose.

"M-milk," she stammered.

He inclined his head, added a portion of milk to one cup, set cup and saucer in front of her. He was an exceedingly calm man, she reflected, prodigious patient: he permitted her several swallows of the hot, strong tea before he leaned back in his chair and laced his long fingers over his ribs.

"Trevor," he mused. "I am familiar with but one family of that name. Are you Sir Ambrose's daughter? Major Trevor's daughter? The Reverend Mr. Trevor's daughter?"

"They are my uncles," Molly replied. "I am Stephen Trevor's daughter."

"Ah, the moneylender." His tone was unmistakably grim. "Then I daresay I can interpret your peculiar remark. I fancy you intended to say that you had found a way to collect James's debt. I must own myself somewhat surprised that he cannot live on his income; I should estimate it at nearly six thousand a year. Surprised but not astonished: James was ever a spendthrift. Did he fall victim to women or to gaming? Never mind; that is not your concern, is it, Miss Trevor? You're no doubt aware that you've no legal means of coercing me to meet my grandson's obligations, but I am compelled to grant you considerable credit for your perseverance. Advise me what James owes you, and I shall write a check at once."

"You have quite misconstrued the purpose of my call, Lord Andover," Molly said. "It has nothing to do with Lord Durham."

"Then I fear you've put yourself to a great deal of effort for naught," the marquis said, not unkindly. "I have no other grandson, Miss Trevor."

Molly hesitated. The words she had blurted out before her faint had altogether obviated an oblique approach; at this juncture, she could only attempt to be gentle. "Are you absolutely certain of that?" she said. "Is it not possible, remotely possible, that your elder son sired a child prior to his death?" She paused again. "I recognize that my inquiry is a delicate one: as your son was unwed, the child would naturally be illegitimate—"

"Unwed?" Lord Andover had paled; like Jon's, his freckles seemed very pronounced. "But John was not unwed, Miss Trevor; he married some four years before he died."

"Good God!" This exclamation was hardly subtle either, and Molly struggled to contain her burgeoning excitement. "I collect you did not approve the marriage," she said as levelly as she could.

"Approve?" he echoed bitterly. "No, I *dis*approved most violently. The young woman styled herself an actress, from which circumstance you must not infer that she graced the stages of Covent Garden or Drury Lane. No, she performed in traveling troupes and in bawdy entertainments conducted at country taverns . . ."

"She spoke extremely well . . . but she had nothing to say." Jon's words rang in Molly's ears, drowning Lord Andover's continuing discourse. His mother had spoken well because she had been trained to do so; however limited her talents, she had been an actress . . .

" . . . a beautiful girl," the marquis was saying, "or so I am given to understand. In any event, John was utterly besotted with her, and when it became clear he couldn't be talked round, I recommended he make her his mistress. Provide her a comfortable household with all the accouterments. But John was a . . . a romantic, and he insisted on wedding her."

"Leaving Oxford to do so," Molly suggested.

"You're excessively well-informed, Miss Trevor." His lordship gave her a wry nod of approval. "Yes, John abandoned his education, married his actress, and I—as any proper father would—disowned him." A sardonic smile. "I could not dis*inherit* him, of course—the Durham earldom and much of my own estate is entailed —but I refused to see him again or to receive his wife. And John, romantic that he was, disowned me in turn, me and all his background. He declined to occupy any of his estates, declined to spend a farthing of his income. He and his wife settled in London, and I can only suppose they lived off the fruits of her labor and whatever funds John was able to earn."

"And then he . . . he died," Molly said.

"He was killed," Lord Andover corrected. "Killed in a brawl of some sort; I never learned the details. Can you imagine my feelings, Miss Trevor? Had I accepted her, accepted his wife, they would surely have resided at Durham Wood, not five miles along the road." He vaguely tossed his head. "Resided safely in the country, surrounded by neighbors John had known all his life. With my example, the neighbors might eventually have accepted her as well. As it was, John and his wife were thrown among the demimonde—I use the term in its broadest sense—and I daresay the result was inevitable." He stopped, and his pale eyes grew distant. "John was killed nearly thirty years since, and I have scarcely left this house from that day to this."

"I . . . I am sorry," Molly murmured.

"Yes, I was sorry too." The marquis dragged his eyes back to her. "I dispatched Henry, my second son, to London to see John's widow and provide for her financial needs. Though I must confess that even in my grief, I keenly wished to forestall any scandal. When Henry returned, he reported complete success: he had paid the girl a handsome settlement and persuaded her to change her name and emigrate . . ."

Which explained why Lord Durham had been so interested in the appearance of Jon's mother, Molly thought. He had noted the striking resemblance between Jon and Lord Andover, had realized at once that they were somehow related. But only the earl's legitimate cousin posed a danger—the son of the woman his father had met and described. It was additionally clear why Lord Durham had never inquired their mother's name— a signal omission Molly had failed to remark.

". . . but," Lord Andover concluded, "Henry made no mention of a child."

It was her chance—perhaps her last and only chance— to be subtle after all. "Maybe she was . . . was in a delicate condition and didn't know it," she said.

"Well, we can readily settle that point. How old is the person you fancy to be my grandson?"

"Eight . . ." But she could not lie on this head either. "Thirty," she replied. "I do not know his birthday, when he will be thirty-one—"

"It doesn't signify," his lordship interjected. "John was killed in October of 1787. Your pretender would have been"—he stopped, frowned, moved his fingers in calculation—"twenty months of age at the least."

But Lord Durham's father had not ascertained that, Molly reflected. He had been so horrified by the news of a male heir that he had neglected to ask the boy's age; the earl merely knew that his cousin was between eight-and-twenty and thirty-two. Since his father had not mentioned a second child, a daughter, Lord Durham could only assume that Molly had been born posthumously. Born no later than the summer of 1788, which was why he had further assumed her to be lying about her age.

"It is scarcely surprising that your second son failed to advise you of the child's existence," she said. "The boy would have been Earl of Durham in Henry's stead, would he not?" She frowned a moment as well. "I do wonder, though, why the widow agreed so meekly to surrender her son's inheritance."

"I can but speculate," the marquis said. "She was an ignorant young woman, and Henry may well have convinced her there *was* no inheritance, that I could legally deny the boy his estate and title. Or he might have taken precisely the opposite tack, threatened to remove the child from her care and bring him up as befit a young peer." He stopped, his pale eyes narrowing. "All of which presumes that you have, in fact, found my grandson, Miss Trevor. It occurs to me that I have not inquired your interest in the situation."

"Jon had puzzled out that my father was dead," she began. She was not bound to volunteer the *whole* truth, she decided, and she related a considerably abbreviated version of her and Jon's first meeting, describing only the theft and the note that had prompted him to initiate a search for his father. "And I consented to assist him," she finished.

"For a price, of course," his lordship said dryly. "I cannot suppose that Trevor and Company has taken to dispensing charity."

"No, we have not," Molly concurred. "I am a woman of business, Lord Andover." It felt good, felt wonderfully good, to be herself again. "At the least, Jon was to repay my investment. If he discovered himself the heir to an estate, I was to receive a percentage of its value."

"I see." The marquis nodded. "Then I fancy you have come to collect your share of the Durham earldom." Molly opened her mouth to protest, but he flew on. "And while I am, again, compelled to grant you credit for your ingenuity, you must understand that any payment is quite out of the question. To begin with, I could not spend a groat from the estate even did I desire to do so; it is not mine to spend. In the second place, I cannot entirely dismiss the possibility of fraud. Your father was reputed to be a thoroughly honest man, and though I've no reason to believe you otherwise, I cannot dismiss the possibility. I suspect you maintain careful records of the nation's leading families; you could have learned of John's unfortunate marriage and manufactured a long-lost son."

"I could have, but—"

"Third," he continued relentlessly, "you yourself may have been deceived, taken in by a Canadian adventurer. And finally, if you have said the truth, if *he* has said the truth, there is still no proof of his identity. I shall own that your pretender *could* be my grandson, but without proof . . ." He stopped once more and spread his hands.

"No, there is no proof," Molly acknowledged. "I believe the ring might have proved Jon's parentage, but as it is gone—"

"Ring!" Lord Andover bolted up in his chair, the blood draining from his face. "What ring!"

Molly could hardly conceive that she had forgotten to mention it, and she now described it as best she could, omitting the small detail that she had located it while covertly searching Jon's bedchamber.

"The frog," his lordship said softly. "A family legend

surrounds that humble emblem, Miss Trevor; whether it is true or not, I cannot say. The story is that when Charles II made the first William Wentworth a marquis, he—William, that is—set about designing a suitable coat of arms. And as he debated among dragons and lions and similarly magnificent creatures, his young son bore a frog in from the garden and proposed *that* as a symbol. It wouldn't do, of course—a frog was far too undignified for William's purpose—but to appease the boy, he declared the frog the official emblem of the Andover heir and commissioned a ring with that device. Later, or so the tale has it, the ring was enlarged and customarily presented to the heir on his twenty-first birthday. It was strictly a family tradition, unknown to those outside . . . Dear God, Miss Trevor, you *have* found my grandson."

The marquis' mouth began to tremble, and Molly detected a sparkle of moisture in his pale eyes and looked hastily downward. She wondered if she should leave the room, leave him alone with his emotions, but he soon cleared his throat.

"But the ring is gone, you say?"

His voice remained a trifle unsteady, but he seemed to have regained his composure, and Molly raised her own eyes.

"Yes, it was stolen." She told him of the "robbery," of the attack on Jon, and his mouth hardened as she spoke.

"James's doing, I fancy," he said grimly when she had finished.

"He . . . he had observed the ring just before the incident occurred . . ." She stopped and bit her lip; he was sufficiently clever to deduce the obvious without a lengthy explanation to augment his distress.

"You have found my grandson," Lord Andover repeated, his voice now tinged with awe. "And you must tell me everything about him, Miss Trevor, everything you know."

"Everything?" Molly wriggled to the edge of her chair and placed her elbows on the table. "I have already relayed what *he* told *me*: that he was given his stepfather's name and raised in Canada, where he was in the fur trade." She elected not to add that he had once been quite friendly with a woman named "Kitty." "From my own knowledge, I can say that he's prodigious handsome. Very tall and very lean, and he has auburn hair just touched with gold and excessively light blue eyes. In short, he looks exactly like you."

His lordship's lips quivered a bit, and Molly realized that her latter remark sounded like the most shameless flattery.

"Well, he *is* prodigious handsome," she said defensively, her cheeks growing warm. "And terribly clever and extremely amusing, and he *can* be very kind. Though he is inclined to mock me from time to time, and I must admit we've had the occasional quarrel. But he keeps his room exceedingly neat." She didn't wish to exclude a single one of Jon's superior qualities.

"I collect you're quite fond of my grandson," the marquis said.

"I am . . . am monstrous fond of him," Molly conceded, "as you will be when you meet him. He cannot yet travel, Lord Andover, so I implore you to return with me to Brighton. If you do not, you cannot make his acquaintance for some days—"

"You need scarcely implore me, Miss Trevor," his lordship interposed. "To the contrary, I shall insist on accompanying you back."

"Excellent!" Molly leapt to her feet. "If we leave within the hour, we can be there shortly after dark."

The marquis shook his head, his mouth twitching again. "No, Miss Trevor, you are in no condition to undertake the journey yet today. You must rest here through the night, and we shall depart at dawn tomorrow."

Molly started to object, but, to say the truth, she had discovered her knees alarmingly weak, and she sank back in her chair. As she did so, she remembered the excessively grave complication she had thus far neglected to bring to his lordship's attention.

"There . . . there is one other matter, Lord Andover,"

she said. "Since our arrival in Brighton, I have been posing as Jon's sister, calling myself Miss Shelton."

"Whyever should you want to do that?" He knit his brows, and Molly observed that they were still quite auburn, nearly as dark as Jon's.

"I . . . I . . ." But there was no escape; she must reveal the truth in this regard as well. She confessed her *tendre* for Lord Ogilvie, pointing out to the marquis that any connection between the very respectable Eltings and the highly *un*respectable Miss Trevor was altogether unthinkable.

"How peculiar." He once more wrinkled his forehead. "I had fancied . . ." His voice trailed off.

"Fancied what?" Molly pressed.

"Never mind. I shall not expose you, Miss Trevor. Though I daresay, if you are to be my granddaughter, I should call you Molly, eh?" He flashed a grin, Jon's engaging grin, then sobered. "You and my grandson must settle his debt between you. For my part, I owe you far more than money; permitting your imposture to continue is small recompense indeed for the joy you've given me. And perhaps—if you can understand this—I perceive you as a way to satisfy my obligation to John and his wife. Perhaps they taught me that in the end *respectability* signifies nothing."

He lapsed into silence, and Molly cast about for a response, but, upon reflection, she did not believe he expected one.

"So I shall not expose you," he reiterated. "Quite the reverse, in fact: I shall *abet* your . . . ah . . . enterprise insofar as I can. For the present, however, you must rest, and I calculate you've just enough strength to manage the stairs."

Not quite enough, as it happened. She was compelled to lean on him more and more as they ascended the staircase towering up from the center hall, traversed the endless corridor on the first floor; and Molly thought he virtually carried her from the bedchamber door to the great curtained bed. But at last her head met the pillow,

and Lord Andover gently tucked the bedclothes round
her neck.

"Sleep well, Molly," he whispered.

"Thank you, L . . . Thank you, Grandpapa."

She closed her eyes and did not even hear the click of
the door.

The door creaked open, and Molly sprang out of the
Adam chair, ramming her heel most painfully into one of
the lion-claw feet.

"What are they at now?" she hissed.

"The same thing they were at when you last inquired
fifteen minutes since," Mrs. Mulvaney whispered dryly
back. "The same thing they have been at these past three
hours: they are conversing in Mr. Shelton's bedchamber.
No, I beg your pardon, they recently finished their
dinner and rang for brandy, which I have just
delivered." She glanced at the dressing table, where
Molly's own dinner tray sat untouched. "You have not
eaten a bite, Miss Shelton," she said reprovingly. "With
all your traveling about, you will grow quite ill without
proper nourishment."

"I am too nervous to eat," Molly snapped.

This was entirely true—indeed, the very sight of food
rendered her faintly nauseous—and as she sank back into
the chair, she shoved the tray well to one side. She and
Lord Andover had departed, as scheduled, shortly after
dawn that morning, and during the first hours of their
journey, he had put her at ease—chatting of his life and
hers and Jon's and the state of the world in general. As
Molly related her and Jon's experiences in Brighton, the
marquis managed to elicit a complete accounting of Lord
Durham's intervention in their affairs, at the end of
which he declared there was no doubt whatever that
James had commissioned the attack on his cousin.

"What . . . what will you do to him?" Molly asked.

"I shouldn't suppose I shall have an opportunity to do
anything," his lordship replied. "Whatever his defi-
ciences, James is far from stupid, and I am confident he

has puzzled out the situation by now. Puzzled it out and fled abroad unless I badly miss my guess. In anticipation of that eventuality, I visited my solicitor yesterday afternoon and placed a hold on James's accounts. Except for the cash in his possession and those items he can readily sell, he will be unable to divest the estate of any assets."

Molly was inclined to agree that Lord Durham would trouble them no further, but her relief was short-lived. She had assumed that Jon would be as thrilled as she, as thrilled as Lord Andover, by the discovery of his parentage, but as they crossed the border of East Sussex, she was compelled to own she might be wrong. However fortunate the outcome of her endeavor, she had pursued it behind Jon's back, and she shuddered to contemplate the magnitude of his possible displeasure. By the time the landau clattered to a stop in Ship Street, her hands were visibly trembling with fright, and she looked desperately at the marquis.

"I daresay it would be best if I were to see him alone. When I have explained how very well you represented his interests, he cannot conceivably be angry."

As was often the case with his grandson, Lord Andover appeared to have read her mind, and Molly gave him a grateful nod.

And that, as Mrs. Mulvaney had stated, had been three hours ago, though it seemed to Molly that she had been skulking in her bedchamber for a period of years. The first hour had been relatively bearable, for the housekeeper had demanded a complete recounting of Molly's search for Jon's father—the *whole* story, starting from the moment she had found the mysterious ring.

"You were excessively brave, Miss Shelton," she said when Molly had finished. "To go to Lady Ogilvie, I mean, and then to Hampshire, not knowing what Lord Durham might do. I . . . I am monstrous sorry I accused you of neglecting Mr. Shelton."

"That is all right," Molly murmured.

She could only hope Jon would view her activities in an equally favorable light—a hope she attempted to sustain

as the next two hours dragged interminably by. She stole
a glance at the mantel clock, wondering if it had stopped.
But it was ticking merrily, maddeningly away, so
perhaps only the *hands* had ceased to function—

"Miss Shelton?"

Molly leapt to her feet again, this time smashing her
ankle into one of the chair's cabriole legs. Mrs. Mulvaney
had left the door ajar, and Woodson was peering across
the threshold.

"Their lordships want to see you now."

Their lordships, Molly marveled. She still had not
registered the fact that Jonathan Shelton—the ragged fur
trader who had burst into her life under a month since—
was actually Jonathan Wentworth, Earl of Durham. She
tottered along the corridor in Woodson's wake and, when
he opened the door, stepped cautiously into the master
bedchamber.

They did not see her for a moment, and Molly used the
moment to study them, astonished anew at their
remarkable resemblance. They were seated side by side
on the edge of Jon's bed, and they might truly have been
one man—a man painted in his prime and again in his
old age. In the intervening years, the auburn hair had
gone mostly white, the eyes had faded, the facial bones
had grown a trifle sharper, but it was the same man.
They chanced to raise their brandy glasses simultaneously, and Molly observed that even their hands, even
their gestures, were alike.

"Molly!"

Jon crashed his glass on the bedside cabinet, jumped
up, strode toward her, and, before she could surmise his
intention, pulled her into his arms.

"Molly," he whispered against her hair. "It was an
idiotish thing you did; I should never have permitted it
had you asked. And I should never have forgiven myself
if you'd come to harm. As it is, I shall be forever in your
debt . . ."

He stopped, drew a bit away, gazed down at her, and
she experienced that strange, wonderful, terrible
sensation that she had turned to water. He still bore the

marks of the attack, she noted distantly—though the cut
on his face had scabbed over and the bruises had started
to fade—but he had regained his color. And, as she had
told Lord Andover, he was prodigious handsome, which
must explain the weakness in her knees, the pounding of
her heart.

"You . . . you aren't angry then?" she stammered.

"Angry? How could I be angry?"

He released her, walked to the dressing table, plucked
up the chair, and carried it toward the bed, beckoning
her to follow. He set the chair beside the bed, seated her,
resumed his own place; and he and the marquis regarded
her in silence for a time. Molly could not but recollect
several unhappy incidents in her childhood: whenever
her conduct had been particularly reprehensible, Papa
and Mrs. Mulvaney had sat her down just so . . .

"I do not wish to imply that I shall remain *financially*
in your debt," Jon said at last. "I sought Grandpapa's
counsel on that head, and we have, we believe, devised
an appropriate solution. Subject to your approval, of
course."

"I am not concerned about the money—"

"No, we quite *insist* on payment," Lord Andover interposed. "However, as I am sure you realize—being a
woman of business—these are not the best of times, and it
would be unwise to sell any of Jon's principal in the
present environment. We consequently propose to pay
you ten percent . . . Was that not the figure, Jon?"

"Yes, ten percent." Jon nodded.

"To pay you ten percent of the *income* in perpetuity,"
the marquis went on. "Naturally Ogilvie will assume it
the income of your dowry; he need never know your
background."

"That . . . that is exceedingly generous," Molly
muttered. "But there is really no need—"

"No," Jon said firmly, "a bargain is a bargain. And as
Grandpapa pointed out, the prospect of a handsome
settlement is sure to kindle Ogilvie's interest."

"I also pointed out that his interest is sure to be stirred

by your beauty and charm," the marquis said gallantly. "To say nothing of your presumed connection with me. Yes, if I may be immodest, Molly, I am not an unimportant figure, and if I remember Grace Elting aright, she will be fairly *wild* to promote your marriage to her son."

"But . . . but . . ."

Molly's voice trailed off. Lord Andover was beaming, Jon was beaming, and she wondered why she felt so . . . so *empty*. Her dream was nearly within her grasp; why should she entertain an absurd notion that she was being nudged along against her will?

"But we must not think of Lord Ogilvie till Jon is fully recovered," she said. "In a week or two, a month perhaps—"

"But I shall be recovered by Thursday!" Jon interjected brightly. "Amidst all the excitement, I failed to advise you of Dr. Dunn's morning visit. He assures me I shall be quite myself again by Thursday."

"Thursday," Molly echoed dully. Thursday was but two days hence. "Very well; we shall consider Lord Ogilvie then. We shall require some time to plan a proper entertainment—"

"I fear that is out of the question." The marquis regretfully shook his head. "I should like to return to Hampshire on Friday. As you are aware, I departed in a considerable rush, with insufficient attention to my affairs. No, I must go Friday, and we needn't plan a *grand* entertainment in any case. With your permission, Molly, I shall host a small dinner party here Thursday evening—you and Jon, the Ogilvies, of course, and . . . Who is your friend, Jon? Ah, yes, Lady Ellen Palmer."

"But . . . but—"

"No, I insist on this as well," Lord Andover interrupted kindly. "It is the very *least* I can do. Though I must prevail on you to write the invitations, Molly; I'm afraid my script isn't all it was. So if you will procure the cards, I shall dictate the message, and we shall dispatch the invitations at once, eh?"

"But . . ."

But further argument was clearly useless, and Molly nodded and rose and trudged across the hall to her bedchamber. Wondering, again, why she should want to argue, why her feet had turned to lead, why her heart was a great stony lump in her chest.

—13—

"That is the most astonishing story I have ever heard!"
Lady Ogilvie declared.

She beamed at Lord Andover, who was seated at the
head of the table, at Jon on his right, at Molly on his left,
and—for good measure—at Lady Palmer, Viscount
Ogilvie, and Mrs. Mulvaney. The inclusion of the latter
in their gathering had been a subject of considerable
controversy, sparked when Molly gently informed the
housekeeper that her presence at table simply wouldn't
do. Mrs. Mulvaney greeted this pronouncement with a
four-and-twenty-hour sulk, followed by a day of fitful
sobbing, at which juncture Jon entered the fray. It was
altogether possible, he said, that Canadian custom *did*
permit the head of staff to sit at table, and if it did not,
Lady Ogilvie would never know the difference. Molly
now suspected that the contretemps had been for naught,
suspected her ladyship would have welcomed Lord
Andover's hunting dogs at table had the marquis wished
to seat them.

"Though I am not *personally* astonished in the least,"
Lady Ogilvie amended. "From the instant I met your
grandchildren, Lord Andover, I was quite persuaded of
their excellent breeding." They might have been two
horses she had spied at Tattersall's. "Did I not say as
much, Andrew? Did I not say there was no doubt whatever that the Sheltons came from a splendid family?"

"Yes, Mama."

The viscount nodded, consumed the final bite of his mincemeat pie, and pushed his dessert plate aside. The recounting of Jon and Lord Andover's tale had required the entire meal, and Molly had been nearly as fascinated as their guests, for the facts had perforce been substantially embroidered. "Perforce" arising from the circumstance that Jon and the marquis had agreed not to divulge Lord Durham's role or that of his father. Consequently, in their telling, Jon's mother had elected for unknown reasons not to reveal the existence of her son, and Jon had been attacked by a band of anonymous robbers. By a great stroke of fortune, one of the Regent's servants had been previously employed at Andover Castle, had recognized Jon's ring, and had come to Ship Street the afternoon following the robbery to advise Jon of its significance. As Jon himself was unable to travel, he had promptly dispatched Molly to Hampshire to visit Lord Andover. Apart from these modifications, the rest of their narrative had been true, though Molly was somewhat pressed to identify what "rest" remained.

"A *splendid* family," Lady Ogilvie repeated. "How sad it is that James could not be here to share in the joy of your reunion. However, he departed very suddenly on Monday morning. He and Andrew were chatting of one thing and another, and James abruptly decided to go abroad. Did he not, Andrew?"

Chatting of her call on Lady Ogilvie, Molly thought, as the viscount once more inclined his head.

"Though James's joy would be tempered a bit, wouldn't it?" her ladyship said. "Since he is no longer Earl of Durham, I mean. Well, I am sure you will ease his disappointment, Lord Andover. I am sure that when James returns, you will provide appropriate compensation."

"If James returns, I shall ensure he receives all he deserves," the marquis said grimly.

"How very generous." Lady Ogilvie beamed about the table again. "For the present, I trust you share my own joy on another head, Lord Andover. I hope you are as delighted as I by the prospect of a connection between our families."

Molly's mouth dropped open; she could scarcely credit even Lady Ogilvie with such utter lack of subtlety. But as her cheeks warmed with mortification, she perceived that her ladyship was smiling fondly at Jon and Lady Palmer.

"Which is not to suggest that I have been empowered to make an *announcement*," she said coyly, transferring her eyes back to the marquis. "However, I daresay Mr. Shelton has mentioned . . . But what am I saying? Mr. Shelton indeed! I daresay *Lord Durham* has mentioned his . . . his friendship with my dear niece Ellen."

"So he has," Lord Andover concurred.

He and Jon exchanged a long, unreadable look, and Molly clenched her hands in her lap.

"Then we need only see to *Miss* Shelton's future, need we not?" her ladyship said brightly. "Miss Shelton; I am at it again." She emitted an apologetic little laugh and gazed across the table at Molly. "I should suppose, dear, that you'd prefer to be called Lady Mary; it is somewhat more dignified than—"

"No!" Molly interposed sharply.

Though she could not have explained precisely why, Jon's discovery of his identity had rendered the loss of hers infinitely more distressing. She had surrendered her surname, surrendered her profession; she would not let them have the last shred of herself.

"No," she muttered, "Lady Molly will do very well."

"As you wish, dear," Lady Ogilvie said kindly. "In any event, I am well aware of Lady Molly's concern for her future because she recently paid me the *great* compliment of soliciting my counsel. However, I fancy she will agree that her circumstances have since altered most dramatically."

She had played her part to perfection, Molly reflected. She had represented herself as an ambitious young woman seeking to wed as well as she could, and Lady Ogilvie quite expected her to lose interest in the now penniless Mr. James Wentworth. She waited for a rush of relief, a surge of triumph, but nothing came.

"We can therefore set about launching Lady Molly *properly* into society," her ladyship continued. "With your permission, Lord Andover, Lord Durham, I shall conduct her come-out ball during the forthcoming London Season. Of course"—she essayed a frown—"the Season is some months away yet. In the interim . . ." She affected great deliberation, the dawning of a brilliant notion. "In the interim, and again with your approval, I shall appoint Andrew to take Lady Molly under his wing. He will be eager to do so, I assure you; he was remarking only this morning that he keenly desired to further their acquaintance. Were you not, Andrew?"

"Yes, Mama."

How very remarkable, Molly marveled: within the space of a few minutes, Miss Baird had been summarily dismissed and Lady Molly thrust in her place. She stole a peep at Lady Palmer, wondering her reaction to her stepdaughter's sad and sudden fate, but her ladyship's face was altogether blank.

"I approve your proposal most enthusiastically indeed, Lady Ogilvie," Jon said heartily. "And who knows what might happen between now and the beginning of the Season? It occurs to me that a come-out might prove unnecessary after all. Yes, Molly might well meet a suitable young man right here in Brighton."

"Why, so she might!" Lady Ogilvie clapped her hands, as if overwhelmed by Lord Durham's clever, novel observation. "It is settled then, and there is no time to waste. I daresay Lady Molly would enjoy a small tour of the town to start, Andrew." Evidently she had elected to overlook the circumstance that Lady Molly had resided in Brighton above two weeks. "Perhaps you could drive her round a bit tomorrow?"

"I should be delighted." The viscount smiled, displaying his excellent teeth. "Would ten o'clock be satisfactory to you, Lady Molly?"

"Yes," Molly mumbled. "Yes, ten would be fine."

Lord Ogilvie smiled again—indeed, all of them were

smiling—and Molly managed a weak grin of her own. But the emptiness, that gnawing emptiness, remained, and she could not quell an awful fear that it might never go away.

But go away it did, or at least she so persuaded herself when she woke the following morning. She was not exactly giddy with excitement, she conceded, padding to the window to check the weather, but she was now sufficiently rested from her journey to define her feelings and judge them entirely natural. Yes, she assured herself as she hurried to the wardrobe, it was altogether natural that she should experience a sense of anticlimax: after all the weeks of dreaming and scheming, her endeavor was at last nearing fruition. Furthermore—she tugged out the black bombazine carriage dress she had never worn—it was inevitable that the viscount's imminent courtship should precipitate a prodigious attack of nerves. Once the initial awkwardness had subsided, her *tendre* would blossom anew, and she would be even happier than she had imagined.

In this optimistic frame of mind, Molly dressed with excessive care, and it was half-past nine before she descended to the breakfast parlor. To her great, though inexplicable relief, it was deserted, and she choked down a piece of toast and two rashers of bacon and fled up the stairs again before anyone could join her. She found her bedchamber door ajar, and as she slipped inside, she literally collided with Mrs. Mulvaney.

"Ah, Miss . . . Lady Molly," the housekeeper said. "I was just searching for you. Lord Andover is ready to depart, and he wished to bid you good-bye."

Molly had forgotten that the marquis planned to return to Hampshire today, and when she glanced at the mantel clock, she discovered it lacked but ten minutes to ten. She dashed back to the wardrobe, snatched out her black French bonnet, and tied the ribbons with trembling fingers. When she turned away from the glass, she met Mrs. Mulvaney's keen dark eyes, and at length the housekeeper nodded.

"You look very taking," she declared, "and I've no

doubt Lord Ogilvie will be completely *bouleversé.*"

She had uttered these words on so many occasions in the past that, in other circumstances, Molly might have laughed. As it was, she entertained the odd but familiar notion that she was somehow being prodded along against her will.

"Very taking," the housekeeper repeated. "However . . ." She stopped and bit her lip.

"However, what?" Molly demanded.

"Are you absolutely certain you are doing the right thing?" Mrs. Mulvaney blurted out. "I mean no slight to Lord Ogilvie: he's handsome enough, and he seems a . . . a sweet person. But—"

"Absolutely certain," Molly interposed firmly. Her optimism was too new, too untested to withstand the housekeeper's criticism, whatever it might be. "So if you will please excuse me, I shall bid L . . . I shall bid Grandpapa farewell."

The marquis was waiting in the vestibule, and he greeted her with a warm smile, clasping her hands in his.

"Mrs. Mulvaney located you, I collect," he said. "Pray forgive me if I interrupted your toilette, but I could not leave without seeing you."

"You . . . you interrupted nothing," Molly lied. Despite the brevity of their acquaintance, she had grown monstrous fond of him as well, and she blinked back a threat of tears.

"Come now, Molly." He released her hands and brushed her eyes with one gloved fingertip. "I forbid you to cry, for I'm confident we'll meet again in the very near future. Indeed, as my dutiful granddaughter, how could you avoid me? If nothing else, you will surely be compelled to invite me to your wedding."

Her wedding; there it was again. They were rushing her, propelling her dizzyingly ahead . . .

"Which is not to suggest you must delay your return to Andover Castle till then." His lordship's smile briefly widened; then he sobered. "I can never repay my debt to you, Molly." His voice was so low she could scarcely hear him. "I could give you *all* my riches now, this instant, and my debt would remain unpaid. You must consequently remember that if you should ever need me—at any time and for any reason—you are to come to me at once. Do you promise you will do so?"

"Yes, Lord Andover." She emitted a great, indelicate sniffle.

"Grandpapa," he hissed.

The doorbell pealed, and he patted her shoulder, and Molly hastily dabbed at her own eyes. She assumed it was the marquis' coachman who rang—he had followed them from Hampshire in one of his lordship's carriages—but when Lord Andover opened the door, Lord Ogilvie stepped into the entry hall.

"Good morning, Lord Andover." The viscount's tone was exceedingly polite, but he regarded Grandpapa's cloak, his beaver hat, with unmistakable dismay. "Did you intend to accompany us on our excursion? If so, I regret to report that I drove my curricle—"

"No, I am at the point of traveling back to Hampshire," the marquis interjected. "However," he added sternly, "you must not suppose that my physical absence in any way implies an absence of *concern* for my dear granddaughter." He sounded astonishingly like Jon, Molly thought as he patted her shoulder again. "No, I caution you to treat Molly with the utmost consideration, Ogilvie; if you do not, you will answer to me."

"Oh, I shall, sir," the viscount gulped.

Grandpapa gave him a regal nod, and one of the footmen materialized with Molly's black velvet pelisse; even the servants seemed to be urging her inexorably along. The three of them trooped outside and separated at the street, the marquis proceeding to his berlin, Lord Ogilvie assisting Molly into the passenger seat of his curricle. At least, Molly reflected—as the viscount took the driver's place and clucked his team to a start—at least Grandpapa's presence had eased the first uncomfortable moments of her and Lord Ogilvie's official courtship.

"Well, I observe that you are very punctual," his lordship remarked, whipping the horses to a trot. "I much admire that in a woman, Lady Molly."

It seemed a rather backward compliment, but Molly forced a smile. "Thank you," she murmured.

Silence; they clattered toward North Street in silence. Molly waited for him to point out the sights of Brighton as they passed them—though she had seen them all long since, of course—but he said nothing. She groped for some topic of conversation, and it occurred to her that she could have conjured up a hundred things to say to Jon. But most of those would have led to an argument, she reminded herself, and, at any rate, Jon was her *brother.* She recollected their "lesson," recollected that the viscount had evinced no interest whatever in frozen meat, and cleared her throat.

"I was delighted to have this opportunity to converse with you, Lord Ogilvie," she said. She immodestly congratulated herself for her well-chosen, well-spoken words. "I have long wished to inquire your opinion of the Corn Laws."

"The Corn Laws?" he echoed quizzically.

"Not the *laws* so much as their *effect,*" she amended. "I am extremely alarmed by the prospect of further rioting. What is your view?"

"I'm afraid I have none." He turned the carriage east on North Street. "I sit in the House as seldom as possible, for I find the proceedings excruciatingly dull. No, I have much more important matters to occupy my time."

"Well, you would, of course," Molly agreed eagerly. "I am given to understand that you have a house in town and an estate in Warwickshire, to say nothing of your home here." She vaguely tossed her head, but unfortunately they had just reached the intersection of Bond Street, the very spot where Jon had been attacked, and she rushed on. "I daresay the management of your property does quite occupy your time."

"Happily, it does not." The viscount's smile was, indeed, a happy one. "Happily, I have an excellent man of business. He is Ellen's man of business as well; I fancy your brother has mentioned him. His name is Scruggs."

"No, Jon has not mentioned him," Molly muttered.

"No? Then I must own myself surprised: Ellen is

inclined to rave of his talents. Scruggs is an orphan, or so he claims—self-raised in the streets of London, self-educated . . . But that is neither here nor there, is it? Whatever his background, Scruggs is a splendid man of business, and *he* manages my property."

"Then what . . . what do *you* do?" Molly asked.

"Do?" He sounded rather more puzzled than he had when she'd mentioned the Corn Laws. "I spend the winter in Brighton and the Season in London, go to Warwick for the summer and fall, return to town for the Little Season, and come back to Brighton. It's a hectic schedule but one I thoroughly enjoy."

"Enjoy what?" Molly snapped. She belatedly regretted her sharpness, but he did seem a trifle obtuse. "That was my question, Lord Ogilvie: what do you *do* that you so enjoy?"

"Please forgive me, Lady Molly." He turned the curricule north again, and they trotted past the Pavilion. "I had forgotten that you are unaccustomed to our ways. You must simply trust me when I say that the entertainments you've enjoyed in Brighton are but a pale shadow of those in London, where one must often choose among three or four routs on the same night. Must choose among the theater, the opera, Almack's, one's club . . . By the end of the Season, it all becomes quite exhausting, and I am delighted to retire to Warwick, to my racing and my shooting and only the *occasional* ball. But when autum comes, I am equally delighted to return to town. And that—the constant change of scene—is what renders my life so very pleasant."

Change of scene? Molly could not but wonder at Lord Ogilvie's reaction if he were suddenly cast into the Canadian wilderness. Which was wretchedly unfair, of course: respectable people were not required to trap beaver, to venture hundreds of miles through ice and snow to the merest outpost of civilization . . .

"But tell me of yourself, Lady Molly," the viscount said, guiding the horses into Church Street. "Tell me of your life in Canada."

Fortunately, Molly and Jon had anticipated such an

inquiry when they planned the details of their charade, and she recited what he had told her of the small settlement of York—hardly a difficult task inasmuch as the community comprised a fort, a collection of rough cottages, and a population of seven hundred persons. She thought she acquitted herself quite well, but she soon realized that the viscount was attending her discourse only vaguely if, indeed, he was listening at all. She suspected she could add that, by the by, she was not Lady Molly Wentworth, that she was, in fact, Miss Molly Trevor, the infamous moneylender, and Lord Ogilvie would continue to drive in silence, a vacuous smile on his handsome face.

In short, she reflected as they turned south on King Street, jogged across North and back into Ship, it was clear that Viscount Ogilvie had no more interest in Lady Molly than he'd had in the anonymous Miss Shelton; and she experienced a curious rush of relief. She had had her opportunity—she need never regret on that head—and she had failed to captivate his lordship after all. He had obeyed his mother's directive, nothing had come of it, and he would now bid Lady Molly a polite farewell and return his attentions to Miss Baird—

"Well, this has been a most enjoyable interlude, Lady Molly." He halted the curricle in front of the house, clambered out, assisted her down, escorted her to the door. "I daresay you and Lord Durham are invited to Lady Ellis' assembly this evening?"

Since the startling revelation of Jon's identity, the console table had grown fairly heaped with cards of invitation, and Molly had no doubt Lady Ellis' was among them. "I daresay we are," she murmured.

"Then I should very much like to accompany you there," the viscount said. "I shall call for you at a quarter before nine if you've no objection."

"I . . . I . . ." But what objection could she offer? "I should be delighted," she finished lamely.

"Excellent."

He flashed his bland smile, opened the door, bowed away, and Molly hurried into the vestibule.

Following Lady Ellis' ball, Lord Ogilvie engaged Lady Molly for another drive on Saturday, during which he proposed himself as her escort to Mrs. Hunter's card party that evening. He took her to church on Sunday, then to dine with his mother, who could not hide her keen pleasure at the splendid progress of the courtship. Indeed, her ladyship went so far as to comment that she was somewhat reluctant to schedule Lady Molly's come-out ball as she believed "the situation" might well have changed by May. Molly, for her part, did not believe it would take till May, for by Tuesday evening it appeared certain that Lord Ogilvie would shortly offer for her hand. Or so the Honorable Mr. Sloane implied when he sought her advice on an extremely delicate matter.

"I shouldn't want Ogilvie to think I am trying to cut him out with Miss Baird," he explained in a whisper. Since the viscount had remained devotedly at her side, Mr. Sloane had been forced to accost her as she returned from the ladies' withdrawing room. "But I fancy that is no longer a factor, eh? *On dit* that you and he will probably be engaged before the Season, and I should hate to lose my chance. My father has recovered from his most recent attack," he added glumly.

"I . . ." Molly had started to tender her condolences but decided this would be somewhat inappropriate. "I am pleased to hear it," she said.

She went on to assure him that Andrew (for so the viscount had requested her to address him during his afternoon call) would not be in the least distressed if Mr. Sloane elected to court Miss Baird, and he bounded eagerly back into Lord Cunningham's ballroom. Despite the embarrassing nature of their interchange, Molly was considerably relieved because she had suffered more than a few qualms of conscience for Miss Baird's abrupt abandonment. As it was, she fancied Miss Baird and Mr. Sloane would be quite happy together, and there remained no conceivable obstacle to her and Andrew's own happiness.

No obstacle except . . . Except what? Molly asked herself desperately, as Andrew's courtship neared the end of its second week. They had been together almost constantly for twelve consecutive days, yet she felt she knew him no better than she had the night they met at his mother's assembly. Their conversations tended to blur in her mind, but she did not count that surprising, for they seemed always to talk of the same things, to talk of the orchestra and the food and the people they were with. And what else *could* they talk of? she wondered; what else could they ever talk of? Andrew's entertainments were his life, and her own life must forever remain her secret.

"*You're a hard woman, Molly.*" Jon's voice echoed in the darkness of her bedchamber, and she closed her eyes and wearily conceded him right. She must be a hard woman, for she had never encountered a man who could melt the ice inside her—not Mr. Sloane or Mr. Crawford or Lord Durham when she had thought him her suitor, not even Andrew. No man but Jon, and him she regarded as a brother. So if she was ever to marry, it would be without a great *tendre*; it would be an arrangement, much like the numerous business arrangements she had concluded over the years. And viewed in that light, Andrew was an excellent risk: attractive and personable, kind and pleasant, dependable and respectable. Yes, Andrew was a splendid risk, and she could ask for nothing more.

It remained, then, only to await his offer, and Molly suspected that might come at Lady Reeves's ball. The assembly was scheduled for Valentine's Day—a circumstance Lady Ogilvie had coyly remarked upon for several days past. Molly had by now exhausted her wardrobe, and she reverted to the gown she had worn at her ladyship's ball, calculating that Andrew was unlikely to recollect it since, at that juncture, he had hardly registered her name. Evidently her calculation was correct, for the viscount complimented her attire at prodigious length and sat excessively close to her in his barouche as they proceeded to the Reeveses' home in Richmond Place.

The significance of the date had clearly not escaped Lady Reeves's attention either: the saloon was awash with bouquets of red roses, and a little cupid had been perched in each of the potted palms. It soon became additionally clear that the orchestra had been instructed to play primarily waltzes and the caterer directed to supply endless quantities of champagne. As a result of these efforts, the atmosphere had grown decidedly romantic by half-past ten; indeed, Molly feared Jon was at the point of assaulting Lady Palmer in full public view. She trod on Andrew's foot and hastily returned her eyes to him. She and Jon had had no private conversation since the evening of their dinner party, and if he was not interested in the progress of her courtship, she was *certainly* not interested in the status of his. The set ended, and Andrew cleared his throat.

"Do you not find it a trifle warm?" he said. "May I propose a breath of air?"

Molly quelled a hysterical inclination to advise him that he had taken her part, that *she* was supposed to complain of the heat. But her heart had jumped into her throat—she could not have spoken had she dared—and she nodded and mutely trailed him down the stairs, through the lower parlor, and out the rear door.

The weather had moderated again since the foul day of her arrival in Hampshire: the sky was clear, and the fig trees in the garden were bathed in moonlight. But it was not so warm as it had been the night of the Regent's party, and Molly swallowed another insane laugh as she felt the onset of a chill. He would shortly place his arm around her . . .

"Are you cold?" the viscount murmured, seating her on a stone bench just off the gravel path. "I should have thought to bring my cloak, but as I did not . . ."

He took the place beside her, draped one arm rather awkwardly over her shoulders, and Molly waited for her heart to accelerate, her knees to weaken. But his arm merely warmed her body; inside, she was as cold and dead as the stone of the bench.

"Ahem." He cleared his throat again. "I should hate you to judge my . . . my confession premature, Molly, but I wished you to know that during the past weeks, I have grown quite . . . quite fond of you."

"I have grown quite . . . quite fond of you as well, Andrew," she mumbled. She realized she was speaking to one of the fig trees, and she forced herself to turn her head. "I have grown quite fond of you as well," she repeated shrilly.

"Then if I am fond of you, and you are fond of me . . ."

He rotated on the bench a bit, pulled her closer, laid his lips on hers; and Molly now awaited that wonderful jolt, waited for the ice to melt away. But there was nothing, nothing—his mouth was firm and cool—and she wildly surmised that she wasn't *cooperating* sufficiently. She coiled her free arm around his neck, parted her lips, and he sighed and pulled her nearer yet. But still there was nothing—only that terrible, lingering chill— and insofar as she could think, she understood that she couldn't wed him. Barring all else, she deserved the physical magic; barring all else, the ice must melt when he touched her—

"Ogilvie!"

Jon's tone was one of infinite shock, nay, *horror*, and Andrew sprang to his feet. Leapt up so rapidly that Molly nearly tumbled off the bench, and when she regained her balance, she found Jon peering down at her, shaking his head, his hair red and silver in the moonlight.

"Molly," he said sorrowfully. "But I can hardly hold you accountable, can I? No"—he shifted his pale gaze to the viscount, drew himself indignantly up—"no, I hold *you* accountable, sir. You were to take my dear sister under your wing, introduce her into society, and instead you have taken the most shameless advantage of my confidence . . ." His voice sputtered off, and he squared his broad shoulders. "Were I entirely recovered from my wounds, I should be compelled to demand you go out with me at once. In the circumstances, such satisfaction will have to wait—"

"*Please*, Lord Durham," Andrew bleated. "You have entirely misconstrued the situation."

"Misconstrued?" Jon barked. "I discovered you in the very act of seducing my sister; what have I miscontrued?"

"My *intentions*; my thoroughly honorable intentions. I am—"

"Prepared to offer for Molly?" Jon sagged with relief, seized the viscount's hand, wrung it. "Why did you not say so? That is welcome news indeed—a match I heartily approve."

"No!" Molly said frantically. "That is to say, I cannot—"

"Do not tease yourself about it, dear," Jon interposed kindly. "You need not justify your behavior; it is obvious you were overcome with passion. Which is not to suggest"—he wagged an admonitory finger—"that I shall tolerate similar lapses of conduct in future. No, Ogilvie, you are to treat Molly most circumspectly until your marriage. But that needn't be long, eh?" He threw a fraternal arm across Andrew's back and began steering him up the path. "With your permission, I shall call on you tomorrow so as to discuss the . . . er . . . financial details."

"Permission?" The viscount giggled. "To the contrary, Lord Durham, I *insist* you call tomorrow . . ."

Their words deteriorated to a buzz as they strode toward the house, faded away as they disappeared inside. By the time Molly left the bench, bestirred herself to follow, clouds had raced across the moon, and her teeth were chattering with cold.

—14—

"How dare you?" Molly hissed.

She had waited for Jon in the library, waited in the dark, and she was childishly gratified to see him start.

"How dare I what?" he asked coolly, pulling the front door closed behind him.

"How dare you take . . . take . . ."

Her voice was shaking with anger, shrill with rage, and she glanced warily around the vestibule, wondering if any of the servants was about. Evidently Jon shared her concern, for he brushed past her, strode into the library, and she was compelled to follow. He lit the lamp on the bow-fronted commode beside the door, shut the door, flung his cloak on the sofa, stalked to the liquor cabinet, unstopped one of the decanters with a fearful clang, and filled a glass.

"Well, I am waiting," he snapped, whirling back round. "What have I done to elicit your displeasure this time?"

"You simply seized control of my life; that is all." Her fury had put her dangerously near to tears, and she gulped down a great lump in her throat. "You treated me like a cockleheaded schoolgirl, forced Andrew to offer for me—"

"I collect, from the cozy scene I interrupted, that he was at the point of offering in any case."

"Perhaps he was," Molly agreed, "but without your intervention, I could have declined."

"Declined?" He raised his auburn brows. "Then I do most abjectly beg your pardon; I was not aware you had changed your mind."

"I . . ."

But she could not give him that ultimate satisfaction, could not admit her last and gravest error. If she must inevitably wed a man she didn't love, it might as well be Andrew as another; she might as well emerge with her pride at least intact.

"I have not changed my mind," she said haughtily. "I merely resent being . . . being rushed."

"Then I apologize again. I judged it best not to delay; one never knows when Ogilvie might meet the grand-daughter of a *duke*." Molly clenched her hands. "Conse-quently, when·I discovered that he had . . . ah . . . com-promised you—"

"He had not compromised me!" Molly screeched. "No more than you . . ."

She stopped and bit her lip, for he couldn't possibly recall the moment in his bedchamber. He could not remember, and she could not forget, and her knees grew as weak as if he were touching her now. As, indeed, he might have been, so intent were his eyes on her face, and she groped for some escape.

"I wonder how you chanced to make your discovery," she said frostily. "I wonder how you chanced to be in the garden at that particular time."

"Oh, there was no chance about it," he said airily. "You must recollect that I once counseled you to entice Ogilvie into just such a situation, and when I saw you leave the saloon, I followed. After which, events unfolded precisely as I'd anticipated."

"How clever of you." He was still watching her, and she felt her own eyes narrow. "In fact, you were so very clever that it occurs to me there might be another reason for your prodigious hurry. It occurs to me that Lady Palmer might look most favorably on a connection be-tween your sister and her cousin. That such a connection might impel her to accept *your* suit."

"Well, Ellen *is* excessively fond of Ogilvie."

"What a beast you are," Molly whispered. "To . . . to manipulate me with no regard for my wishes—"

"I thought that was your wish, Molly. To wed Ogilvie, I mean."

His voice was so low she could scarcely hear him, his eyes on her face still unwavering, and she would not be trapped. "So it is," she said stiffly.

"Then no harm was done, was it?"

"No, no harm was done," she muttered, "except that I bitterly mislike being used. But I daresay I should accustom myself to that, for I've no doubt you'll continue to turn my circumstances to your advantage." She suddenly remembered Mrs. Mulvaney's allusion to a double wedding. "Indeed, I daresay you might choose to announce your engagement in conjunction with mine."

"I shouldn't dream of stealing any part of your grand moment," Jon said kindly. "Furthermore, I fear Lady Ogilvie would object most strenuously to any diversion of attention from Andrew's splendid match."

"Lady Ogilvie?" Molly echoed sharply. "The betrothal was not to be formal till tomorrow."

"She succeeded in wheedling the news from Ogilvie while you were in the withdrawing room. You may recall that you spent the better part of the evening there," he added pointedly. "Following the . . . er . . . incident in the garden." Molly once more clenched her hands. "In any event, Lady Ogilvie desired me to advise you that she will call on you tomorrow, and unless I badly miss my guess, she will come quite early. So if you've nothing else to say, I might recommend that you retire."

"No, I've nothing else to say." No, he had utterly outwitted her again.

"Good night then. And please do accept my sincere congratulations."

She was too tired to ascertain whether he was mocking her or not; she nodded, opened the door, and fled into the vestibule. She had reached the first landing when she heard the resounding ring of the decanter as he once more unstopped it, and she hesitated. But there was no reason for her to care if he drank himself into insensibility, and she hurried on up the stairs.

"Molly!"

Lady Ogilvie leapt out of the satinwood chair, bounded across the saloon, and seized Molly's hands in hers. As Jon had predicted, it was quite early—not yet ten—and Molly fancied that must explain why she still felt so very tired.

"You will not object if I call you Molly?" her ladyship said anxiously. "I realize the engagement is not yet official, but I am confident it will be shortly, for your dear brother was arriving in West Street just as I drove off. And I can conceive no possible obstacle to your and Andrew's union."

Molly could conceive no obstacle either; not when Jon was fairly dying to wed her to Lady Palmer's cousin. "No, you may certainly call me Molly," she muttered.

"Then ring for tea, dear, and come sit with me. I've something of excessive importance to say."

Molly had already alerted Mrs. Mulvaney to the need for refreshment, and she obediently tugged the bell cord before trailing Lady Ogilvie on into the drawing room. Her ladyship sank onto the Adam sofa and eagerly patted the place beside her.

"What I wished to say, dear"—she beamed as Molly took the designated seat—"is that you will find me a most accommodating mother-in-law. You shall function as mistress of Andrew's households with absolutely no interference from me. You may, of course, choose to solicit my *advice* from time to time, but apart from that, I shall behave quite like a guest."

Molly had hoped that her mother-in-law would elect to establish her own residence, but barring that, her attitude did seem acceptably "accommodating." "I appreciate your cooperation, Lady Ogilvie," she murmured aloud.

"No interference whatever," her ladyship reiterated. "Though I do pray you don't plan to use any of Chudleigh's furniture; I never much cared for his taste."

To say the truth, Molly did not much care for Lord Chudleigh's furniture either, but she cared even less for Lady Ogilvie's disdainful nod about the saloon. Fortunately, before she was compelled to respond, Mrs. Mulvaney bustled in, deposited a tea tray on the sofa table, and hurried out again.

"A pleasant woman—your Mrs. Mulberry," her ladyship said. Molly bit back a correction. "However, as I am sure you understand, we cannot tolerate her presence at *our* table. But then I daresay she will remain in your brother's employ."

"Mrs. Mulvaney will come with me as my abigail," Molly said tightly.

"Do you think that is wise, dear?" Lady Ogilvie knit her brows with concern. "It would be a great step downward for her, and servants can be *so* difficult when they're crossed. Well, we shall see. My point was that you are to have *complete* control of the household, and should there be any doubt of that in your mind, I shall prove my intentions at once. Yes, I shall grant you *total* authority to plan your engagement ball."

"Engagement . . . ball."

Molly was hard put to imagine anything she less desired, but as she cast about for a credible objection, she perceived, instead, an advantage. If the ball was to be held during the Season, the announcement of her and Andrew's engagement would be delayed some months.

"In lieu of my come-out ball, you mean." She hoped the ragged relief in her voice bore some resemblance to excitement. "That is an excellent notion, Lady Ogilvie—"

"No, dear, we certainly shouldn't wish to postpone the announcement till *May*." Molly wondered what it was her ladyship feared. An earl? A marquis? "No, we must announce your engagement as quickly as we can, and I consequently took the liberty of reviewing my social calendar. By a great stroke of luck, nothing is scheduled for tomorrow week, so we shall hold our assembly then."

"Tomorrow . . . week." Molly began groping for objections again and, miraculously, found one. "That is exceedingly kind of you, Lady Ogilvie, but you conducted a ball just a few weeks since. A *magnificent* ball, I might add, and I could not permit you to have another—"

"Nor shall I," her ladyship interposed happily. "Lady Calder will conduct the assembly."

"Lady . . . Calder."

"You have not met her, dear; she has been abroad and returned only Tuesday. Be that as it may, Lady Calder— Dorothea—is Andrew's godmother, and she will be *thrilled* to hold an engagement ball in his honor. Furthermore, she has the most *splendid* facilities: a great mansion in Preston. The village is but a short drive from Brighton, but it will *seem* a complete change of scene. Which is imperative to the theme of the assembly."

"The . . . theme."

"A Gypsy carnival!" Lady Ogilvie clapped her hands with delight. "Is that not a marvelous idea, Molly? Everyone will be masked, but in addition to that, we shall all dress as Gypsies—in bright gowns and great gold earrings." Molly distantly wondered what the *men* were to wear. "And we shall have Gypsy music—though I am not certain what sort of music they favor; and Gypsy food —though I can't say precisely what they eat. We shall have a painted wagon or two drawn up outside the house, and perhaps we can locate a *real* Gypsy to tell fortunes. Is it not a marvelous idea?" she repeated.

Molly judged it quite possibly the worst idea she had ever heard, but before she could formulate the proper, delicate way to say so, Lady Ogilvie once more clapped her hands.

"I knew you would agree, and as you are to plan it, you must begin without delay. I shall assist you, of course," she added kindly. "We shall go to the printer this afternoon to order the invitations. Naturally the actual *purpose* of the assembly will be kept a secret; there will be a surprise announcement of your engagement at the very stroke of midnight, in conjuction with the unmasking. In any event, as I stated, we shall visit the printer this afternoon. Then, tomorrow, we shall begin interviewing the various purveyors, and they will ensure that every detail of the ball is *authentically* Gypsy."

But this was not to be, for none of the purveyors knew the slightest thing about Gypsies; there was even an argument with the printer as to how the word was spelled. That conflict was speedily resolved by a search through his dictionary, but the florist had no such reference at hand. No reference and, not numbering any Gypsies among his clientele, no notion what plants and/or flowers they fancied.

"Then I daresay unadorned palms will do very well." Molly snapped at length.

"Palms?" Lady Ogilvie echoed dubiously. "It strikes me, dear, that *ferns* are rather more Gypsy-like than palms."

The orchestra leader was equally at a loss: an exhaustive examination of his music revealed not a single piece by a Gypsy composer.

"Perhaps we could use selections from eastern Europe then," Molly suggested. "From Hungary and Austria and Russia—"

"Russia?" Her ladyship frowned. "With all due respect to Countess Melnikoff, I should suppose the Gypsies prefer *Spanish* music."

The caterer's only opinion of Gypsy cuisine was that it must be quite varied since they reputedly stole everything they ate. Molly interpreted this as a *carte blanche* to order anything she liked, but as she issued her instructions, Lady Ogilvie thoughtfully tapped her teeth with one forefinger.

"No, consider what they would be most likely to steal, dear," she counseled at last. "They would be most likely to steal chickens and eggs and to poach the occasional deer, and then they would cook it all in spicy sauces."

The caterer shook his head with admiration; even *he* had not realized the Gypsies' keen partiality to spicy sauces.

By the time Molly and Lady Ogilvie reached the mantua-maker, on the Monday prior to the ball, they found the poor woman altogether immersed in a sea of gaudy fabrics and ruffled, half-finished garments. She could permit them no fittings, Miss Fowler cautioned; as she had been quite flooded with orders for Gypsy attire, an initial measurement would have to suffice. However, she hastened to assure them, this did not signify a whit because Gypsy women invariably wore very loose-fitting ensembles. Molly wryly marveled to discover such an accomplished scholar posing as a humble seamstress.

"Now for the hair," Miss Fowler said after she had noted their measurements. "You are probably aware that *all* Gypsies have black hair. Well, the old ones gray as we do, so you will pass, Lady Ogilvie. Which is not to imply you are *old*," she rapidly amended, apparently noting her ladyship's fearsome scowl. "But"—she turned quickly back to Molly—"Gypsies are *never* blond. Fortunately, having realized that, I ordered a supply of black wigs from London, and if you would care to try one on . . ."

But Molly did not need to try one on; she had long since recognized that if she was to participate in Lady Ogilvie's ludicrous charade, she must somehow cover her hair. She exited the shop, wig box in hand, and trailed her ladyship to the jeweler, where—by Molly's reckoning—they did try on at least a thousand pairs of great golden earrings.

By Thursday evening—after return visits to the florist and the caterer, after numerous trips to Preston to oversee the preparation of Lady Calder's house—Lady Ogilvie pronounced everything in readiness.

"You have performed wonderfully well, my dear," she continued as the Ogilvies' coachman handed Molly out of the Ogilvies' barouche. "I've no doubt our ball will be the pinnacle of the Brighton season, and you planned it *all by yourself.*"

Molly felt it in her throat—the threat of a wild, mad giggle—and lest she grow altogether hysterical, she nodded and rushed up the steps.

"Umm." Mrs. Mulvaney stood back and cocked her gray head. "You look very . . . very . . ."

Molly clenched her hands; if the housekeeper said "taking," she was persuaded she would scream. However, she soon perceived that there was little likelihood of this, for Mrs. Mulvaney's lips were twitching most furiously.

"Very *Gypsy-like*, I fancy," she concluded with a snort of laughter.

Molly glowered into the mirror. Whether she looked Gypsy-like or not, she couldn't say, but there was no doubt she looked totally absurd. She suspected Miss Fowler had fashioned her dress out of whatever scraps of fabric chanced to remain in her inventory: the bodice was a hideous marigold in hue, and the striped skirt was done in various clashing shades of red. It appeared quite possible that the mantua-maker had also confused Molly's measurements with those of another client; the top of the dress was so tight that she sincerely feared to breathe while the skirt could comfortably have accommodated the Prince Regent. And the numerous deficiencies of her own hair paled to insignificance when compared to the long, limp black wig which trailed into her eyes and around her shoulders.

"Pack me another dress, Mrs. Mulvaney," she said. "I will *not* have my engagement announced in this; I shall change just before midnight."

"Ah, yes, your engagement." Mrs. Mulvaney sobered, withdrew Molly's valise from beneath the bed, plucked her blue muslin gown from the wardrobe, laid it in the case. "Yes, I daresay you are quite beside yourself with joy; it is a dream come true, is it not?" She hesitated a moment. "Although . . ." She stopped, closed the valise, and tugged it briskly off the bed.

"You have the most maddening habit," Molly snapped. "The most maddening habit of dropping but a single shoe. Come now; what were you going to say?"

"Say?" The housekeeper's black eyes darted about as if to ensure that they were alone. "I was going to say that I had rather entertained a hope you might end by wedding Mr. Shelton. Lord Durham, that is."

"Wed *Jon?*" Molly tried to laugh, but she discovered

her mouth peculiarly dry. "However did you conceive such a ridiculous notion, Mrs. Mulvaney?"

"Never mind," she mumbled.

"No, I demand an answer. How could you possibly imagine I should wish to marry Jon?"

"Because I thought you were falling in love with him," the housekeeper said in a rush. "Indeed, I thought you *had* fallen in love with him. If you could see yourself as I do, see the way you look at him, and you seemed so very jealous of Lady Palmer—"

"I am not in the least jealous of Lady Palmer!" Molly screeched.

"Then I was mistaken," Mrs. Mulvaney said levelly, "so we shall talk no more about it." The mantel clock began to chime. "Nor have we the time to do so, for I fancy Lord Ogilvie has already come to fetch you." She paused once more. "I wish you happy, Miss Molly," she whispered.

Miss Molly. It was the last time, the very last time, she would ever be herself, and she choked down a rising wave of panic. She rushed to the dressing table and snatched up her mask, dismayed to observe that her hands were trembling, then seized her valise.

"Thank you, Mrs. Mulvaney," she murmured. Her voice was unsteady as well, and there was a swelling lump in her throat, and before she could altogether dissolve, she hurried out of her bedchamber and down the stairs.

Molly was somewhat annoyed to note that Andrew did not look nearly so ludicrous as she: he was clad in a pair of black pantaloons, a loose white shirt, and—the only major concession to the Gypsy motif—an exceedingly garish waistcoat. Furthermore, as his hair was naturally dark, he had not been compelled to wear a wig. In short, she thought grouchily, he looked almost *decent,* and she was enormously thankful she had decided to bring a change of attire.

"What is in the case?" he asked as the carriage rumbled to a start.

Molly briefly explained her intention.

"But I think you make a perfectly lovely Gypsy," he protested gallantly, patting her knee.

She had once threatened to knock Jon halfway to hell if he patted her knee again, Molly recollected. And he had chided her for her shocking language, mocked her as he always did . . . *"I thought you were falling in love with him."*

"Though I must own I shall be glad when the ball is over," Andrew went on. "You and Mama have been so occupied, I've scarcely had a chance to see you. She is immensely pleased with you, by the by, Molly; you have quite won her over."

"I said you would find it damnably difficult to live a lie for the rest of your life." "I thought you were falling in love with him." Molly's heart began to thud, dully thud, against her ribs.

"And as soon as the ball is over, we must turn our attention to the wedding, eh?" Andrew said. "Mama and I should very much like to have it in town, during the Season." *" . . . live a lie for the rest of your life."* "Naturally your brother will give you away, and in light of that, Mama had an excellent idea. Since you've no close friends in England, she suggested Ellen attend you—"

"No!" Molly interposed sharply. *"You seemed so very jealous of Lady Palmer."*

"No?" the viscount echoed quizzically. "Do you and Ellen not get on? That would be most unfortunate."

"We get on well enough." *" . . . so very jealous of Lady Palmer."* Her heart was racing now, crashing in her throat, pounding in her neck. "I . . . I should merely prefer to select my own attendant."

"Well, of course, dear," Andrew said kindly, once more patting her knee.

"I collect you're quite fond of my grandson." Lord Andover's voice rang in Molly's ears. *"I am . . . am monstrous fond of him." "Indeed, I thought you had fallen in love with him."* Dear God. Her palms had grown quite soaked, and she gazed desperately at Andrew.

"You needn't make your choice *now*," he assured her.
"No, after all your effort, you quite deserve to enjoy our
engagement ball. We shan't start planning the wedding
till tomorrow. The ceremony and our wedding trip . . ."

He chattered on, but his words were entirely lost
among all the other voices clamoring round her. It could
not be true; it simply could not; but the voices were
shouting at her, shrieking at her . . .

"And here we are," the viscount said brightly.

This did, indeed, appear to be the case, for the
barouche was stopping just behind the gaudy wagon
which—after much debate—Lady Ogilvie had
determined to position precisely at the entry of the ballroom. Molly and Andrew donned their masks, and he
assisted her out of the carriage. She must get a grip on
herself, she thought frantically, her knees briefly
buckling as her feet touched the pavement. She had
reached her decision long since, long before Jonathan
Shelton/Wentworth had burst so unceremoniously into
her life.

Another carriage clattered up behind the barouche,
and Molly's eyes narrowed as she recognized her own
landau, recognized Lewis on the box. But Mrs. Mulvaney
had mentioned that, she belatedly recalled, had
mentioned that Lady Palmer's coachman was ill, and Jon
desired to use the carriage. He exited first—she would
have known him anywhere, even in his dreadful waistcoat, his black wig, his black satin mask—then handed
Lady Palmer out. Molly was delighted to observe that her
ladyship's dress was quite as grotesque as her own;
indeed, upon closer inspection, it was almost exactly *like*
her own. However, as was the case with her cousin, Lady
Palmer had required no wig . . .

"Hurry!" Andrew hissed with boyish enthusiasm. "If
they see us beside the carriage, they will penetrate our
disguises."

Molly had not supposed the disguises would prove very
effective at any rate, but she was shortly compelled to
own herself wrong, for the costumes were so prodigious
unimaginative that everyone looked precisely the same as

everyone else. Evidently all of Brighton's tailors had
agreed that proper garb for a male Gypsy comprised dark
pantaloons, a flowing white shirt, and a brilliantly
colored waistcoat. A waistcoat in *several* brilliant colors,
preferably dissimilar; the men were a veritable
monument to execrable taste. Meanwhile, the town's
mantau-makers had conspired to dress all their clients in
bodices of a single hue and striped or patchwork skirts—
the only absolute requirements being that the colors must
not match and the gowns must not fit. Added to which,
all those guests without dark hair (or gray if one was
"old") had been rigged out in horrid black wigs. On the
whole—in the dim light of Lady Calder's half-lit chandeliers, masks in place—the Brighton *ton* might well have
been mistaken for a marauding band of genuine Gypsies.

And they seemed to adore it, Molly realized as the
evening progressed. They seemed to love stamping about
to Lady Ogilvie's Spanish music, stumbling into the ferns
from time to time, wolfing down the spicy chicken and
venison and raw red wine the caterer had supplied.
Tonight they could be anonymous Gypsies; tomorrow
they would be themselves again. No, never themselves;
tomorrow they would be *respectable* again. " . . . *live a
lie for the rest of your life.*"

"It is half-past eleven," Andrew whispered, consulting
his watch. "If you wish to change before the announcement, perhaps you should be about it."

"Yes; thank you."

Molly hurried out of the ballroom and paused to get
her bearings. She had left her valise in the ladies' withdrawing room, which was directly across the foyer from
the ballroom, but she now perceived that she was not *in*
the foyer. She was, instead, in a narrow corridor,
servants bustling back and forth about her; obviously the
kitchen wing lay on the opposite side of the hall. She
sighed, squared her shoulders to traverse the ballroom
again, and beheld a door ahead of her. The door gave
access to the garden, she surmised, and it was open, for
despite the relative chill of the night, the ballroom had
grown fearfully warm.

"And then you would remark that the room had grown altogether too warm." He was there, Jon was there— haunting her, mocking her; and perhaps the cool night air would forever clear her mind. She proceeded along the corridor, nearly colliding with one of the busy footmen, and slipped outside.

Initially the fresh air was wonderfully bracing, and Molly struck aimlessly out upon one of the gravel pathways. Within the space of a minute, however, within twenty yards of the house, she realized that it was, in fact, quite cold. Cold and excessively dark: though the winter sky blazed with stars, there was no moon. It wouldn't do to become lost, to be wandering round Lady Calder's garden at the magical stroke of midnight; and as Molly gazed apprehensively over her shoulder, marked the lights of the house, she barked her knee on an obstacle in the path. She spun her head back and saw a stone bench, much like the one where Andrew had kissed her, the bench to which Jon had followed them.

"Indeed, I thought you had fallen in love with him."

"Please." Though there was no one to hear, Molly was whimpering aloud. "Please leave me alone—"

"Ah, this time I find you alone."

There was no mistaking his voice, no mistaking his accent, and when Molly's eyes darted up, he was standing beside her. Standing perhaps three feet away, cloaked in darkness, the upper portion of his face invisible behind his mask.

"Yes, I am alone."

She waited for him to say something more, but he did not. He stood, stood for an eternity, it seemed, then took one step forward. It was to be left to her, she thought wildly; how like him to insist that she admit her error. If, in truth, she had erred, and she would never know unless she accepted his challenge. She moved one step ahead as well—at least she had intended only one—but suddenly there was no more space between them. She was in his arms, crushed against his chest, her own arms coiled around his neck, and it was exactly as it had been before.

No, not exactly, she amended distantly, as he took her

mouth, forced her lips apart. Then he had been weak, barely conscious, and now he was fearfully strong; she fancied she could feel every muscle in his arms, his back, his legs. His hands had begun to explore her body—lean, powerful, urgent hands—and his mouth on hers was hungry. He could snap her in two if he wished, she reflected, but he would not, for there was a delicacy in his hands, a softness to his lips, a deep gentleness beneath that terrible strength.

His mouth moved to her throat, to her shoulder, and she nearly cried out with sheer relief. She was not a hard woman after all; she was simply, utterly, hopelessly in love with him. Had been from the start probably; had been from the moment his bold, pale eyes swept across her desk. He lifted his head and looked down at her, his eyes now glowing through the slits in his mask, and Molly swallowed the last shred of pride. This, too, must be left to her.

"I . . . I—" She was interrupted by three great echoing chimes. The church-tower clock was striking a quarter before midnight; her engagement was to be announced in fifteen minutes. "Andrew!" she gasped.

Jon stiffened, then flashed his easy smile; she could see his teeth even in the darkness. "We need hardly be considering your cousin yet," he drawled. "Nor my sister, come to that. No, Ellen, the announcement is still a quarter-hour away; we've plenty of time."

He lowered his head again, and somehow, as the world crashed down around her, Molly twisted out of his grasp and fled up the gravel path.

—15—

Molly raced through the garden door, glancing fearfully over her shoulder for Jon's pursuing figure, and when she spun her head back round, it was too late: she crashed into one of the bustling footmen, and he, she, and his tray of glasses thudded to the floor. Fortunately, the latter landed some distance away, spattering Molly and her fellow casualty with only a few drops of red wine and no broken glass at all. However, the servant did not seem to appreciate their immense good luck; he stared at the debris for a long, dazed, horrified moment before struggling to his feet and tugging Molly up beside him.

"Are you all right?" he demanded through gritted teeth.

"I . . ." But it wouldn't do to undertake a lengthy conversation; Jon might appear at any instant. "No, I am not," she said. "In point of fact, I am excessively ill, and I was searching for the ladies' withdrawing room."

As she had hoped, the potential ramifications of her "excessive illness" galvanized the footman to immediate action: he began dragging her along the hall with such alacrity that she was hard put to keep pace. They rushed past the ballroom entry—he evidently judging that speed was of the essence—and followed the corridor on around to its intersection with the foyer.

"The withdrawing room is just there," he said, indicating a door on the opposite side of the vestibule. "Shall I . . . er . . . wait?"

"No," Molly panted. "No, I am likely to be inside fo some time."

He nodded with unmistakable relief, dropped her arm hurried back down the hall; and Molly scurried across the foyer and into the ladies' withdrawing chamber. She wa initially gratified to find it empty, but she soon surmisec the reason for this: it could not lack more than fiv minutes to midnight, and everyone was no doub assembling in the ballroom for the unmasking. She sagged against the door a moment, her mind churning She could not go through with the engagement—tha much was certain—and the honorable course was to seel Andrew out and forthrightly announce her change o heart. But, upon reflection, she doubted she would be granted the opportunity; as soon as Lady Ogilvie spiec her future daughter-in-law, she would surely begir calling the guests to attention. No, the only sure way to prevent the announcement was not to return to the ballroom, to flee at once, and Molly dashed on into the withdrawing chamber and retrieved her valise. She then proceeded to the adjacent cloakroom, where her hear plummeted at the sight of perhaps a hundred pelisses anc pelerines hanging on an endless rack. There was no time to locate her own; she would have to "borrow" one and trust that its owner would count Molly's midnight-blue velvet an adequate substitute. She snatched the neares garment—a black Russian wrapping cloak, it proved— hastily donned it and raced back to the door, cracked the door and peered into the vestibule. It, too, remained deserted, and she ran to and out the front door, noting that the orchestra had ominously fallen silent.

The church-tower clock started to chime even as Molly passed the painted wagon, and she fairly galloped toward the coach yard. She would be safe a few minutes more, she calculated; Andrew would assume she was still changing and would not immediately grow alarmed. But only a few; he would shortly send someone to assist her . . .

She reached the yard, fighting for every breath, and her heart sank once more, for a veritable sea of carriages extended well out of sight in the darkness. As Jon and Lady Palmer had been among the first to arrive at the ball, it seemed logical that Molly's landau would be near the far end of the yard, and she stumbled ahead as quickly as she could, dodging vehicles and horses and knots of coachmen gathered to while away their long wait in conversation. It took her a full five minutes, she estimated, to traverse the first two-thirds of the yard, and she decided she could waste no further time.

"Lewis!" she shrieked. "Malcolm Lewis! Where are you!"

She continued to shout as she darted along, and at length a dark figure detached itself from a group ahead and hurried forward to meet her.

"Miss Trevor?" he gasped, reaching her side.

"Yes, it is I," she wheezed. Despite the dreadful incident in the garden, despite her present precarious circumstances, she felt as though she had shed a great burden: she was, now and forever, herself again. "It is I, and we must depart at once, Lewis."

"Depart?" he echoed suspiciously. He craned his neck and evidently glimpsed her valise. "We are going to Hampshire again?" he wailed. "At this time of night?"

In point of fact, Molly had not considered where she would go, and she briefly hesitated. If she returned to Ship Street, she would gain not a moment of respite; Mrs. Mulvaney would be awaiting her, eager to know the details of the ball, and Andrew and/or Jon would undoubtedly arrive within the hour. An escape to London would be little better: once Mrs. Mulvaney learned of her flight, she would guess London to be her destination and take the next stage to town. But it might be several days before anyone thought to seek the wayward bride-to-be at Andover Castle, several days of rest and peace, which Molly most desperately required. She had promised the marquis to come to him if ever she needed him, and she would not, could not, ever need him more.

"Yes, that is precisely where we are going, Lewis," she said crisply.

"But what of Lord Durham and—"

"To *hell* with Lord Durham!" Molly hissed. "Come now, Lewis; if we make it in good time, there will be a five-pound bonus for you at the end of the journey."

The coachman appeared remarkably restored by this prospect: he plucked Molly's case from her hand and set out at a dead run, leaving her to totter along in his wake. Fortunately, she hadn't far to go—the landau stood only a few yards ahead—and within the space of perhaps five more minutes, Molly and her valise were ensconced inside, and Lewis had threaded their way out of Lady Calder's coach yard. They were passing the church as the tower clock struck a quarter past the hour, and five minutes after that they were out of Preston altogether, pounding westward on the dark and deserted highway. Molly gazed nervously out the rear window until they reached the vicinity of Hove, at which juncture she dared to believe that her escape would prove successful. She tore off her wig and mask, pulled the purloined cloak more firmly about her, burrowed into the leather squabs, and closed her eyes. But exhausted as her body was, her head was still whirling, and eventually she opened her eyes again and gazed sightlessly at the rear-facing seat.

How could she have been so cockleheaded? she wondered, her cheeks flaming even in the darkness, even in her solitude. How could she have been seduced by Mrs. Mulvaney's chatter? Though it was unfair to blame the housekeeper, Molly owned; Mrs. Mulvaney had never implied that Jon might reciprocate her emotion. No, Molly had conceived that absurd notion quite unaided, had conveniently forgotten his attachment to Lady Palmer, had invited the resulting humiliation. It was clear, in retrospect, that Jon had followed "Ellen" to the garden, and Molly could only infer from his remark that it was not his first such quest. "*Ah, this time I find you alone.*" No, he had trailed Lady Palmer before; how delighted he must have been to find her, indeed, alone and so exceedingly receptive to his physical charms. Molly was compelled to grant her ladyship a good deal of credit: apparently she had held Jon off, whetted his

appetite, during their many drives, their many hours
together at her house . . . Which rendered his comment
rather odd, Molly reflected, for he and Lady Palmer had
repeatedly been alone. So perhaps he had been referring
to an encounter earlier this evening; perhaps her ladyship
had previously been in the garden with Miss Baird or one
of her numerous friends.

Whatever the case, it really didn't signify, Molly
thought wearily, once more closing her eyes. Jon had
kissed her twice, both times fancying her to be someone
else, and there would be no third opportunity. In fact,
with any luck, she would not be required to see him
again; she certainly had no intention of accepting ten
percent of his income "in perpetuity." She took some dim
satisfaction in the awareness that her defection would be
most embarrassing for her dear "brother"; he would be
hard pressed to explain her scandalous conduct. But Lady
Palmer, smitten as she was, would soon forgive him, and
then he could start explaining why his "sister" had altogether vanished from the face of the earth . . .

Yes, that was a pleasant note, and Molly drifted into
an uneasy sleep, waking when they negotiated a particularly poor stretch of road, when they stopped to rest and
water the horses, then tumbling into oblivion again. And
dreaming confused dreams of Gresham and Mrs.
Mulvaney, of Andrew and Lady Ogilvie, of Lady Palmer
and Miss Baird, of the erstwhile Lord Durham and Mr.
Sloane and the Prince Regent. And of Jon—mostly of
Jon—and when she opened her eyes for the last time, it
was morning, and the landau had stopped.

"It is eight o'clock, Miss Trevor," Lewis announced,
opening the carriage door.

"By your watch?" Molly said dryly, knowing full well
he possessed no timepiece.

"I have been checking our progress at every opportunity." The coachman spoke with great wounded
dignity. "And as it was only seven when we passed
through Fareham—"

"Never mind." Her fitful sleep had provided no real
rest; were it not for the position of the sun, she would

readily have believed it was any time he chose to tel her. As it was, she did gauge it to be about eight, and she managed a grateful smile. "Well done, Lewis; you shall have your ten pounds."

"*Ten* pounds! Thank you very much indeed, Miss Trevor."

He handed Molly out of the carriage and bounded up the front steps; one might well have collected he had spent the preceding eight hours in a warm and comfortable bed. Molly, for her part, was able only to trudge behind him, belatedly questioning the wisdom of her course. She recalled from Lord Andover's visit to Brighton that he was an early riser, but this she viewed as a mixed blessing, for she remained far too overwrought to conduct a sensible conversation. On the other hand, she was not at all sure Tanner would remember her, so if his lordship *was* still abed . . . She hurried up the steps, thinking to advise Lewis that they would drive on to Eastleigh, but as she tugged his sleeve, the great front door creaked open.

"Miss Trevor!" Obviously the butler did recollect her, and his eyes widened with shock as he studied her garish, wine-spattered dress. "Is something amiss?" he inquired anxiously.

Nothing except that my whole life has fallen apart . . . "No," she murmured aloud. "Nothing we need trouble Lord Andover about at any rate. If you could just show me to one of the guest rooms, I shall speak with his lordship later—"

"Molly?"

There was a tap of rapid footfalls in the entry hall, and she ground her fingernails into her palms.

"I thought I recognized your voice," the marquis said, stepping up next to Tanner. He sounded peculiarly jovial, and his smile seemed warmer than one of mere welcome. "But where is Jon?" he asked, frowning over her head.

"Jon?" she echoed bitterly, not pausing to reflect why he should pose such an odd question. "I fancy he is still asleep, for he must have had a long and exhausting night.

Attempting to apologize to Lady Ogilvie and Lady Palmer. Attempting to explain why his sister fled her own engagement ball."

"Fled the ball?" Lord Andover's frown deepened. "Why . . . ?" His pale eyes darted to Tanner, to Lewis, who were following the conversation with rapt attention. "Please order tea, Tanner," he said pleasantly. "And see that Miss Trevor's man is settled."

The servants plodded away, clearly shattered to be deprived of the forthcoming *on-dit*, and his lordship guided Molly across the threshold and closed the door.

"I daresay you would much prefer a soft bed to a cup of tea," he whispered, taking her cloak, "and I shan't keep you up for long. However, if you can forgive an old man's curiosity, I do wonder why you . . . er . . . *fled* the assembly."

"It was a cowardly thing to do," Molly confessed. She walked weakly to the middle of the hall and sank onto the Egyptian sofa, and the marquis sat beside her. "But it was nearly midnight, and I did not believe Lady Ogilvie would grant me a chance to advise Andrew of my change of mind."

"But that was my question, dear," he said gently. "Why did you change your mind?"

Why indeed? Molly once more clenched her hands. "I . . . I had discovered that my affection for Andrew was insufficient to permit our marriage."

"I see." Lord Andover appeared remarkably unsurprised. "Would you care to tell me how you reached that conclusion?" Molly bit her lip. "No, I perceive that you would not, so I shall venture a guess. I suspect you came to realize that you are terribly in love with my grandson."

Molly's mouth dropped open, and she hastily snapped it shut again.

"My dear child." He shook his white head with fond exasperation. "The situation was abundantly clear to me the day of your first visit; that was why I was so astonished when you professed a *tendre* for Ogilvie. And why I . . ."

He stopped, and Molly distantly reflected that he and Mrs. Mulvaney would have made a splendid pair, forever dangling half-finished sentences in one another's ears.

"I collect," the marquis went on at last, "that you did not inform Jon of your feelings."

How he could have collected this, Molly could not imagine; she was beginning to think Lady Ogilvie should have engaged *him* to read fortunes at the ball. "No, I did not," she replied stiffly. "I was at the point of doing so when . . . when"—she decided to borrow his own words —"when it became abundantly clear to me that Jon's affections lay elsewhere."

"I see," Lord Andover said again, but his auburn brows were knit in another frown. "Well, as I promised, I shan't keep you up. Do you remember the location of the room you previously occupied?" Molly nodded. "Then if you would not judge me frightfully remiss, I shall ask you to make your own way. As you no doubt recall from your earlier stay, my household is ill-equipped for company."

"I shan't impose on you for long," Molly assured him, heaving herself wearily erect. "Indeed, I shouldn't have come at all except that I wished a few days' rest, and I was certain Mrs. Mulvaney would follow me to London. Had I gone to London, that is. But after a few days, I shall proceed to town."

"Oh, I shouldn't suppose it will take *days* . . ." His lordship's voice once more trailed off; yes, he was quite as maddening as Mrs. Mulvaney. "In any event, do ring when you wake; I shall assign someone to attend you."

Molly inclined her head, toiled up the great staircase and down the endless corridor, and collapsed, fully clothed, in the curtained bed.

The mantel clock was striking three when Molly woke, and as Lord Andover had instructed, she wriggled upright and tugged the bell cord beside the bed. Her summons was answered by an exceedingly elderly woman, so very old and frail that Molly hesitated to request a bath. But she was persuaded she would fairly die without one, and her guilt was considerably assuaged when two young, strapping maids actually delivered and filled the tub. Molly soaked for fully half an hour, during which interval her valise was brought to the bedchamber and laid upon the bed. She donned the fresh muslin dress, combed her hair, and grudgingly conceded that she might survive the day after all.

She crossed to the window and parted the draperies. As she had remembered, her room was situated on the park side of the house, Lord Andover's manicured grounds extending as far as the eye could see, and, perversely enough, the weather was magnificent. Molly hurried out of the bedchamber, back along the hall and down the stairs, and eventually located a door in the conservatory. She slipped outside, gratified to note that the day was warm as well as clear, and strolled into the garden.

Though the marquis' garden was vastly larger, it was very similar to the Reeveses', very similar to Lady Calder's, and Molly hesitated at the head of the main pathway. But she could not avoid gardens for the rest of her life—not if she was *ultimately* to survive—and she ventured cautiously down the path. As she had anticipated, she soon reached a stone bench, and this, too, seemed some sort of test. She sat gingerly down, and to her unutterable relief, nothing happened: none of the marble deities around her came to life, no ghosts leapt from the bushes, no warning clap of thunder crashed overhead.

So she had been right to come, Molly reflected, gazing toward the end of the garden, the point at which it turned to park. She had been right to come, and after a few days' rest, she would return to London, and everything would proceed precisely as it had before. She would, again, be Molly Trevor, the cleverest money-lender in England; it would be as though Miss Shelton and Lady Molly had never been. As, of course, they never *had*; they had been creations as cold and dead as the statues in the garden.

Molly contemplated the resurrected Miss Trevor a moment more, then frowned. At some juncture, Trevor and Company's clientele would expect Stephen Trevor to grow infirm, to die; and Gresham would be compelled to retire. So perhaps it would be best to start establishing a new facade at once, and Molly almost laughed aloud as she glimpsed the perfect solution. A brother! Yes, she must have a brother; she would instruct Gresham to begin casually referring to "young Mr. Trevor" during his client conversations. And then, in a few years, she would actually engage a discreet, ambitious young man, train him to her exacting standards; and when the time came, he would serve as her disguise. Serve until she herself was a doddering old woman, at which point the fate of Trevor and Company would no longer signify.

And by then, surely by then, she would have forgotten Jonathan Shelton/Wentworth. Yes, by then she would not have seen him for forty or fifty years, and she might well have forgotten his *name*. He and Lady Palmer would be long married, and perhaps one of their sons, a rackety lad, would apply to Trevor and Company for a loan. And Molly would say, with perfect honesty, "Wentworth? I am not familiar with that name, but I shall certainly consult my files . . ."

Oh, Jon, Jon. Molly's cheeks had grown wet, and she furiously scrubbed her fists in her eyes. She had neglected to advise Lord Andover that she would not accept their terms of repayment, she recalled; she must definitely do so before she left for London. She would take what Jon had cost her, not a farthing more, and she screwed her eyes closed in calculation. For his clothes, his food— five hundred pounds? Nearer a thousand maybe; she didn't seem to be thinking very clearly. But it would hardly be unfair if she erred a bit on the high side: she was entitled to something for her trouble, for her discovery of his inheritance. So she would ask for a thousand pounds, and even as she settled on the figure, she heard footsteps in the gravel. Excellent; the marquis would find a fully recovered Miss Trevor, a shrewd woman of business entirely in control of her destiny—

"Ah, I find you alone again."

She was so startled that she scarcely registered his words, registered nothing but his voice, his distinctive accent. She spun her head in disbelief, but it was not a dream: he was there. There in such disreputable splendor as to remind her of their first meeting—still clad in his outlandish Gypsy garb, his auburn hair hopelessly tousled, a sprouting of red-blond whiskers on his chin and upper lip.

"You . . . you look like hell," she muttered. She could think of nothing else to say.

"Am I never to correct your language?" He attempted a grin, but it was decidedly shaky round the edges, and he lowered himself wearily to the bench beside her. "I daresay you'd look like the devil too had you been on the road for fifteen hours."

"I presume you hired a chaise," she said. "And if it required fifteen hours to come from Brighton, you were most fearfully cheated. Were I you, I should have declined even to pay the mileage, and I certainly shouldn't have tipped the postboy—"

"Will you hush?" he interposed mildly. "How was I to guess you'd come to Hampshire? I assumed you'd gone to London, and that was my initial destination. It was not until Gresham advised me he hadn't seen you that I thought of Grandpapa and turned back round. I exhausted fully three dozen horses, I fancy . . ." He stopped and raked his long fingers through his hair.

"Well, you quite wasted your time and the horses' energies as well," Molly snapped. "I collect you persuaded Andrew and Lady Ogilvie and Lady Palmer to forgive me if I could be brought to see the error of my ways. If you could convince me to return immediately to Brighton and proceed with the engagement. And I will not; you could chase me round the world, and I would not."

He stared at her for a long moment, then shook his head, his hair glinting red-gold in the sunlight. "Can you possibly believe that?" he said. "Can you possibly have failed to perceive . . ."

His voice again trailed off, and, as so often happened, he moved before she could surmise what he was at. He reached out and gathered her into his arms and laid his mouth on hers—his lips warm and soft, gentle and hungry all at the same time. Molly felt that familiar melting weakness, and she desperately willed herself not to respond.

"How very disappointing." Jon released her and once more shook his head. "You were considerably more . . . ah . . . cooperative during our previous encounters."

"Our previous encounters?" Molly's jaw sagged. "You *knew?* There was no . . . no 'Kitty'?"

"I did not say there was no Kitty. In point of fact, Kitty is a barmaid in York, an excessively . . . er . . . friendly girl—"

"Jon," Molly said warningly.

"However, I knew quite well who it was I was kissing."

"But why?" Molly demanded. "Why would you pretend?"

"What else was I to do? I had employed every conceivable approach, and you had invariably rejected my overtures. The night we drove to Lady Ogilvie's ball, when I told you how very handsome you looked, you turned away. When I attempted to persuade you that Ogilvie would never accept you, you decided to deceive him permanently about your background. When I conducted our . . . our lesson, you ran away. When I threatened to leave, just prior to the attack, you seemed prepared to let me go. What else was I to do?" he repeated.

"And last night?" Molly said. "You were pretending then as well? Pretending to mistake me for Lady Palmer?"

"How could I *not* have been pretending? How could I ever mistake you for Ellen? You are half a head taller than she and very"—he coughed—"very differently constructed."

Molly's cheeks warmed, and her discomfiture was in no way alleviated by the infuriating twitch at the corners of his mouth. "But why?" she said again, with as much dignity as she could muster.

"Because I thought you had mistaken me for Ogilvie."

"Mistaken you for Andrew!" she screeched. "You are *nearly* half a head taller than he, and you were wearing that ludicrous wig . . ." She sputtered off and cast him a glare of keen vexation.

"So I now realize." He sketched a sheepish grin. "At the time, however . . . Well, be fair, Molly: the clock started to strike, and you said 'Andrew,' and I reached what seemed the obvious conclusion. Later, when it became clear you'd fled the ball, I recognized my error. But enough of them—I didn't drive all night and across half of England to discuss Ogilvie and Ellen."

He lapsed into silence, and Molly's heart began to thud against her ribs, to crash into her throat; if he delayed a moment more, she feared it would altogether burst.

"Have you no mercy?" he said ruefully. "Must I make a full confession?"

"A confession of . . . of what?"

"Oh, Molly." He took her hand, and despite the warmth of the day, she shivered. "I hardly know where to start; my head hasn't stopped spinning since I met you. I'm mad for you, smitten, *bouleversé*—choose your word. I love you; it's as simple as that. And what was I to do? You had set your cap at Ogilvie, and much as I regretted your disappointment, I could only pray he would never pay you the slightest attention."

"But you didn't attempt to keep us apart," Molly protested. "To the contrary, it was you who accepted the invitations to Lady Palmer's ball and the Regent's party and all the other functions."

"That was a gamble," Jon said, "but I judged the odds vastly in my favor. I was reasonably confident that Ogilvie would continue to ignore the anonymous Miss Shelton, and each time he did so, your disappointment was sure to increase. Until, or so I calculated, you abandoned hope and were ready to entertain my suit. The great danger was that you would cease to be anonymous. Did it not occur to you to wonder why I was so very reluctant to pursue my quest for my father? Even after you discovered the ring? I didn't *want* to confirm Nell's tale because if Ogilvie believed you the daughter of an earl, he was certain to initiate a most enthusiastic courtship."

"And then I forced you to wear the ring," Molly said.

"Yes, you forced me to wear it; had I refused to do so, I suspected you might well send me packing. I wore it, and after that, the matter was out of my hands: my clever little 'sister' speedily located Grandpapa. As you can imagine, I had mixed emotions when he arrived, but it was he who set me straight. After I had revealed my feelings, that is. I could not do battle with a dream, he said; we must throw you at Ogilvie's head and let you learn for yourself you didn't love him."

"Grandpapa!" Molly gasped. "You and he were scheming against me!" But, upon reflection, she was not entirely surprised; it explained Lord Andover's odd reaction this morning, explained his tantalizing, incomplete remarks.

"Scheming very hard indeed," Jon said cheerfully. "Yes, we determined to drive you into Ogilvie's arms and await your inevitable disenchantment. Though Mrs. Mulvaney was strenuously opposed to the plan."

"Mrs. Mulvaney! She was plotting with you?"

"Actually, she had been independently plotting for some time, or so she said. Attempting to point out my many virtues, which, of course, would not be difficult." He flashed a wry smile. "Trying to make you jealous of Ellen—"

"I was not in the least jealous of Lady Palmer," Molly interjected primly. But his mouth was twitching again, and she could not repress a grin of her own.

"In any event, Mrs. Mulvaney thought our plan was fraught with hazard," Jon continued. "She feared your pride was such that you might wed Ogilvie before you'd own to your mistake. And you damned near did, didn't you?"

"Would you have permitted it?" Molly countered question with question. "Would you never have confessed your feelings?"

"Not if I believed you truly loved him; I've my pride

too. But you don't; you love me. Admit it, Molly: you love me as much as I love you."

His tone was light, but there was a flicker of apprehension in his pale eyes, and she swallowed a burgeoning lump in her throat.

"Oh, very well, I do. Though why I should, I cannot conceive. You're a dreadful scoundrel, always mocking me . . ." But she could not go on, and she buried her face in his shoulder.

"Molly," he whispered.

He wrapped his fingers in her hair, and his other arm slipped round her, and for a time he merely held her. Then he tilted her head back and covered her mouth with his, and at last there were no shadows between them. No doubts, no fears, and she parted her lips, strained against him, moaned as his hands insistently roamed her body. They would always have this, she marveled, this magic they shared, this and more; and she shuddered with the force of his desire, the force of her own. He was trembling as well, for all his strength, and at length he drew away.

"One reason you love me," he said hoarsely, unsteadily, "is that you very much like to kiss me. Fortunately, that suggests a means by which we can avoid the sort of disagreements that have plagued us in the past. We shall simply spend our entire married life in bed—"

"Jon!"

Her cheeks were positively aflame, but she could not repress a giggle. A giggle nor another shiver of pure joy, for this was the real dream: to wed the only man she had ever loved, ever could; to belong to him utterly . . . She suddenly recollected one of their numerous "disagreements," and she stiffened.

"You once said you wouldn't marry me," she reminded him. "Wouldn't wed me no matter how much money I had."

"I said *what?*" His frown was one of complete bewilderment, but eventually he nodded. "I said, Molly, that had I sought to wed *only* for money, I could have wed you. I need scarcely have devised a complex charade to meet another rich woman. I could have attempted to win you that very first day, and in retrospect, I'm deuced sorry I didn't."

"You're not," Molly chided. "Had you done so, we should never have found Grandpapa, never discovered you're an earl."

"I should regret not knowing Grandpapa," he said, "but I don't care a damn for the title. But ask me again tomorrow." He gave her his easy smile. "Ask me tomorrow because today I don't care a damn for anything in the world but you."

He broke into his terrible whistle, but it was the sweetest of music in Molly's ears, and she snuggled into the curve of his arm, now draped around her shoulders. There were no shadows, all her doubts were truly laid to rest, but she could not quell an intense curiosity, and at length she cleared her throat.

"I wonder what will become of Lady Palmer?" she said casually.

"Lady Palmer," he echoed. "I should adore to tell you that I expect her to pine quite away without me, but that is far from being the case. Ellen is not Lady Palmer, you see; she is actually, and most happily, Mrs. Scruggs."

"Scruggs?" Molly gasped. "She wed her man of business?"

"Ah, I did mention him then; I did not recall that I had." In point of fact, it was Andrew who had mentioned Mr. Scruggs, but Molly did not judge it the proper time to issue a correction. "Yes, she wed him with rather indelicate haste following Palmer's demise. If one would term ten days 'indelicate.' "

"Ten days? They have been married above a year? Does she intend to keep it permanently a secret?"

"Oh, no, indeed; no, as I once told you, Ellen attaches scant importance to convention. *She* does not, but others do—most particularly Lady Ogilvie. Ellen calculated that it would quite destroy Maria's chances with Ogilvie if his mother learned of her scandalous marriage, so she

decided to keep the secret through the forthcoming
Season. I presented a splendid red herring: it could be
made to seem that Ellen was being courted by a wealthy
and possibly titled man. And our interests were identical,
of course; I was as eager as Ellen to promote Ogilvie's
relationship with Maria."

"Well, I daresay it is too late for that." Molly sighed
with genuine regret.

"Oh, I fancy not. Evidently—and surely for the first
time in her life—Lady Ogilvie held her tongue. Evidently
no one knew of the impending engagement beyond our
two families and Ellen."

"And Lady Calder," Molly said.

"Then she maintained her silence as well. At any rate
—and at the risk of wounding your sensibilities—I am
obliged to report that at half-past twelve last evening,
when it became clear you'd fled the assembly and were
unlikely to return, Ogilvie turned to Maria for solace. By
the time I myself left, they were stamping quite merrily
about to that horrid Spanish music. Naturally I shouldn't
wish to imply that Ogilvie's heart was unbroken"—his
mouth quivered again—"but it does appear to have
mended with wonderful speed."

Poor Mr. Sloane, Molly thought; all his projects
seemed to reach a premature and disastrous end. "And
Lady Ogilvie?" she said aloud. "How did she react?"

"It was she who discovered you were gone; Ogilvie dispatched her to the withdrawing room to assist you with
your clothes. And when she came stalking back to the
ballroom, she—and, again, I hate to wound you—she
was far more distressed by the disappearance of her cloak
than she was by your departure."

"Her cloak?" Molly shrieked with laughter. "It was
Lady Ogilvie's cloak I stole?"

"You stole a cloak?" Jon clicked his tongue against his
teeth. "I must add theft to your already lengthy catalog
of sins? Really, Molly, I may have to rescind my rash
offer."

He essayed a mischievous grin, but it died aborning,

and Molly realized that he was too tired to talk, almost too tired to hold himself erect. She gently shrugged his arm away, stood and tugged him up beside her, threw her own arm round his waist, and began ushering him up the path.

"You must sleep," she said soothingly, "and later we shall decide precisely what to do."

"Sleep, yes," he agreed groggily. "Though I am given to understand that my bedchamber is just across the hall from yours, so I fancy no one would notice if you cared to join me."

"Jon!" She suppressed another giggle.

"No, that would be highly unrespectable, wouldn't it? You—impossible woman that you are—will doubtless insist on marriage before you succumb to my charms. Well, I shall speak with Grandpapa after I've slept; perhaps he can bribe the local rector or some such thing."

"Respectable!" Molly suddenly perceived the one obstacle she had not considered, and exhausted as he was, she drew him to a halt and whirled to face him. "We can never be respectable, Jon. Once our marriage is known, it will be equally known I posed as your sister. And when Lady Ogilvie ferrets out my true identity, we shall *never* be accepted in polite society."

"I should wager my last groat that we shall," he said. "With Grandpapa's position and my own title, with our combined fortunes . . . Do you realize, Molly, that we shall be nearly as wealthy as the Scruggses?" He managed a smile at last, albeit a trifle weak. "Yes, I should wager that when Lady Ogilvie discovers herself connected to Mr. Scruggs, she will judge him and the former Miss Trevor as respectable as any two people in England."

"But if she does not?" Molly pressed. "She and all the *ton?* If they do *not* accept us?"

"Then it will be entirely their loss, will it not? I myself do not care a damn. And if you ask me about *that* tomorrow, I shall give you exactly the same answer."

They started weaving up the path again, he sagging increasingly against her, and for some reason, Molly glanced up. She thought she saw a tall figure in one of the upper windows, thought it raised its hand in a little gesture of triumph. And though it might have been her imagination, she raised her hand in turn before she guided Jon, guided her love, on toward the house.

About the Author

Though her college majors were history and French, Diana Campbell worked in the computer industry for a number of years and has written extensively about various aspects of data processing. She had published eighteen short stories and two mystery novels before undertaking her first Regency romance.

JOIN THE REGENCY READERS' PANEL

Help us bring you more of the books you like by filling out this survey and mailing it in today.

1. Book title:_____

   Book #:_____

2. Using the scale below how would you rate this book on the following features.

Poor		Not so Good			O.K.			Good		Excellent
0	1	2	3	4	5	6	7	8	9	10

                                                          Rating

Overall opinion of book . . . . _____
Plot/Story . . . . _____
Setting/Location . . . . _____
Writing Style . . . . _____
Character Development . . . . _____
Conclusion/Ending . . . . _____
Scene on Front Cover . . . . _____

3. On average about how many romance books do you buy for

   yourself each month?_____

4. How would you classify yourself as a reader of Regency romances?
   I am a ( ) light ( ) medium ( ) heavy reader.

5. What is your education?
   ( ) High School (or less)   ( ) 4 yrs. college
   ( ) 2 yrs. college   ( ) Post Graduate

6. Age_____   7. Sex: ( ) Male ( ) Female

Please Print Name_____

Address_____

City_____State_____Zip_____

Phone # (   )_____

Thank you. Please send to New American Library, Research Dept, 1633 Broadway, New York, NY 10019.

More Regency Romances from SIGNET

*Prices slightly higher in Canada

**Buy them at your local
bookstore or use coupon
on next page for ordering.**